Quantum Blockchain

Scrivener Publishing
100 Cummings Center, Suite 541J
Beverly, MA 01915-6106

Publishers at Scrivener
Martin Scrivener (martin@scrivenerpublishing.com)
Phillip Carmical (pcarmical@scrivenerpublishing.com)

Quantum Blockchain

An Emerging Cryptographic Paradigm

Edited by

Rajesh Kumar Dhanaraj
Vani Rajasekar
SK Hafizul Islam
Balamurugan Balusamy
and
Ching-Hsien Hsu

Scrivener
Publishing

WILEY

This edition first published 2022 by John Wiley & Sons, Inc., 111 River Street, Hoboken, NJ 07030, USA and Scrivener Publishing LLC, 100 Cummings Center, Suite 541J, Beverly, MA 01915, USA
© 2022 Scrivener Publishing LLC
For more information about Scrivener publications please visit www.scrivenerpublishing.com.

Wiley Global Headquarters

111 River Street, Hoboken, NJ 07030, USA

For details of our global editorial offices, customer services, and more information about Wiley products visit us at www.wiley.com.

Limit of Liability/Disclaimer of Warranty

While the publisher and authors have used their best efforts in preparing this work, they make no representations or warranties with respect to the accuracy or completeness of the contents of this work and specifically disclaim all warranties, including without limitation any implied warranties of merchantability or fitness for a particular purpose. No warranty may be created or extended by sales representatives, written sales materials, or promotional statements for this work. The fact that an organization, website, or product is referred to in this work as a citation and/or potential source of further information does not mean that the publisher and authors endorse the information or services the organization, website, or product may provide or recommendations it may make. This work is sold with the understanding that the publisher is not engaged in rendering professional services. The advice and strategies contained herein may not be suitable for your situation. You should consult with a specialist where appropriate. Neither the publisher nor authors shall be liable for any loss of profit or any other commercial damages, including but not limited to special, incidental, consequential, or other damages. Further, readers should be aware that websites listed in this work may have changed or disappeared between when this work was written and when it is read.

Library of Congress Cataloging-in-Publication Data

ISBN 978-1-119-83622-3

Cover image: Pixabay.Com
Cover design by Russell Richardson

Set in size of 11pt and Minion Pro by Manila Typesetting Company, Makati, Philippines

Printed in the USA

10 9 8 7 6 5 4 3 2 1

Contents

Malathy S., Santhiya M., Rajesh Kumar Dhanaraj
and Sanjeevikumar Padmanaban

Preface

Quantum cryptography is the science of exploiting quantum mechanical properties to perform cryptographic tasks. Quantum cryptography attributes its beginning to the work of Stephen Wiesner and Gilles Brassard in the early 1970s. The best-known example of quantum cryptography is quantum key distribution, which offers an information-theoretically secure solution to the key exchange problem. Quantum cryptography uses individual particles of light, or photons representing binary bits, to transmit data over fiber optic wire. The security of the system relies on quantum mechanics. The best-known developed application of quantum cryptography is quantum key distribution (QKD), which is the process of using quantum communication to establish a shared key between two parties. The security of QKD can be proven mathematically without imposing any restrictions on the abilities of an eavesdropper; something not possible with classical key distribution.

Quantum cryptography enables users to communicate more securely compared to traditional cryptography. After keys are exchanged between the involved parties, there is little concern that a malicious actor could decode the data without the key. Quantum cryptography is a fast-evolving field that combines elements of quantum optics, pattern recognition, and electrical engineering, which proposes a significant shift in the foundation for security from numerical complexity to the basic physical nature of the communication platform by combining the major quantum mechanical laws of single photons with various aspects of cognitive science. Post-quantum cryptography refers to cryptographic algorithms that are thought to be secure against an attack by a quantum computer. These complex mathematical equations take traditional computers months or even years to break. However, quantum computers running Shor's algorithm will be able to break math-based systems in moments.

The applicability of quantum cryptography is explored in this book. In a key field, such as authentication, we show that quantum cryptography performs better in classical cryptography. Authentication can be done solely through quantum methods, contrary to the popular perception. Quantum cryptography has become a particularly active study subject in recent years due to growing worries about the security of our data. By utilizing unique quantum features of nature, quantum cryptography methods offer everlasting security.

Quantum key distribution, which permits secure interactions between different users, is the most widely used protocol. The goal of this book is to draw attention to current QKD and show how it has recently been generalized to multiple users with a quantum conference key agreement. In addition, we've created quantum security measures in unusual environments. Our approach secures both the message content and the identification of the nodes, making it possible to detect a node scanning incursion. The foundations of quantum theory, quantum algorithms, quantum entanglement, quantum entropies, quantum coding, quantum error correction, and quantum cryptography are all covered in this book. The only prerequisites are a basic understanding of mathematics and basic algebra.

This book is an introduction to post-quantum cryptography for students, engineers, and researchers in the realm of information security. Above all, it explains the mathematical ideas that underpin the methods of post-quantum cryptography security. The first section of the book gives important context by quickly outlining the key principles of quantum computation, which solves the factoring issue. The second half, on the other hand, discusses a variety of potential post-quantum public-key encryption and digital signature techniques. Highlighting most of the research directions in security era, this book is most suitable for cybersecurity and AI researchers, machine learning and data analysts, ethical hackers, students and academicians.

Rajesh Kumar Dhanaraj
Vani Rajasekar
SK Hafizul Islam
Balamurugan Balusamy
Ching-Hsien Hsu
May 2022

Introduction to Classical Cryptography

Vani Rajasekar[1]*, Premalatha J.[2], Rajesh Kumar Dhanaraj[3] and Oana Geman[4]

[1]Department of CSE, Kongu Engineering College, Tamil Nadu, India
[2]Department of IT, Kongu Engineering College, Tamil Nadu, India
[3]School of Computing Science and Engineering, Galgotias University,
Greater Noida, India
[4]Department of Health and Human Development Computers,
University of Suceava, Suceava, Romania

Abstract

In today's world, with societies of information that transmits a growing number of personal data via public channels, the protection of information is a global challenge. It is the technique used to authenticate users among two parties in the public environment, where there are unauthorized users and suspicious activities. Two types of process involved in classical cryptography are encryption and decryption, which are performed at the sender and receiver sides, respectively. Encryption is the method by which legible data or plain text is combined with key (additional information) and converted into an illegible data or cipher text. Decryption is the method by which cipher text is again transformed to plain text. Classical cryptography depends on mathematics and on the complexity of computing factorization in large numbers. The two major categories of classical cryptography are symmetric key cryptography and asymmetric key cryptography. In symmetric classical, both encryption and decryption are done using same key called private key [1]. In asymmetric classical, the sender uses public key to encrypt the message and the receiver uses private key to decrypt the message. The most widely used conventional cryptographic scheme is Data Encryption Standard (DES), Advanced Data Encryption Standard (AES), and Rivest-Shamir-Adleman (RSA). These algorithms have a primary advantage of flexibility and their protection, based on computational and validated security claims. The disadvantage relies on security of protocols against adversary.

*Corresponding author: vanikecit@gmail.com

Rajesh Kumar Dhanaraj, Vani Rajasekar, SK Hafizul Islam, Balamurugan Balusamy and Ching-Hsien Hsu (eds.) Quantum Blockchain: An Emerging Cryptographic Paradigm, (1–30)
© 2022 Scrivener Publishing LLC

Message authentication code (MAC) plays an important role in classical cryptography. MAC value ensures the authenticity and data privacy of message, and it will detect any changes in the transformed messages. Secure Hash Algorithm, also known as SHA, is a family of cryptographic approaches that is used to keep the information secured [2]. SHA and MAC functions generally include bitwise operations, compression functions, and modular operations. All cryptographic approaches should fulfill the security features such as confidentiality, integrity, privacy, reliability, authentication, and non-repudiation. Cryptography tools are far more effective in the instances of signatures confirmation, user authentication, and to conduct other cryptography practices. The most extensively used classical cryptographic tools are security token, Java Cryptographic Libraries (JCA), Docker, and authentication keys. The major applications of cryptography implies banking, digital currencies, military communications, secure network communications, disk encryption, health care, education, software, and marketing.

Keywords: Security, cryptography, authentication, privacy, key agreement

1.1   Introduction

The term "cryptography" is used to refer to the branch of science that sprang from historical secret writing. Secret writing is just one of many challenges for which cryptography has provided a solution. Cryptographic primitives relate to the answers to various cryptographic difficulties. The term "symmetric encryption" relates to a cipher in which the transmitter and receiver maintain a common secret key, allowing them to exchange a message in such a way that an adversary cannot decipher the message even if he witnesses it. In cybersecurity, a classical cipher is a form of encryption that has been employed in the past but has mostly fallen out of favors. Most classical ciphers, unlike modern cryptographic techniques, can be effectively calculated and decoded manually. However, with technological advances, they are usually fairly easy to break. The various classical ciphers are substitution cipher and transposition cipher.

1.2   Substitution Ciphers

A substitution cipher is a type of encryption in which plaintext elements are substituted with cipher text in a predetermined order using a key. The key units can be single letters, groups of letters, triplets of letters, combinations of the above, and so on. To retrieve the original message, the receiver uses the reverse substitution technique to decrypt the text. The plaintext elements are reorganized in a different, generally very complex order in a transposition cipher, but the elements themselves remain unaffected [3]. In a substitution cipher, on the other hand, the plaintext elements are kept in the same order in the cipher text, but the values themselves are changed.

1.2.1   Caesar Cipher

Caesar cipher, also referred as the shift cipher, Caesar's coding, or Caesar shifting, is among the most basic and extensively used encryption algorithms. It is a substitution cipher where each letter in the plaintext is chosen to replace that is a certain number of places down the alphabet. The conversion can be visualized by aligning the alphabets. The cipher letter is the plain letter rotated by a certain range of positions left or right. For example, here, a Caesar cipher uses a three-place left rotation, which is identical to a three-place right shift.

Encryption:
The encryption can alternatively be described using modular arithmetic by converting the letters into integers using the $A = 0$, $B = 1$, ..., $Z = 25$ technique. The mathematical formula for encrypting a letter x with a shift n is

$$E(x) = (x + n) \bmod 26 \qquad (1.1)$$

Similarly, the decryption is

$$D(x) = (x - n) \bmod 26 \qquad (1.2)$$

Plain	A	B	C	D	E	F	G	H	I	J	K	L	M	N	O	P	Q	R	S	T	U	V	W	X	Y	Z
Cipher	D	E	F	G	H	I	J	K	L	M	N	O	P	Q	R	S	T	U	V	W	X	Y	Z	A	B	C

Example:
Sample plain text: HELLO WORLD
Cipher Text: OLSSV AVYSK

In a cipher text–only environment, the Caesar cipher is easily broken. There are two scenarios to consider:

1. An attacker is aware that a simple substitution cipher has been employed.

2. An attacker recognizes the presence of a Caesar cipher but is unaware of the shifting value.

1.2.2 Polyalphabetic Cipher

Any cipher based on substitution that uses numerous substitution alphabets is known as a polyalphabetic cipher. Although it is a reduced particular case, the Vigenère cipher is possibly the best illustration of a polyalphabetic encryption [4].

1.2.2.1 Working of Polyalphabetic Cipher

- Select a keyword
- Construct the Vigenère table as shown in Figure 1.1.
- Write the key for plain text
- For each letter of plain text and a letter in key, look at the Vigenère table
- Trace down all the letters and finally write the cipher text

ROW																										
0	A	B	C	D	E	F	G	H	I	J	K	L	M	N	O	P	Q	R	S	T	U	V	W	X	Y	Z
1	B	C	D	E	F	G	H	I	J	K	L	M	N	O	P	Q	R	S	T	U	V	W	X	Y	Z	A
2	C	D	E	F	G	H	I	J	K	L	M	N	O	P	Q	R	S	T	U	V	W	X	Y	Z	A	B
3	D	E	F	G	H	I	J	K	L	M	N	O	P	Q	R	S	T	U	V	W	X	Y	Z	A	B	C
4	E	F	G	H	I	J	K	L	M	N	O	P	Q	R	S	T	U	V	W	X	Y	Z	A	B	C	D
5	F	G	H	I	J	K	L	M	N	O	P	Q	R	S	T	U	V	W	X	Y	Z	A	B	C	D	E
6	G	H	I	J	K	L	M	N	O	P	Q	R	S	T	U	V	W	X	Y	Z	A	B	C	D	E	F
7	H	I	J	K	L	M	N	O	P	Q	R	S	T	U	V	W	X	Y	Z	A	B	C	D	E	F	G
8	I	J	K	L	M	N	O	P	Q	R	S	T	U	V	W	X	Y	Z	A	B	C	D	E	F	G	H
9	J	K	L	M	N	O	P	Q	R	S	T	U	V	W	X	Y	Z	A	B	C	D	E	F	G	H	I
10	K	L	M	N	O	P	Q	R	S	T	U	V	W	X	Y	Z	A	B	C	D	E	F	G	H	I	J
11	L	M	N	O	P	Q	R	S	T	U	V	W	X	Y	Z	A	B	C	D	E	F	G	H	I	J	K
12	M	N	O	P	Q	R	S	T	U	V	W	X	Y	Z	A	B	C	D	E	F	G	H	I	J	K	L
13	N	O	P	Q	R	S	T	U	V	W	X	Y	Z	A	B	C	D	E	F	G	H	I	J	K	L	M
14	O	P	Q	R	S	T	U	V	W	X	Y	Z	A	B	C	D	E	F	G	H	I	J	K	L	M	N
15	P	Q	R	S	T	U	V	W	X	Y	Z	A	B	C	D	E	F	G	H	I	J	K	L	M	N	O
16	Q	R	S	T	U	V	W	X	Y	Z	A	B	C	D	E	F	G	H	I	J	K	L	M	N	O	P
17	R	S	T	U	V	W	X	Y	Z	A	B	C	D	E	F	G	H	I	J	K	L	M	N	O	P	Q
18	S	T	U	V	W	X	Y	Z	A	B	C	D	E	F	G	H	I	J	K	L	M	N	O	P	Q	R
19	T	U	V	W	X	Y	Z	A	B	C	D	E	F	G	H	I	J	K	L	M	N	O	P	Q	R	S
20	U	V	W	X	Y	Z	A	B	C	D	E	F	G	H	I	J	K	L	M	N	O	P	Q	R	S	T
21	V	W	X	Y	Z	A	B	C	D	E	F	G	H	I	J	K	L	M	N	O	P	Q	R	S	T	U
22	W	X	Y	Z	A	B	C	D	E	F	G	H	I	J	K	L	M	N	O	P	Q	R	S	T	U	V
23	X	Y	Z	A	B	C	D	E	F	G	H	I	J	K	L	M	N	O	P	Q	R	S	T	U	V	W
24	Y	Z	A	B	C	D	E	F	G	H	I	J	K	L	M	N	O	P	Q	R	S	T	U	V	W	X
25	Z	A	B	C	D	E	F	G	H	I	J	K	L	M	N	O	P	Q	R	S	T	U	V	W	X	Y

Figure 1.1 Vigenère table.

Example:
Key: KEYKEYE
Plain text: TRYTHIS

Then, based on the steps described above and from the Vigenère table, it is identified that the cipher text as follows:

Cipher: DVWDLGW

1.2.2.2   Cracking of Cipher Text

- Look for repeated sequences of letters in the ciphertext; the longer the sequences, the stronger. Make a note of where they are by underlining or marking them in the some fashion [5, 6].
- Determine how many letters are between the first letters in the string and add one for each appearance of a repetitive string.
- Factor the number obtained in above calculation.
- Create a table of common components by repeating this method with each repeated string that has found. The length of the phrase used to encrypt the cipher text is perhaps the most common factor.
- Count the number of times each letter appears in the cipher text. There should be n separate frequency counts in the end.
- To determine exactly how much each letter was displaced, compare these counts to regular frequency distribution.
- Shift should be undoing and the message can be read.

1.2.3   Hill Cipher

Hill cipher is a linear algebra–based polygraph substitution cipher. A value modulo 26 is assigned to each letter. The basic scheme A = 0, B = 1, …, Z = 25 is frequently employed, although it is not a requirement of the encryption [7]. Encryption is done by multiplying plain text matrix with the key matrix as nXn. The decryption is done by inverting the key matrix and it should be multiplied with cipher text to produce the plain text.

Example: Encryption
Plain text: ACT
Key: GYBNQKURP

$$Plaintext = \begin{bmatrix} 0 \\ 2 \\ 19 \end{bmatrix} \text{ and } Key = \begin{bmatrix} 6 & 24 & 1 \\ 13 & 16 & 10 \\ 20 & 17 & 15 \end{bmatrix}$$

$$Ciphertext = \begin{bmatrix} 6 & 24 & 1 \\ 13 & 16 & 10 \\ 20 & 17 & 15 \end{bmatrix} \times \begin{bmatrix} 0 \\ 2 \\ 19 \end{bmatrix} \mod 26$$

$$= \begin{bmatrix} 15 \\ 14 \\ 7 \end{bmatrix}$$

Cipher Text: POH

Example: Decryption
Cipher Text: POH
Find the inverse of key as follows:

$$Key^{-1} = \begin{bmatrix} 6 & 24 & 1 \\ 13 & 16 & 10 \\ 20 & 17 & 15 \end{bmatrix}^{-1} \mod 26 = \begin{bmatrix} 8 & 5 & 10 \\ 21 & 8 & 21 \\ 21 & 12 & 8 \end{bmatrix}$$

$$Plaintext = \begin{bmatrix} 8 & 5 & 10 \\ 21 & 8 & 21 \\ 21 & 12 & 8 \end{bmatrix} \times \begin{bmatrix} 15 \\ 14 \\ 7 \end{bmatrix} \mod 26$$

$$= \begin{bmatrix} 0 \\ 2 \\ 19 \end{bmatrix}$$

Plain Text: ACT

1.2.4 Playfair Cipher

The Playfair cipher was the very first digraph stream cipher to be used in practice. Unlike standard ciphers, Playfair cipher encrypts a pair of alphabets (digraphs) rather than a single alphabet. It starts by generating a 5*5 matrix key table. The matrix comprises alphabets that serve as the plaintext's encryption key. It is important to remember that no alphabet should be duplicated. Another thing to keep in mind is that there are 26 alphabets and only 25 blocks to fit a letter into. The message is encrypted digraph by digraph with the Playfair cipher. As a result, the Playfair cipher might be considered a digraph substitution cipher [8, 9].

1.2.4.1 Rules for Encrypting the Playfair Cipher

- To begin, divide the plaintext into digraphs (pair of two letters). Insert the letter Z to the start of the plaintext if it has an odd number of letters.
- If the letters in digraph appears twice then add X in between the letters
- To figure out the cipher text, make a 5*5 key matrix or key table and complete it with alphabet letters.
- Then, the condition to be followed is a) replace each letter of the digraph with the letters adjacent to their right if a pair of digraph appears in the same row; b) replace each letter of the digraph with the letters below them if a pair of digraph appears in the same row; c) in this scenario, select a 3*3 matrix from a 5*5 matrix and present the elements at the two opposite corner if digraph appears in a different row and column.

Example:
Plain Text: COMMUNICATION
Key: COMPUTER

- Split the plain text into digraphs as CO MX MU NI CA TI ON
- Construct 5*5 key matrix as follows

C	O	M	P	U
T	E	R	A	B
D	F	G	H	I
K	L	N	Q	S
V	W	X	Y	Z

- For the first digraph, CO, the cipher is OM; for the second digraph, MX, the cipher is RM; for the third digraph, MU, the cipher is PC; for the fourth digraph, NI, the cipher is SG; for the fifth digraph, CA, the cipher is PT; for the sixth digraph, TE, the cipher is ER.
- The final cipher text is OMRMPCSGPTER

1.3   Transposition Cipher

A transposition cipher is an encryption technique in which the positions of plaintext units often characters or groups of letters are shifted according to a regular pattern, resulting in the cipher text being a permutation of the plaintext. That is, the elements' order is altered that is the plaintext is reordered. To encrypt, a bijective function is applied to the locations of the letters, and to decrypt, an inversion function is applied [10].

1.3.1   Columnar Transposition

In a columnar transposition, the information is typed out in fixed-length rows and then called out column by column, with the columns picked in a random sequence. A keyword is commonly used to determine the width of the rows and the recombination of the columns. Any empty spaces in a standard columnar transposition cipher are completed with nulls; any empty spaces in an uneven columnar transposition cipher are left blank. Finally, the information is recited in columns according to the keyword's sequence.

Example:
Keyword: ZEBRAS
Order is: 6 3 2 4 1 5
Plain Text: WE ARE DISCOVERED FLEET AT ONCE

The columnar grid is as follows:
6 3 2 4 1 5
W E A R E D
I S C O V E
R E D F L E
E A T O N C
E Q K J E U
In regular case, after filling the (QKJEU) values, the cipher text is EVLNE ACDTK ESEAQ ROFOJ DEECU WIREE.

In the irregular case, the left-out column values are not completed by null.

The columnar grid is as follows:
6 3 2 4 1 5
W E A R E D
I S C O V E
R E D F L E
E A T O N C
E
The cipher text value is EVLNA CDTES EAROF ODEEC WIREE.

To decipher it, the receiver must divide the message length by the key length to determine the column lengths. Then, rewrite the statement in columns, reformatting the key phrase to reorder the columns.

1.3.2   Rail Fence Transposition

The rail fence encryption is a type of transposition cipher named after the technique in which it is encoded. The plaintext is placed vertically and diagonally on consecutive "rails" of an imagined fence in the rail fence cipher, then moved up to the bottom.

Example:
Plain text: HELLO WORLD
Rail Fence Format:
H   L   O   R   D
    E   L   W   L
Cipher Text: HLORD ELWL

1.3.3   Route Cipher

The plaintext is printed out in a grid of required dimension in a route cipher and then taken off in a sequence specified in the key.

Example:
Key: Clockwise spiral inward starting from top right
Dimension: 3
Plain Text: HELLO WORLD HOW ARE YOU
H L O D W E U
E O R H A Y X
L W L O R O Z
Cipher Text: UXZOROLWL EHLODWE YAHROE

1.3.4   Double Transposition

A simple columnar transposition could be exploited by predicting possible column lengths, putting the information in columns, and then hunting for anagrams. As a result, a double transposition was frequently utilized to strengthen it [11]. It is just a columnar transposition done twice. Both transpositions can be done with the same key or with two distinct keys.

Example:
Keyword: STRIPE
Permutation: 564231
6 3 2 4 1 5
W E A R E D
I S C O V E
R E D F L E
E A T O N C
E
Cipher Text: CAEEN SOIAE DRLEF WEDRE EVTOC

1.4   Symmetric Encryption Technique

Symmetric encryption is a type of cryptography that uses only one key, known as the secret key, to encrypt and decrypt the information. The key must be exchanged between the organizations communicating using symmetric encryption so that it may be utilized in the decryption process. This encryption method varies from asymmetric encryption, which encrypts and decrypts messages using a key pair, one public and one private. Data is changed to a format that can be read by anybody who does not have the unique key to decrypt it using symmetric encryption methods. Once the message has been delivered to the intended receiver who holds the key, the algorithms reverses its effects, returning the message to its original and comprehensible state. The secret key used by both the sender and receiver can be a particular login credentials or a randomized string of numbers and letters created using a secure random number generator (RNG) [12, 13]. There are two different kind of symmetric algorithms such as block and stream ciphers.

- Block Cipher:
  By the use of a secret key, fixed sequences of bits are encrypted in electronic communications blocks. While the data is encrypted, the system stores it in memory while waiting for entire blocks.
- Stream Cipher:
  Rather than being stored in the system database, information is secure as it streams.

Although symmetric encryption is an outdated kind of encryption, it is quicker and more accurate than asymmetric encryption, which strains networks due to data capacity limitations and excessive CPU usage. Symmetric cryptography is frequently included in bulk encryption or encoding enormous amounts of information due to its greater efficiency and greater speed. In the case of a network, the secret key may be used to encrypt or decrypt data exclusively by the database. Reported plaintext attacks, chosen-plaintext attacks, differential cryptanalysis, and linear cryptanalysis have all been known to be vulnerable to symmetric cyphers in the past [14]. The functions for each round should be carefully constructed to limit the odds of a successful attack. In the case of a database, the secret key may be used to encrypt or decrypt data exclusively by the database.

1.4.1   Key Management

The maintenance of cryptographic keys in a crypto algorithm is referred to as key management. Handling with the creation, transmission, storage, usage, removal, and restoration of keys falls under this category. Cryptographic protocol development, key servers, user procedures, and other pertinent protocols are all covered. Key management is the process of keeping track of cryptographic keys in a crypto algorithm. This includes dealing with the production, transfer, storage, use, removal, and recovery of keys. The construction of cryptographic protocols, key servers, user processes, and other relevant protocols are all discussed. Various types of keys are used by various authentication systems, and some systems utilize more than one. Asymmetric or symmetric keys are examples of these. The keys used in a symmetric key algorithm are the same for both encoding and decoding a message. Keys should be chosen carefully, disseminated, and stored in a secure manner. In contrary, asymmetric keys also known as public keys are two separate keys that are mathematically linked. They are usually used in tandem to communicate.

1.4.2 Key Generation

The process of producing keys in cybersecurity is known as key generation. To encode and decode whatever information is being encrypted or decrypted, a key is used. A key generator, often known as a keygen, is a device or program that generates keys. Prescriptive algorithms and public key algorithms are both used in modern cryptography systems. A single shared key is used in symmetric-key methods, and keeping information secret necessitates keeping this key secret as well. A public key and a private key are used in public key algorithms. Anyone can have access to the public key. A sender uses encryption with the receiver's public key, which can only be decrypted by the owner of the private key. Wireless techniques like TLS and SSH utilize a mixture of the two since public key algorithms are substantially lower than conventional algorithms. One party obtains the other's public key and encodes a short bit of data.

1.4.3 Key Exchange

Key exchange, also known as key establishment, is a contractual method of exchanging cryptographic keys among parties involved to enable the usage of a cryptographic algorithm. If the transmitter and recipient choose to send and receive encrypted communications, then they both need to be able to encrypt and decrypt messages. The key exchange challenge is exchanging whichever keys or other data is required to establish a confidential channel of communication that no one else can copy. To share information confidentially, parties involved must first interchange the secret key, which allows each party to encrypt and decrypt the data before sending or receiving them. The main issue with symmetrical cryptography, also known as single-key cryptography, is that it necessitates the transmission of a secret key via authorized couriers, diplomatic luggage, or any other safe communication route.

1.4.4 Data Encryption Standard

The Data Encryption Standard (DES) is a symmetric key technique for digital information encryption. Despite the fact that its small key length of 56 bits renders it unsecure for applications, it has had a significant impact on cryptography. Following the publishing of an NSA-approved encryption standard, it was quickly adopted around the world and subjected to extensive scholarly investigation. Controversy emerged due to confidential design features: the symmetric key block cipher design's relatively short key length, and the NSA's involvement, creating concerns about a backdoor. The NSA constructed the S-boxes that sparked those suspicions to remove a backdoor they knew about. The NSA, on the other hand, made sure that the key size was dramatically lowered so that a brute force attack could be used to break the cipher. The algorithm was subjected to a lot of academic scrutiny throughout time, which led to the contemporary understanding of block ciphers and their cryptanalysis.

1.4.4.1 Structure of DES

DES is a method that generates a fixed-length sequence of plaintext bits and converts into another cipher text bit string of the same size using a series of difficult operations. The block size throughout the case of DES

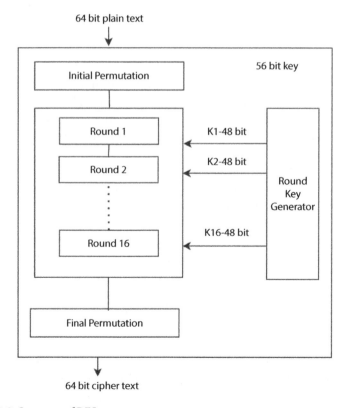

Figure 1.2 Structure of DES.

is 64 bits. DES also employs a key to modify the transformation, implying that decryption can only be accomplished by those who have access to the encrypting key. The overall structure of DES is specified in Figure 1.2. There are 16 rounds of operation, each with 16 identical phases. There are also inverses of the initial and final permutations, known as IP and FP. The block is broken into two 32-bit into halves treated simultaneously before the major rounds; this crossing is known as the Feistel scheme. Decryption and encryption are relatively comparable procedures according to the Feistel structure. The F-function encrypts a half-block and a portion of the key. The F-output function is then mixed with other half of the block before the following cycle, and the two strands exchanged [15]. The halves are exchanged after the final round; this is a property of the Feistel structure that makes encryption and decryption procedures identical.

1.4.4.2   Fiestel Function

The structure of Fiestel function is shown in Figure 1.3. The steps involved in the Fiestel function are shown in the following.

- Expansion:
  By replicating 50% of the bits, the 32-bit half-block is extended to 48 bits using the extension permutation, marked E in the image. The output is composed of eight 6-bit (86 = 48 bits) parts, each of which contains a copy of four general input bits as well as a copy of the directly adjacent bit of each of the input bits on each side.
- Mixing of key:
  An XOR function is used to merge the outcome with a subkey. To use the key schedule, sixteen 48-bit subkeys are produced from the main key, one in each round.
- Substitution
  The block is separated into eight 6-bit parts after adding in the subkey before even being processed by the S-boxes or substitution boxes. As shown in a non-linear adjustment available in the form of a lookup table, every one of the eight S-boxes substitutes its six input bits with 4 output bits. The S-boxes are at the heart of DES's security. The cipher would be linear and computationally breakable without them.
- Permutation
  Finally, the P-box rearranges the 32 outcomes from the S-boxes as shown in a predetermined permutation. This is structured such that the bits from each S-output box's in this round are

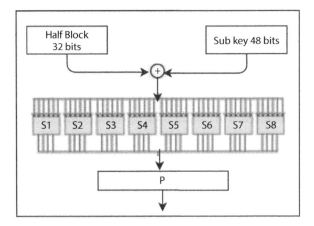

Figure 1.3 Structure of Fiestel function.

divided among four distinct S-boxes for the next round after recombination.

1.4.5   Advanced Encryption Standard

The Advanced Encryption Standard (AES), popularly known as Rijndael in its original form, is a standard for digital information encryption [16]. AES is based on a partial replacement network design idea and is effective in both hardware and software. AES is not using a Feistel network, unlike its predecessor DES. AES is a Rijndael variation with a 128-bit constant block size and a session key of 128, 192, or 256 bits. The state is a four-by-four column major-order matrix of bytes used by AES. The majority of AES calculations are performed in a finite field. The following is the number of rounds:

- For 128-bit keys, there are 10 rounds.
- For 192-bit keys, there are 12 rounds.
- For 256-bit keys, there are 14 rounds.

1.4.5.1   Operation in AES

The steps involved in the AES are described as follows:

- Key Expansion
  By using AES key schedule, round keys are produced from cypher keys. Each round of AES requires a distinct 128-bit rounds key block, with one additional.

- Initial Round Key
  Bitwise XOR is used to combine every byte of the value with a byte of the round key.
- Round operation
  1. Sub bytes
     Using an 8-bit substitution box, every byte in the state array is replaced with a sub byte in the sub bytes step. The cipher's non-linearity is provided by this process. The multiplicative inverse is often used to create the S-box. The S-box is built by merging the inverse function with an invertible affine transformation to resist assaults based on the simple mathematical features.
  2. Shift rows
     The shift rows step works on the state's rows, shifting the bytes in each row circularly by a given offset. The first row is unaffected for AES. The second row's bytes are displaced one to the left. Similarly, the third and fourth rows have two and three offsets, accordingly. As a result, each column of the shift rows step's output sequence is made up of bytes from each column of the input state. The purpose of this step is to prevent the columns from being encrypted separately, which would cause AES to devolve into four separate block ciphers.
  3. Mix column
     In the mix columns phase, an invertible transformation function is used to aggregate the four bytes of each state column. The mix columns function takes 4 bits as input and produces four bytes, with each input byte affecting each of the four output bytes. Mix columns in conjunction with shift rows enable cipher dispersion.
  4. Add round key
     The subkey is coupled with both the state in add round key step. Using Rijndael's key schedule, a subkey is generated from the main key for every round; each subkey is the same length as the state. The subkey is created by using bitwise XOR to combine each byte of the state with the appropriate byte of the subkey.
- Final Round
  The final round operation contains sub bytes, shift rows and add round key.

1.4.6   Applications of Symmetric Cipher

1. Financial applications such as banking transactions and smart card applications
2. Authentication applications
3. Hash code generation
4. Random number generation

1.4.7   Drawback of Symmetric Encryption

1.4.7.1   Key Exhaustion

Symmetric encryption has a flaw in which each use of a key "leaks" some information that could be exploited by an attacker to rebuild the key. The establishments of a key hierarchy to guarantee that master or key encryption secrets are not overused, as well as the proper rotation of keys that do encrypt large amounts of data, are two defenses against this behavior. Both of these techniques require competent key-management procedures to be traceable, as data might be compromised if an expired encryption key can still be recovered.

1.4.7.2   Key Management at Large Scale

When only some few keys, for example, tens to low hundreds are included in a scheme, the administration overhead is minimal and can be managed through manual, human work. With a large estate, however, keeping track of expiration dates and coordinating key rotation rapidly becomes impossible.

1.4.7.3   Attribution Data

With exception of asymmetric certificates, symmetric keys lack associated metadata such as an expiration date or an Access Rights to identify the key's intended usage in encryption but not in decryption.

1.5   Asymmetric Encryption Technique

Asymmetric key algorithms are comparable to symmetric key algorithms in that plaintext is coupled with a key, passed through an algorithm, and cipher text is returned. The main distinction is that the keys used for encryption and decryption is distinct, resulting in the algorithm's asymmetry. A private key and a public key make up the key pair. Public key cryptography and digital signatures are the two most common applications of asymmetric key methods. Anyone can transmit an encrypted communication within a trusted network of users using public key encryption. The sender encrypts the communication with the receiver's public key, leaving only the receiver with his or her own shared secret key to decrypt it. In such a scheme, anyone can encrypt the message that use the designated receiver's public key, but only the recipient's private key can access this information. This allows server software to construct a cryptographic key for compatible symmetric key cryptography and then encrypt that freshly generated symmetric key using a client's openly provided public key. Robust authentication is also achievable with public key cryptography. A sender can construct a brief digital signature on a communication by combining it with a private key. Anyone having the sender's public key can compose a message with a claimed digital certificate, and if the signature is equal to the message, the message's origin is validated.

1.5.1   Rivest-Shamir-Adleman Encryption Algorithm

The Rivest-Shamir-Adleman (RSA) algorithm utilizes asymmetric cryptography, which means it employs both a public and a private key. A public key can be shared openly, but a private key is kept private and must not be communicated with anybody. The steps involved in the RSA are described as follows:

- Key Generation
  1. Select two large prime number p and q
  2. Compute $n = p \times q$
  3. Compute the totient function as $\phi(n) = p - 1 \times q - 1$
  4. Identify the integer e such that $1 < e < \phi(n)$
  5. Compute d such that $e.d = 1 \bmod \phi(n)$
- Encryption
  1. Given a plain text message m, the cipher text c is calculated as $c = m^e \bmod n$
- Decryption
  1. Given the cipher text c, the plain text can be identified as $m = c^d \bmod n$

1.5.2   Elliptic Curve Cryptography

Elliptic curve cryptography (ECC) is a public key cryptography technique based on the analytical solution of elliptic curves over finite fields. In comparison to non-EC encryption, ECC allows for smaller keys. Key agreement, digital signatures, pseudo-random generators, and other jobs can all benefit from elliptic curves. By integrating the key agreement with a symmetric encryption algorithm, they could be used for encryption effectively. To utilize ECC, both parties will agree on all of the characteristics that compose the elliptic curve, i.e., the agreement's domain parameters. In the prime case, the data is characterized by p, and in the binary case, the pair of m and f. The elliptic coefficient is drawn by the characterizing equation's parameters a and b. Domain parameter creation is typically not performed by each individual because it requires computing the amount of instances on a curve, which is time-consuming and difficult to execute. As a result, various standard bodies produced elliptic curve domain parameters for a variety of field sizes. "labeled curves" or "standardized curves" are terms for domain parameters that can be referred by name or by the unique object identification defined in the standard standards. The structure of elliptic curve is shown in Figure 1.4.

1.5.2.1   Elliptic Curve

ECC is a comprehensive cryptography technology that is an alternative to RSA. It uses elliptic curve mathematics to generate security between key pairs for public key encryption. RSA uses prime numbers instead of elliptic curves to achieve a similar result, but ECC has recently gained prominence due to its reduced key size and ability to retain security. In opposition to RSA, ECC builds its public key cryptography techniques on the algebraic structure of elliptic curves over finite fields. As a result, ECC generates keys

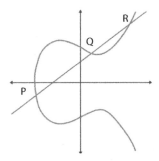

Figure 1.4 Elliptic curve.

that are computationally harder to break. As a result, ECC is regarded the next level of public key cryptography, and it is more secured than RSA. It also makes perfect sense to use ECC to keep both reliability and functionality at a high level. This is because ECC is becoming more widely used as websites aim for improved online security in client data while also improving mobile optimization. The demand for a concise guide to ECC grows as more sites use ECC to encrypt data. For modern ECC applications, an elliptic curve is a graphical method over a finite field composed of points obeying the formula:

$$y^2 = x^3 + ax + b$$

Whatever point on the curve can be duplicated over the x-axis in this ECC demonstration, and the curve will remain the same. Any non-vertical line that intersects the curve in three or fewer locations will be considered non-vertical.

1.5.2.2   *Difference Between ECC and RSA*

The size of RSA and ECC encryption keys differs significantly in terms of security output. In other terms, a 384-bit ECC key provides the same measure of protection as a 7,680-bit RSA key. The lengths of ECC and RSA keys do not have a linear relationship. That example, doubling the size of an RSA key does not result in doubling the size of an ECC key. This significant difference demonstrates that ECC key length and signing are far faster than RSA, as well as the fact that ECC utilizes less memory than RSA. Furthermore, unlike RSA, where both private and public keys are numbers, the private and public keys in ECC are not interchangeable equally. Conversely, the public key in ECC is a curve line, while the secret key is indeed an integer. ECC has shorter cipher texts, keys, and signature, as well as quicker key and signature production. It has a reasonably fast decryption and encryption performance. By computing signatures in two steps, ECC achieves lower latency than inverse. ECC has solid standards for authenticated key exchange, and the technology has a lot of backing.

1.5.2.3   *Advantages and Security of ECC*

The methods used in public key cryptography are simple to process in one direction but complicated to perform in the other. For example,

RSA makes use of the fact that combining prime numbers to generate a larger number is simple, but converting massive groups back to primes is significantly more complex. Elliptic curve encryption has a significant strength advantage, which translates to even more power for smaller, smart phones. Because factoring is easier and takes less energy than solving for an elliptic curve discrete logarithm, RSA's factoring authentication is more susceptible for two keys of same length. ECC has various flaws, notably side-channel attacks and twist security attacks. These types try to compromise the ECC's secret key security. Exploitable vulnerabilities are common as a result of side-channel attacks such as differential power assaults, fault analysis, normal power attacks, and simple temporal attacks. All sorts of side-channel attacks have simple responses. The twist security vulnerability, also known as a fault attack, is another sort of elliptic curve attack. Invalid-curve attacks and small-subgroup attacks are examples of such assaults, and they can expose the victim's secret key. Twist security threats are often averted by carefully validating parameters and selecting curves.

1.5.3 Hyperelliptic Curve Cryptography

In the same way that the Jacobian of an elliptic curve is an Abelian group with which to do computation, hyperelliptic curve cryptography (HECC) is analogous to ECC in that the Jacobian of a hyperelliptic curve is an Abelian group in which to do computation. An hyperelliptic curve over g is given by

$$C:y^2 + h(x)y = f(x)$$

The Jacobian of C, written J(C), is a division group; therefore, its elements are similarity classes of divisors of degree 0 under the connection of linear equivalence, rather than points. This is consistent with the elliptic curve situation, because the Jacobian of an elliptic curve can be proven to be isomorphic to the set of points on the elliptic curve. Neal Koblitz pioneered the use of hyperelliptic curves in encryption in 1989. Despite being released only three years after ECC, few cryptosystems use hyperelliptic curves since the arithmetic application is not as effective as with elliptic curves or factoring. Like an Abelian group, the Jacobian on a hyperelliptic curve could be used to solve the discrete logarithm issue (DLP). This allows for the usage of Jacobians of relatively low order, making the service more effective. However, if the hyperelliptic curve is chosen incorrectly, then the DLP becomes trivial to solve. The DLP in the Jacobian of hyperelliptic curves could be attacked using any generalized attack on the discrete logarithm in finite Abelian groups, such as the Pohlig–Hellman technique and Pollard's rho approach. Another approach that can be used to resolve DLP in some cases is the indexing calculus algorithm. There is an index calculus assault on DLP for Jacobians of hyperelliptic curves. The approach will be more effective than Pollard's rho if the genus of the curve grows too large. In light of numerous DLP attacks, it is feasible to compile a list of hyperelliptic curve characteristics that should be ignored. However, as shown, DLP in this addition group is straightforward to solve. These curves, referred to as anomalous curves, are likewise not to be employed in DLP.

1.6   Digital Signatures

A digital signature is a computational method for verifying the integrity and validity of a message, program, or digital document. It is the virtual counterpart of a written document or a stamped seal, but it comes with a lot more security built in. The purpose of a digital signature is to prevent manipulation and deception in electronic communications. Electronic papers, transactions, and digital messages can all benefit from digital signatures as proof of origin, identity, and position. They can also be used to affirm informed permission by signers. Digital signatures are a ubiquitous feature of most cryptographic protocol suites, and they are often used for cloud hosting, financial transactions, contract software solutions, and other situations where forgery or tampering must be avoided. Digital signatures are a ubiquitous feature of most cryptographic protocol suites, and they are often used for cloud hosting, financial transactions, contract software solutions, and other situations where forgery or tampering must be avoided. Asymmetric cryptography is used in electronic certificates. They give a layer of validation and security to communications sent via an insecure channel in several cases: A digital signature, when properly implemented, gives the recipient reason to assume the communication was transmitted by the stated sender. In many ways, digital signatures are comparable to conventional handwritten signatures.

1.6.1   Working of Digital Signature

Public key cryptography, often known as cryptographic algorithms, is used to create digital signatures. Two keys are produced using a public key algorithm like RSA resulting in a mathematically connected pair of keys, one secret and one public. The two or more mutually authenticating encryption algorithms of public key cryptography are used to create digital signatures. The person who makes the digital signature encodes signature-related data with a secret key, which can only be decrypted with the signer's public key. If the receiver cannot open the documents using the signer's public key, then there is an issue with the signature or the message. Digital signatures are verified in this way. All parties must trust that the person who creates the signature has maintained the private key secret in order for digital signature technology to work.

Typically, a digital signature approach consists of three methodologies:

- A key generation technique that chooses a private key from a collection of potential private key at random. The technique generates both a private key and a public key.
- Given a text and a private key, this signing method generates a signature.
- A signature verification algorithm that tries to determine the message's claim to legitimacy based on the message, public key, and signature.

1.6.2   Creation of Digital Signature

Signature software, such as an email application, is used to produce a digital signature by providing a one-way hash of the digital information to be signed. An algorithm generates a fixed-length bunch of numbers and integers called a hash. The hash is then encrypted using the private key of the digital signature originator. The digital signature is comprised of the encoded hash, as well as other characteristics such as the hash function. Because a hash function can turn any input into a specified result, which is usually significantly shorter, it is preferable to encode the hash rather than the full message or document. Hashing is much quicker than signing; therefore, this saves the time. A hash's value is distinct to the data it hashes. Any modification in the data, even a specific character modification, will result in a new value. This property allows others to decode the hash using the signer's public key to verify the information's authenticity. It shows that the data has not altered since it was verified if the decrypted hash matches a subsequent computed hash of the same data. If the two hashes does not equal, then the data was either changed with and is now vulnerable, or the signature was made with an encryption key that does not match the decryption key supplied by the signer, resulting in an authentication problem. The process of creating digital signature is denoted in Figure 1.5.

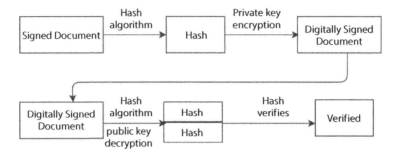

Figure 1.5 Process of creating digital signature.

A digital signature could be used with any type of message, if encrypted or not, to ensure that the sender's identity is verified and that the message was delivered intact. Because the digital signature is distinctive to both the document and the signer, it connects them altogether; it is hard for the signer to dispute finally signed something. Non-repudiation is the term for this characteristic. Digital signatures and message authentication are not the same thing. A digital certificate is a digital document that includes the granting CA's digital signature. It connects a public key to an individual or entity's identification which can be used to validate that a person belongs to that individual or persons. Digital signatures and digital certificates are supported by most web-based email applications, making it simple to sign any outgoing emails and authenticate digitally signed receiving communications. Digital signatures are also widely employed to give assurance of validity, integrity of data, and non-repudiation of online interactions and experiences.

1.6.3 Message Authentication Code

A message authentication code (MAC), also referred as a tag in cryptography, is a brief piece of knowledge used to authenticate a message—that is, to ensure that it originated from the specified sender and has not been modified. By enabling verifiers to identify any modifications to the message content, the MAC value safeguards both the data integrity and the validity of the communication. The MAC algorithm is a communication authentication symmetric key encryption mechanism. The transmitter and receiver exchange a symmetric key K to initiate the MAC process. A MAC is an encoded checksum computed on the underlying message being sent along with message. The sender enters the information and the secret key K into a publicly available MAC algorithm and generates a MAC value. The MAC function compressing an arbitrary lengthy input into a fixed size output, similarly to the hash function. The key difference among hash and MAC is that MAC compresses using a shared secret. The message is forwarded together with the MAC by the sender. We will assume the information is sent in the clear because we are only interested in message origin verification, not message secrecy. If message confidentiality is essential, then the message must be encrypted. The receiver inserts the received message and the sharing secret key K into the MAC technique and recomputed it after receiving the message and the MAC. The receiver now compares the newly computed MAC to the MAC received from the sender to ensure that they are equal. If they are identical, then the receiver receives the message and is confident that it was sent by the intended sender. If the calculated MAC differs from the MAC given by the sender, then the recipient is unable to tell if the message has been tampered with or whether the origin has been forged. In the end, a recipient can reasonably conclude that the message is not real.

1.6.3.1   Limitation on MAC

- Establishing shared secret: It can authenticate messages between pre-determined legitimate individuals who share a key. Prior to using MAC, a shared secret must be established.
- Lack of non-repudiation: The guarantee that a message originator cannot disavow any previously communicated messages, agreements, or acts is known as non-repudiation. A non-repudiation service is not provided by the MAC approach. MACs cannot give verification that a communication was sent by the sender if the transmitter and recipient have a disagreement about message origination.

1.6.3.2   One Time MAC

As soon as the key is only used once, global hashing and, in particular, bilateral separate hash functions provide one reliable message authentication. This can be thought of as an authenticating one-time pad. The random key, key = (a, b), is the shortest pairwise independent cryptographic algorithm, and the MAC tag for a message m is calculated as tag = (am + b) mod p, where p is prime. For k-ways autonomous hashing functions, k-independent hashing functions give a secure MAC if the key is utilized less than k times. In the context of quantum cryptography, hash function and data access control have also been proposed. In contradiction to other cryptographic tasks, such as digital certificates, quantum resources have been demonstrated to have no advantage over absolutely secure one-time conventional MACs over a rather extensive class of quantum MACs.

1.6.4   Secure Hash Algorithm

Secure Hash Algorithm (SHA) is a group of cryptographic techniques that are used to keep data safe. It operates by converting data with a hash function, which is a bitwise operations, modular additions, and compression function–based method. The hash function then generates a fixed-length string that bears no resemblance to the original. These techniques are one-way functions, which mean that it is nearly impossible to change them back into its original data once they have been changed into their feature vectors. SHA-1, SHA-2, and SHA-3 are three algorithms of importance, each of which was built with increasingly prominent encryption in reaction to hacker attempts. Because of its widely known flaws, SHA-0 is currently considered obsolete [17]. A common application of SHA is to encrypt passwords, as the server side just needs to maintain track of a physical requirements hash value, rather than the actual password. If the database is hacked, an attacker will only be able to see the hash functions, not the real credentials. Furthermore, SHAs display the avalanche effect, in which a small change in the encrypted letters causes a large change in the output; or, conversely, vastly dissimilar strings yield comparable hash values. As a result of this consequence, hash values do not provide any information about the input string, such as its initial size.

1.6.4.1   Characteristics of SHA

Pre-image resistant, second pre-image resistance, and collision resistance are three key safety features used by cryptographic algorithms to keep the information secure. The supply of pre-image resistance particularly makes it difficult and time-consuming for an attacker to find an original comment given the hash value and is the cornerstone of cryptography algorithms. The structure of one-way functions, which is a crucial component of SHA, provides this security. To fend off brute force assault from strong machines, pre-image resistance is required [18]. Second pre-image resistance is a security measure offered by SHA when a communication is known but it is difficult to locate another message that hashes algorithms to the same value. Collision resistance is the final safety feature, which is given by methods that make it much more difficult for an adversary to locate two very different communications that hashes to the same hash value. In addition to provide this feature, there must be a comparable number of potential inputs as random variables, as more inputs than outputs will inevitably result in potential collisions according to the pigeonhole principle.

1.6.4.2   Applications of SHA

TLS and SSL, PGP, SSH, S/MIME, and IPsec are just a few of the security applications and devices that use SHA-1. MD5 and SHA-1 are both developed from MD4 and can be used in those applications. The hash techniques SHA-1 and SHA-2 are legally required for use in certain defense department applications, including use inside other cryptographic methodologies, in order to secure sensitive confidential information. FIPS PUB 180-1 also recommended private and commercial enterprises to adopt and use SHA-1.

1.6.5   Advantages and Disadvantages of Digital Signature

If some crucial conditions are handled both before and during the signing and verification procedure, then digital certificates are legally enforceable [19, 20]. To begin, signers must establish their identification before the document may be considered legally enforceable.

1.6.5.1   Advantages of Digital Signature

- A digital signature is more secure than an electronic system because it uses unique identification keys to construct and validate the signature.
- The time-consuming process of creating a digital signature offers a higher level of security, which is suitable for sensitive data.
- Digital signatures are widely accepted around the world and are legally enforceable in the majority of countries.
- Unauthorized users cannot change digitally signed papers or information.

1.6.5.2   Disadvantages of Digital Signature

- The technology utilized to establish a digital signature will have a big impact on it. If technology develops at its current rate, digital signatures must evolve at the same rate or risk losing their effectiveness.

- Digital signatures need the purchase of digital certificates, which can be rather costly.
- Users must also invest in verification software.

1.6.6   Conclusion

This chapter represents the various classical cryptographic techniques. Classical cryptography depends on mathematics and on the complexity of computing factorization in large numbers. The two major categories of classical cryptography are symmetric key cryptography and asymmetric key cryptography. In symmetric classical, both encryption and decryption are done using same key called private key. SHA is a group of cryptographic techniques that are used to keep data safe. It operates by converting data with a hash function, which is a bitwise operations, modular additions, and compression function–based method.

References

1. Yin, J., Li, Y.-H., Liao, S.-K., Yang, M., Cao, Y., Zhang, L., Ren, J.-G., *et al.*, Entanglement-based secure quantum cryptography over 1,120 kilometres. *Nature*, 582, 7813, 501–505, 2020.
2. Arnon-Friedman, R., Dupuis, F., Fawzi, O., Renner, R., Vidick, T., Practical device-independent quantum cryptography via entropy accumulation. *Nat. Commun.*, 9, 1, 1–11, 2018.
3. Shenoy-Hejamadi, A., Pathak, A., Radhakrishna, S., Quantum cryptography: key distribution and beyond. *Quanta*, 6, 1, 1–47, 2017.
4. Wang, L.-J., Zhang, K.-Y., Wang, J.-Y., Cheng, J., Yang, Y.-H., Tang, S.-B., Yan, D., *et al.*, Experimental authentication of quantum key distribution with post-quantum cryptography. *NPJ Quantum Inf.*, 7, 1, 1–7, 2021.
5. Rajasekar, V., Premalatha, J., Sathya, K., Multi-factor signcryption scheme for secure authentication using hyper elliptic curve cryptography and bio-hash function. *B. Pol. Acad. Sci. Tech.*, 68, 923–935, 2020.
6. Larocque, H., Gagnon-Bischoff, J., Mortimer, D., Zhang, Y., Bouchard, F., Upham, J., Grillo, V., Boyd, R.W., Karimi, E., Generalized optical angular momentum sorter and its application to high-dimensional quantum cryptography. *Opt. Express*, 25, 17, 19832–19843, 2017.
7. Shang, T., Tang, Y., Chen, R., Liu, J., Full quantum one-way function for quantum cryptography. *Quantum Eng.*, 2, 1, e32, 2020.
8. Rajasekar, V., Jayapaul, P., Krishnamoorthi, S., Cryptanalysis and enhancement of multi factor remote user authentication scheme based on signcryption. *Adv. Math. Commun.*, 1–19, 2020. doi:10.3934/amc.2020103

9. Kumar, D.R., Krishna, T.A., Wahi, A., Health Monitoring Framework for in Time Recognition of Pulmonary Embolism Using Internet of Things. *J. Comput. Theor. Nanosci.*, 15, 5, 1598–1602, 2018.

10. Buchmann, J., Braun, J., Demirel, D., Geihs, M., Quantum cryptography: a view from classical cryptography. *Quantum Sci. Technol.*, 2, 2, 020502, 2017.

11. Rajasekar, V., Premalatha, J., Sathya, K., Cancelable Iris template for secure authentication based on random projection and double random phase encoding. *Peer Peer Netw. Appl.*, 14, 2, 747–762, 2021.

12. Moizuddin, M., Winston, J., Qayyum, M., A comprehensive survey: quantum cryptography, in: *2017 2nd International Conference on Anti-Cyber Crimes (ICACC)*, IEEE, pp. 98–102, 2017.

13. Velliangiri, S., Manoharn, R., Ramachandran, S., Rajasekar, V.R., Blockchain Based Privacy Preserving Framework for Emerging 6G Wireless Communications. *IEEE Trans. Industr. Inform.*, 2021. doi: 10.1109/TII.2021.3107556.

14. Lakshmi, P.S. and Murali, G., Comparison of classical and quantum cryptography using QKD simulator, in: *2017 International Conference on Energy, Communication, Data Analytics and Soft Computing (ICECDS)*, IEEE, pp. 3543–3547, 2017.

15. Billewar, S.R., Londhe, G.V., Ghane, S.B., Quantum cryptography: Basic principles and methodology, in: *Limitations and Future Applications of Quantum Cryptography*, pp. 1–20, IGI Global, Mumbai, 2021.

16. Rajasekar, V., Premalatha, J., Sathya, K., Saračević, M., Secure remote user authentication scheme on health care, IoT and cloud applications: A multilayer systematic survey. *Acta Polytech. Hung.*, 18, 3, 87–106, 2021.

17. Dhivya, M.N. and Banupriya, M.S., Network Security with Cryptography and Steganography. *Int. J. Eng. Res. Technol.*, 8, 3, 1–4, 2020.

18. Krishnasamy, L., Dhanaraj, R.K., Ganesh Gopal, D., Reddy Gadekallu, T., Aboudaif, M.K., Abouel Nasr, E., A Heuristic Angular Clustering Framework for Secured Statistical Data Aggregation in Sensor Networks. *Sensors*, 20, 17, 4937, 2020.

19. Keserwani, P.K. and Govil, M.C., A Hybrid Symmetric Key Cryptography Method to Provide Secure Data Transmission, in: *International Conference on Machine Learning, Image Processing, Network Security and Data Sciences*, Springer, Singapore, pp. 461–474, 2020, July.

20. Gupta, M., Gupta, M., Deshmukh, M., Single secret image sharing scheme using neural cryptography. *Multimed. Tools Appl.*, 79, 1–22, 2020.

2

Quantum Cryptographic Techniques

Malathy S.[1*], Santhiya M.[2], Rajesh Kumar Dhanaraj[3]
and Sanjeevikumar Padmanaban[4]

[1]Computer Science and Engineering, Erode, India
[2]Electronics and Instrumentation Engineering Kongu Engineering College,
Erode, India
[3]School of Computing Science & Engineering, Galgotias University,
Greater Noida, Uttar Pradesh, India
[4]Department of Business Development and Technology, Aarhus University,
Herning, Denmark

Abstract

Cryptography is the technique of scrambling plain text, i.e., encrypting data so that only those with the appropriate "key" can read it. By extension, quantum cryptography encrypts data and transmits it in an unhackable manner using quantum mechanics principles. The complexity of quantum cryptography [1] lies in the ideologies of quantum mechanics, which is given as follows: The particles that make up the space are intrinsically insecure, and they can exist in multiple places or states at once. In one of two quantum states, photons are generated at random. It is possible to clone some quantum qualities of a particle, but not the complete particle. It is impossible to measure and analyze a quantum property without disturbing or changing it.

Keywords: Quantum cryptography, post quantum cryptography, entanglement, quantum key distribution, attributes of quantum key distribution, protocols in quantum key distribution, Heisenberg Uncertainty Principle, no-cloning theorem

Corresponding author: ksmalathy@gmail.com

Rajesh Kumar Dhanaraj, Vani Rajasekar, SK Hafizul Islam, Balamurugan Balusamy and Ching-Hsien Hsu (eds.) Quantum Blockchain: An Emerging Cryptographic Paradigm, (31–54)
© 2022 Scrivener Publishing LLC

2.1   Post-Quantum Cryptography

Cryptographic techniques that are expected to be secure on a quantum computer assault are referred to as post-quantum cryptography [3–6].

2.2   Strength of Quantum Cryptography

- Quantum cryptography employs quantum mechanics to convey secure messages and is truly unhackable, unlike mathematical encryption.
- Quantum cryptography [2] encrypts data using quantum physics principles, making it essentially unhackable.

2.3   Working Principle of Quantum Cryptography

Quantum cryptography, which is also defined as the quantum key distribution (QKD), is a method of transmitting data through a fiber optic cable using a succession of photons (light particles) as shown in Figure 2.1. By relating the percentage of measurements and properties of these photons, the two endpoints can fix the safer key which could be used. The steps will be explained to the core as follows.

1. Photons pass via a filter, which assigns one of four polarizations and bit designations:

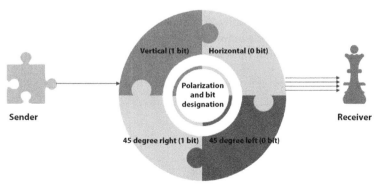

• The photons read with the incorrect beam splitter are eliminated
• The state of the photon will change if it is read or copied in anyway by an eavesdropper

Figure 2.1 Overview of quantum cryptography.

- vertical (1 bit)
- horizontal (0 bit)
- 45° right (1 bit), or
- 45° left (0 bit)

2. The photons are transmitted to a receiver, which reads the polarization of each photon using two beam splitters. The receiver must estimate which beam splitter to utilize for each photon because it does not know which to use.

3. After sending the stream of photons to the receiver, it informs the sender about the type of beam splitter used for each photon in the sequence. Then, the sender matches this information to the polarizer sequence for conveying the key. The photons matched with the incorrect beam splitter are eliminated, and the resulting bit sequence will be determined as the key.

4. If an eavesdropper reads or copies the photon in any way, then the status of the photon will change. The endpoints will be able to detect the change. To put it another way, you cannot read a photon and then forward it or replicate it without being discovered.

2.4   Example of Quantum Cryptography

The overall working principle of quantum cryptography is illustrated in Figure 2.2.

1. Allow two persons, "XX" and "YY", to send each other a secret message that no one else can read.

2. A succession of photons that have been polarized is sent by "XX" to "YY" across a fiber optic connection using QKD. Because photons have a randomized quantum state, this wire does not need to be secured.

3. If an eavesdropper (Say Eve) tries to overhear the conversation between "XX" and "YY", then she has to read each photon in order to figure out what is being said.

4. Then, Eve has to pass that photon to "YY".

5. Eve changes the quantum state of the photon by reading it, introducing faults into the quantum key.

6. This informs "XX" and "YY" that someone is overhearing their conversation, which leads to change the key for communicating further.

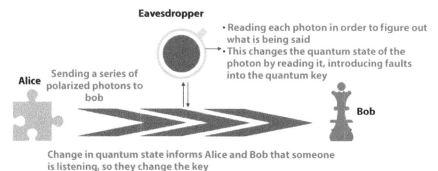

Figure 2.2 Working principle of quantum cryptography.

7. "YY" will be able to read the secret if "XX" sends him another new key, which has not been compromised.

2.5   Fundamentals of Quantum Cryptography

Quantum mechanics is a set of principles or mathematical foundation for constructing physical theories. Even specialists find quantum mechanics' laws perplexing, and the former environments of quantum computation and information might be drawn back to physicists' long-lasting desire to comprehend quantum mechanics in a better way.

2.5.1   Entanglement

Entanglement is one of the significant resources in quantum mechanics, which plays a vital role in most of the exciting quantum computation applications. In recent years, a great deal of effort has gone into better understanding the features of entanglement, regardless of information, entropy, energy, and any of the other ultimate resource. A complete entanglement theory has not yet been developed. However, still, significant progress is achieved in realizing this essential feature of quantum mechanics.

2.5.1.1   Entanglement State

Direct interactions between subatomic particles are the most common cause of entanglement. These encounters can take a variety of shapes. One of the most common methods for producing polarized photons is impulsive parametric down-conversion. Other techniques include using a fiber coupler to limit and fuse photons, using quantum dots to capture electrons until they decay. The intertwined particles were created using atomic forces in the first testing of Bell's theorem. Entanglement swapping can also be used to produce entanglement prevailing among quantum systems that have not interact directly.

It is impossible to identify which system belongs to a distinct pure state when the composite system is in this condition. The subsystem entropy measure should be more than zero practically, despite the fact that the von Neumann entropy of the overall state is estimated as zero. The systems are "entangled" in this sense. Interferometry suffers from distinct empirical repercussions as a result of this. It is worth noting that the following example is one of four maximally entangled pure states known as Bell states.

2.6   Problems With the One-Time Pad and Key Distribution

There is an unbreakable code in traditional cryptography. Gilbert Vernam invented it in 1918 [14], and it is called the one-time-pad. In the one-time pad technique presented in Figure 2.3, "XX" converts a message into binary form using a publicly known mechanism. A set of binary string that is equal to the message's length is determined as a key. "XX" encrypts plain text by using XOR to combine each message bit with the corresponding key bit to produce the cipher text.

"XX" then uses a broadcast channel to send the cypher text to "YY". The encryption text can be obtained by anyone, including an eavesdropper. The cypher text, on the other hand, is completely random without the key, and it does not have any information regarding the plain text. "YY", who shares the same key as "XX", can recover the plain text by performing another XOR between the encrypted text and the associated key bit.

The one-time pad approach is impenetrable, but it has a major flaw: it assumes that the sending agent and receiving agent share a random sequence of string that is same as the message at first. As a result, the one-time pad just pushes the challenge of establishing the communication securely to key distribution [8]. This is the main issue with dissemination.

Public key cryptography is one proposed solution to the issue of key distribution. The key distribution issue can be solved using quantum mechanics. Using nonorthogonal quantum states, a random key for the process of encryption is generated between the sender and the receiver in QKD. The no-cloning theorem in quantum mechanics states that even an

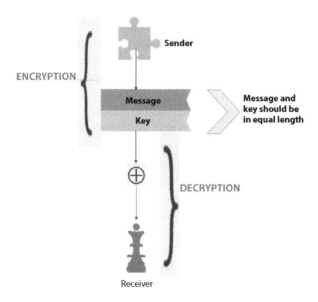

Figure 2.3 One-time pad operation.

eavesdropper is unable to produce the duplicate of an unidentified quantum state. As a result, any attempt by an unauthorized person to obtain a key in a QKD process will cause disruption, which "XX" and "YY" can identify by examining the error rate of raw data transmission.

2.7   Quantum No-Cloning Property

The quantum no-cloning theorem is defined as the direct outcome of quantum physics' linearity. It also states that, if a measurement provides a knowledge on the state of a quantum system, then the quantum system's state will be disturbed in general, unless it is known in advance that the original quantum system's possible states are orthogonal to each other.

At first glance, the inability to create exact replicas of unknown quantum states appears to be a flaw. Any attempt tried by the unauthorized listener to understand the quantum mechanically encoded information would disrupt the quantum state and reveal her presence. The features of the quantum no cloning theorem is shown in Figure 2.4 and is presented below.

1. Conventional error correction techniques cannot be used on quantum states because of the no-cloning theorem. The backup copies of a state cannot be used either to fix

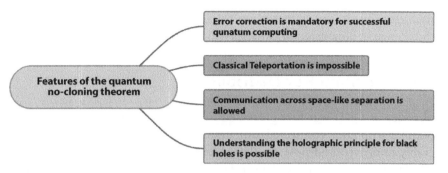

Figure 2.4 Features of quantum no-cloning theorem.

subsequent faults or in the middle of a quantum computation. Error rectification is necessary for successful quantum computing, and it was once regarded to be a fatal flaw.

2. Cloning would also be a violation of the no teleportation theorem, which states that classical teleportation is impossible. Quantum states cannot be properly measured.

3. The no-cloning theorem does not preclude superluminal message via quantum entanglement since cloning is adequate technique but not a required condition for such communication. This allows the users to establish the process of communication across space-like separations.

4. The no-cloning theorem stops us from understanding the black hole holography principle as two distinct copy of data residing at the event horizon and inside a black hole at the same time. As a result, more radical interpretations emerge, such as black hole complementarity.

2.8   Heisenberg Uncertainty Principle

The Heisenberg Uncertainty Principle (HUP) is a key idea in quantum physics that serves as the foundation for the preliminary realization of basic uncertainties lying in an experimenter's capacity to detect more than one quantum variable at the same time.

Quantum communication is the transmission of information at the quantum level. the transmission of encrypted messages that are unhackable by computers, because the instructions are conveyed by minute light particles called photons, this is conceivable. If a spy or a third person tries to recite the message while it is in transmission path, then the disturbance will produce the change in dimension of particles will be detected as a result of the HUP.

2.9 Quantum Key Distribution

The idea of QKD was first presented in early 1970s, but it was becoming popular when it is connected with entanglement. Since then, it is considerably improved and now developed as an effective quantum technology [3]. Data security is critical in today's digital society, both during communication and storage in various fields such as e-health, e-banking, e-government, and e-business channels.

With the advancement of quantum computers, which have the capacity to break this protection, the threat to everyone is becoming more real. QKD is the only technology that can genuinely handle the issue of enduring security, especially when it comes to health records, which may need to be safeguarded for the rest of a person's life [9].

Similarly, vital infrastructure that supplies services such as energy must handle this danger, and quantum technologies hold the key once again. The current challenge is integrating these QKD systems into existing are as follows.

- Network organization, which is being worked on by multi-disciplinary teams of network operators, telecommunication and QKD-related equipment manufacturers, digital security professionals, infrastructure providers, and scientists.
- QKD allows you to distribute and share secret keys, which are required for cryptographic protocols. It is important to keep the keys private between the conversing parties.
- QKD, which is based on quantum physics concepts, offers an absolutely safe mechanism to dispense random keys via unsecure channels.
- To improve information security, the secure and safe key created by QKD might be used in most of the encryption techniques.

Example:
The section explains the phases of secret key generation as illustrated in Figure 2.5.

1. "XX" can select to translate them in a system of bit sequence using either of the two different states, such as vertical (V)

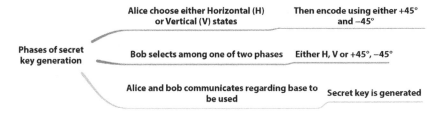

Figure 2.5 Phases of secret key generation.

or horizontal (H) polarization, and also choose to translate in two separate states, such as +45° and −45°.

2. "YY" then selects one of two bases: H, V or +45°, −45°. If Robert measures in a different base than the one "XX" used to formulate, then his resultant value will be different one than the actual value and so it will be discarded; however, if they both picked the same base, both will precisely correlated results: "XX" sends hand, "YY" senses H, and the values are saved.

3. This final phase necessitates "XX" and "YY" communicating about the type of the base used. It does not reveal any data about the message and serves as the key to be used secretly between them.

These steps generate a secret key, which must then be put into cryptographic protocols in order to assure safety in the many applications where it is utilized. The quantum physics is potential enough to identify flaws and disclose them if a hacker attempts to capture the key generation. This occurs prior to any data being encoded or sent.

2.10   Cybersecurity Risks Prevailing in Current Cryptographic Techniques

Authentication and secrecy are two features that our cybersecurity architecture demands. Authentication allows users to trust and validate the content of their interactions from afar. Public key signature systems are commonly used to implement it. Any transmission of private information necessitates confidentiality. It is frequently carried out in two steps. The users must first exchange a shared secret key.

This is based on the key exchange mechanism, which is a public key protocol. A symmetric key encryption algorithm is then employed with the secret key. Both functions rely on asymmetric or public key cryptography, which uses comparable cryptographic principles.

Cybersecurity entails a lot more than just cryptography. All contemporary hacks and security failures are due to defective implementation, social engineering, and the like, rather than inadequate encryption. Today, we put our faith in cryptography and work hard to ensure that it is implemented correctly.

Today's point of cryptographic vulnerability is public key cryptography, which uses techniques like RSA or elliptic curve to both authenticate data and safely exchange encryption keys. The quantum computer's processing capacity allows it to answer these mathematical problems exponentially quicker than traditional computers, breaking public key cryptography.

As a result, current public key cryptosystems are unsuitable for securing data that requires long-term confidentiality. By attacking the public keys, an adversary might indeed record encrypted data and wait for a quantum computer to decipher it.

2.11   Implementation of Quantum-Safe Cryptography

Public cryptography, also known as asymmetric algorithms, is the most vulnerable. It is used for digital signatures and key exchange. Once a universal quantum computer is accessible, quantum algorithms such as the well-known Shor's algorithm can break RSA and elliptic curve methods.

The Grover method, another well-known quantum technique, targets symmetric cryptography. Grover, fortunately, can be defeated by simply increasing the key size. The AES symmetric encryption system with 256-bit keys, for example, is deemed quantum-safe.

Two pillars will be used to combat the quantum computing danger as shown in Figure 2.6.

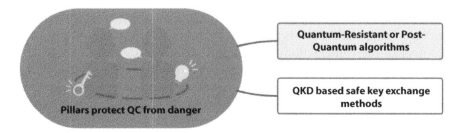

Figure 2.6 Two pillars protects QC from danger.

1. The first is the creation of new classical algorithms that will withstand the quantum computer. These are known as quantum-resistant or post-quantum algorithms [5, 7].
2. QKD, which provides quantum-safe key exchange based on completely distinct concepts, is the second pillar, which is currently available.

2.12   Practical Usage of Existing QKD Solutions

The majority of QKD solutions now include key distribution equipment and link encryptors [4]. The secret keys are distributed to the link encryptors by the QKD appliances. The keys are used by the link encryptors to encrypt massive volumes of data, usually up to 100 Gb/s.

In the most basic scenario, two QKD appliances are connected via optical fiber and continuously disseminate key material, which they store at each end-point until the encryptors require it. Depending on the quality of the optical network, these solutions work up to an optical attenuation in the fiber of 18 dB, which equates to a range of around 80 km. As a result, these systems are commonly found in Local and Metropolitan Area Networks, such as corporate campuses and datacenter interconnects.

Through the deployment of so-called Trusted Nodes, these applications have been expanded across much greater distances. Key hopping is a process in which keys are generated at a starting node and securely moved from node to node until they reach the destination node. Instead of relying on the security of the entire transmission line, each node must have its own security. Various forms of QKD networks, including as ring networks and star networks, can also be built using a similar technology.

This necessitates more complicated Key Management Schemes that distribute keys from and to any network node. The Trusted Nodes can be implemented in satellites with free-space QKD for global reach. Many encryptor manufacturers now provide "quantum enabled" devices that take keys from QKD appliances [12]. These encryptors work with Ethernet and Fiber Channel, with a connection bandwidth of up to 10 Gbps and a combined bandwidth of up to 100 Gbps.

2.13   Attributes of Quantum Key Distribution

QKD is a new class of security solutions that does not depend upon computational assumptions for apparently challenging issues. QKD networks, on the other hand, must be incorporated into the current environment and match with specific requirements and circumstances [9]. Figure 2.7 states some of the most common QKD network requirements.

1. Key rate
2. Length of the link
3. Key material protection
4. Robustness
5. Usage of the key

2.13.1   Key Rate

The average key rate of a QKD network is one of the most important factors in defining a QKD system. Because encryption and decryption activities are not possible without enough key material, the rate at which key material is recorded in the key storage against the rate at which it is used for encryption and decryption actions has a significant impact on network performance. With enhanced optical components and better electronics, primarily in the usage of detectors, a constantly rising secret key rate has been achieved over the last 20 years. Digital signal processing in FPGA was improved for attaining the record-high speeds of about 10 Mbps. By eliminating restrictions without using an FPGA, the throughput of measured qubits has been increased to improve key rates, especially for shorter connections.

Another research is in underway to achieve longer single-span transmission lengths based on protocol improvements and technology advancements that result in detectors with lower dark count rates. In the future, an ideal solution will considerably outperform current key rate and distance values, despite the fact that the race between key material creation and consumption will continue.

Figure 2.7 Attributes of key distribution.

2.13.2   Length of the Link

The major issue in the QKD network is the length of the link over which the key material can be created. The link length restricts the capability of the quantum channel to a particular distance. The longest connection in the DARPA QKD network was a 29-km link between Harvard and Boston Universities through an optical switch. The longest link in SECOQC was 82 km between the BREIT and St. Pölten nodes, whereas the longest link in Tokyo was a record-breaking 90 km between the Koganei-1 and Koganei-2 nodes. The distance over which QKD connections may be efficiently applied in existing optical fiber networks is restricted to about 100 km.

2.13.3   Key Material Production

The security of the established key material is the fundamental reason for interest in QKD. This means that a QKD network's nodes must be protected with a greater probability that the key material produced is unique and unavailable to other parties. The confidentiality of key material is assessed not only at its generation, but also during its management, storage, and final usage. As a result, it is critical to protect each level of the QKD network design.

2.13.4   Robustness

QKD networks are gradually taking part in conventional and daily communications systems because of their low cost and ease of installation. It is crucial to maintain reliability, which is demonstrated by the progressive and smooth inclusion of additional nodes and the development of new linkages [10]. To avoid faulty nodes or nodes experiencing heavy attack, a QKD network must provide enough alternative routes. Regardless of the security measures used, it is vital to remember that attackers may simply terminate optical links and disrupt QKD connections. In such cases, a QKD network must have a sufficient response.

2.13.5   Usage of the Key

Due to limited resources, network communication is kept at a bare minimum, since each subsequent packet requires the usage of already generated key material. Because communication is generally done hop by hop, requiring the integrity of every nodes along the way, the shortest routing path must be chosen to reduce the number of nodes that may be seized or targeted by an unauthorized person. Longer routes also demand a larger consumption of key materials. To minimize the possibility of leaks, expired key material is voluntarily discarded during network congestion or communication difficulties, and new key material for retransmission is applied. As a result, reducing the number of hops is preferred.

2.14   Quantum Key Distribution Protocols

Quantum cryptography protocols are developed with the intent of having their security ensured by quantum physics principles [11, 13]. Quantum cryptography techniques must be fully investigated at an amount of precision that is near to that of actual implementation. For the study and verification of communication systems and protocols, computer researchers have designed a variety of methodologies and tools.

The majority of encrypted online traffic is controlled by using commodity security protocols. Despite the fact that these protocols are defined, they lack a common application programming interface (API), and a variety of implementations are available for these protocols. The most commonly used QKD protocols [12] are explained in the forthcoming section. The general model of QKD protocol model is shown in Figure 2.8.

2.14.1   BB84 Protocol

Charles Bennett and Gilles Brassard designed the Bennett-Brassard protocol BB84 QKD channels in 1984. This protocol is the first developed in quantum cryptography. The protocol is highly robust because it focuses on two scenarios: the quantum characteristic that data collection is only

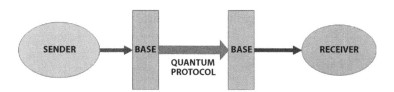

Figure 2.8 QKD model protocol.

feasible at the cost of signal disturbance if the two states being differentiated are not orthogonal and the occurrence of authenticated public traditional channel. This is generally described by privately sending a security code from one client to the other that can be used in one-time pad encryption.

2.14.2 Decoy State Protocol

This protocol is desirable because it necessitates minor changes to the current hardware used for the BB84 protocol. Hwang was the one who initially proposed this framework. Photon pulses coming out from the attenuated laser beam with a differing mean photon number are called as "decoy" pulses. These pulses are added in parallel to the photon pulses that are used to deliver key data. The key data can be called as signal pulses. In signal pulse channel, decoy pulses are dynamically overlapped. The decoy state protocol provides absolute security and allows for transmission lengths of over 140 km.

2.14.3 T12 Protocol

Lucamarini proposed a novel "T12" protocol that is both secure and efficient in the finite size situation. T12 protocol's security verification is defined by the finite size security proofs established and has a number of advantages. To begin with, it enables uniformly configurable security, which indicates that the key is protected regardless of the function for which it is employed. Second, it does not necessitate a random permutation of the clients' text before the conventional post-processing process nor does it necessitate encrypting error-corrected data.

2.14.4 SARG04 Protocol

The four states of polarization are utilized in the BB84 protocol. When these states are encrypted with unique data, a distinct protocol called SARG04 is developed. This protocol is robust toward the photon-number-splitting attack. These attacks will usually happen if attenuated laser pulses are utilized as a replacement for single-photon sources. According to computations and data previously published about this protocol, the average "Quantum Bit Error Rate" for N = 2 is about 75%, which is higher than 50% for the BB84 protocol. It is predicted that a free space link with a transmission distance of up to 144 km would be possible.

2.14.5 Six-State Protocol

Six-state protocol was created by Pasquinucci and Gisin. This consists of addition of two polarization states. This protocol's polarization states are divided into three categories: x, y, and z. It is comparable to BB84's well-known four states (0°, 90°, +45°, and −45°), but with the addition of two polarized basis as shown in Figure 2.9. In 2001, Nicolas Gisin said that this technique is extremely secure and reduces the amount of disturbance induced by Eve's attempt to access the information. When calculating with single photon, the QBER is 33% for this SSP protocol and 25% for the BB84 protocol.

2.14.6 E91 Protocol

It works on the concept of quantum entanglement. The method is based on two entanglement characteristics. Firstly, in which Alice A produces a set of photons, which are dispersed by both of them, and they end up with a single photon. These entangled photons are conceptually coupled; if both compute their photons' vertical or horizontal polarization states, then they receive a 100% chance of getting the same result. Second, any effort by Eve to listen in on Alice and Bob's communications breaks these relationships in a way that Alice and Bob can recognize [12].

2.14.7 COW Protocol (Coherent One-Way Protocol)

In this Coherent One-Way (COW) Protocol, a key is established and an interferometer is built on an additional observing line using the predicted photon arrival time on the detector data line. The aim of this line is to allow for the detection of a secret agent attempting to disrupt consistency through an attack.

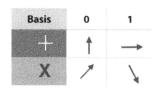

Figure 2.9 Polarization states (rectilinear and orthogonal).

2.14.8   HDQKD Protocol (High-Dimensional Quantum Key Distribution)

This High-Dimensional Quantum Key Distribution (HDQKD) protocol can be deployed by using the same degrees of freedom of qubits. By creating an expanded set of states corresponding to a d-dimensional Hilbert space, high-dimensional QKD algorithms have recently been proposed, demonstrating how bits of information may be securely encrypted on each single photon [15]. Qudits are the name for such states. The increased information capacity of qudits enables for more efficient use of the photon budget at the transmitter while simultaneously reducing the risk of saturation in single-photon detectors at the receiver. Furthermore, employing high-dimensional states enhances the communication's resilience to noise, allowing for a larger quantum bit error rate threshold value (QBER). As a result, when compared to conventional QKD protocols with binary encoding, high-dimensional QKD achieves a higher secret key rate and the total losses are reduced to limit the randomized dark counts at the receiver to a minimum level.

2.14.9   KMB09 Protocol

This belongs to the category of high–error rate QKD protocol. This sort of cryptographic protocol employs two sets of bases and is known as prepare and measure. When Alice gives Bob a set of photons in one of the specified states, Bob estimates the photons' arrival on an independently defined basis. A conventional route, which Alice employed for the encryption of the photon, allowed her to provide some information about the index of the base state in order to create a strong connection. KMB09 similarly achieves a 25% transmission rate of key, but at the cost of a large error rate in the presence of an eavesdropper. When using KMB09, the bit error rate is around 50%.

2.14.10   B92 Protocol

This protocol uses only two nonorthogonal states, and it is proposed by Charles Bennett in 1992. It differs from BB84 in such a way that it only employs two distinct photon states (one in H-polarization and one in +45°-polarization) as opposed to four in BB84.

2.14.11   MSZ96 Protocol

MSZ96 is a QKD technique that uses four nonorthogonal quantum states for its operation. In this protocol, the cryptographic key bit is encrypted by using these states and that are characterized by noncommuting quadrature phase amplitudes of a weaker optical field. Here, there is no need for photon polarization as in BB84 Protocol or entangled photons as in E91 protocol.

2.14.12   DPS Protocol

Kyo Inoue suggested this Differential Phase Shift Protocol in 2003 and tested it on two nonorthogonal states. Sender Alice uses a Poisson distribution to send a randomized modulated cohesive train of pulses ranging between 0 and π. Bob, the receiver divides each pulse into two paths and then merges those pulses using a beam splitter. When the beams are merged, the computed phase difference between those two trains of pulses can either be 0 or π. The sender and the receiver can fix their key bits and reject all other bits based on the occurrences of the detector of the proper findings. In addition, the DPS protocol is resistant to a PNS assault.

2.14.13   Three-Stage Quantum Protocol

In 2006, this quantum cryptography technique was originally suggested, and in 2012, it was realized. It is an asymmetric cryptography-based system in which each user encrypts messages delivered across public channels with their own secret key. In contradiction to the BB84 protocol, which transfers a single stream of quantum bits in one way before switching to traditional data, the message will be in quantum throughout all the stages. There is a chance that multi-photon quantum cryptography will be used. This technique uses several photons to exchange signals between sender and receiver for improving data transfer.

2.14.14   S09 Protocol

Eduin Esteban Hernandez Serna demonstrated this S09 protocol, which employs both private and public key encryption. This protocol ensures that information is safely sent across an open network. The transmission stays quantum at all stages. In this protocol, the enormous key distribution occurs between the n − 1 devices and a key distribution center. Because it is not employing the traditional channels, it is immune to the middle-in-the-man attack and other subsequent attacks. This protocol allows for the transfer of qubits in any condition.

2.15   Applications of Quantum Cryptography

Computers and the internet are now used mostly by everyone. The internet is closely associated with business activities, online purchase, online games, and advertising. Despite the fact that the internet has made our lives easier, we are indeed concerned about our confidentiality and protection. As a result, many are hoping for certain highly secured techniques

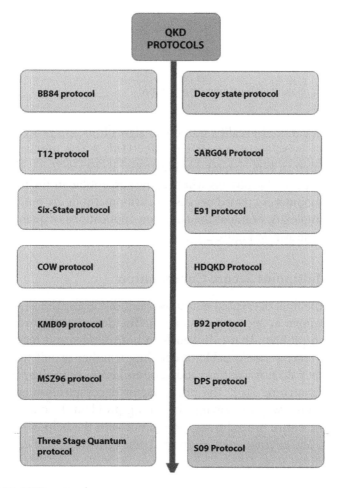

Figure 2.10 QKD protocols.

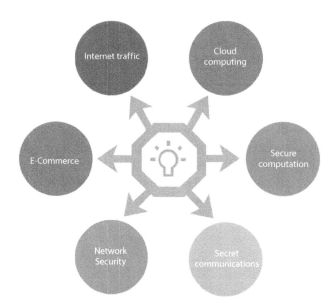

Figure 2.11 Applications of quantum cryptography.

for communication. In reality, numerous algorithms and procedures have been created by scientists to offer privacy [16]. A few important protocols mentioned in this chapter are illustrated in Figure 2.10. These standard algorithms and protocols will become susceptible in the future if the quantum computer is created because security methods are built on mathematical complexity. Some of the common applications of quantum cryptography are shown in Figure 2.11.

2.15.1   Multipoint Secure Computation

Acquiring the final decrypted output without disclosing the needed information is known as secure computation. The dating problem is a secure computation problem that is linked with both sender and receiver. Both sender and receiver are capable of deciding whether or not to date each other, but they do not want anybody else to know about their plans save for the end outcome [16]. The prime factor decomposition approach is the conventional way for solving the dating problem. In quantum cryptography, the entire procedure is carried out with the help of four entangled qubits. The entanglement property is the only thing that can assist us solve the dating difficulty. The dating problem can be solved using standard computing methods; therefore, we focus on quantum security for this issue. Mathematical complexity is used in the conventional technique. It indicates that, if we had a supercomputer, then we can figure out the solution quickly. The security features of physics are used in all operations that employ quantum technologies. Because it is uncrackable, this type of security seems to be more dependable than the previous.

2.15.2   E-Commerce

Quantum theory may also be used to tackle communication problems. Solving these difficulties with traditional approaches is difficult and wasteful. Quantum mechanics provides a simple and effective solution to these issues. Some individuals have been motivated by quantum theory to create algorithms that replicate the superposition and entanglement phenomena in traditional computers. The majority of such simulated algorithms are really good at tackling such difficult issues, and yet we still had to work on improving them. In the upcoming years, the quantum algorithms may give enhanced security and reliability.

2.15.3   Cloud Computing

Because of internet's fast and substantial growth, there is an increase in the emergence of computation and storage technologies. As a result of these storage and SaaS improvements, a new computing model has emerged: cloud computing. Given that such an application relies on a traditional network for its data transport, several users can store their data on the same server, with resource allocation and scheduling being handled by the cloud service provider, making cloud security a critical problem. Security breaches at Apple and Dropbox have made cloud security a hot issue in recent days as hackers attempt to get access to one or more cloud services. Some scientists are proposing a novel "hybrid" security architecture for cloud computing that takes advantage of both existing protocols and quantum cryptography's security advantages. The storage system effectively meets the criteria of data integrity, data secrecy, and packet delivery due to the tight interaction of encoding, encryption, and forwarding. The storage servers execute coding and re-encryption actions separately, while the key servers handle partial decryption actions in totally independent way.

2.16   Conclusion

The technique of scrambling plain text or encrypting data so that only those with the proper "key" may read it is known as cryptography. Quantum cryptography uses quantum physics concepts to encrypt and transmit data in an unhackable manner. Quantum cryptography, also known as QKD, is a way of sending data via a fiber optic cable by employing a series of photons (light particles). Entanglement is a key resource in quantum physics that plays an important role in many interesting quantum computing applications. The most prevalent source of entanglement is direct interactions between subatomic particles. One suggested solution to the problem of key distribution is public key cryptography. Quantum mechanics can be used to address the key distribution problem. In QKD, a random key for the encryption process is produced between the transmitter and the receiver using nonorthogonal quantum states. The quantum no-cloning theorem is referred to as direct result of the linearity of quantum physics. The HUP is a fundamental concept in quantum physics that constitute the basis for the preliminary understanding of fundamental limitations in an experimenter's ability to detect multiple quantum variables at the same time. Our cybersecurity architecture necessitates authentication and confidentiality. The common attributes of the QKD network are key rate, length of the link, key material protection, robustness and usage of the key. Quantum cryptography protocols are developed with the intent of having their security ensured by quantum physics principles. The most commonly used protocols are BB84, three-state quantum protocol, COW protocol, and so on. Some of the common applications of quantum cryptography are secure data sharing, cloud computing, future e-commerce, secure internet communication, network security, quantum machine learning, and quantum security–based IoT approach.

References

1. Yin, J., Li, Y.H., Liao, S.K. *et al.*, Entanglement-based secure quantum cryptography over 1,120 kilometres. *Nature*, 582, 501–505, 2020.
2. Routray, S.K., Jha, M.K., Sharma, L., Nyamangoudar, R., Javali, A., Sarkar, S., Quantum cryptography for IoT: A Perspective. *2017 Int. Conf. on IoT and Application*, pp. 1–4, 2017.
3. Pirandola, S., Andersen, U.L., Banchi, L., Berta, M., Bunandar, D., Colbeck, R., Englund, A.D., Gehring, T., Lupo, C., Ottaviani, C., Pereira, J.L., Razavi, M., Shamsul Shaari, J., Tomamichel, M., Usenko, V.C., Vallone, G., Villoresi,

P., Wallden, P., Advances in quantum cryptography. *Adv. Opt. Photonics*, 12, 1012–1236, 2020.

4. Dhanaraj, R.K., Krishnasamy, L., Geman, O., Izdrui, D.R., Black hole and sink hole attack detection in wireless body area networks. *Comput. Mater. Con.*, 68, 2, 1949–1965, 2021.

5. Borges, F., Reis, P.R., Pereira, D., Comparison of Security and its Performance for Key Agreements in Post-Quantum Cryptography. *IEEE Access*, 8, 142413–142422, 2020.

6. Dhanaraj, R.K., Lalitha, K., Anitha, S., Khaitan, S., Gupta, P., Goyal, M.K., Hybrid and dynamic clustering-based data aggregation and routing for wireless sensor networks [JB]. *J. Intell. Fuzzy Syst.*, (Preprint), 1–15, 2021.

7. Alagic, G., Alperin-Sheriff, J., Apon, D., Cooper, D.A., Dang, Q., Kelsey, J., Liu, Y.-K., Miller, C., Moody, D., Peralta, R., Perlner, R., Robinson, A., Smith-Tone, D., A Status Report on the Second Round of the NIST Post-Quantum Cryptography Standardization Process, A NIST Internal Report (NISTIR) 8309, National Institute of Standards and Technology, Gaithersburg, MD, 2020.

8. Mitra, S., Jana, B., Bhattacharya, S., Pal, P., Poray, J., Quantum cryptography: Overview, security issues and future challenges. *2017 4th Int. National Conf. on Opto-Electronics and Applied Optics (Optronix)*, pp. 1–7, 2017.

9. Balygin, K.A., Zaitsev, V., II, Klimov, A.N. *et al.*, Practical quantum cryptography. *JETP Lett.*, 105, 606–612, 2017. https://doi.org/10.1134/S0021364017090077.

10. Mehic, M., Niemiec, M., Rass, S., Ma, J., Peev, M., Aguado, A., Martin, V., Schauer, S., Poppe, A., Pacher, C., Vozňák, M., Quantum Key Distribution: A Networking Perspective. *ACM Comput. Surv.*, 53, 5, 1–41, 2020.

11. Zhou, T., Shen, J., Li, X., Wang, C., Shen, J., Quantum Cryptography for the Future Internet and the Security Analysis. *Secur. Commun. Netw.*, 2018.

12. Kong, P.-Y., A Review of Quantum Key Distribution Protocolsin the Perspective of Smart GridCommunication Security. *IEEE Syst. J.*, 2020.

13. Gyongyosi, L., Bacsardi, L., Imre, S., A Survey on Quantum Key Distribution. *Infocommunications J.*, 11, 2, 14–21, 2019.

14. Ramakrishnan, V., Chenniappan, P., Dhanaraj, R.K., Hsu, C.H., Xiao, Y., Al-Turjman, F., Bootstrap aggregative mean shift clustering for big data anti-pattern detection analytics in 5G/6G communication networks. *Comput. Electr. Eng.*, 95, 107380, 2021.

15. Vagniluca, I., Lio, B.D., Rusca, D., Cozzolino, D., Ding, Y., Zbinden, H., Zavatta, A., Oxenløwe, L., Bacco, D., Efficient time-bin encoding for practical high-dimensional quantum key distribution. *Phys. Rev. Appl.*, 14, 1, 014051, 2020.

16. Chen, C.-Y., Zeng, G.-J., Lin, F.-J., Chou, Y.-H., Quantum Cryptography and Its Applications over the Internet. *IEEE Netw.*, 29, 64–69, 2015.

3

Evolution of Quantum Blockchain

Dinesh Komarasamy[1]* and Jenita Hermina J.[2]

[1]*Department of Computer Science and Engineering, Kongu Engineering College, Perundurai, India*
[2]*Department of Computer Science and Engineering, Er. Perumal Manimekalai College of Engineering, Hosur, India*

Abstract

Blockchain is the mechanism that makes security harder or difficult to hack, alter, or scam the system. Blockchain is very familiar because it has a digital transaction ledger distributed across the network. Every block in the chain has many new transactions that are added to the ledger. The ledger is maintained in the decentralized database by multiple participants, which is termed as Distributed Ledger Technology (DLT). DLT is secure, distributed, immutable, and time-stamped. Similar to classic databases, blockchain also stores a copy of blocks. The key features of quantum blockchain are performance and safety. Moreover, quantum blockchain has faster processing speed and safer transactions based on quantum mechanics. To corrupt a system, every block in a chain has to be changed. Hence, the system is highly secured.

Keywords: Blockchain, quantum computers, quantum cryptography

3.1 Introduction of Blockchain

Blockchain is one type of database, which is shared among the users by giving the rights to the users through transacting valuable assets in a public environment without depending on the intermediary authority or central authority. The blockchain collects information and stores it in any specific

Corresponding author: dinesh.nova@gmail.com

Rajesh Kumar Dhanaraj, Vani Rajasekar, SK Hafizul Islam, Balamurugan Balusamy and Ching-Hsien Hsu (eds.) Quantum Blockchain: An Emerging Cryptographic Paradigm, (55–82)

location, which is termed as blocks. Therefore, the blocks are interconnected with each other to form a blockchain in which each block has certain storage capacities. A fresh block has been created and appended with the blockchain whenever new information or transaction is processed. The blocks in a blockchain are stored in a network by creating specific nodes. Each node has a copy of the chained block which can also be updated when a new block is added. After creating a block, each hash has its own hash code embedded with a timestamp. The hash codes are randomly generated using a predefined function by the combination of letters and strings. The hash code is appended with the timestamp, and it has been added with the blockchain [1].

Nowadays, every user prefers to store their information in a digital mode. Even although the users store their data in digital mode in any network, the end-users sometimes worry about information security. The end users have the following queries to store the data or information online. The queries are as follows: (i) How the information is securely transmitted and stored in a network; (ii) Who is authorized to handle the information; and (iii) Where the information is stored in the network. In order to resolve the queries, blockchain technology has emerged, which stores the information securely. The information stored in the blockchain is secure and immutable.

The ultimate objective of the blockchain is to record digital information and distribute it through the network. Even though the digital information is distributed, blockchain does not allow the end-user or hackers to modify the information stored in the database. Sometimes, the users update their information. Even though users update their information, a new block will be created instead of changing the data in the existing blocks. The blocks are replicated in the network and so if a hacker changes any data in the network, the data that exists in the remaining nodes are violated. Therefore, the information stored in the blockchain is much more secure. Since the data is replicated throughout the network, the blockchain is costlier and not preferable for all applications.

Therefore, blockchain has a public distributed database that holds encrypted ledgers to store authorized information. Ledger is created by software in which the data is distributed throughout the network in an encrypted manner. Since the ledger is distributed throughout the network, every user has a copy of the data. Even though the blockchain is costlier, blockchain is preferred for banking applications to securely store the data. For banking applications, the ledger will maintain the following information such as account number and balance amount of the people in a network. After each transaction, the details of the transaction will be updated in the ledger of each network. Even though any minor transaction takes place in the bank application, the ledger needs to be updated. The ledger will be updated after each successful transaction. For example, if any user wants to withdraw the amount from the bank, then the transaction will be recorded only if the users have a sufficient balance for any transaction. In similar to that, the bitcoin technique is introduced to replace the banking transaction [2].

In bitcoin, a ledger is maintained to record all the transaction details with the help of a minor. A minor is the one who records and maintains the ledger by initiating and completing the transaction. A transaction is initiated only when the person has sufficient bitcoins. The minor does not support multiple transactions at the same time. Instead of supporting multiple transactions at the same time, the minor permits the transaction to take place sequentially. The minor will validate the balance only after the completion of each transaction and the minor approves the other transaction only if there is a sufficient amount of bitcoins in their account. Each transaction is recorded in a blockchain by creating a block. Therefore, all the successful transactions are recorded in bitcoin. In bitcoin, the blocks are initially validated and the amount is debited to an end-user. After the successful transaction, the ledger will be updated and encrypted with the information. The information is stored in a block, in which the blocks are connected to form a blockchain. In a blockchain, the blocks are interconnected by establishing hash maps.

The hash map creates and stores the information in a block. The information is stored once it is verified and validated. Therefore, all the transactions are recorded in a hash table, and, thereby, the hash table will grow in size based on the number of transactions. The ultimate objective of the blockchain is to create a unique hash code for each block using the hashing algorithm. The effective hashing algorithms will generate an efficient hash code. The hash function will generate a unique code dynamically, and, thereby, it is difficult to read or hack the code using the hash function. However, predicting the hash code is not possible in a blockchain. Therefore, blockchain is preferred for bitcoin because of the secure encrypted algorithm. Minor avoids the deadlock occurrence because all the transactions are processed sequentially in bitcoin. Due to encrypted security and no deadlock, the blockchain technique is preferred in the banking sector.

The present banking system faces the following issues like high transaction fee, security, deadlock, and double-spending. Among these, the current banking system spends huge amounts on security to protect the data or information of the end-users from hackers. Therefore, the current banking system has a high transaction fee for online transactions. With these connections, the current banking system uses several encrypted algorithms to enhance security. Even though the current banking algorithms deploy several algorithms, hackers can crack the algorithms. In addition to that, the current banking system sometimes faces a deadlock issue. Sometimes, the amount can be detected multiple times from the user account for the failed transaction. The debited amount will be credited back to the user account within a stipulated time period which is called double-spending. Therefore, double spending is one of the major problems in the banking sector [3]. Figure 3.1 represents the transaction. Consider a user A has 1,000 rupee in the account. A initiates two transactions T1 and T2 parallelly at the same time. In T1, A initiates a transaction for transferring rupee 800 to the other user named B. However, due to any technical or logical issue, T1 transaction fails. In T2, A initiates a transaction for transferring rupee 500 to the other user C. At that time, the transaction will fail due to the deficiency of balance. The above-mentioned type of transaction is termed double-spending in which the user permits to do multiple transactions at the same time. In order to overcome this deficiency, the banking system prefers the blockchain technique.

Figure 3.2 represents the two transactions in the blockchain. Blockchain technique is used to overcome the above-mentioned problem. Figure 3.2 shows the basic flow of blockchain. The major advantage of using blockchain in the banking sector is that it does not allow multiple transactions. Since multiple transactions are not allowed in the blockchain as a result double spending is restricted in the blockchain. Therefore, blockchain

Scenario 3.1:

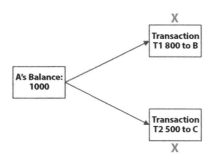

Figure 3.1 Transaction.

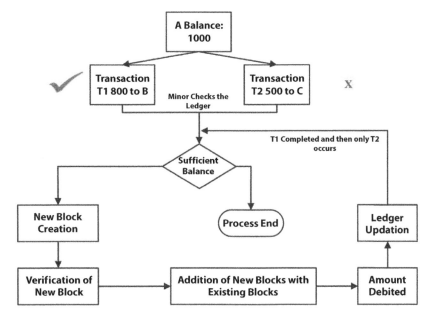

Figure 3.2 Two transactions in a blockchain.

supports only the sequential manner in which one transaction can take place after another.

In the above scenario, user A tries to do multiple transactions T1 with 800 and T2 with 500 to different users B and C, respectively, at the same time. In the traditional case, T1 fails but the amount is debited from A's account and T2 fails due to the insufficient balance. However, blockchain processes the transaction sequentially and blockchain updates the ledger only after a successful transaction. Therefore, transaction T1 or T2 can be processed in any scenario in the blockchain.

The steps are mentioned below:

Step 1: First transaction T1 is checked by the Minor in the Ledger. The Ledger holds the details of the user and their balance along with the time-stamp of the transactions. At this time, the transaction T2 will be waiting for the first transaction to complete.

Step 2: Based on the amount of sufficiency, the process continues. The process ends if there is no sufficient balance.

Step 3: The process continues only when there is a sufficient balance.

Step 4: User A has a sufficient balance as result new block will be created.

Step 5: Verification of the newly created block is carried out.

Step 6: After verification, the new block is added with the existing blocks. This makes the chain of blocks.

Step 7: The amount is debited from the account.

Step 8: After the successful transaction, the ledger will be updated.

Step 9: After the ledger is updated, the new or next waiting transaction T2 takes place in the same way.

Figure 3.3 represents multiple failed transactions. Let us consider the concept of an online ticket booking system. User A has a balance of 1000. A tries to book a ticket in the transaction T1. Due to some failure, the transaction T1 failed but the amount gets debited from the account, now the balance in A becomes 500. Due to the failed transaction T1, the ticket is not booked. After some time, A again tries to book the ticket and the transaction T2 also fails due to some technical issue. Later, A cannot book tickets because of insufficient balance. The debited amount will be credited back to the user account after a sufficient time.

Figure 3.4 represents avoiding transaction failure in the blockchain. Even though the amount will be debited from the user account, the ledger will be updated only after a successful transaction. Therefore, if A tries for another transaction at the same time, then the multiple transactions cannot be initiated in the blockchain. In the case of blockchain, the amount

Scenario 3.2:

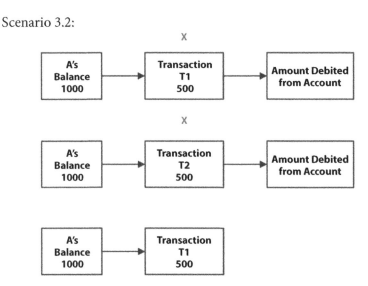

Figure 3.3 Multiple failed transactions.

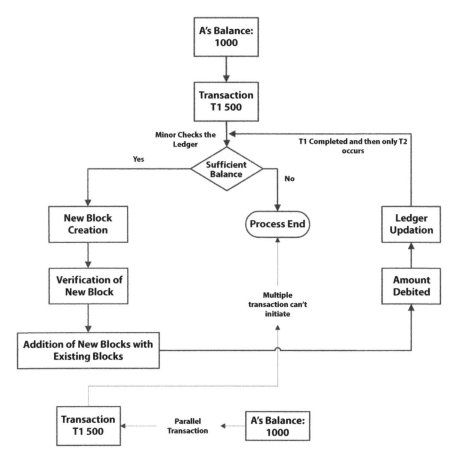

Figure 3.4 Avoiding transaction failure in blockchain.

gets debited only if the transaction is successful. The process was carried out in a similar way as previously mentioned.

Figure 3.5 represents a shared transaction. Let us consider the scenario where the user's A and B jointly transfer the sum of 3,000 to user C which is considered as T1. After some time, User B initiates another transaction T2 in which B transfers 500 to A. In transaction T1, A has a balance of 1,000 and B has a balance of 2,500. In the traditional case, T1 fails due to insufficient balance. As a result, user C does not get the amount either from A and B. Hence, the balance of C remains 0. To handle deadlock in transactions, a locking mechanism is used in the traditional approach. Moreover, User B is locked in Transaction T1, and T2 also does not take place.

Scenario 3.3:

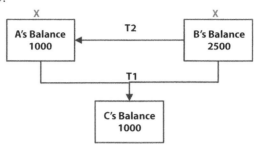

Figure 3.5 Shared transaction.

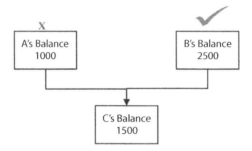

Figure 3.6 Shared transaction in a blockchain.

Figure 3.6 shows the shared transaction in the case of blockchain. In a blockchain, the transactions take place sequentially. T1 transaction does not take place due to insufficient balance in A. Hence, user B is released and T2 will take place. After completing T2, User A and B have a sufficient balance to transfer the amount to C. As a result, at least a transaction has taken place with the help of blockchain.

3.2   Introduction of Quantum Computing

Quantum computing is gaining popularity due to its ability to solve complex problems that classical computers cannot solve effectively, namely, quantum chemistry simulation [2, 3] and integer factorization [4]. Quantum computers are used to resolve the difficulties that exist in different mechanism such as Hamiltonian Simulation Algorithms, Shor's algorithm and Grover's algorithm. These algorithms are briefly explained later in this chapter. However, a collaboration between quantum hardware and software is carried out in quantum computers. The quantum computers are developed using the circuit model along with quantum control micro architecture interfaces and Quantum Instruction Set Architecture (QISA) [5]. Researchers initially proposed QISA for predicting and detecting non-fault tolerant Noisy Intermediate Scale Quantum (NISQ) devices. Along with QISA, quantum control microarchitecture is also used in it. However, Fault-Tolerant (FT) quantum computing needs to perform logical operations and to measure the repeated quantum error correction at run-time.

In addition to that, the present quantum control microarchitectures cannot handle a large number of necessary logical operations. Therefore, this work integrates a large number of quantum bits with microarchitecture. Therefore, this work supports the full compilation of large quantum bits and also computes the quantum error correction at runtime. With these connections, the proposed work greatly reduces quantum program code size and improves scalability [6]. A large number of quantum bits are called qubits.

3.2.1 Background and History of Quantum Computers

Table 3.1 represents timeline for the invention of quantum computers. Quantum computing arose at the start of 1980, at first Benioff came up with the idea of designing a computer-based on quantum mechanics. He started by designing small and simple circuits that fulfill quantum mechanics. Quantum mechanics is basic physics that describes the physical characteristics of atoms. Even though it uses quantum mechanics, it was more similar to the traditional turning machine. Therefore, it is similar to the Turing machine, and it does not give high performance to quantum computers. Quantum computers must have high performance when compared

Table 3.1 Timeline for the invention of quantum computers.

Year	Inventor	Description
1980	Benioff	He designed simple circuits that fulfill the quantum mechanics.
1982	Feynman	He gave the solution for features of the photons.
1998	Gershenfeld and Chuang	They designed a 2-qubit quantum computer.
2001	IBM	The built 7-qubit NMR quantum computer.

to traditional computers. Thus, the findings of quantum computing may not be considered as having a high impact on the invention of quantum computers but it paved the way for others to come up with similar ideas to design quantum computers. In this sequence, in the year 1982, Feynman introduced the examples of the physical features of the photons that are considered as the basis for the development of quantum computers. In addition, he also stated that quantum computers must have a functional method that follows basic principles of quantum.

The principle of quantum mechanics basically follows the principles of electromagnetic energy, Pauli Exclusion Principle, the uncertainty principle, and the wave theory of particles. This principle follows the action of the nuclear particles between smaller distances. However, the complete solution for the quantum computers was not given by him. After a long year gap again professor Gershenfeld and Chuang at MIT in the year, 1998 introduced a 2-qubit quantum computer which is focused on Nuclear Magnetic Resonance (NMR). This is considered as the very first development of the quantum computer. The design and development of quantum computers are achieved by imposing the nucleus into a constant magnetic field [8]. Furthermore, in the year 2001, IBM was successful in building a 7-qubit NMR quantum computer. IBM also implemented Shor's algorithm. Shor's algorithm is considered the core concept in the quantum computer. This makes quantum computers more powerful than the 2-qubit quantum computer.

Computers are designed to reduce human activity and increase performance. Traditional computers operate using binary values such as 0 or 1. With the use of only 0's and 1's, traditional computers cannot perform huge calculations like the factorization of a number. Factorization of a small number might be simple in traditional computers but the factorization of a huge number may take much time to solve. Hence, to overcome the issue, quantum computers have been developed to solve such problems as factorization of a number. Unlike traditional computers, quantum computers use qubits, which makes it efficient to solve vast calculations. The qubits are created using the electron's spin or the photon's path. Furthermore, quantum computers not only solve complex problems like factorization but also perform well in the cryptography phase. The minute decoding of the code by quantum computers is said to take many years for a traditional computer to decode [4]. Thus, with the rise of quantum computers, the security of blockchain can be reduced.

3.2.2   Scope of Quantum Computers in Blockchain

Blockchain has been used in a wide range of applications because of its performance, reliability, and authenticity. Among the several applications, blockchain is mostly preferable for cryptographic systems such as backing and online booking. The cryptographic systems generate asymmetric key algorithms and hash functions to achieve these characteristics. The encryption present in blockchain can be decrypted using Shor's algorithm, which is being used in the rapidly growing technology of quantum computing. Shor's algorithm has a time complexity in terms of polynomial time for the factoring problem which can crack the public key cryptography in the blockchain. Furthermore, quantum computers generate hashes using Grover's algorithm, allowing the entire block in the blockchain to be recreated. As a result, the blockchain's security is compromised with the advent of quantum computers. Therefore, this necessitates a renovation of the current blockchain to survive the quantum attack. In order to safeguard the blockchain's security, quantum-resistant cryptosystems can be used instead of following the traditional cryptosystems [7].

3.3   Restrictions of Blockchain Quantum

In order to withstand the rise of quantum computers, the existing blockchain must be quantum-resistant to secure the blockchain. There are mainly two approaches to make the blockchain quantum resistant. They are quantum cryptography and post-quantum cryptography.

3.3.1   Post-Quantum Cryptography

Post-quantum cryptography is also termed quantum-resistant cryptography because it secures blockchain cryptography from quantum computers with the aid of mathematical algorithms. Post-quantum cryptography uses mathematical algorithms rather than quantum properties. The mathematical algorithms in post-quantum cryptography are Lattice Cryptography, Multivariate Cryptography, Hash Cryptography, and Code Cryptography [8].

3.3.1.1 Lattice Cryptography

The Figure 3.7 represents the lattice and basis of the given sample space R_n. The term lattice is denoted as L, which means a data point on the given sample space R_n. The lattices are only the integers and do not contain factors. V1, V2, and V3 are the vectors. A vector is the point or coordinates [13]. For example, (2, 3) is a vector. If v1, v2, …, Vn belongs to the space R_n, then it is called basis.

Figure 3.8 represents the Shortest Vector Problem. SVP finds the shortest vector with respect to the origin. Figure 3.8 shows the SVP problem in

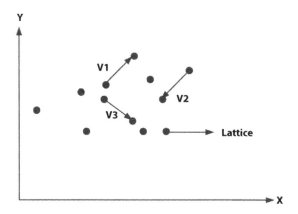

Figure 3.7 Lattice and basis.

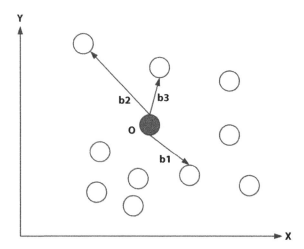

Figure 3.8 Shortest vector problem.

a two-dimensional plane. Here, the basis b1 is the shortest vector from the origin O. Whereas b2 and b3 are farthest from the origin. SVP cannot solve quantum computers because it is difficult to find the shortest distance in the n-dimensional plane.

Closest Vector Problem (CVP) is similar to the SVP problem. CVP finds the lattice point which is nearest to the target with the lattice submitted as the input. Figure 3.9 represents the CVP, which is explained in a two-dimensional plane. Here, the basis b1 and b3 do not connect the lattice which is nearby the target T. Whereas the basis b2 connects the lattice which is nearby the target T. Hence, it can resist the quantum attack in the blockchain. CVP cannot be solved by quantum computers because it is difficult to find the closest lattice in the n-dimensional plane. Shortest Independent Vector Problem (SIVP) finds the maximum number of short independent vectors in the given lattice that is linearly in nature.

Figure 3.10 represents SIVP, which shows the SIVP problem in a two-dimensional plane. Here, the basis b1, b2, and b3 are the shortest vectors rather than b4 and b5. SIVP is obviously polynomial time reducible to SMP [10]. Hence, it cannot be solved by quantum computers. Therefore, some algorithms are introduced in mathematical approaches. They are N^th Degree Truncated Polynomial Ring Unit (NTRU) and Ring learning with errors (Ring LWE). Hence, the lattice-based cryptography gives more security to the blockchain in the quantum attack and thus resists the quantum attack [9]. NTRU and Ring LWE approaches are discussed below.

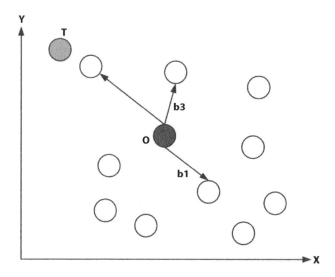

Figure 3.9 Closest vector problem.

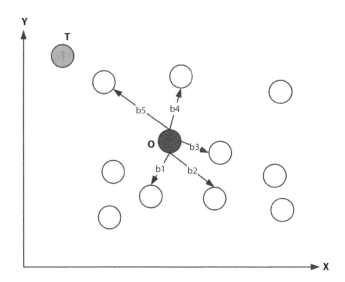

Figure 3.10 Shortest independent vectors problem.

NTRU:

NTRU is an approach based on SVP. It is a lattice-based public-key crypto-system. NTRU uses NTRUEncrypt to encrypt the information which has three parameters, namely, N, p, and q whereas p and q are prime numbers. N represents truncated polynomials degree. Mostly, q > p and q will be in the form of 2^n.

i) **Key Generation**
  - A small polynomial function $f(x)$ and $g(x)$ are chosen randomly
  - Calculate $f_q(x)$ and $f_p(x)$ where $f_q(x)$ is inverse of product of $f(x)$ and $\mod q$ and $f_p(x)$ is inverse of product of $f(x)$ and $\mod p$
  - Public key $h(x)$ is generated by $p * f_q(x) * g(x) \mod q$

ii) **Encryption**
  - The encryption is carried by encoding the message m to a ternary polynomial function named as $m(x)$.
  - The small polynomial $r(x)$ has been chosen randomly.
  - The encrypted message $e(x)$ is given by $h(x) * r(x) + m(x) \mod q$ [17].

Ring LWE:

The worst-case problem in lattice cryptography is Learning With Error (LWE). Therefore, it can withstand quantum attacks.

i) **Key Generation**

- Let r_1 and r_2 be the two polynomials taken from a discrete Gaussian sampler.
- Perform $\tilde{r}_1 \leftarrow NTT(r_1); \tilde{r}_2 \leftarrow NTT(r_2); \tilde{p}_1 \leftarrow \tilde{r}_1 - \tilde{a} * \tilde{r}_2$.
- The private key represents as $\tilde{r}_2$ and the public key denotes $(\tilde{a}, \tilde{p})$.

ii) **Encryption**

- Let the message be m. m is encoded to a polynomial $\tilde{m} \in R_q$.
- $e_1, e_2, e_3 \in R_q$ are caused through discrete Gaussian sampler, where e1, e2, and e3 are the error polynomials.
- Perform $\tilde{e}_1 \leftarrow NTT(e_1); \tilde{e}_2 \leftarrow NTT(e_2) (\tilde{c}_1, \tilde{c}_2) \leftarrow \tilde{a} * \tilde{e}_1 + \tilde{e}_2; \tilde{p} * \tilde{e}_1 + NTT(e_3 + \bar{m})$ [18].

3.3.2 Multivariate Cryptography

Multivariate polynomials through finite field F are used in these schemes. It is an NP-hard or NP-complete problem. The biggest benefit is that they make use of a very brief signature, which can be used for authentication in various small devices. Rainbow, a modern signature scheme based on multivariate cryptography introduced by J. Ding and D. Schmidt in 2005, is based on Oil and Vinegar schemes.

Building Blocks for Rainbow Schemes

The following operations are necessary to produce a Rainbow signature:

1. Computing affine transformations, $y = Ax + b$ where A represents matrix and b denotes a vector.
2. Calculating core map transformations, evaluating or solving multivariate polynomials using linear equations.

Key Generation:

1. There are two invertible affine maps $L_1:K^m{\to}K^m$ and $L_2:K^n{\to}K^n$, as well as the map $F = \left(f_{v1+1}(x),...,f_n(x)\right)$ make up the private key.
2. The number of components of F is given by $m = n_{v1}$.
3. The public key is made up K field and the composed map $P(x) = L_1{\circ}F{\circ}L_2(x) : K^n{\to}K^m$.

Signature:

1. To compute the value $h = h(d){\in}K^m$ for a document d, it has hash function h: $K{*}{\to}K^m$.
2. Also, compute $x = L_1^{-1}(h), y = F^{-1}(x)$ and $z = L_2^{-1}(y)$ recursively.
3. The document's signature is $z{\in}K^n$.
4. In this case, $F^{-1}(x)$ denotes the discovery of one (of many) pre-images of x.

Signature verification

1. To check the validity and verify the signature using $h = P(z)$.
2. Compute the document's hash value, $h = h(d)$.
3. The signature is accepted if $h = h$ holds true; otherwise, it will be refused [8].

3.3.3   Hash Cryptography

Hash cryptography uses Merkle's hash-tree, which is the public-key signature system Figure 3.11 shows the merle tree. The key will be generated

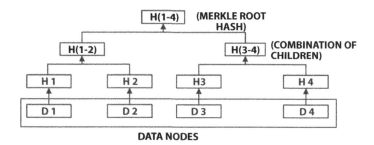

Figure 3.11 Merle tree.

based on the signature schemes such as the Lamport signature scheme, which are one-time signatures. Merkle system limits the number of keys generated and it is a binary tree.

To generate a public key:

1. Generate public keys and private keys X_i and Y_i respectively with 2^n single time signature.
2. The hash tree creates private key Y_i using the hash function $h_i = H(Y_i)$.
3. Each tree node is specified by $A_{i,j}$, where i signifies the node's height and j signifies the node's left-to-right location. Hence, the root is i = n and the leaf is i = 0.
4. The inner node is represented by the combination of its children.
5. Merkle key is constructed with 2^n leaves and 2^{n+1} nodes. The root node represents the public key for Merkle signature.

To generate the signature:

1. The leaf node represents the one-time public key X_i.
2. Determine the path P from root to the leaf in the generated tree. The path consists of n+1 nodes.
3. To find P, all the child nodes $(C_1, C_2, ..., C_n)$ are considered. C_i is the child of C_{i+1}. That means C_{i+1} is the parent node.
4. To find the path of P_{i+1}, find the children of C_{i+1}.
5. The node P_{i+1} is called $auth_i$. Hence, $C_{i+1} = H(C_i \| auth_i)$.
6. These auth node and the one time signature node makes Merkle scheme [8].

3.3.4   Code Cryptography

Code cryptography is used to secure blockchain from quantum computers. It is a mathematical approach that is used to generate the public key cryptosystem. The algorithm used in achieving the security is McEliece Public-Key Encryption (MPKE) and Quasi-Cyclic Moderate-Density-Parity-Check (QC-MDPC). The idea behind the McEliece is to use a ciphertext or cyphertext word selected from the Linear Error Correcting Code (LECC) [11]. The ciphertext is the outcome of the encryption, and the encryption is carried out using an algorithm called a cipher. Thus, it gets the name ciphertext. Cipher is one of the symmetric public key algorithms. There are two security considerations in McEliece. These are as follows:

1. Decryption complexity in a random linear code.
2. The indistinct Goppa codes needed for public-key systems.

Since the MPKC's secret key is a Goppa message. The efficiency of the error-correcting algorithm for choosing code class combined with its permutation is trapdoor for McEliece cryptosystem. Goppa code is also known as algebraic geometric code. In Goppa code, the code is generated by using the algebraic curve. The advantage of McEliece is that the security measures are heavy, effective, and faster since the encryption and decryption methods are simple and straightforward. The major drawback of McEliece is it has a huge size of keys [12]. Due to the drawback, QC-MDPC comes into the picture. QC-MDPC codes make it possible to represent a key in a very small amount. Although it gives small keys, the secret code may be released [13].

3.4   Post-Quantum Cryptography Features

A post-quantum cryptosystem has to support the blockchain with the following key features

- Signature and the hash length should be short. A blockchain maintains a digital ledger that helps to track data transactions such as user signatures and data/block hashes. As a result, the length of signatures/hashes grows the size of the blockchain.
- The execution of the post-quantum cryptosystems should be fast. It needs to be faster in order to support the blockchain for processing large numbers of transactions in a short time span. Thereby, high computational speed for processing the large dataset in blockchain minimizes the low computational cost.
- The generated private keys and public keys should be small to make the computational process less complex [7].

3.5   Quantum Cryptography

Quantum cryptography is mainly based on physics instead of mathematical problems. Hence, it is proved that quantum cryptography withstands quantum attacks and is unbreakable by quantum computers. The theory of quantum mechanics is used in quantum cryptography. The quantum properties like uncertainty principle and no-cloning theorem. Quantum mechanics employ the uncertainty principle, which states that photons may be produced in one of two polarized states, namely, basis or conjugate. The state of the photon is said to be the basis if the property is based on the single-photon. The state of the photon is said to be conjugate if quantum mechanics determines that evaluating one property totally randomizes the other. The no-cloning theorem indicates that there is no way of creating duplicate states. Quantum cryptography uses the process called Quantum Key Distribution (QKD), which sends the key between the sender and receiver. The transmission is done only if the channel is established between them. This channel is called a quantum channel. QKD is secure since it transmits only the key but not the data [14].

3.5.1   Working of QKD

Let us consider two parties A and B who agrees to send the keys. It should not be eavesdropped on by the other parties like E during the transmission of the keys. In the traditional cryptographic systems, the digital transmission can be monitored by the eavesdroppers E. E eavesdropped on the communication between A and B even without the knowledge of A and B. However, in quantum cryptography, the digital data is replaced by photons. Hence, E cannot eavesdrop. A and B share the keys in the form of polarized photons in the quantum channel of quantum cryptography. The quantum channel is built to avoid eavesdroppers. In this channel, the eavesdroppers can watch the communication between A and B but cannot alter or modify the data being transmitted by A and B. Figure 3.12 shows the information that A sends to B.

1. A randomly sends series of five photons to B. The photons are in the basis state. Basis states may be horizontal, vertical, diagonal, and anti-diagonal. Here, horizontal and vertical comes under rectilinear. Whereas diagonal and anti-diagonal come under diagonal. Figure 3.13 represents message transferring in QKD and Figure 3.14 represents Quantum key representation.

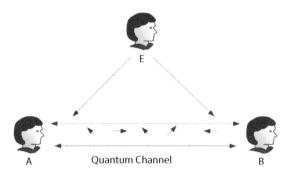

Figure 3.12 Message transferring in QKD.

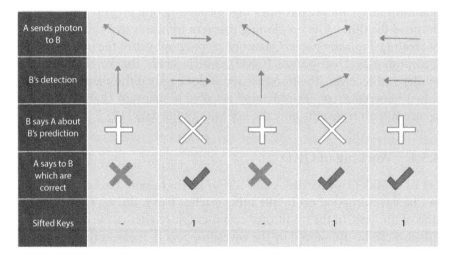

Figure 3.13 Sifted key.

2. The photon states are transferred to B through a quantum channel.
3. B also randomly computes the photon state.
4. B says A about the measurement of the photon state through the quantum channel.
5. A and B decide whether to proceed or abort the process based on the comparisons.
6. To discard the wrong measurement of basis state, B performs sifting with A.
7. B sends the list of measurements that B made.
8. A says the correct measurements that B made. By this, they discard the wrong measurements.

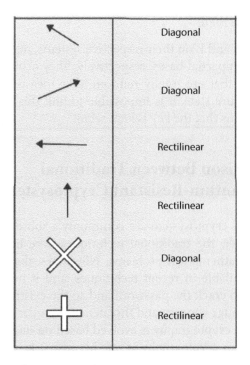

Figure 3.14 Quantum key representation.

9. In between, if the eavesdroppers read the information, then demolish it. Then, in the sifting process, that photon state will be discarded.

10. If eavesdroppers try to copy the state of the basis state and try to modify it, then quantum cryptography does not allow due to the no-cloning theorem [14, 15].

3.5.2 Protocols of QKD

The protocols used in QKD are as follows:

1. Prepare-and-measure
2. Entanglement

3.5.2.1 Prepare-and-Measure

In this protocol, sender A prepares the basis state of the polarized photon. In addition, receiver B measures the photon sent from A. Hence, this QKD protocol is called prepare-and-measure [16].

3.5.2.2 Entanglement

In this protocol, A and B on their respective systems, make measurements in two mutually impartial bases, respectively. They achieve perfectly correlated outcomes that are totally random after measurement. Since the source creates a pure state, it is impossible to link this state to an eavesdropper. This means that the key is kept secret.

3.6 Comparison Between Traditional and Quantum-Resistant Cryptosystems

Cryptography and cryptosystem are commonly a subset of mathematical problems. However, the traditional techniques have limited computing power to solve mathematical problems. Nowadays, the huge computing power can be available in recent techniques, and it needs only a small instance of time to crack the password and so the existing cryptography's security is under huge concern and threatened. In order to resolve the difficulties, quantum cryptography is evolved based on quantum mechanics. Therefore, quantum cryptography is safe because it generates encryption using physical principles. However, in a real environment, it is a very crucial task to ensure the safety of the key which cannot be modified or stolen by a third party (e.g., eavesdroppers) at the time of data transmission and distribution. The attackers are effectively spotlighted in quantum cryptography while transmission and distribution of data through the network. Thereby, quantum cryptography safeguards the security of communication channels [5]. In traditional cryptography, the security of the systems is proven and experimented. Since quantum-resistant algorithms are still in their early stages of development, their security has yet to be established, and it is not possible to replace the existing cryptographic algorithms with quantum-resistant cryptosystems.

These quantum-resistant cryptosystem computers have the potential to revolutionize information technology by providing significant benefits and increased speeds. However, they are being designed in particular for surveillance machines that have never been seen before. In traditional cryptography, only the conventional methods are used which are slow and have few benefits.

3.7   Quantum Blockchain Applications

The applications of the quantum blockchain are as follows:

- Quantum digital currency
- Electronic voting
- Online auction and multiparty lotteries

3.8   Blockchain Applications

Blockchain technology is implemented in multiple industries including financial and non-financial industries.

3.8.1   Financial Application

Blockchain is preferred in financial applications because the transaction cannot be duplicated in financial applications like e-transaction and banking. In addition to that, blockchain also registers and validates a transaction. Therefore, blockchain is preferred for financial applications. Blockchain can act as a secure registry for the completed financial transactions. Some financial applications are digital currencies, stock trading, insurance marketplace, peer-to-peer global financial transactions, and so on.

Digital Currencies: Digital currency is nothing but the currency that is available in electronic form. Digital currency is termed either digital money or electronic money. The digital currency does not have any intermediate for trading. Nowadays, more than 500 digital currencies are currently available in the world as of January 2015. Later, bitcoin was the first cryptocurrency released in 2009.

Stock Trading: Stock trading is carried out by a centralized authority by exchanging market values by tracking all trades and settlements. The central authorities will charge extra charges for settlements. In order to address the issue, a new platform is created using blockchain to reduce costs and settlement delays to increase transparency and audit ability.

Insurance Marketplace: Blockchain is also used for the insurance marketplace in which is used for negotiating, buying and registering new insurance policies. It is also used for submitting, uploading and processing insurance documents. Most of the insurance documents are automated with the aid of smart contracts. The smart contracts have digital protocols to automate the insurance policies and thereby reduce the processing charge.

Global Financial Transactions: The Global Financial Transactions have been carried out with the help of a peer-to-peer network in which is a financial transaction takes place between people who have to go through any form of authentication in any financial institute for verification [19].

3.8.2   Non-Financial Application

Blockchain is also used in non-financial applications. Blockchain is preferred in the network wherever information security is required. It is used to protect the data over the network. The non-financial applications are telecommunication, construction, pharmaceutical industries, and agriculture. Blockchain is also an application in healthcare applications.

Healthcare Applications: Nowadays, healthcare applications are one of the major phenomena to secure information from a third party. In healthcare applications, patients' history needs to be maintained confidentiality because patients do not want to share their personal health records. Due to the evolution of recent technologies, patient information is maintained on the internet as Electronic Medical Record (EMR). Moreover, the information is scattered in several servers and handled by several healthcare providers and thereby it is difficult to secure the information. However, there are several security and privacy problems for sharing EMRs among multiple providers. With the help of blockchain, EMRs data can be securely transmitted among the providers.

Logistics Management Applications: Blockchain is also used in logistics management applications, which is software used to maintain the information about the product, delivery of raw material, and services which is considered as transactions. Blockchain maintains the records about the transaction between the producers and the consumer destinations. It needs to organize, schedule, coordinate, monitor, and validate the activities of the users [20].

3.9   Limitations of Blockchain

Some of the challenges in the technical and non-technical parts of Blockchain are as follows:

Technical limitations:

- High costs: Blockchain is costlier than the existing algorithms because it replicates the data in the network. In addition to that, blockchain maintains the entire history of transactions which is also replicated in the network. Therefore, blockchain is computationally expensive.
- Latency: The new block can be added and the subsequent transaction records will be stored in the blockchain. The blockchain contains several nodes in which it stores and maintains all the records of completed transactions in order to ensure network security. However, maintaining the details in the blockchain is computationally expensive.

Non-technical limitations:

- Migration of blockchain needs an executive commitment and significant investment over a non-significant length of time.
- The regular and legal authorities have a lack of acceptance.
- Does not have user acceptance

3.10 Conclusion

Blockchain is the mechanism that makes security harder or difficult to hack, alter, or scam the system. Quantum blockchain breaks our current encryption systems used for protecting the information. The key features of quantum blockchain are performance and safety. Moreover, quantum blockchain has faster processing speed and safer transactions based on quantum mechanics. To corrupt a system, every block in a chain has to be changed. Hence, the system is highly secured. It also cracks the RSA algorithm. RSA is used for encryption, based upon the hardness of solving the factorization problem.

References

1. Soni, S. and Bhushan, B., A comprehensive survey on blockchain: Working, security analysis, privacy threats and potential applications. *2019 2nd*

International Conference on Intelligent Computing, Instrumentation and Control Technologies (ICICICT), vol. 1, IEEE, pp. 922–926, 2019 Jul 5.

2. Chatterjee, R. and Chatterjee, R., An Overview of the Emerging Technology: Blockchain. *2017 3rd International Conference on Computational Intelligence and Networks (CINE)*, pp. 126–127, 2017.

3. Pérez-Solà, C., Delgado-Segura, S., Navarro-Arribas, G., Herrera-Joancomartí, J., Double-spending prevention for bitcoin zero-confirmation transactions. *Int. J. Inf. Secur.*, 18, 4, 451–63, 2019 Aug.

4. Jain, S., Quantum computer architectures: A survey. *2015 2nd Int. Conf. Computing Sustain. Global Dev. (INDIACom)*, 2165–2169, 2015.

5. Gao, Y.L., Chen, X.B., Xu, G., Yuan, K.G., Liu, W., Yang, Y.X., A novel quantum blockchain scheme base on quantum entanglement and DPoS. *Quantum Inf. Process.*, 19, 12, 1–15, 2020.

6. Fu, X., Lao, L., Bertels, K., Almudever, C.G., A control microarchitecture for fault-tolerant quantum computing. *Microprocess. Microsyst.*, 70, 21–30, 2019 Oct 1.

7. Fernández-Caramès, T.M. and Fraga-Lamas, P., Towards post-quantum blockchain: A review on blockchain cryptography resistant to quantum computing attacks. *IEEE Access*, 8, 21091–21116, 2020.

8. Roy, K.S. and Kalita, H.K., A Survey on Post-Quantum Cryptography for Constrained Devices. *Int. J. Appl. Eng. Res.*, 14, 11, 2608–15, 2019.

9. Regev, O., Lattice-based cryptography, in: *Annual International Cryptology Conference*, Springer, Berlin, Heidelberg, pp. 131–141, 2006, August.

10. Blömer, J. and Naewe, S., Sampling methods for shortest vectors, closest vectors and successive minima. *Theor. Comput. Sci.*, 410, 18, 1648–65, 2009 Apr 17.

11. Sendrier, N., Code-Based Cryptography: State of the Art and Perspectives, in: *IEEE Security & Privacy*, vol. 15, pp. 44–50, 2017.

12. Heyse, S., Von Maurich, I., Güneysu, T., Smaller keys for code-based cryptography: QC-MDPC McEliece implementations on embedded devices, in: *International Conference on Cryptographic Hardware and Embedded Systems*, Springer, Berlin, Heidelberg, pp. 273–292, 2013 Aug 19.

13. Chou, T., QcBits: Constant-Time Small-Key Code-Based Cryptography, in: *Cryptographic Hardware and Embedded Systems – CHES 2016. CHES 2016. Lecture Notes in Computer Science*, vol. 9813, B. Gierlichs and A. Poschmann (Eds.), Springer, Berlin, Heidelberg, 2016, https://doi.org/10.1007/978-3-662-53140-2_14.

14. Bennett, C.H., Bessette, F., Brassard, G. *et al.*, Experimental quantum cryptography. *J. Cryptology*, 5, 3–28, 1992, https://doi.org/10.1007/BF00191318.

15. Elliott, C., Quantum cryptography. *IEEE Secur. Priv.*, 2, 4, 57–61, 2004 Oct 4.

16. Nurhadi, A.I. and Syambas, N.R., Quantum key distribution (QKD) protocols: a survey, in: *2018 4th International Conference on Wireless and Telematics (ICWT)*, IEEE, pp. 1–5, 2018 Jul 12.

17. Liu, B. and Wu, H., Efficient architecture and implementation for NTRU Encrypt system, in: *2015 IEEE 58th International Midwest Symposium on Circuits and Systems (MWSCAS)*, IEEE, pp. 1–4, 2015 Aug 2.

18. De Clercq, R., Roy, S.S., Vercauteren, F., Verbauwhede, I., Efficient software implementation of ring-LWE encryption, in: *2015 Design, Automation & Test in Europe Conference & Exhibition (DATE)*, IEEE, pp. 339–344, 2015 Mar 9.

19. Al-Jaroodi, J. and Mohamed, N., Industrial applications of blockchain, in: *2019 IEEE 9th Annual Computing and Communication Workshop and Conference (CCWC)*, IEEE, pp. 0550–0555, 2019 Jan 7.

20. Hughes, L., Dwivedi, Y.K., Misra, S.K., Rana, N.P., Raghavan, V., Akella, V., Blockchain research, practice and policy: Applications, benefits, limitations, emerging research themes and research agenda. *Int. J. Inf. Manage.*, 49, 114–2, 2019 Dec 1.

4

Development of the Quantum Bitcoin (BTC)

Gaurav Dhuriya[1]*, Aradhna Saini[1] and Prashant Johari[2]

[1]Department of Computer Science and Engineering, Noida Institute of Engineering and Technology, Greater Noida, Uttar Pradesh, India
[2]School of Computing Science and Engineering, Galgotias University, Greater Noida, Delhi-NCR, India

Abstract

A basic well-balanced model/system was created to analyze the compressed blueprint of a cryptocurrency model, which was exertion on the principle of blockchain. This system is integration into the transaction data of BTC in order to function in a quantitative assessment of the entire exertion of the idea. The formulation of the all the important aspects of this system is then noted down and written in a formulated form: the blockchain keeps the history of all the transactions and so on; updating is done through distribution of information and consensus through the process of automatic system update. Through observation, it is clear that, unlike cash, a cryptocurrency model is not allowing an immediate or ultimate settlement. Moreover, the BTC model that is currently in practice corresponds to a loss (welfare) of 1.4% of the total consumption. This loss or more of its kind can be reduced by up to 0.08% if we begin implementing the optimal processes, which will reduce the loss related to extract as it depends upon the growth of sum instead of the fees for transacting extract finances. A significant feature of quantum cryptocurrency is that extract is economical a good general deed, while double-spending to defraud the cryptocurrency corresponds to the individual incentives to reverse a particular transaction. As a result, a cryptocurrency acting as BTC and so on is heavily in use and is at its peak when the integer of transactions as a whole is in the larger value instead of individual transactions (e.g., as in a retail payment system).

Keywords: Bitcoin, quantum computing, cryptocurrency, blockchain, cryptography, hashing, decentralization, immutability

*Corresponding author: gauravdhuriya10047@gmail.com

Rajesh Kumar Dhanaraj, Vani Rajasekar, SK Hafizul Islam, Balamurugan Balusamy and Ching-Hsien Hsu (eds.) Quantum Blockchain: An Emerging Cryptographic Paradigm, (83–108)
© 2022 Scrivener Publishing LLC

4.1   Introduction of BTC

The new value flood of BTC has caught the consideration of general society about digital forms of money and their position later on. Large integers of the appealing excessive lights of digital forms of money approach from the absence of an outsider controlling the cash, taking into consideration superiorities, for example, lower exchange expenses, speed, worldwide use, and preservation. While its utilization as an everyday strategy for exchange is slightly restricted, the ascent of BTC esteem has served to draw in extraordinary absorption to it, which BTS promoters would propose is the initial move with regard to general acknowledgment. Simultaneously, over the most recent a period, there has been a developing influx of idealism regarding quantum processing [1]. It is currently normal to catch remarks recommending that quantum figuring innovation has arrived at a level where versatility is reachable something incomprehensible even five years prior. Cryptography is the notable of the core BTC, and quantum PCs are especially acceptable at troublesome matters like looking and code-breaking. This opens up numerous inquiries in regard to what quantum figuring will mean for BTC. Will a quantum PC be utilized to colliery BTC?

Are quantum computers able to bargain the BTC frame exertion? How well a quantum PC in some unacceptable hook may be utilized to get hold of BTC? This has been a worry in the BTC local area for quite a while, although a hypothetical concern at this juncture. In this chapter, we separation a portion of these matters and see precisely what the ramifications of the post-quantum figuring world to BTC are. BTC is a companion-to-peer (p2p) computerized money frame exertion. The BTC p2p grid carries out a conveyed timestamp administration that records exchange in a general record, and this is also known as blockchain. The timestamp activity is computationally costly, requiring confirmation of exertion to check exchange and supplement it into the blockchain. In remuneration for this exertion, the BTC convention empowers the hubs to mint coins, i.e., to add into the record exchange for self-credit. This appropriated stamping activity is the wellspring of one more cash, shedding the demand for a focal backer. Huge quantities of clients at present carry out in BTC, taking part in altogether measured exchange [2, 3]. The decentralized idea of BTC, wherein trust in the respectability of the general record emerges by the helpful idea of cooperation in the middle of the members, is a basic part of its prosperity: BTC eliminates the demand for all essential to consent to trust any single substance. Be that as it may, the opposite is likewise evident: BTC does not offer an inherent instrument to fuse reliability from true elements into the frame exertion. Namelessness in the BTC Protocol: In the BTC cryptographic ledger, clients are distinguished exclusively by addresses, which are pseudonymous general key fingerprints marks. It is feasible for the client controlling a BTC address to stay unidentified—until the data is deliberation uncovered in the course of a buy or in different conditions. Consequently, BTC has been now and again picked as an installment mechanism for unlawful business. Some governments are additionally worried that BTCs could be utilized to skirt capital jurisdiction laws. Then, again, authentic clients covetous of protection ought to be aware of the way that it is feasible to connect elements that offer money streams. We can perceive how an examination of the blockchain may uncover that a similar genuine element is behind various BTC addresses. Along these lines, acting as clients ought to totally isolate their BTC addresses among their various personas. BTC's objective of disposing of the requirement for a believed focal gathering is based on the conjunction of four ideas: decentralization, permanence, cryptography, and confirmation of exertion. We will examine every one of them exhaustively.

The preservation of the decentralized advanced cash, BTC, depends on the Asymmetrical Curve Advanced Signature Algorithm (ECDSA) and the Proof-of-Exertion (PoW) calculation. ECDSA permits approval of the payer. PoW keeps a payer from paying with similar cash more than once. BTCs are moved in the middle of clients through exchange beginning with one location then onto the next; the location being is a hashish of a beneficiary's general key or content. The general key of the operator is uncovered when the exchange is appropriated over the BTC organization [4]. The possessing of BTCs sums to the responsibility for the personal key of the relating address. The computerized signature, which is put on the exchange, is the verification of proprietorship.

The cryptographic strength of the ECDSA depends on the intricacy of the discrete logarithm matter in the gathering of asymmetrical bend focuses (ECDLP), which is tackled in outstanding time; i.e., it is hard for a traditional PC. Shor's quantum calculation for estimation of the discrete logarithms in limited fields permits the computation of the personal ECDSA key through the general key in polynomial time; this is fundamentally simpler. This compromise addresses a non-zero equilibrium that was recently utilized for spending and exchange that have not yet been remembered for a square. At the point when the exchange is dispersed over the organization, the general key is unveiled. This offers a window for an assault foregoing to the exchange is remembered for the following square to ascertain the personal key utilizing a quantum PC and fashion one more exchange with a substantially advanced mark.

Luckily, there are matters that are appropriate for advanced mark plots and are adequately unpredictable for both old-style and quantum PCs. Looking for the pre-image of the hashish applies to these matters. Grover's quantum calculation for looking through an unsorted data set permits tackling the matter identified with the hashish pre-image looking on the schedule of request the square base of the old-style time, which is an extraordinary speed increase. Not with standing, the intricacy of the matter stays remarkable. Along these lines, the fundamental preservation level is accomplished by utilizing a hashish capacity of the proper length. This permits the hashish-based cryptographic frame exertions to be viewed as quantum-safe. As indicated by the PQCRYPTO proposals (The European A consortium of Universities and Companies for Post-Quantum Cryptography Matters), the all-inclusive Merkle signature plot (XMSS) ought to be utilized as a quantum-safe advanced mark since it joins excessive preservation, worthy key age time, and the dimensions of the signature, interestingly with the other post-quantum computerized signature calculations offered by established re explorers.

BTC Post-Quantum (BPQ) is a trial part of BTC's primary blockchain utilizing quantum-safe advanced marks. Later on, the experience of BPQ might be valuable for the acquaintance of quantum-safe cryptography with the fundamental part of BTC. Moreover, BPQ serves the current requirements for a reinforcement blockchain in case of an unexpected jump in innovative improvement that could bargain the preservation of the most conventional cryptographic forms of money.

There is mounting proof that quantum PCs will turn out to be adequately amazing to break famous cryptographic plans within a reasonable time frame, despite the fact that it is difficult to precisely foresee when it will occur. Blueprint of realities exhibits the idealness of our turn of events.

- In 2015, the US National Preservation Agency (NSA) reported the designs for the development to post-quantum cryptographic calculations: Shockingly, the development of craggy bend use has to knock facing the reality of proceeded with development in the exploration on quantum figuring, which has clarified that asymmetrical bend cryptography is not the drawn-out arrangement numerous once trusted it would be.
- In 2016, IBM gave [2] the main cloud-based quantum PC, IBM Q, with five qubits, available to any individual who demands to rehearse quantum programming.

- In 2016, Intel engineers reported the exertion on a quantum processor with millions of qubits.
- In 2016, Google Chrome designers carried out the post-quantum key trade calculation New Hope, and, in 2017, Google anticipated the commercialization of quantum innovation inside the following 5 years.
- In April 2018, the designers carried out the post-quantum calculation of the XMSS computerized signature for the OpenSSH 7.7 update.
- In June 2018, Microsoft attached post-quantum key trade calculations and marks to their OpenVPN fork.

4.2 Extract

One of the advances that BTC depends on is the Secure Hashish Algorithm (SHA)–256, a cryptographic hashish capacity that transforms discretionary information into a 256-cycle string (the "hashish"). This is a single direction exertion with the goal that it is not difficult to track down the hashish from an information however not the opposite way on all side. Figure 4.1 shows the Bitcoin extraction explained. BTC extract comprises of the pursuit matter of discovering information (the "nonce")

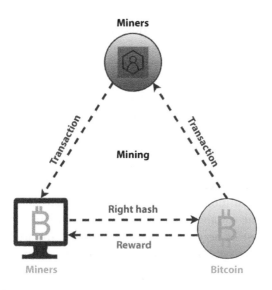

Figure 4.1 Bitcoin extract.

joined with data of the latest square that produces a hashish that is not exactly an objective worth T, the most extreme integer that is adequate to be considered a substantial BTC hash. The objective worth is constantly being corrected to acting as an extent that the normal time in the middle of blocks is 10 min (at the hour of composing the objective is roughly T = 8.9*10^{11}, a lot more modest than 2^{256} = 1.2*10^{77}). On the off chance that it was feasible to discover a quantum calculation to transform SHA-256 proficiently [5]. Nonetheless, the worth of BTC approaches from the trouble of discovering acting as arrangements, which offers it "evidence of exertion". At present, it is accepted that near is no productive calculation, old style or quantum, which can modify SHA-256. Thus, the lone process is a savage power explore, which traditionally implies attempting various contributions until a good arrangement is found.

Quantum mechanically, we have Grover's explore, which is by all accounts an ideal answer for this sort of matter and has a quadrilateral quantum acceleration. Allow us to perceive how competently this system functions, meanwhile, contrasting it with extract with a traditional PC. Traditionally, the achievement likelihood of extract a square with supposes is offer by $Trt/2^{256}$, "r represents the hashish remuneration (the quantity of estimates made each second), and t represents the time in a moment or two. For a quantum digger organization Grover's calculation, the achievement likelihood is sin2(2r$_q$ $\sqrt{T/2^{256}}$) [2], where r$_q$ is the integer of a Grover cycles each second, which we can term the "quantum hashish remuneration".

Presently, there is an alternate energetic in the middle of the traditional and quantum excavator on the grounds that BTC is intended to track down one more square on normal at regular intervals (=600 s) and, henceforth, the idea of the inquiry matter exchange in this pattern. In arrangement to the Grover system to offer excessive achievement likelihood, a quantum digger demands to run their calculation for a period t foregoing to the matter exchange and afterward make estimation. In the meantime, the oldstyle digger has, in this time, been trying however a large number of present moments as could be expected under the circumstances [6–8]. Hence, the quantum digger is trusting that none of the traditional excavators have discovered an answer yet in the course of the Grover advancement. Since the stretch in the middle of blocks follows a remarkable dispersion, the likelihood that the square is still mineable is offered by e$^{-t/600}$. Expecting a consistent expense of organization, a quantum PC for an offered measure of time, the productivity of quantum BTC extract is then, at that point

$$Re^{t/600} sin^2 \left(2\sqrt{rtT/2^{256}} \right) tCt$$

where R is the award (right now equivalent to the cost of 12.5 BTCs in addition to exchange expenses) and C is the expense of organization the quantum PC.

Allow us currently to assess several conceivable integers to see whether quantum BTC extract is productive. We expect a quantum PC that costs something very similar to utilize each hour as a traditional PC and utilize the present BTC value, block prize, and extract trouble. We gauge that quantum BTC extract gets beneficial at a quantum hashish pace of 48 kilo-hashish/s. Contrasting with the current best old-style BTC extract equipment with a hashish pace of 125 kilo-hashish/s, these integers may seem promising, yet we demand to remember that traditional BTC excavators can accomplish tremendous hashish remunerations in light of the fact that the arbitrary estimate extract calculation can be effectively complemented. The matter is that the quantum superiority does not surpass the component $\sqrt{2^{256}/T}$, regardless of the integer of qubits one has. Accordingly, while there is a quantum superiority, it is anything but outlandish enough that traditional side by side cannot hit it. For a quantum PC with an unhurried hashish remuneration than the insignificantly productive 48 kilo-hashish/s, single would then have to fall back on the old-style parallelization of quantum PCs. For instance, if the quantum hashish remuneration is 3 kilo-hashish/s, then one would require 1,300 quantum PCs to be comparable to traditional best extract equipment that could be bought this day. Accordingly, for quantum extract to be productive, one would require rather a quick quantum hashish remuneration or, potentially, a substantially more critical quantum hurry up. This might be in any case occur later on, however for the present, traditional extract appears to be hard to beat.

4.3   Preservation

To guarantee that BTC is spent simply by its legitimate proprietors, the asymmetrical bend computerized signature calculation (ECDSA) is utilized. Hence, it depends on open key cryptography where BTC proprietors can remarkably sign exchange utilizing their personal key and further can check that it is veritable utilizing their general key. Asymmetrical bend cryptography is defenseless against quantum registering. Shor's calculation can be effortlessly exchanged to unscramble messages sent with asymmetrical bends [3], for example, a quantum PC could then be utilized to track down the personal key from a general key. This seems to uncover a weakness; however, there are a few shields incorporation into BTC that forestall this. First and foremost, general keys are not uncovered by your location.

The BTC convention produces addresses by placing the general key through SHA-256 and afterward through RIPEMD-160. Since the general key is possibly uncovered when BTCs are spent, it gets defenseless against an assault by a quantum PC solely after the general key is uncovered in an exchange. The present circumstance is promptly cured by producing one more location after every exchange (as is current best practice at any remuneration). When quantum PCs are approach typical, most BTC customers will probably exchange to programmed key age after every exchange. This may diminish the comfort of specific applications. For instance, you would not print out a location QR cipher and utilize it is anything but a sales register. Deplorably (as we will forego to long see), this attach is just impermanent.

One more chance is that, one time, a general key is uncovered in a forthcoming exchange, a pernicious entertainer, even with a quantum PC that could get hold of the BTCs foregoing to the exchange, is finished. In head, Eve just has 10 min to track down the personal key foregoing to the exchange is concluded. Practically speaking, BTC exchange regularly sits in an informal forthcoming pool (the "mem-pool") for an hour or additional. Proos and Zalka gauge that for 256-digit ECDSA about 1,500 qubits are required and $6 \ 10^9$ one-qubit augmentations are essential (each and every one-qubit expansion get hold of nine quantum entryways) [3]. Hence, to carry out this sort of assault inside an hour, the quantum PCs require to carry out door tasks speed of on all side 660 MHz. All the more, as of late, Roetteler *et al.* tracked down that 2,330 qubits are essential and $1.26 * 10^{11}$ Toffoli door activities are essential (note: non-Toffoli entryways are accepted to get hold of unimportant time in this exertion) [10]. By this gauge, regardless of requiring more qubits, the quantum PC would just have to run at 350 MHz to pull off the assault. Regardless, the requests on the quantity of qubits and rate put together this assault unthinkable for untimely ages of quantum PCs.

Expecting you could shatter one and the other SHA-256 and RIPEMD-160, then, at that point, accompanied a current location, it is not difficult to remove the cash from one more person's possession. Nonetheless, notice that this matter is basically equivalent to the matter of discovering hashish impacts to add squares to the blockchain (for example, extract). The hypothesis goes that insofar as the registering power expected to get hold of BTCs is a lot excessive than the processing power expected to mine BTCs, any individual who could get hold of would rather mine.

Quantum figuring does not alteration this rationale in the absence of question. Doing a hashish crash assault on an old-style PC requires producing wallets thoroughly, although, in a post-quantum world, crude contribution to the hashish capacity can be examine and afterward personal keys perceived sometime later. In this manner, a steady calculate speedup impact assaults is gotten. Past that consistent factor, the current preservation of BTC against hashish impact assaults actually up right [9]. While there is no verification that different weaknesses do not exist, right now, there is no motivation to accept that there is. The solitary affirmation that we have is that BTC has existed for quite a long time in the absence of anybody hacking it regardless of tremendous monetary motivating forces to do as acting as. While we do not preclude the chance of novel quantum calculations being concocted for hacking or extract, it shows up profoundly non-paltry most definitely.

4.3.1 The Role of Cryptography in BTC

We characterized a computerized coin as a chain of advanced marks. Every proprietor moves the coinage to the following before carefully marking a hashish of the past exchange and the general key of the following proprietor and attaching these to the furthest limit of the coinage. A cashier can confirm the marks to check the shackles of proprietorship. The matter obviously is the cashier cannot confirm that one of the proprietors did not twofold spend on the coin. As we have perceived foregoing to, your personal key empowers you to concoct a general key. While your personal key empowers you to think of your general key, it is difficult to utilize the general key to derive the personal key. Our #1 similarity is the one utilized by blockchain reporter Don Tapscott in a meeting that was (amusingly) consequently got by the US moderator John Oliver [10]. Tapscott thinks about the interaction with chicken McNuggets, noticing that it is not difficult to transform a chicken into a McNugget, yet hard to transform the McNuggets turn into a chicken. This component is basic to keeping up with the preservation of BTC exchange (Figure 4.2).

What is an advanced mark? In the conventional world, one would sign an assessment to make it legitimate. We as a whole realize that faking a mark made by hand is incredibly simple, particularly on the grounds that you generally utilize a similar mark. It is honestly to some degree clever that we actually look for written by hand marks nowadays. In the crypto space, any individual who can discern your general key can confirm that the mark was made by the holder of the related personal key in the absence of the require to realize the personal key by and of as such. To proceed with our

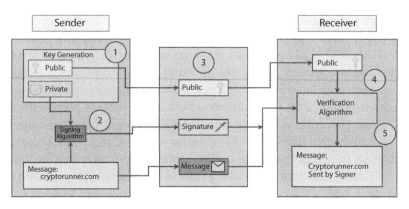

Figure 4.2 Cryptography.

McNugget model, it would resemble realizing that McNugget approaches along with a particular chicken, however in the absence of uncovering the chicken's mysterious name. This is an entertaining similarity; however, ideally, it serves the point.

Likewise, as the mark is substantial for a particular exchange, it cannot be reordered on one more piece of information in the absence of the mark being negated. Hence, if one somehow happened to get hold of the mark on the above McNugget and put it on an alternate McNugget by an alternate chicken, then the mark would be infirm. This is not finished by an abstract careful decision, however by unadulterated science. For anybody keen on becoming familiar with computerized marks, there is an abundance of data effectively open on the web.

Presently, continuing onward to the hashish, it is the hashish of the exchange that is marked, not simply the exchange [11]. In any case, what is a hashish? A hashish is a calculation utilized in cryptography that get hold of a contribution of any dimensions and go back a fixed-length succession of integers. This is significant as paying little heed to the extent or the dimensions of the information, you will get secure dimensions hashish. Hashish can be created from some section of information; however, the information cannot be produced from the hashish. Essentially, it just exertions single method and you cannot figure the contribution by taking a gander at the hashish. Additionally, regardless of whether an extremely slight swap is assembling in the information, the hashish will be unique.

The SHA-256 is a genuine illustration of a hashish exertion that is manufacturing quality. Initially planned by the National Preservation Agency (NSA), it is utilized in different spots in the BTC organization. With regard to BTC exchange, you are practically speaking utilizing your personal key to indication the hashish of the exchange (not simply the exchange), which empowers you to have a little trademark regardless of whether the hidden information beyond the hashish is immense. This is the thing that demonstrates proprietorship to others in the organization as they realize that it is the individual with the right personal key that marked the exchange. Indeed, there are various articles and writing on the web on hashish's and their set of experiences for anybody intrigued. Yet, while the above tackles the possession matter, it does not settle the twofold spend matter. The matter untimely is that the payee cannot affirm that one of the holders did not twofold spend on the coin. A run of the mill course of action is to initiate a trusted in middle force, or mint, that examine each trade for two fold pay out.

In the trade, the coin ought to be go back to the mint to offer one more coin, and, simply, coins gave sprightly from the mint are trusted not to be twofold consumed. The matter with this course of action is that the predetermination of the whole money structure hangs on the association organization the mint, with each trade going through them, particularly similar to a bank. We demand a way for the payee to understand that the foregoing owners did not indication any premature trades. For our inspirations, the soonest trade is the one that is important, so we were unable to think often less about later undertakings to twofold spend. The most ideal approach to assert the deficiency of a trade is to think pretty much all trades. As referenced, the twofold go-through matter is managed in the conventional world by having banks and other confided in focal specialists. However, how might we have this in a decentralized world?

4.3.2   The Role of Decentralization in BTC

While we could manage the twofold expend matter by having an organization of accountants, we would likewise require an "ace clerk" or some sort of guardian (a decent relationship are quality setters in the bookkeeping calling this day or the law social orders for attorneys). In any case, this makes the frame exertion concentrate (Figure 4.3). Along these lines, the arrangement in the BTC grid is to permit anybody to be a clerk and to have a similar arrangement of volume and documentation as any other person. These accountants are called hubs [12, 13]. All exchange is communicated to the different hubs in the BTC blockchain, permitting anybody and everybody to see them and modernize their "books". However, then, at that point how might we make certain of the request for this exchange? While everybody can see every one of the exchanges, we demand to concede to a

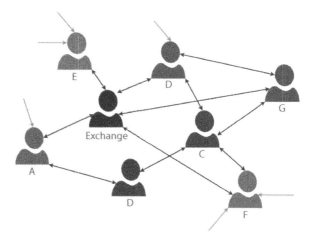

Figure 4.3 Decentralization.

specific request of exchange. To achieve this in the absence of a confided-in party, exchange should be freely declared, and we demand a frame exertion for members to concede to a solitary the past of the request where they were accepted. The BTC grid does this through hunk. On the off chance that the BTC grid is one monstrous book, each square is a sheet. For everybody to be in total agreement (in all seriousness), the accountants demand to know what the last sheet is and how it peruses. It would resemble a major book club where no one actions to the following sheet until everybody in the gathering has conceded to what the end sheet says or, for the BTC blockchain, what each square says.

4.3.3   The Role of Immutability in BTC

Nonetheless, how might we guarantee that no one returns and can exchange a sheet of the book? We recommend that each new sheet demands to hold the hashish of the relative multitude of past sheets. The arrangement that we put forward begins with a timestamp exertion. A timestamp exertion by proceeds hashish of a square of things to be time stepped and generally distributing the hashish. The timestamp demonstrates that the information probably breathed at that point, untimely, to get into the hashish. Each and every timestamp incorporates the past timestamp in its anything but, a chain, with every extra timestamp building up the ones preceding it. As we have seen foregoing, regardless of whether a solitary small detail is exchanged in any piece of information, its hashish will be extraordinary. Along these lines, remembering the hashish of the multitude of past sheets for each and every sheet makes it hard to modify the record, since, for somebody to exchange a past sheet, she should exchange each and every sheet past to that sheet. In the BTC blockchain, one more square (or an authority sheet of the book in our similarity) is made on all side every 10 min and attached to the chain, guaranteeing that when any new snippet of data is attached to the blockchain, then, at that point, it gets exchange less.

However, in the event that everybody will utilize a similar book and no one will push ahead until we have all consented to the substance of the last sheet, then, at that point, who will choose what that last sheet will hold? We could have an "ace" supervisor or expert clerk, however that would make the frame exertion unified indeed, opposing the motivation behind BTC. That is when proof of exertion approaches in.

4.3.4   The Role of Proof-of-Exertion in BTC

The proof-of-exertion instrument is actually the mystery ingredient of the BTC organization. The proof of exertion includes extract for a worth that when hashish, for example, with SHA-256, the hashish begins with various zero pieces. The normal exertion essential is dramatic in the quantity of zero pieces essential and can be confirmed by executing a solitary hashish. For our timestamp grid, we carry out the verification of exertion by augmenting a nonce in the square until a worth is discovered that offers the square's hashish the necessary zero pieces. When the CPU exertion has been used to cause it to fulfill the evidence of-exertion, the square cannot be exchanged in the absence of re-trying the exertion [14, 15]. Later, squares are fastened after it, and the exertion to exchange the square would incorporation re-trying every one of the squares after it. This interaction is the thing that is regularly called "extract". It includes four separation bits of information: hashish of the exchange on that square, the hashish of the past block, the time, and an integer called the nonce. A nonce is an irregular integer that is isolated from the exchange that is set out on that square.

Thus, an "excavator" will get hold of these four factors and expectation that the hashish yield will meet the vital necessity of the quantity of beginning zeros. That yield is known as the brilliant hashish. The digger can begin with a nonce of 0, then, at that point, attempt a nonce of 1, then, at that point, a nonce of 2, etc. The more nonces that an excavator can test, the more possibilities the digger demands to track down the "brilliant hashish" that meets the prerequisites and will permit him to add that square to the

BTC blockchain. This implies tracking down the right hashish turns out to be absolutely a matter of possibility. Anybody can, in principle, turn into a digger and track down the following brilliant hashish. The more various nonces an excavator can test, the excessive the odds she has of tracking down the brilliant hashish and getting new BTCs as an award. The remuneration at which latest nonces can be tried is known as the hashish remuneration which is extensively the times each second that a PC can run those four factors through a hashish exertion and determine one more hashish. To remunerate these diggers for their diligent effort, they are compensated with BTC. That exchange is known as the coin base exchange and is the primary exchange of each square. At the hour of composing, the prize is 12.5 BTC per block, yet this award gets split each 210,000 squares. For instance, the following splitting will occur in May 2020 where the award will diminish to 6.25 coins. To proceed with our clerk similarity, the digger would be a reviewer who will figure out what is the right last sheet of exchange (the square) to be utilized and the accountants will utilize that to add their new exchange until the inspectors affirm one more sheet. However, for an examiner to have the option to verify that her sheet will turn out to be essential for the authority book, she would have to toss a couple of dice and whoever gets a twofold six would have the option to add her sheet to the book. Obviously, the chances of an evaluator tossing two six-sided dice with the objective of in the end getting a twofold six are generally acceptable. With regard to genuine BTCextract, the chances are fundamentally more modest. The reason for this award is to remuneration excavators, yet in addition to make new BTCs. This day there are on all side 1,800 new BTCs made each day (roughly six new squares for every hour × 12.5 BTC per new block × 24 hours = 1,800 new BTCs). Yet, this raises a matter. In the event that the key to getting new BTCs is to dominate at this match of possibility, while this may sound engaging, it would cause financial expansion as it would significantly expand the stockpile of BTC.

Then, at that point, the organization makes it harder to track down the brilliant hashish by adding zeros to the hashish that is essential. This is known as the "trouble". This exchange is done generally like clock exertion with an objective of diggers tracking down the brilliant hashish in about 10 min. Thus, roughly every 10 min, one more square is attached to the chain. This is the place where the beginning of the name blockchain approaches from, yet it is imperative that Satoshi never utilized the word "blockchain" in the BTC whitepaper (more on this later). As should be obvious, "The organization is hearty in its unstructured effortlessness. Hubs exert at the same time with little coordination." In principle, anybody can interface with the BTC organization, download past blocks, monitor new exchange, and attempt to crunch the information to track down the brilliant hashish. This is one of the vital superiorities of the BTC organization. In any case, extract BTC chasing brilliant hashish has now gotten very troublesome. Just connecting your PC and expecting to track down the brilliant hashish is incredibly impossible. The innovation utilized for extract has developed decently fast from CPUs in PCs and graphical handling units (GPU) in realistic cards to application-explicit coordinated circuits (ASIC). To place things in context, probably, the best ASIC gadgets that are accessible available at the hour of composing have hashish paces of more than 13 TH/s, permitting you to crunch information and yield a hashish 13 trillion times a second. (Imagine tossing those dice at that speed!) Many of these extract tasks are likewise situated where there is modest power as extract activities this day devour a great deal of energy.

4.4   The Growth of BTC

The initially reported acquisition of products through BTC is dated May 2010. What could be compared to US$41 at the time? By 2017, those 10,000 were worth millions, apparently making it the costliest pizza request ever. May 22 is presently celeb remuneration by numerous individuals in the worldwide crypto local area as "BTC Pizza Day".

In the course of the last decade, BTC consistently begin acquiring energy, encountering a significant blast toward the finish of 201,324 when its value rose to about US$1,000. However, exactly when things appeared to be removed, the value began to fall. It kept on encountering a consistent decrease and dove back to about US$200 throughout the following 2 years. Those were troublesome occasions for the BTC people group because of numerous general occasions, incorporating the relationship with the Silk Road commercial center captures, just as the hack of a BTC trade, called Mt. Gox. Notwithstanding, the use of BTC expanded in the course of that time, with the quantity of affirmed day-by-day BTCexchange, untimely multiplying each year, coming to more than 100,000 by 2015. However, following these occasions, the tide began gradually changing for BTC and the more extensive crypto ecosystem. At the beginning of crypto resources, the purchasers, dealers, and clients of these resources were a specialty gathering of people. These people went from experienced cryptographers and nerds to designers and libertarians. The scene began to exchange rapidly in 2015 and 2016 as an ever-increasing integer of people got keen on digital currencies, from college understudies day exchanging their apartments to untimely adopters who decided to contribute a part of their enhanced portfolio in this new resource class. The year 2017 will be recognized as a game-changing year for BTC and the more extensive crypto ecosystem. BTC's value hit US$10,000 in November 2017—one more excessive that would have been unfathomable for a very long time back. Yet, the craze proceeded with BTC's value coming to almost US$20,000 close to the furthest limit of December 2017. Out of nowhere, BTC was being talked about routinely on media junctures like Bloomberg and CNBC, which thus produced mass measures of worldwide buzz in the crypto space. Numerous retail and institutional financial backers additionally began focusing on and getting truly associated with crypto resources. Individuals began to extract BTC in the course of supper and at family social occasions. For instance, US-based trade coin base opened more than 100,000 new records over the 2017 Thanksgiving holiday. Demand was excessive to the point that numerous trades demanded to quit taking on new customers or were overwhelmed with demands when they did. For instance, the Hong Kong–based trade Binance opened on all side 250,000 new records in an hour after it returned its foundation in 2017. The cost of BTC and numerous other crypto-resources fell in 2018. BTC shut the year at marginally over US$4000, a long way from the excessive it saw in 2017.

This resuscitated the discussion in the middle of BTC adherents and its cynics. For instance, Nobel laureate Nouriel Roubini gave a show at a US Senate Committee considering BTC the "mother", everything being equal. Others have begun to get hold of a more nuance; see the International Monetary Fund's overseeing chief Christine Lagarde reference that it could exchange how individuals save and invest. Others have accepted digital forms of money all the more proactively: for instance, a few rumored worldwide associations began tolerating BTC. PwC's Hong Kong department acknowledged BTC installment in 2017 for its warning services. Accessible travel booking juncture, Expedia, permits clients to book a few inns by means of BTC, while Microsoft permits clients to purchase content from Windows and Xbox stores through BTC. Many accept that we have passed the final turning point with BTC as well as more extensive crypto-resources and that they are staying put. Nonetheless, others accept that a portion of the difficulties, as we will talk about beneath, is not kidding road obstructions and that we actually have far to go foregoing to BTC and other crypto-resources be approach standard.

4.5   Quantum Computing (History and Future)

The field of quantum figuring offers a great deal of hypothetical guarantee to the calculation of expert matters. The utilization of Shor's calculation has been promoted as a finish to encryption and computerized marks, in any event as we probably are aware of them now. Since the 1980s, matter open-minded quantum registering (FTQC) has been an advancement that is practically on all side the bend. Quantum figuring is a huge scope and costly exercise. In this paper, we address both the matters with blunders in quantum processing and the plausibility of acting as a frame exertion and afterward keep on taking a gander at the financial effect of acting as a machine. From this investigation, we show that the best case for quantum processing is a long way from under extract toward cryptology whenever soon and afterward, truth be told, it could be infeasible.

The fascinating thing with Moore's law and cryptography is that we twofold in computational force like clock exertion and figure out how to expand the length of a key we can sensibly break at a similar remuneration. The out approach is that keys expressed to last huge integer of years are just suitable for a little part of that time. This is not an out approach of some legendary quantum frame exertion; rather it is anything but a factor of old-style calculation and the advances in innovation. We cannot anticipate breaking 256-bit ECC in the following 10,000 years, utilizing any current present day traditional PC frame exertion. However, in the event that we just wait1, we would have a home PC in less than 200 years that could promptly and rapidly address ECC and any remaining general-personal keys plans in regular use. Now, we might have moved to 512- or even 1,024-bit ECC, and we would in any case be secure from assault. The necessities for scrambling information approach from the following: the time frame that the data should be gotten, the measure of time it would get hold of to exchange to one more calculation or to build key dimensions, how long we can hope to have, and a calculation that endures assaults (counting from quantum frame exertions if these are created).

4.6   Quantum Computation

Quantum PCs are theoretical machines that depend on a few hypothetical dimensions from quantum mechanics in physical science. Assuming these guesses from and others demonstrate that remuneration is valid, it is conceivable that quantum PCs could dominate traditional computation on an electro-mechanical PC. A significant part of the current generality originates from Shor's discovering of a polynomial quantum calculation that gets hold into account the factorization of the chosen classes of integers and calculations (particularly those related with cryptographic cycles). Figure 4.4, this figure explain quantum computing. Likewise, with all lacking yet

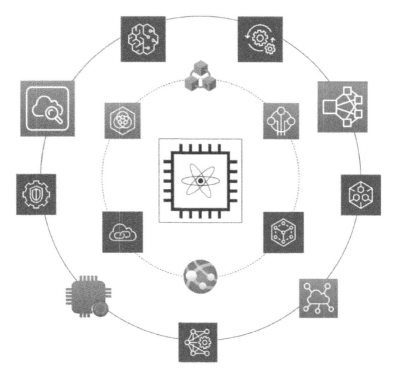

Figure 4.4 Quantum computing.

conceivably encouraging advancements, the reexploreers make these over-sell the close term capacity. This is not out of the ordinary. In the absence of subsidizing, they could never approach to exist. The out approach is that there are numerous simply hypothetical assaults right now that are blaming quantum computation so as to move individuals into new and untested regions. On acting as space of assault has been in cryptographic money and BTC where numerous bogus bits of gossip have been spread. A portion of this announcing (purposefully) darkens the types of computation expected to break a frame exertion perplexing the peruser into a deception that the end is excessive. Actually, the contentions are misleading, best case scenario, to say the least, they are deliberately intended to hoodwink. We exhibit the defects in these contentions and show that frame exertions (like BTC) are good for any remuneration in the following not many years and perhaps forever from acting as an assault.

4.7   The Proposal of Quantum Calculation

The venturesome guess that "Computational gadgets dependent on quantum mechanics will be computationally better looked at than advanced PCs". This was get hold further by the announcement that quantum PCs will be equipped for considering integers in polynomial time. Quantum frame exertions are innately loud. A few, including Shor, accept this to be a minor matter with decoherence being a straightforward matter. Different specialists are a long way from certain (4). No organization or exploration bunch has made even the least difficult of all-inclusive quantum PCs yet. The frame exertions are completely specific frame exertions and false quantum computers. This is as no frame exertion has had the option to hold cognizance to make even a solitary legitimate qubit for any measure of time. IBM marketing has reported that they "expect(s) to have a 5- to 8-qubit general frame exertion by 2020" [5]. Of course, this has been a predictable refrain since the 1980s with a frame exertion to break 256-cycle ECC that should have at any remuneration of 20,000 intelligent Qubits to be compelling in figuring enormous integers. A significant part of the hypothesis shows that a 100,000 to 1 million coherent qubit machine would be demanded to approach existing frame exertions that factor enormous primes. To do what is essential for ECDSA breaking in near-continuous (under 60 min), this could be just about as extensive as a 10 million consistent qubit machine.

The speculation of matter open-minded quantum calculation (FTQC) states that, under those conditions, the limit hypothesis on the normal assumptions for measurable freedom over the pace of commotion will prompt the likelihood that the clamor per sensible qubit could be adequately low per PC cycle to empower an FTQC to exertion (Aharonov and Ben-Or, 1999. Different analysts are finished doubters and do not accept that FTQC is even possible and would not ever be accomplished [6]. Kalai (2008) stands firm on a footing he calls the "postulate of clamor: quantum frame exertions are loud", which he guesses that cannot permit the formation of a huge FTQC. He holds that "computationally prevalent quantum PCs rely upon acknowledging quantum blunder revision codes, which are not seen in nature, debilitates the underlying reasoning offern for quantum PCs".

One of the essential worries with the recuperation of data from quantum frame exertions is credited to blunder recuperation. In none quantum frame exertions, blunders are conveyed as repetitive sound. The conveyance of small transaction is autonomous and indistinguishably circulated data that is stochastically differed on all side the main matter at a time. This varies altogether from a large part of the out approaches found in quantum processing. As indicated quantum states are, by and large, discovered to be caught. This meddles with the recuperation of data as existing factual devices do not deal with the partition of data and misget hold ofs from exceptionally corresponded data well overall.

4.8   What Are Quantum Computers and How They Exertion?

The total meaning of quantum mechanics and quantum registering is a long way past the extent of this paper. We will address just the nuts and bolts and direct the peruser toward a few notable papers on the theme. A portion of the essential matters with the comprehension of any quantum frame exertion get straightforwardly from the basic principles of quantum mechanics. The simple perception of a marvel exchanges the result of the occasion that will be estimated. Any communication with a quantum molecule (on account of a quantum PC, the qubit) on a very basic level and irreversibly adjusts the condition of the frame exertion that will be estimated. This out approach is in the matter of not knowing whether a quantum frame exertion is acting as we would anticipate. In principle, we can make frame exertions that exertion toward arrangements with boundless exactness permitting us to do matters like the factorization of enormous integers.

This matter requires the improvement of a widespread quantum PC. To make acting as a frame exertion, it is demanded to carry out quantum doors that action the grid vibrations or, potentially, the core been of the individual particles related with the qubits to be estimated. This, obviously, prompted the revelation of presented decoherence impacts. This impact presents stochastically factor data that makes a degree of misget hold ofs in any estimation. The proposed arrangement in the improvement of an FTQC has been to settle on a blunder remuneration and plan on all side it. This blunder remuneration cannot be totally get hold out; nonetheless, the scholars accept that the presentation of extra qubits will offer adequate misget hold of revision to empower the formation of a functioning quantum PC. The formation of qubits is a troublesome undertaking; the acquaintance of numerous qubits with structure a solitary intelligent qubit is gradually more troublesome. A portion of the current execution recommendations requires the joining of seven physical qubits into the formation of a solitary first layer coherent qubit. To diminish the blunder remuneration on computations adequately at any remuneration, two layers of legitimate qubits are recreated to make a variety of 49 qubits that go about as a solitary matter safe sensible qubit. The main thing to note here is that we have not made a frame exertion with more than five qubits as of now, so the making of a coherent qubit with one or the other seven or 49 actual parts stays theoretically best case scenario. There is numerous propositions that detail the novel methods of making physical qubits (7). These are at present conceivable at a limited scale. The trouble approaches from the way that we do not have a clue how proportional these nor regardless of whether it is feasible to scale a quantum PC into the domains of what is explained inside the hypothesis.

An exertion, versatile quantum PC would require an answer for the matter of quantum decoherence first. Any quantum frame exertion should be secluded from all-encompassing cooperation's as any impacts from encompassing particles will bring about the molecule decal hearing or falling into a double state similar to an old-style PC. For all the promotion, no quantum PC has at any point been judged exactly to be functioning as the hypothesis would state. Quantum figuring is not deterministic. The coding of a quantum frame exertion essentially prompts a probabilistic out approach. We are accustomed to organization a program in acquiring the very out approach for every cycle that we draw in with a piece of similar information. Quantum frame exertions are intrinsically unique in relation to this. To acquire an exact out approach, the estimation on a quantum PC should be run as a hashish circle commonly until the probabilistic probability of an alternate out approach is limited. This is the motivation behind why quantum PCs department I little benefit over numerous types of calculation. The enchanted properties of quantum PCs have been connected to hypothetical calculations that are proposed to offer factorization arrangements in the domain of cryptography (this is recuperating prime elements of huge integers and related matters). The following matter with the probabilistic frame exertion is that it is anything but vital that it is possible to decide whether it has been created. While we can get hold of the out approaches related to the age of a cryptographic personal key and check on an old-style PC whether this worth comparing to the satisfying personal key is looking to factor, it is absolutely impossible to decide if any of the yields is right prior to testing. The out approach is essentially organization numerous emphases prior to having the option to decide if the out approach is right. Some guarantee has been proposed on all side the stremunerationgy of "daze quantum computing" [8]. This procedure has been shown to deal with a limited scale utilizing a full qubit quantum PC to check the after effects of a subsequent PC. As Scott Aaronson noted in Science [9], "As practically all current quantum registering tests, this presentation has the situation with a pleasant exhibit verification of idea, instead of anything straightforwardly valuable yet". Proposition exists for the making of numerous quantum PCs comprising double caught qubits. The matter with these propositions is that these are not exclusively the arrangements outside the scope of present innovation, however, that we could not say whether the principal particles that we try to snare exist.

4.9   Post-Quantum Cryptography

A post-quantum cryptosystem is one that is secure against a quantum assault. The known calculations of post-quantum cryptography with a general key depend on different methodologies, including hashish capacities, super singular asymmetrical bends isogenies, misget hold of adjusting codes, cross sections, and multivariate quadratic conditions.

The preservation level of a hashish-based computerized mark is decreased to the first and second pre-image opposition of a hashish exertion. On an exemplary PC, the recuperation of n bits hashish is bound to a beast power explore [intricacy O(2n)], while on a quantum PC, it is restricted to Grover's hunt [intricacy O(2n/2)]. Along these lines, we can pick a reasonable hashish exertion that offers the essential traditional and post-quantum preservation level. Other ways to deal with post-quantum cryptography depend on numerical matters that are viewed as quantum-safe however can be settled on an old-style PC in an out approach of a forward leap in the advancement of math.

As indicated by the PQCRYPTO proposals, the computerized signature conspire XMSS with boundaries from RFC 8391 is utilized to accomplish 128-bit post-quantum cryptography in BTC Post-Quantum. The superiority of the XMSS conspire is that it is anything but a predetermined integer of marks, which relies upon the tallness of the Merkle tree utilized. Notwithstanding XMSS, the PQCRYPTO suggestions incorporate remunerating the SPHINCS conspire, which has no limitations on the quantity of marks. Nonetheless, for a 128-cycle preservation level, the dimension of acting as a mark is on all side 41 kB, which is too costly to even consider utilizing in a blockchain and is more reasonable for validation frame exertions. The dimensions of the XMSS mark is about 2.5 kB, which is very huge contrasted and the ECDSA signature (71 bytes), and requires an expansion in the square dimensions; be that as it may, this is the most suitable choice for post-quantum signature in a blockchain.

4.10   Difficulties Facing BTC

Regardless of its numerous advancements, BTC is not awesome. A few observers contrast BTC with the car Model T's motor; in 1908, it is planned by Ford Motor Organization. While development at that point, it was generally sluggish (about 40 miles per hour), which is not a lot quicker than a pony's organization velocity. Additionally, the motor was not proficient and it was excessive energy-serious. In any case, we have made some amazing development from that point forward to the present Tesla electric vehicles.

Many expect that crypto-resources will move through a similar advancement. Presently, BTC faces numerous difficulties. For instance, its cost is as yet unstable. While unpredictability is extraordinary for theorists and merchants, it is anything but useful for a resource that can be utilized as a store of significant worth. Individuals purchase blue-chip stocks or gold to some extent due to their soundness. Much expectation that as BTC selection increments and the quantity of institutional financial backers develop, instability will decay, however that is not the situation yet. The instability is likewise a snag to having more inescapable acknowledgment, for example, from dealers.

One more matter is legitimate, administrative, and particularly charge lucidity. It is extremely hard for a resource for acquire standard acknowledgment whether financial backers do not have the foggiest idea what the expense effect will be for any addition or misfortune that they make. Likewise, one necessity to have conviction on the legitimate and administrative system prior to placing her existence investment funds in that resource. The uplifting message (as will be examined later in this section) is that loads of governments, controllers, and duty specialists are taking a gander at resolving these matters; however, this does not occur incidentally, sadly.

A portion of the difficulties is likewise specialized, for instance, the adaptability of BTC. At present, the BTC organization can just measure less than six or seven exchange each second. Just via examination, Visa's organization can measure on all side 24,000 for every second. While there have been drives to address this matter in the BTC grid with hard forks (for example, BTC Cash) or delicate forks (for example, Isolated Witness), this is as yet a remarkable matter. BTC additionally faces genuine natural difficulties as extracts get hold of an inconceivable measure of energy. Beginning at 2018, the organization is essential to devour about 2.55 giga-watts (GW) of power untimely. In examination, the whole nation of Ireland on normal devours about 3.1 GW of power and gauges show that, in the foregoing year, the quantity of terawatt-hours (TWh) utilized by the BTC grid every year may have expanded by as much as 400%.

The power utilization demanded by the confirmation of exertion instru-ment is unmistakably not versatile in a reasonable manner. While numer-ous other digital forms of money use stremunerationgies that are not as energy-serious as evidence of exertion (for example, confirmation and purchase), this day is as yet a matter for BTC.

4.11   Conclusion

Since the commencement of BTC, the digital currency market has devel-oped forcefully. It has additionally brought up significant matters that, specifically, are digital currencies the eventual fate of money-related frame exertions. We strived to address this puzzler according to a specialized point of view by zeroing in on the preservation concerns, protection mat-ters, and their trade-offs versus the exchange postponement of BTC. These worries are key factors in deciding the fate of digital forms of money. To address these worries, we initially presented the foundation of BTC and elucidated its significant structure squares and conventions. Then, we dove into critical preservation concerns. We begin by talking about the twofold spending assault and extract its likelihood of accomplishment. Utilizing this investigation, we further assessed the productivity of a likely assault. We showed that anybody possessing not exactly 50% of the absolute computational force will ultimately lose eventually while playing out the assault. Furthermore, we investigated the significant organization-related preservation matters of the hidden shared organization. Our conversation showed that these organizational assaults are unavoidable since there is no stremunerationgy to limit noxious hubs from interfacing with the organi-zation. We further investigated stockpiling preservation by exploring the wallet foundations and the various methods of capacity. We inferred that there is a trade-off in the middle of capacity preservation and common sense. Past the preservation offers that BTC endures, we explored the pro-tection impediments innate to the frame exertion. We exposed the confu-sion of BTC's namelessness and audited significant stremunerationgies for preservation assurance. We likewise hoped to extend the peruser's infor-mation on arising altcoins with cutting-edge preservation and protection excessive lights. A broad examination is as yet essential in the blockchain space to completely comprehend and upgrade the preservation and protection of acting as applications. However, numerous applications focus on further improving preservation or potentially protection; the clients stay suspicious because of different application-explicit prerequisites. As exploration propels in these fields, it is conceivable that blockchain-based frame exertions may help reform and override the incorporated remuneration frame exertions that we depend on this day.

References

1. Nakamoto, S., Bitcoin: A Peer-to-Peer Electronic Cash System, Bitcoin Project 2008, *Decentralized Business Review*, 21260, 2020. Dostupno na: https://bitcoin.org/bitcoin.pdf (pristupljeno 16. 8. 2018.).
2. Huang, H.Y., Kueng, R., Preskill, J., Information-theoretic bounds on quantum advantage in machine learning. *Phys. Rev. Lett.*, 126, 19, 190505, 2021.
3. Fosso Wamba, S., Kala Kamdjoug, J.R., Epie Bawack, R., Keogh, J.G., Bitcoin, blockchain and fintech: a systematic review and case studies in the supply chain. *Prod. Plan. Control*, 31, 2–3, 115–142, 2020.
4. Singh, S., Rajput, N.K., Rathi, V.K., Pandey, H.M., Jaiswal, A.K., Tiwari, P., Securing blockchain transactions using quantum teleportation and quantum digital signature. *Neural Process. Lett.*, 1–16, 2020.
5. Jogenfors, J., Quantum bitcoin: An anonymous and distributed, and secured currency secured by the no-cloning theorem of quantum mechanics, *IEEE International Conference on Blockchain and Cryptocurrency (ICBC)*, 245–252, 2016. arXiv:1604.01383.
6. Aggarwal, D., Brennen, G., Lee, T., Santha, M., Tomamichel, M., Quantum attacks on BTC, and how to protect against them, 2017. arXiv:1710.10377.
7. Dhanaraj, R.K., Lalitha, K., Anitha, S., Khaitan, S., Gupta, P., Goyal, M.K., Hybrid and dynamic clustering-based data aggregation and routing for wireless sensor networks [JB]. *J. Intell. Fuzzy Syst.*, (Preprint) 1–15, 2021.
8. Roetteler, M., Naehrig, M., Svore, K.M., Lauter, K., Quantum resource estimates for computing elliptic curve discrete logarithms. In *International Conference on the Theory and Application of Cryptology and Information Security*, Springer, Cham, 241–270, 2017. arXiv:1706.06752.
9. Aharonov, D. and Ben-Or, M., Fault-tolerant quantum computation with constant error. *STOC'97, ACM*, pp. 176–188, 1999.
10. Nerurkar, P., Patel, D., Busnel, Y., Ludinard, R., Kumari, S., Khan, M.K., Dissecting bitcoin blockchain: Empirical analysis of bitcoin network (2009–2020). *J. Netw. Comput. Appl.*, 177, 102940, 2021.
11. Beck, R., *Beyond bitcoin: The rise of blockchain world. Computer*, vol. 51, pp. 54–58, 2018. https://www.computer.org/csdl/magazine/co/2018/02/

12. Truby, J., Decarbonizing Bitcoin: Law and policy choices for reducing the energy consumption of Blockchain technologies and digital currencies. Energy research & social science, in: *Stabilizer codes and quantum error-correction*, vol. 44, Gottesman, D. (Ed.), pp. 399–410, 2018, Ph. D. Thesis, Caltech, quant-ph/9705052.

13. Kher, R., Terjesen, S., Liu, C., Blockchain, Bitcoin, and ICOs: a review and research agenda. *Small Bus. Econ.*, 56, 4, 1699–1720, 2021.

14. Krishnasamy, L., Ramasamy, T., Dhanaraj, R., Chinnasamy, P., A geodesic deployment and radial shaped clustering (RSC) algorithm with statistical aggregation in sensor networks. *Turk. J. Elec. Eng. Comp. Sci.*, 29, 95, 3, 2021.

15. Yin, W., Wen, Q., Li, W., Zhang, H., & Jin, Z, An anti-quantum transaction authentication approach in blockchain. *IEEE Access, 6*, 5393– 5401, 2018.

5

A Conceptual Model for Quantum Blockchain

Vijayalakshmi P.[1]*, Abraham Dinakaran[2] and Korhan Cengiz[3]

[1]Department of Artificial Intelligence and Data Science, KL Deemed to be University, Green Fields, Vaddeswaram, Guntur District, A.P., India
[2]Department of Computer Science and Applications, KL Deemed to be University, Green Fields, Vaddeswaram, Guntur District, A.P., India
[3]Department of Electrical-Electronics Engineering, Trakya University, Edirne, Turkey

Abstract

Blockchain and Distributed Ledger Technologies (DLTs) have progressed considerably in recent years with their significance in the development of applications related to the ability to produce transparency, redundancy, and responsibility. Technological progression guarantees the expansion of computers in terms of principles related to quantum physics and is not adequate to the principles of conventional physics. Quantum computing focuses on developing technology that supports the principle of quantum theory and gains monumental processes through multiple states and performs tasks simultaneously with reasonable permutations. Quantum blockchain framework simplifies the event and deployment of applications with minimized customization. The quantum blockchain framework ensures to yield a quantum-based system reliable, manageable, adaptable, and cost-efficient. This chapter consists of three phases for the design consideration of the quantum blockchain framework. In the foremost phase, the hardware components of a system, *viz.*, processors, and its interconnecting network devices are evaluated. The second phase identifies the underlying components that underpin the quantum blockchain system for the current communication task performed. The last phase presents the essential integrant of the system's behavior. This chapter also elaborates the significant and complementary ways that a framework of quantum blockchain is represented and quantified.

*Corresponding author: viji.syon@gmail.com

Rajesh Kumar Dhanaraj, Vani Rajasekar, SK Hafizul Islam, Balamurugan Balusamy and Ching-Hsien Hsu (eds.) Quantum Blockchain: An Emerging Cryptographic Paradigm, (109–126)
© 2022 Scrivener Publishing LLC

Keywords: Distributed ledger technology, quantum theory, quantum blockchain, layering, security

5.1   Introduction

Blockchain and quantum computing are cutting-edge technologies that remodel the information industry and optimize its security. However, blockchain implements security measures for securing information in its information base, and quantum computers take advantage of the quantum principle, which will override blockchain's security. Quantum-resistant cryptography and quantum computing eliminate blockchain's security measures [5]. Incorporations of the two technologies bring the ultimate quantum blockchain or quantum time machine to make every single operation secure.

The purpose of this chapter is to introduce the requirements for designing a framework for quantum blockchain with considering the hardware composition of the quantum computer, computational elements, architectural patterns, and fundamental Integrants. Section 5.2 introduces distributed ledger technology (DLT) with examples of blockchain and quantum blockchain and also the evolution of quantum computing, and Section 5.3 introduces the core components of quantum computers. Section 5.4 depicts framework styles of quantum blockchain. Section 5.5 presents the fundamental integrants that should be considered during the implementation of quantum blockchain.

5.2   Distributed Ledger Technology

The database exists across several locations or among several participants that gives control of all its information and transactions to the users and promotes transparency. DLT is the component of the "Internet of Value" that enables interactions and it transfers to an end-to-end communication with no centralized database. A *value* in the DLT infers to a record in database such as money, securities, health information, and other personal information. The DLT is also called as a Shared ledger. Figure 5.1 highlights the applications, *viz.*, voting, financial services, energy, law, insurance, music, healthcare, public records, supply chain management, real estate, cloud computing, and retail where the DLT can be utilized.

Voting   Financial   Energy   Law   Insurance   Music
          Services

Healthcare   Public   Supply Chain   Cloud   Retail   Real Estate
              Records   Management   Computing

Figure 5.1 Utilization of DLT in industries.

5.2.1   Features of DLT

The DLT features [8] that are considered as key to the technology are outlined as follows.

a) **The distributed nature of the ledger:** It can be referred to as one-copy update semantics used in conventional file systems. The one-copy update semantics method depicts the concurrent access and updates to the ledger contents by network participants. However, the consistency of the ledger contents is maintained in the ledger database.

b) **Consensus mechanism:** The consensuses are rules and procedures that nodes validate across a distributed ledger. It is a method used for authentication and validation without the need to trust a central authority.

c) **Cryptographic mechanisms:** The security of the ledger is maintained cryptographically through encryption to control access to the distributed ledger. This mechanism supports confidentiality during communication before transmission occurs between source and destination. We now look at concepts of blockchain, quantum computing, and quantum blockchain.

5.2.2   Quantum Computing

The term quantum computing is a progressive field with the intersection of mathematics, physics, and computer science. We present here an introduction to the growth of quantum computing, significant differences between classical and quantum computing, and also exploring the concepts of blockchain and quantum blockchain.

5.2.2.1 Growth of Quantum Computing

Richard Feynman, a theoretical physicist, proposed quantum computing. During a presentation in the year 1981 at MIT, he witnessed a statement on quantum computing that reveals "The evolution of quantum systems are efficient enough and they cannot be simulated by classical computers". As a result, a core framework model was proposed for experimenting with simulation in quantum computers. This framework also highlights the possibility of how quantum computers can overtake classical computers. However, quantum computing was revolutionized by the design of Shor's algorithm that prevails success to quantum computation.

In 1994, Peter Shor proposed an algorithm named Shor. The Shor is capable of factorizing complex integers efficiently in quantum computers. This algorithm executes effectively faster than traditional algorithms on machines. Quantum computers make computations faster than classical computers. The Shor can break cryptosystems efficiently, as it factorizes integers into polynomial time.

In 1996, the invention of the quantum database search algorithm by Lov Grover opened for a variety of problems concerning time and space in business and science applications. The problem that uses random [15] and brute-force search methods can execute faster compared to classical search algorithms.

In 1998, a 2-qubit quantum computer was developed, and it implements quantum algorithms such as Grover's algorithm and produces better results. The computing power by quantum computers paved way for many applications in the field of research.

In 2017, IBM took the initiative to build the first commercial quantum computer (IBM Q). IBM Q computes systems for business and science applications for the commercial platform. IBM Q systems and services are marketed by IBM Cloud. This also paved the way to access quantum processors in public and to serve as an empowering utility in scientific research, repository access to university classrooms, and also as a channel of interest in information analysis [14].

5.2.2.2 A Comparison of Classical Computing and Quantum Computing

In classical computing, a piece of information is represented as a bit, known as 0 and 1. These are commonly realized by the ON or OFF state

$$|0\rangle = [1\ 0\ ]\quad |1\rangle = [1\ 0\ ]$$

Figure 5.2 Representation of qubit.

of a transistor. In quantum computing, two quantum states, 0 and 1, can define a basic unit of information known as *qubits* (*quantum bits*). The representations of qubits are shown in Figure 5.2.

The two possible states in classical computing are either 0 or 1. However, in quantum computing phenomena, it can be 0, 1, or a superposition of 0 and 1. This leads to a large number of possibilities to store information. The properties of quantum mechanics help to store, represent, and perform operations in quantum computers. These operations work efficiently in quantum computers compared to classical computers. The conceptual rules and mathematical manifestations play a vital role in the behavior of particles in quantum mechanics. The behavior of particles uses the properties [2], *viz.*, *entanglement*, *superposition*, and *interference* for quantum computing. *Superposition* is defined as the capability of a qubit to exist in multiple states or different positions at a period. *Entanglement* is the strong correlation of two quantum particles that exits between physical properties and qubits. The *interference* allows the content of the qubit to remain stable in multiple states.

5.2.3 Blockchain and Quantum Blockchain

A blockchain stores stable information that can neither be modified nor hacked. A blockchain is considered a digital ledger of transactions that is replicated and distributed among the network. Each transaction is an immutable cryptographic signature termed a *hash*. The structure of the block consists of a cryptographic *hash*, a timestamp, and the transaction data. Since the blocks are interconnected, the changes made to one block reflect apparently to its neighborhood blocks. If an unauthorized user tries to corrupt a blockchain system, the changes need to be included in every block of chain and also across its distributed versions. This enables blockchain systems to record information securely. The primary limitation of blockchain is that the data on the network is immutable and protected [2].

5.2.3.1 Characteristics of Blockchain

The characteristics of blockchain, *viz.*, distributed ledger, chronological and time-stamped, and consensus method [13], are discussed in the following.

a) **Distributed Ledger:** It is accessible and managed by a group (cluster) of computers.

b) **Chronological and Time-Stamped:** The block is a storehouse of information about data transactions. The chronological chain forms a link to the previous block transactions and maintains a record for the underlying transaction.

c) **Consensus Method:** The purpose of the consensus method is to define a validation process for all network users in blockchain to determine the block's validity. After successful validation, the users are added to a new block of their respective ledgers. The modifications made to the ledger are replicated among the whole network and therefore a copy of the entire ledger is attained by each user of their respective network.

5.2.3.2   Quantum Blockchain

The computers that performed quantum computing are termed "Quantum Computers". These computers lack circuits to embed components, *viz.*, integrated circuits, transistors, and logic gates involved in the computation. They use subatomic particles like atoms, electrons, photons, and ions as qubits to represent information. The spin and state of qubits are parts of qubit information. The information can be superposed that presents various combinations by using the property of *superposition*. Therefore, quantum computers are powerful and can execute instructions in parallel using their memory efficiently.

Del Rajan and Matt Visser at Victoria University of Wellington have suggested a method named quantum blockchain, and it prevents blockchain from hacking using quantum computers. The quantum blockchain is used to secure Bitcoin. Bitcoin is a blockchain technology used to record the financial transactions of a user securely. Bitcoin can be referred to as a cryptocurrency, a virtual currency, or a digital currency. Quantum computing can easily break the security implemented by Bitcoin; therefore, quantum blockchain is used to prevent hacking that takes place by quantum computing. Quantum blockchain [17, 19] uses time entanglement and a quantum attack–resistant cryptographic algorithm to prevent and secure blockchain from attacks of quantum computing. Quantum computing has the potential of breaking encryption deployed in blockchains and cryptographic codes. Quantum blockchain [1] also uses entanglement for applications that involve time and space. Now, we look into the hardware composition of the quantum computer [9].

5.3   Hardware Composition of the Quantum Computer

The quantum computer consists of memory, a processor, and an input/ output unit for manipulating the states of qubits. The qubit manipulation allows quanta to propagate the (photonic energy) bits among quantum computers to enable qubit assembling. The qubit stores 1, 0, or 0-1 as quanta states. Multiple qubits are clustered to form registers. These registers assist in storing and manipulating quanta data quantum systems.

The logic gates form as the processor in a quantum computer. The qubit logic gates are designed to execute composite (complex) operations. The combination of logic gates performs single or multiple operations that support unitary and rotation operations. Qubits and control devices function together as memory and processor. As quantum computers contain multiple states by the property of superposition, it enables parallelism for rapid computing [2]. We look into the framework of quantum blockchain.

5.4   Framework Styles of Quantum Blockchain

The framework of a quantum blockchain enables the integration of modules that can be reused for developing quantum blockchain applications. The framework formulates the system as reliable, manageable, adaptable, and cost-effective for developing domain-specific functionality. The framework [4] needs to fulfill the characteristics such as transparency, consistency, availability, confidentiality, and performance.

5.4.1   Computational Elements

The computational elements describe qubits and quantum gates and their computation the building blocks in quantum blockchain computation.

5.4.1.1   Qubits

The computational elements in quantum blockchain are blocks, data, and timestamps that are stored on a decentralized network and operate through quantum methods. In quantum blockchain, data is encoded using qubits. The qubits can also be referred to as photons. Photons are electromagnetic radiation that comes from light or radio waves. Superdense coding is used to write a block. This method is used to send two bits as (00, 01, 10, or 11) in a single qubit format.

Consider, when user A wants to send information to user B, the information is sent as two entangled qubits. User A applies a quantum gate to its qubit that sets the entanglement between the two qubits to a certain Bell state. The Bell state is also known as the entangled state. The Bell states [2] are a way to measure the entangled quantum states between two photons. There are four possible Bell states (00, 01, 10, 11) based on the spin of the qubit that maps to the four possible 2 bits of information that one user (user A) has to send to another user (user B). The sender (user A) sends a qubit to an receiver (user B) and therefore, user B measures the Bell state between the two qubits and decodes the two-bit message sent by user A.

A block of data in quantum blockchain is called a GHZ (Greenberger–Horne–Zeilinger) state. A GHZ is a collection of entanglements between all the qubits in the block. The block is shared to all nodes on the network to verify the block's validity by a verifier node. The verifier node is chosen randomly from the network by using a quantum random number generator. The block's validity is verified by implementing the protocol in the quantum network. The protocol implemented in the network verifies whether the block contains Genuine Multipartite Entanglement (GME). GME is a type of entanglement that can exist if all qubits in the GHZ state were involved that were formed during the creation of the state. The verifier generates a set of random angles and sends them to the network to entangle with one single GHZ state. The block of data that is entangled will be the new GHZ state [18]. The entire history of the blockchain is now encoded into this new GHZ state. Now, the information can be extracted as the entanglements for the encoded data that can have access to the entire blockchain. The older qubits no longer exist and therefore the history of entanglement cannot be changed and if any changes are initiated the entanglement gets separated and the entire chain falls apart.

5.4.1.2   *Quantum Gates and Quantum Computation*

The language of quantum computation describes the changes in a quantum state. As discussed in Section 5.2.2.2, under quantum blockchain, a quantum computer is constructed with a quantum circuit consisting of wires and primary gates to control quantum information. The quantum gates and their models are discussed in the following.

In classical computers, the information is carried out in a single-bit logic gate. It defines the truth table as 0 to 1 and 1 to 0, where the states 0 and 1 are exchanged mutually. A quantum circuit (quantum array or quantum network) replaces the primary gates, *viz.*, AND, OR, and NOT by primary quantum gates. The gates used for carrying the one qubit information are the phase flip gate Z and bit flip gate X and the Hadamard gate H. The two-qubit gate is named controlled-NOT (CNOT). The gate with a three-qubit is called Toffoli gate (CCNOT controlled-controlled not), which negates the third bit if the first two bits are 1. These CCNOT circuit gates can be simulated for any classical computation by using auxiliary wires and giving values according to the classical Boolean circuit.

The qubits record many states of information but the properties of quantum measurement restrict to yield of a single bit of information for the extraction from the state change that occurred.

To deal with quantum computations, there are three classes of algorithms, namely, classical algorithms, quantum search algorithms, and quantum simulation. Different models are required for computation and these models require different resources too. To understand a problem concerning the model and the requirements asymptotic notation is developed. The asymptotic notation summarizes the behavior of a function in a problem. Suppose we are interested in the count of the gates necessary for adding two n-bit numbers, exact counts of the number of gates will not be clear. A specific algorithm requires $24n + 2[logn] + 16$ gates to execute this task. The essential behavior of the algorithm scales for the number of operations performed on a function.

5.4.2   The Architectural Patterns

These patterns focus on building computational components for building quantum blockchain applications and securing mechanisms for the transactions in the quantum blockchain.

5.4.2.1   *Layered Approach*

The architectural patterns are built on primitive computational elements that offer partial insights to develop a solution for domain-specific problems. In architectural patterns, the concept of layering is discussed. A composite system is partitioned into layers, the highest layer offer services to the lowest layer. However, the level of abstraction is offered by the layers, and although the higher layers are unaware of the implementation process of its lower layers.

In quantum blockchain, services are offered in the vertical organization [6]. Figure 5.3 presents the quantum blockchain communications. The physical layer is responsible for channel configuration. The link layer is used for sharing the entangled state of qubits. The network layer provides a connection among quantum devices. The qubit transmission is done in the transport layer and the interaction is handled by the application layer [7, 11, 12].

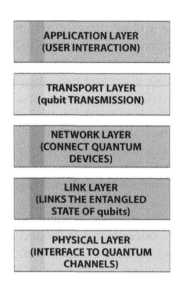

Figure 5.3 Quantum blockchain layers.

5.4.2.1.1   Physical Layer

The physical layer interacts with quantum network devices via the quantum channels. It forwards qubits among network devices. The physical layer interfaces with the quantum channels to transmit to quantum memory and use the quantum channel for communication. A quantum network device stores qubits for transmission. It also uses an optical setup for communication. The physical layer encapsulates the implementation process required for quantum communication. The quantum network converters use various technologies and transmission strategies [6] to flatten the communication.

5.4.2.1.2   Link Layer

This layer performs the process of generating the state of networks. The network state can be static or dynamic; the static state uses the GHZ state for connection whereas the dynamic state uses the quantum linking protocol [16].

5.4.2.1.3   Network Layer

The interconnected network enables various network state requests across quantum networks. This process is enabled and manipulated by the network layer. The quantum routers are used in this layer. They are linked with static states. The network layer [10] enables network state requests across the networks; therefore, routing between different quantum networks can be achieved. To enable an entangled state, a quantum routing protocol is required among the quantum networks of the network state. The network layer interacts with quantum datagrams across network boundaries. Since the routing protocol creates an entangled state among the network devices, it is required to transform the entangled state into a suitable state to connect with the requesting network device.

5.4.2.1.4 Transport Layer

The qubit transmission occurs in the transport layer [10]. This layer performs host-to-host quantum communications. It uses connection and connectionless protocols for the communication between quantum devices, and it also includes error correction for re-transmission of information.

5.4.2.1.5 Application Layer

This layer consists of quantum network applications and their protocols. The application layer is responsible for the exchange of messages between hosts in the network and the messages are divided into qubits and sent to lower layers. In the quantum network, the global state of the quantum blockchain can be random inputs that are unknown to hosts. The application layer of the receiving host will extract the information accordingly [10].

5.4.2.2 Securing Mechanisms for Quantum Blockchain

The securing mechanism includes encryption and decryption, certificates and digital signatures, and quantum-resistant cryptographic algorithms.

5.4.2.2.1 Encryption and Decryption

To initiate a secure communication channel between two individuals a two-step process has to be implemented in the communication path. The two-step processes are encryption and decryption. The implementations of the two-step process between the two individuals are provided with a secure shared key called the key exchange. This key exchange is used for both encrypting and decrypting. This way of message encryption-decryption is termed symmetric encryption. The communication starts between any two individuals by obtaining the shared key. The Transport Layer Security (TLS) Handshake Protocol protects/secures the communication path between individuals. In TLS Handshake, the two individuals share message sequences among one other, and the communication the individuals know through their shared secret key. This key is used to exchange data securely in an asymmetric encryption protocol. The key exchange protocols that contain algebraic issues are intractable. The uncertain problem that exists in key exchange protocol is termed: *discrete-log issue on elliptic curves.* For example, a problem with m bits is computed with an exponential time of m or $2^{m/2}$. During implementation, if the key size is 256, the execution time to break the key exchange protocol varies in time with $2^{256/2} = 2^{128}$; therefore, the execution time is similar to the time required to assault 128 bits. The common encryption method is used by NIST when the blockchain computations are implemented, and the vulnerability is reduced; however, an asymmetric cryptographic algorithm enables a secured communication. To secure communication post-quantum cryptography algorithms are acting as a replacement. Post-quantum cryptography is discussed in Section 5.4.2.2.3.

5.4.2.2.2   Verification of Identity and Key

The verification of identity is done through certificate and digital signature. Integrity is verified by digital signatures to ensure the identity of the individuals involved in communication. In a digital signature system, two entities are involved; the signer and the signature verifier. The signature verifier has the public key correcting to the secret signing key of the signer. The digital signature system verifies message-signature pair is valid and authorizes the message that the signer is valid for the message. The applications of digital signatures where the identity is required are the internet, payment systems, and software authenticity. The identity over the internet is done through the certificate authority (CA). This issues an identity certificate by using a secret key to an individual or an organization to prove and verify the identity. A certificate is a statement that encapsulates an identity to a cryptographic key. In payment systems, the payer holds a secret signing key, the key is used while making payment. The provision is made for the payee to verify the signature and can be viewed by anyone. In software authenticity, the secret signature key is used for software updates. The signature verification is carried out before installing the software; this ensures the software is authentic. In all three applications, an intruder can masquerade as any entity, forge signatures, and spend other people's funds and create malware in software. The most widely used signature algorithms are RSA (Rivest, Shamir, and Adelman) and ECDSA (Elliptic Curve Digital Signature Algorithm). The parameters used in signature algorithms can be broken with the running time 2^{128}. Quantum algorithms used by quantum computers forges both RSA and ECDSA signatures. The impact of a quantum computer in using blockchain will allow forging certificates and digital signatures due to the power of quantum algorithms. There is a requirement for cryptographically agile and novel hashing algorithms to be resistant toward forging by quantum computing systems.

5.4.2.2.3   Quantum-Resistant Cryptographic Algorithms

The cryptographic research community introduces standard replacement algorithms (post-quantum algorithms) [3] toward the encrypted internet traffic which would be vulnerable to the quantum computer. These standard replacement algorithms are executed on readily available classical processors. The replacement algorithms are evaluated by NIST. The core objective of NIST is to design and operate a cryptographic system with the existing communications protocols. This protects the network against the usage of quantum and quantum computers.

The practical deployment challenges to put quantum-resistant cryptographic algorithms in place are:

a) To know the properties of failure cryptographic infrastructure. This is analyzed when quantum algorithms are implemented in quantum computers.
b) More time consumption is involved to design, built, and deploy the new quantum-resistant infrastructure.
c) It is difficult to identify the proper application with the minimized interval in performing operations.

Apart from practical deployment challenges, considering hardware functionality and software components is also essential in addition to hardware functionality, software components are essential to support quantum computing. The need for tools required to perform quantum computer algorithms for programmers, and the design of system software to evaluate these algorithms and sequence them into quantum hardware, supplementary support like simulation tool, debugging tool for the implementation of these algorithms on specific quantum hardware, optimization tools for implementing the algorithms efficiently and verification tools for correctness toward software and hardware. The universal simulators help programmers to create quantum operations to trail the path to reaching a quantum state. To estimate the performance and qubit resources for different algorithms optimization tools like resource estimators are used. This helps a compiler to know the requirement qubit operations required for the hardware.

5.5   Fundamental Integrants

The fundamental integrants contain the essential concepts of understanding and reasoning of relevant assumptions on the quantum blockchain model. The generalization is concerned about the possible and impossible assumptions. The generalization utilizes general-purpose algorithms [13] like searching, sorting that guarantee logical analysis and mathematical proof.

5.5.1   Interaction of Quantum Systems

The interaction model includes communication delay and accuracy in processing. The communication delay should be minimum and the accuracy is independent of quantum blockchain processes is not be limited by delay. Due to superposition, it is difficult to maintain the same state across quantum systems. The challenges considered during the interaction of quantum systems are as follows:

- **Accounting measurement problem**
  The qubit's state flattens the qubit's position and its entanglement. The qubit processing cannot be evaluated until a proper computation is achieved. The determination of the result can be achieved by a protocol that handles the qubit. However, similar methods used by classical computing for error detection and correction cannot be implemented. The quantum error can be validated based on the topological changes.

- **Fidelity in a quantum state**
  Fidelity entangles the quality of a quantum state. Its value ranges between 0 and 1. It measures the closeness of a quantum state created and expresses the probability of entanglement. Fidelity quantifies how a state can be affected by noise from various sources. Quantum applications require a higher application-specific fidelity.

5.5.2   Failure of Quantum Systems

In a quantum blockchain, the process and communication channel deviate from desirable behaviors. The failure of quantum blockchain provides a better understanding of failures due to incorrect functioning of process and network transmission error in the communication channel. The failure can be categorized as omission, arbitrary, and timing. The omission failure occurs when the communication path fails to perform its operations. The arbitrary failure describes any type of error that occurs during a process or incorrect delivery of information. The timing failure results in deviation of time for process execution and takes longer communication time to deliver information. During the design of the Quantum blockchain, the failure issues must are considered.

5.5.3   Security of Quantum Systems

In a quantum blockchain, each pair of nodes is connected by a classical channel and a quantum channel, these pairs of nodes can establish a sequence of secret keys by using secure communication mechanisms which implement the cryptographic protocol for message authentication. For the security of quantum blockchain, a GHZ state with entanglement in time may provide better security and quantum benefit.

5.5.4   Challenges and Opportunities

The quantum computing ecosystem provides challenges and opportunities to quantum blockchain for various reasons:

a) The mapping of quantum blockchain algorithms down to quantum computing hardware systems is crucial for its design and use. A compiler system is developed with the simulations tools and resource estimators. These are significant measures for optimization and designing algorithms. This challenge can bring improvement in the performance of quantum blockchain computation.

b) Quantum computing toolchain resource optimization during quantum blockchain computation should save several qubits and the execution time required to run the algorithm. This allows implementing an algorithm in a smaller quantum computing system in a reduction in execution time.

c) Digital noisy intermediate-scale quantum (NISQ) systems are under the process of development with some source constraints. Therefore, the use of NISQ machines requires communication flow to be tracked for the implementation of algorithms and to simplify the system design.

d) Simulation, debugging, and validation are still challenging and give opportunities to drive research in hardware and algorithm development toward the development of quantum blockchain computation in quantum computing.

5.6   Conclusion

Quantum blockchain has enabled features of safety and efficiency to guarantee communication between quantum devices. This plays a significant role in enabling us to understand and reason about quantum blockchain relating to the framework. This chapter considers the underlying hardware, examination of the computational elements, architectural patterns, and fundamental integrants that emphasize quantum computing.

This chapter has presented a framework design that considers the quantum hardware, computational elements that are fitting in architectural patterns to enable communication with classical computing. The architectural pattern is complimented with fundamental integrants that include interaction, failure, and security models.

References

1. Rajan, D. and Visser, M., Quantum Blockchain using entanglement in time. *Quantum Rep.*, *1*, 1, 3–11, 2019.
2. Nielsen, M.A. and Chuang, I., *Quantum computation and quantum information*, pp. 558–559, Cambridge University Press, New York, 2002.
3. Azzaoui, A.E. and Park, J.H., Post-Quantum Blockchain for a Scalable Smart City. *J. Internet Technol.*, *21*, 4, 1171–1178, 2020.
4. Lapointe, C. and Fishbane, L., The blockchain ethical design framework. *Innov.: TechnoL., Gov., Globalization*, *12*, 3–4, 50–71, 2019.
5. https://www.mitre.org/sites/default/files/publications/17-4039-blockchain-and-quantum-computing.pdf
6. Dai, W., Quantum-computing with AI & blockchain: modeling, fault tolerance and capacity scheduling. *Math. Comput. Model. Dyn. Syst.*, *25*, 6, 523–559, 2019.
7. Jones, N.C., Van Meter, R., Fowler, A.G., McMahon, P.L., Kim, J., Ladd, T.D., Yamamoto, Y., Layered architecture for quantum computing. *Phys. Rev. X, 2*, 3, 031007, 2012.

8. https://www.gsma.com/identity/wp-content/uploads/2018/09/Distributed-Ledger-Technology-Blockchains-and-Identity-20180907ii.pdf
9. Raychev, N., Quantum Blockchain. *Quantum Rev. Lett.*, *1(2*, 2 (2020, 10–37686, 2020.
10. Kozlowski, W., Dahlberg, A., Wehner, S., Designing a quantum network protocol. *Proceedings of the 16th International Conference on emerging Networking EXperiments and Technologies*, pp. 1–16, 2020, November.
11. Pirker, A. and Dür, W., A quantum network stack and protocols for reliable entanglement-based networks. *New J. Phys.*, *21*, 3, 033003, 2019.
12. Dasari, V.R., Sadlier, R.J., Prout, R., Williams, B.P., Humble, T.S., Programmable multi-node quantum network design and simulation, in: *Quantum Information and Computation IX)*. *Int. Society Opt. Photonics*, vol. 9873, p. 98730B, 2016, May.
13. Manzalini, A., Quantum communications in future networks and services. *Quantum Rep.*, *2*, 1, 221–232, 2020.
14. Biamonte, J., Faccin, M., De Domenico, M., Complex networks from classical to quantum. *Commun. Phys.*, *2*, 1, 1–10, 2019.
15. Krishnamoorthi, S., Jayapaul, P., Dhanaraj, R.K. *et al.*, Design of pseudo-random number generator from turbulence padded chaotic map. *Nonlinear Dyn.*, 104, 2, 1627–1643, 2021.
16. Dahlberg, A., Skrzypczyk, M., Coopmans, T., Wubben, L., Rozpędek, F., Pompili, M., Wehner, S., *A link layer protocol for quantum networks*. *Proceedings of the ACM Special Interest Group on Data Communication*, pp. 159–173, 2019.
17. http://guestpostingworld.com/internet-marketing/quantum-blockchain-an-idea-of-ideal-blockchain-development/
18. Edwards, M., Mashatan, A., Ghose, S., A review of quantum and hybrid quantum/classical blockchain protocols. *Quantum Inf. Process.*, *19*, 1–22, 2020.
19. Li, C., Xu, Y., Tang, J., Liu, W., Quantum Blockchain: A Decentralized, Encrypted and Distributed Database Based on Quantum Mechanics. *J. Quantum Comput.*, *1*, 2, 49, 2019.

6

Challenges and Research Perspective of Post–Quantum Blockchain

Venu K.* and Krishnakumar B.

Kongu Engineering College, Department of CSE, Erode, India

Abstract

Cryptography is a fine technology for communicating in a secure way by sending encrypted information to receiver, which will be understood after decrypted. Symmetric key cryptography, hash function, and public key cryptography are general cryptographic techniques available for encrypting and decrypting information. Modern cryptography indulges confidentiality, integrity, non–repudiation, and authentication. As cryptography plays a great roll in secure communication, by same way, this technology can be introduced to transfer the digital currency with at most security, and this is termed as cryptocurrency (or crypto). Bitcoin is also a technique of cryptocurrency, which was designed using the name Satoshi Nakamoto.

Bitcoin technology is an open–source and public key cryptography, which is owned or controlled by nobody but everyone has right on it. Bitcoin is nothing but a digital currency, which is created, circulated, traded, and warehoused with the use of decentralized computers or nodes. Blockchain is a database that records all the transaction of bitcoins like a ledger system.

Blockchain stores the transaction information in the form of blocks with specific capacity and newly filled blocks are chained with the previous blocks in chronological order. Data on the blockchain are immutably stored in distributed network of multiple computers or nodes across the world. Because of this immutability, it is challenging to do any change in the block data. To achieve immutability and timestamping, digital signature and hash function in cryptographic schemes are indulged in blockchain. The problematic part in both hash functions and public key cryptosystems is that their security is easily broken by the evolution of

---

Corresponding author: venu.kalaimagal@gmail.com

Rajesh Kumar Dhanaraj, Vani Rajasekar, SK Hafizul Islam, Balamurugan Balusamy and Ching-Hsien Hsu (eds.) Quantum Blockchain: An Emerging Cryptographic Paradigm, (127–172)

quantum computers. To resist attacks of quantum computing, a special technique is introduced named post–quantum blockchain.

Alhough there are lot of results and researches with post–quantum, this chapter mainly focus on post–quantum blockchain. It is an emerging technique in present days, and hence, lot of researches are focused here. Post–quantum bitcoin is a trial division of Bitcoin's key blockchain, which uses a post–quantum digital signature outline. Another platform of blockchain that is termed as Abilian prevents quantum attack with lattice centered post–quantum cryptographic blockchain. Similarly, another blockchain platform Corda functions using SPHINCS, a specific algorithm of post–quantum blockchain. Thus, this chapter discusses the post–quantum blockchain and gives a wide idea and many useful strategies on security of post–quantum blockchain for future investigators and designers.

Keywords: Bitcoin, blockchain, post-quantum blockchain, quantum computing, cryptography

6.1　Introduction

6.1.1　Cryptocurrency

Nowadays, human life moves around internet in all aspect. Likewise our currencies also moved into digital world. Cryptocurrency is nothing but virtual currency or digital currency, which is securely encrypted by cryptographic algorithms. Using blockchain technology, many cryptocurrencies are in the network of decentralization. An important factor of cryptocurrency is that they are not created and issued by bank or third party authority. Accessing cryptocurrency or using it cannot be control by government or any other central authorities.

6.1.2　Blockchain

Internet development process happened as multiple stages. At these levels, main breakthroughs are the design of the WAN in 1960s, expansion of an E–mailing system in 1970s, next stage that is Ethernet far lengthways in that decade, the initiation of WWW in 1990s, and finally search engines and browsers. Followed by all the above milestones, computer internet has changed abruptly. Really, today, the internet becomes the backbone for our human life.

By this way, blockchain development also divided into multiple stages. This technology grows with the internet as an important development. Even though lot of experts well defined the blockchain, still some more researches are yet to be proceeded. Blockchain can be understood in some different stages.

6.1.2.1   Bitcoin and Cryptocurrencies

Concepts of blockchain are rounding in computer societies; it was the pen name for the development of Bitcoin. Bitcoin is also a technique of crypto-currency, which was designed using the name Satoshi Nakamoto. Bitcoin is P2P e–payment system or decentralized digital currency, where curren-cies can be transferred among the people without the knowledge of bank or government (third party).

Bitcoin is nothing but a digital currency, which is created, circulated, traded, and warehoused with the use of decentralized computers or nodes. Blockchain is a database that records all the transaction of bitcoins like a ledger system. By this way, blockchain technology is initiated by means of the Bitcoin network.

In the most basic stage of bitcoin, Satoshi designed the blockchain as pub-lic ledger for bitcoin transactions; it was of 1–MB block size. Blocks are linked with undisputable chain of specific capacity, and the newly filled blocks are chained with the previous blocks in chronological order. Information stored on the blockchain is immutably stored in distributed network of multiple computers or nodes across the world. To be sure, Bitcoin's blockchain resi-dues are mostly unaffected from these initial efforts.

6.1.2.2   Insolent Bonds

As time goes on, researchers found that blockchain can do something beyond the transaction ledger. Originators of ethereum initially had the awareness that their belongings and the trust contracts could also have some benefit from blockchain technology. By this way, ethereum intro-duces a next stage for blockchain technology.

The key invention for blockchain is done by ethereum's initiation of insolent agreements. Classically, those agreements in business world are maintained by some entities of third party inputs. By this blockchain tech-nology, some events in agreement like passing the agreement messages, making changes as needed, all these are self–managed by themselves.

At this level, the process of coupling unemployed potential of insolent bonds with the blockchain technology. Therefore, this introduces the con-sequent stages for the development of blockchain technology.

6.1.2.3   Imminent Stage

Even though blockchain grows to this level, it faces a main difficulty in scaling. Bitcoin also faces troubles in time while processing transactions, and it becomes blockage for bitcoins at certain time. To overcome this issue, some other cryptocurrencies tried to update their blockchain, which leads to fluctuating marks of achievement. Future researches will be more in blockchain technology to take forward it to next level by overcoming the scalability problem.

Outside this, many new results and applications about blockchain are being implemented and revealed at all the time period. It is hard to say where the innovations will let the cryptocurrency as the whole. Followers of blockchain technology are really very fascinated from their view. Still, the human life is with the radical technology which grows continually.

6.1.3   Physiology of Blockchain

Blockchain network contains many blocks of data, which are sequentially arranged as blocks of transitions. A timestamp, hash value of present block, and hash value of earlier block are available with every block. Blockchain blocks are linked with each other by using the hash values. Blocks are arranged in a chronological order that every block B is arranged after its previous block B–1. When a block is considered to be a legal, then it is hard to modify those confirmed blocks. Figure 6.1 shows the physiology of blockchain's blocks order.

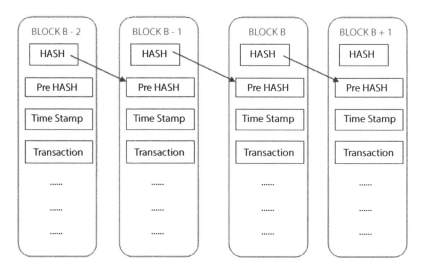

Figure 6.1 Physiology of blockchain.

6.1.4   Blockchain Network

For data consistency, blockchain stores its data blocks into a network consisting of different nodes. Following are the set of processes that each node manipulates the data:

> **Process 1:** New information about transaction is put on air in the network of nodes.
> **Process 2:** Every block nodes collects new information about transaction and saves into its blocks.
> **Process 3:** Proof–of–work algorithm is associated with each block.
> **Process 4:** Every time when a block cracks proof–of–work riddle, that message is passed to each nodes of block every time.
> **Process 5:** When a block gets a broadcast message, it accepts only when the information is new and valid.
> **Process 6:** Acceptance of the transaction by the nodes are expressed as generating a new block in the blockchain using hash value of newly received block as pre–hash value.

6.1.5   Blockchain Securities

Blockchain provides securities that are persistent by digital signature's hash function and public key cryptography as a type of asymmetric cryptosystem.

6.1.5.1   *Public Key Cryptography an Asymmetric Cryptosystem*

Actually blockchain secures transactions among parties with usage of public key asymmetric cryptosystem over done with signatures. In the process of digital signature, the user protects with private key when the publically shared public key is used to authenticate that the digital signature is proved. Hence, when the algorithm for digital signature is authenticated, it can be assured that the person who owns private key only can create such digital signatures.

Asymmetric cryptosystems is important for self–styled cash holders (wallet) that are holder for private keys. Likewise every users in blockchain network has a cash holder (wallet) linked with both keys (private and public) that are used for secure transactions on digital signature. Blockchain rely on bitcoin which has a transaction that halts by sending receiver's public key details that is authenticated with sender's private key. For sending bitcoins, owner should establish their private key, which is the ownership to be transferred. When a receiver receives any bitcoins, it will be authenticated by digital signatures with sender's public key.

6.1.5.2   Digital Signature's Hashing Algorithm

Simple hash functions such as Scrypt or SHA256 are basically availed for blockchains because of its easy check, on the other hand, which are very hard to falsify. This provides the creation for signatures that are used for authenticating users of blockchain by their own or any currency transfers in the presence of any others. Whenever some group of transaction happens at equal instant of time, that blocks of the blockchains are linked using the hash functions in the order that is shown as in Figure 6.1. Hash functions are also used for user address generation and also for filtering public key address information size in blockchains.

6.1.6   Bitcoin Blockchain

As a new researcher, one can easily get into the knowledge of bitcoins without any technical information. At once if anyone installed the bitcoin for the first time on their mobile phone or computer, then it will create their address of first bitcoin. After that using this account they can create any number of bitcoins whenever they need. For each transaction of bitcoins, sender needs the account address to send the bitcoins.

6.1.7   Quantum Cryptography

An excessive extent of digital mark is on the terminology of quantum computers, because such threatens it to the presently following asymmetric cryptographic algorithms. Asymmetric cryptography is a cryptography technique following two key (private and public) pairs which calculate relation among them. Private keys are of secret keys and public keys can be available with anyone publically. By these keys, every user can have a digital signature security with their private keys that will be digitally matched and verified by the key holders (public key). In financial industries, the legitimacy and reliability of transactions are done by these asymmetric cryptographic techniques. One–way function is a scientific principle which gives security for asymmetric cryptographic systems. By using private keys, public keys can be easily derived, but vice versa is not possible which acts as the main principle for these systems. In all classical algorithms, private

Table 6.1 Popular cryptosystems and main blockchains affected by quantum computers.

Algorithm	Blockchains/DLTs affected	Function	Security level		Key size	Hash/signature size
			Pre-quantum	Estimated post-quantum		
SHA–256	Bitcoin, Ethereum, Dash, Litecoin, Zcash, Monero, Ripple, NXT, Byteball	Hash Function	256 bits	128 bits (Grover)	–	256 bits
Ethash (Keccak–256, Keccak–512)	Ethereum		256/512 bits	128/256 bits (Grover)		256/512 bits
Scrypt	Litecoin, NXT		256 bits	128 bits (Grover)		256 bits
RIPEMD 160	Bitcoin, Ethereum, Litecoin, Monero, Ripple, Bytecoin		160 bits	80 bits (Grover)		160 bits
Keccak–256	Monero, Bytecoin		256 bits	128 bits (Grover)		256 bits
Keccak–384	IOTA		384 bits	192 bits (Grover)		384 bits

(Continued)

Table 6.1 Popular cryptosystems and main blockchains affected by quantum computers. (*Continued*)

Algorithm	Blockchains/DLTs affected	Function	Security level		Key size	Hash/ signature size
			Pre– quantum	Estimated post– quantum		
ECDSA	Bitcoin, Ethereum, Dash, Litecoin, Zcash, Ripple, Byteball	Signature	128 bits	Broken (Shor)	256 bits	520 bits
RSA–1024	–	Signature, Encryption	80 bits	Broken (Shor)	1024 bits	1024 bits
RSA–2048	–		112 bits	Broken (Shor)	2048 bits	2048 bits
RSA–3072	–		128 bits	Broken (Shor)	3072 bits	3072 bits
DSA–3072	–	Signature	128 bits	Broken (Shor)	3073 bits	–
SHA–3256	–	Hash Function	256 bits	128 bits (Grover)	–	256 bits
AES–128	–	Symmetric Encryption	128 bits	64 bits (Grover)	128 bits	–
AES–256	–		256 bits	128 bits (Grover)	256 bits	

keys are not able be derive with public keys, which needs non–polynomial time to achieve such a calculation, and therefore, it is not achieved in real world.

Although, in 1994, a researcher Peter Shor found amazing quantum algorithms, which can break those securities of most asymmetric cryptographic algorithms. By this research, anyone can derive the private key from its respective public key using suitably large quantum computers and this results in breaking any kind of digital signatures. Movement of bitcoins among account addresses is referred as transaction which is like transaction of money in bank accounts. While sending the bitcoin, the sender should approve their transfer by giving the digital signature which evidences that they own the account address where the assets are deposited. In this process, if anyone has a quantum computer with the public key, then one can falsify this digital signature and thus possibly send any person's bitcoins.

Cryptographic algorithms can be affected by the quantum computers. Many encryption and decryption algorithms are nullified by the quantum attacks. Table 6.1 compares the basic blockchains and most popular cryptosystems that are attacked by the quantum computers and also shows the key and signature size.

6.1.8   Quantum Blockchain

Blockchain stores the transaction information in the form of blocks with specific capacity, and newly filled blocks are chained with the previous blocks in chronological order. Data on the blockchain are immutably stored in distributed network of multiple computers or nodes across the world. Because of this immutability, it is challenging to do any change in the block data. To achieve immutability and timestamping alone, digital signature, and hash function in cryptographic schemes are indulged in blockchain. The RSA (Rivest–Shamir–Adleman), the large integer factorization problem, or elliptic curve cryptography (ECC) techniques are used for reliable communication, legitimacy, and verification of data in blockchain.

Even though these algorithms are used for security purpose, the calculation of hash function and guess a nonce (value) is done by proof–of–work algorithm, which is frequently used for adding new data to the blockchain. The problematic part in both hash functions and public key cryptosystems is their security is easily broken by the evolution of quantum computers. While protecting blockchain's reliability, Grover's algorithm affects blockchain's security by generating its own hashes and thus recreating the entire blockchain. Shor's algorithm makes digital signature unsafe by breaking it within the polynomial time.

Few quantum computations give some threats to traditional blockchain technology, and some other quantum algorithms effectually give solution to the problems as equivalent to the encryption algorithm. Some NP–complete problems are solved faster by quantum computers; consequently, lot of researches are going on in quantum blockchain. Recipe of quantum skills and blockchain is termed to be quantum blockchain resist such attacks of quantum computing like Shor and Grover, and a special technique is introduced named post–quantum cryptographic blockchain.

6.1.9 Post–Quantum Cryptography

Post–quantum cryptography is an encrypting algorithm which secures against the outbreak of the quantum computers. Likewise, for the resistance of such attacks of quantum computing like Shor and Grover, a special technique is introduced named post–quantum blockchain. Post–quantum blockchain is presently an emerging topic, which has been spoken by lot of researchers.

Post–quantum blockchain secures the blockchain from the attacks of quantum computers. Anti–quantum digital signature proposal is very helpful for improving transaction security in blockchain setup. Some recent researchers have proposed lattice cryptography for resisting the quantum digital signature method for authenticated transactions in blockchain networking system. Likewise, lot of methods have been proposed for quantum attacks, which are secured by potential solutions according to their vulnerabilities.

6.2 Post–Quantum Blockchain Cryptosystems

Post–quantum cryptosystems are of four common types and another type fifth one combines post–quantum cryptosystem with the pre–quantum cryptosystems. This section investigates deeply about effective applications of some cryptosystems for blockchain transaction signature and encrypting cryptographic mechanisms. For detailed summary about these cryptosystems person who reads can refer text books like post–quantum cryptography [10]. As a synopsis, Figure 6.2 shows implementation of different post–quantum cryptosystems with encryption examples, and Figure 6.3 shows the same with digital signatures. For both types, code, lattice–, multivariant–, and isogeny–, and elliptic curve–based is well differentiated and

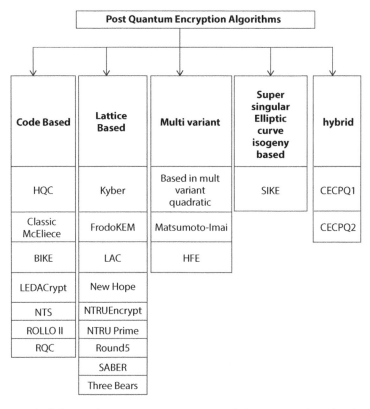

Figure 6.2 Blockchains of post–quantum cryptosystem's (encryption algorithms) catalog for realistic implementations.

hybrid–based is only available with encryption algorithm and hash–based is available only with digital signature. These are discussed as follows.

6.2.1   Post–Quantum Blockchain Cryptosystems Based on Public Keys

6.2.1.1   Code–Based Cryptosystem

This cryptosystem is fundamentally relying on the concepts of ECC in cryptography. Earlier 1970s, code–based cryptosystem is providing the security provided for syndrome decoding problem using the McEliece's cryptosystem (MEC) [14], which provides advantages for performing fast transactions on blockchain by providing pretty fast encryption and decryption. However, private and public keys need to be stored and to maintain many operations with huge matrices in MEC. Keys in matrices space need

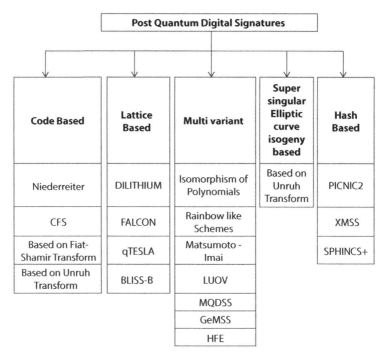

Code Based	Lattice Based	Multi variant	Super singular Elliptic curve isogeny based	Hash Based
Niederreiter	DILITHIUM	Isomorphism of Polynomials	Based on Unruh Transform	PICNIC2
CFS	FALCON	Rainbow like Schemes		XMSS
Based on Fiat-Shamir Transform	qTESLA	Matsumoto - Imai		SPHINCS+
Based on Unruh Transform	BLISS-B	LUOV		
		MQDSS		
		GeMSS		
		HFE		

Figure 6.3 Blockchains of post–quantum cryptosystem's (digital signatures) catalog for realistic implementations.

memory size from 100 KB to several MBs, and it will be a very problematic in the resource controlled systems. To overcome these problems, further proposals are need to be focused in this perspective and the research focus should be on matrix compression technology and some specific coding schemes like QC–LRPC codes, LDPC (Low Density Parity Checker) [15]. Table 6.2 shows classical security in code–based cryptography that provides security stuck between 128 and 256 bits, but, in part of quantum computing, such security levels are reduced drastically. As regards, while comparing the private/public key size has ranges from small size as 320 bits (RQC and ROLLO–II private keys) until 15.5 KB (HQC's public key with highest security). In all time, code–based cryptosystem's private/public keys compared with all other techniques give larger size bits than RSA–based cryptosystem and ECDSA [1]. Overall, while comparing these cryptosystems, it shows that RQC–II gives best substitution between key size and the security, even though it is not under the fastest post–quantum cryptosystems techniques [1, 2].

Table 6.2 Code–based cryptosystem that approved to second round of NIST call.

Cryptosystem	Subtype	Claimed quantum security (Bits)	Claimed classical security (Bits)	Private key size (Bits)	Public key size (Bits)
BIKE–1 Level 1	QC–MDPC McEliece	–	128	2,130	20,326
BIKE–1 Level 3		–	192	3,090	39,706
BIKE–1 Level 5		–	256	4,384	65,498
BIKE–2 Level 1	QC–MDPC Niederreiter	–	128	2,130	10,163
BIKE–2 Level 3		–	192	3,090	19,853
BIKE–2 Level 5		–	256	4,384	32,749
BIKE –3 Level 1	QC–MDPC Ouroboros	–	128	2,010	22,054
BIKE–3 Level 3	QC–MDPC Niederreiter	–	192	2,970	43,366
BIKE–3 Level 5		–	256	4,256	72,262

(Continued)

Table 6.2 Code–based cryptosystem that approved to second round of NIST call. (*Continued*)

Cryptosystem	Subtype	Claimed quantum security (Bits)	Claimed classical security (Bits)	Private key size (Bits)	Public key size (Bits)
Classic McEliece (mceliece8192128)	Niederreiter's dual version using binary Goppa codes	–	256	112,640	10,862,592
HQC Level 1 (hqc–128–1)	Quasi–cyclic and BCH codes	64	128	2,016 (320)	49,360 (25,000)
HQC Level 3 (hqc–192–1)		96	192	3,232 (320)	87,344 (43,992)
HQC Level 5 (hqc–256–1)		128	256	4,256 (320)	127,184 (63,912)
LEDACrypt KEM Level 1 (for 2 circulant blocks)	QC–LDBC Niederreiter	–	128	3,616 (192)	14,976
LEDACrypt KEM Level 3 (for 2 circulant blocks)		–	192	5,152 (256)	25,728

(*Continued*)

Table 6.2 Code–based cryptosystem that approved to second round of NIST call. (*Continued*)

Cryptosystem	Subtype	Claimed quantum security (Bits)	Claimed classical security (Bits)	Private key size (Bits)	Public key size (Bits)
LEDACrypt KEM Level 5 (for 2 circulant blocks)		–	256	6,112 (320)	36928
NTS–KEM Level 1	Based on McEliece and Niederreiter	64	128	73,984	2,555,904
NTS–KEM Level 3		96	192	140,448	7,438,080
NTS–KEM Level 5		128	256	159,376	11,357,632
ROLLO II–128	Based on rank metric codes with LRPC codes	–	128	320	12,368
ROLLO II–192		–	192		16,160
ROLLO II–256		–	256		19,944
RQC I	Based on rank quasi–cyclic codes	–	128		6,824
RQC II		–	192		11,128
RQC III		–	256		18,272

6.2.1.2   Multivariant–Based Cryptosystem

Complexity of solving multivariant equation relies on multivariant–based cryptosystems, which is well explained as an NP–complete or NP–hard problem [10]. Lot of researches need to improve the security level and ciphertext overheads and reduce large key size for providing an efficient security to the quantum attacks [11]. Presently, the research perspective of multivariant–based cryptosystems is based on the usage of random quadratic polynomials in the square matrices vector space; such cryptosystems rely on the Hidden Field Equations (HFE) [12, 13]. Matsumoto–Imai's algorithm is applied for the multivariant–based cryptosystem in random quadratic polynomials.

6.2.1.3   Lattice-Based Cryptosystem

Collection of points in a space of n–dimensional vector is named as lattice. Based on the lattice, this cryptosystem provides its security in an episodic arrangement. This lattice–based cryptosystem supposed to be relying on rigidity of lattice problems similar to an NP–hard problem, which is Shortest Vector Problem whose objective is discovering shortest vector point (only values > 0) within the n–dimensional lattice space. Some other lattice troubles like Shortest Independent Vector or nearby Vector Problem cannot be solved by quantum computing technique these days [3]. For fast black chain transactions, this lattice–based cryptosystem are used, because they are used frequently since they are easy for computation, fast and work in efficient way.

Although it is implemented in other post–quantum cryptosystems, it engages with huge ciphertext overheads because lattice–based cryptosystem needs to save and make utilize of large key sets. Some lattice–based cryptosystems like NewHope [5] and NTRU [4] systems frequently need to maintain and manage the key sets in the classification of some thousand like bits. As of now, all discussed lattice–based cryptosystems have base of Learning With Errors (LWE), polynomial algebra [4, 6, 7] problem with its alternative Lindner Perikert LWE (LP–LWE) or Ring LWE (RLWE) [8, 9].

A lattice–based cryptosystem [1] provides 128 bits to 368 bits of traditional securities and 84 bits to 300 bits of quantum scheme securities, so depending on algorithm the security level differs. While comparing all the cryptosystems, Table 6.3 shows rough calculation of security level is 100 bits, and it shows that Round5 KEM IoT [1] has the very less security key and fast execution by way of comparing to all the cryptosystems.

Table 6.3 Lattice–based post–quantum cryptosystem that approved to second round of NIST call.

Cryptosystem	Subtype	Claimed quantum security (Bits)	Claimed traditional security (Bits)	Private key size (Bits)	Public key size (Bits)	Key references
CRYSTALS Kyber–512	LWE problem with Module Lattices	100	128	13,056 (256)	6,400	[81–84]
CRYSTALS Kyber–512 90s						
CRYSTALS Kyber–768		164	192	19,200 (256)	9,472	
CRYSTALS Kyber–768 90s						
CRYSTALS Kyber–1024		230	256	25,344 (256)	12,544	
CRYSTALS Kyber–1024 90s						
FrodoKEM–640 AES	LWE problem with generic "algebraically unstructured" lattices	–	128	159,104	76,928	[8, 85–87]
FrodoKEM–640 SHAKE						
FrodoKEM–976 AES			192	250,368	1E+05	
FrodoKEM–976 SHAKE						
FrodoKEM–1344 AES			256	344,704	2E+05	
FrodoKEM–1344 SHAKE						

(Continued)

Table 6.3 Lattice–based post–quantum cryptosystem that approved to second round of NIST call. (*Continued*)

Cryptosystem	Subtype	Claimed quantum security (Bits)	Claimed traditional security (Bits)	Private key size (Bits)	Public key size (Bits)	Key references
LAC–128 (CCA)	RLWE	–	128	8,448	4,352	[88]
LAC–192(CCA)			192	16,640	8,448	
LAC–256 (CCA)			256			
NewHope–512 (CCA)		101	128	15,104	7,424	[5, 89–91]
NewHope–1024 (CCA)		233	256	29,440	14,592	
NTRUEncrypt (ntruhrss701)	solving LWE/ Ring–LWE	128–192	–	11,616	9,104	[4, 92, 93]
NTRUEncrypt (ntruhps2048677)				9,880	7,448	
NTRUEncrypt (ntruhps4096821)		192–256		12,736	9,840	
NTRU Prime (sntrup4591761)	RLWE	139–208	153–368	12,800	9,744	[94–96]
NTRU Prime (ntrulpr4591761)		140–210	155–364	9904	8376	

(*Continued*)

Table 6.3 Lattice–based post–quantum cryptosystem that approved to second round of NIST call. (*Continued*)

Cryptosystem	Subtype	Claimed quantum security (Bits)	Claimed traditional security (Bits)	Private key size (Bits)	Public key size (Bits)	Key references
Round 5 KEM IoT	GLWR	88–101	96–202	128	2736	[97, 98]
SABER KEM (LightSABERKEM)	Mod–LWR	114–153	125–169	12,544 (7,936)	5376	[99, 100]
SABER KEM		185–226	203–244	18,432 (10,752)	7936	
SABER KEM (FireSABERKEM)		257–308	283–338	24,320 (14,080)	10,496	
Three Bears (BabyBear CCA)	I–MLWE	140–180	154–190	320	6432	[101]
Three Bears (MamaBear CCA)		213–228	235–241		9552	
Three Bears (PapaBear CCA)		285–300	314–317		12,672	

6.2.1.4   Super Singular Elliptic–Curve Isogeny Cryptosystem

These cryptosystem provides security based on elliptic curves. Normally, elliptic curves are based on the isogeny protocol [16], but it restricts and withstands against the quantum attacks [17]. By this way, lot of post–quantum cryptosystems [18, 19] are available with less key size of few kilo bits [20]. SIKE [21, 22] is the only Isogeny based cryptosystem passed to the NIST's second level. SIKE has the base technique of super singular isogeny protocols graph of pseudo–random walks. SIKE key provides security levels of 2,992 bits for private keys and 2,640 bits for public keys.

6.2.1.5   Hybrid–Based Cryptosystem

Combination of pre–quantum and post–quantum cryptosystem takes the research level toward the post–quantum security with objective of restricting blockchain transaction from quantum system attacks. Currently, this type of cryptosystem's security is tested by researchers and industries, which also have been evaluated by Google [23]. A new hope [5] merged with a scheme ECC rely on DH (Diffie–Hellman) key exchange contract, which is termed as X25519. Next variety of same hybrid–based system is CECPQ2, which can be merged with X25519 and SXY and NTRU. CECPQ2 is the area in which current researchers are focusing and testing [1]. Even though this cryptosystem seems to be very promising, it has to be noted that here combination of two complex schemes lead us to arrange most significant computing resources and it consumes more energy. Consequently, future developers must address into security, resource consumption, and computational complexity on hybrid post–quantum blockchains. Additionally, researchers look in to heavy payload difficulty with this type of schemes when provided with TLS (Transport Layer Security) communications, such problem arises because of huge size of ciphertext size and public key size.

6.2.2   Post–Quantum Blockchain Signatures

6.2.2.1   Code–Centred Digital Signature

Numerous code–centred digital–signature algorithms have been implemented in the times of yore. Few subtypes of this kind of cryptosystems similar to McEliece's scheme are based on CFS [23] and Niederreiter [26]. Such digital signatures have fast verification and shorten length like the McEliece's traditional cryptosystem. However, it has large key size, so it requires most efficient computational resources with high energy conception. Because of this disadvantage, digital signature algorithm may turn out to be inefficient. Other code–based digital signatures are explained in Table 6.4, in which a special code–based signature scheme FST (Fiat–Shamir Transformation) [28], and, in some cases, do better than digital signatures like CFS [29]. On the other hand, at some situations, Fiat–Shamir digital signature schemes is not believed to be absolutely safer against all quantum hits [30]. Unrah transformation [31] is an alternative technique that can be considered for this problem.

6.2.2.2 Multivariant–Based Digital Signature

Multivariant–based digital signature's public keys are created all the way by a doorway access method which is a piece of key termed as private key. These type of schemes have small digital signatures but public keys as very large [10]. Few popular multivariant–based digital signatures rely on MI (Matsumoto–Inmai) algorithm, IP (Isomorphism of polynomials) [32], HFE variants. These types of signatures are capable to create signature size similar to current digital signatures like ECC–based signature and RSA digital signature [33].

Some other related multivariant–based signatures have been analyzed currently; one of the best is based on quadratic equation of pseudo-random multivariant [34] or based on Rainbow–like digital signatures; for example: TRMS [36], TTS [35], and Rainbow [37].

In contrast, some digital signing schemes require improving further more in the conditions onsizes of keys, because they needs multiple 10's of Kilo bytes (KB per each keys). Research [1] relates different multivariant-based signature algorithms that are transferred to NIST calls second round. Among all signature algorithms, MQDSS gives actually small key size, but its digital signature size becomes the largest in the compared signature algorithms. With the signature size from 239 bits to 1,632 bits of shorter size, all other digital signatures provide multiple thousand bytes for each key value.

6.2.2.3 Lattice–Based Digital Signature

Among many lattice–based digital signatures, one of the promising scheme with shorter key size is based on the SIS (Short Integer Solution) [38]. On analyzing the performance, bio–modal lattice digital signature (BLISS–B) paired with ECDSA and RSA [39] gives best signature cryptosystem, which is based on lattices and rely on rigidity of SIS difficulty. While note down

Table 6.4 Post–quantum signature scheme that entered into the NIST second call.

Algorithm	Type	Subtype	Claimed quantum security (Bits)	Private key size	Public key size	Signature size	Key reference
DILITHIUM 1280X1024 SHAKE (recommended)	Lattic–e Based	Based on the "Fiat–Shamir with Aborts" technique	128	–	1,472 bytes	2,701 bytes	[111]
DILITHIUM 1280X1024 AES (recommended)							
FALCON–512		Based on SIS over NTRU lattices and fast Fourier sampling	103	1,314.56 (32) bytes	897 bytes	657.38 bytes	[112, 113]
FALCON–1024			230	2,546.62 (32) bytes	1,793 bytes	1,273.31 bytes	

(Continued)

Table 6.4 Post–quantum signature scheme that entered into the NIST second call. (*Continued*)

Algorithm	Type	Subtype	Claimed quantum security (Bits)	Private key size	Public key size	Signature size	Key reference
GeMSS 128	Multivariant– Based	Built on HFEv–	128	13.44 KB	352.19 KB	258 bits	[114, 115]
GeMSS 192			192	34.07 KB	1,237.964 KB	411 bits	
GeMSS 256			256	75.89 KB	3,040.70 KB	576 bits	
LUOV Level 1 (Chacha8)		Based on Unbalanced Oil and Vineger (UOV)	128	32 bytes	11.5 KB	239 bytes	[116, 117]
LUOV Level 3 (Chacha8)			192		35.4 KB	337 bytes	
LUOV Level 5 (Chacha8)			256		82.04 KB	440 bytes	
MQDSS 31–48		Based on the 5– pass SSH (Sakumoto, Shiraa and Hiwatari) identification scheme	64–128	16 bytes	46 bytes	20,854 bytes	[118, 119]
MQDSS 31–64			96–192	24 bytes	64 bytes	43,728 bytes	

(*Continued*)

Table 6.4 Post–quantum signature scheme that entered into the NIST second call. (*Continued*)

Algorithm	Type	Subtype	Claimed quantum security (Bits)	Private key size	Public key size	Signature size	Key reference
PICNIC2 L1–FS	Hash–based	Realize on zero–knowledge proofs	128	16 bytes	32 bytes	13,802 bytes (max)	[120]
PICNIC2 L3–FS			192	24 bytes	48 bytes	29,750 bytes (max)	
PICNIC2 L5–FS			256	32 bytes	64 bytes	54,732 bytes (max)	
qTESLA–p–I	Lattice–Based	Based on RLWE	128	5,184 bytes	14,880 bytes	2,592 bytes	[24]
qTESLA–p–III			192	12,352 bytes	38,432 bytes	5,664 bytes	

(*Continued*)

Table 6.4 Post-quantum signature scheme that entered into the NIST second call. (*Continued*)

Algorithm	Type	Subtype	Claimed quantum security (Bits)	Private key size	Public key size	Signature size	Key reference
Rainbow Ia	Multivariant–Based	–	128	93 KB	149 (58.1) KB	512 bits	[25]
Rainbow IIIc			192	511.4 KB	710.6 (206.7) KB	1,248 bits	
Rainbow Vc			256	1,227.1 KB	1,705.5 (491.9) KB	1,632 bits	
SPHINCS+ – SHAKE256–128f–simple	Hash based	Stateless signature scheme	128	64 bytes	32 bytes	16,976 bytes	[27, 102]
SPHINCS+ – SHAKE256–192f–simple			192	96 bytes	48 bytes	35,664 bytes	

(Continued)

Table 6.4 Post-quantum signature scheme that entered into the NIST second call. (*Continued*)

Algorithm	Type	Subtype	Claimed quantum security (Bits)	Private key size	Public key size	Signature size	Key reference
SPHINCS+ –SHAKE256–256f–simple			256	128 bytes	64 bytes	49,216 bytes	
SPHINCS+ –SHA 256–128f–simple			128	64 bytes	32 bytes	16,976 bytes	
SPHINCS+ –SHA 256–192f–simple			192	96 bytes	48 bytes	35,664 bytes	
SPHINCS+ –SHA 256–256f–simple			256	128 bytes	64 bytes	49,216 bytes	
SPHINCS+ –Haraka 256–128f–simple			128	64 bytes	32 bytes	16,976 bytes	
SPHINCS+ –Haraka 256–192f–simple			192	96 bytes	48 bytes	35,664 bytes	
SPHINCS+ –Haraka 256–256f–simple			256	128 bytes	64 bytes	49,216 bytes	

clearly, general BLISS [40] under specific conditions is attacked in 2016 by the attack of side–channel [41]. BLISS–B and its subtype disposed into cache attack that can be recovered by secret digital signature keys, which is done followed by 6,000 digital signature generations [42].

In addition with BLISS, other lattice–based digital signatures are based on SIS difficulty but were introduced specially for blockchains [43]. In early 1980s, David Chaum introduced lattice–based blind digital signature [44] for creating undetectable payment transaction system [45]. A research work on lattice–based blind digital signature [46] provides user security and undetectable for blockchain based IoT application in distributed network. Finally, it is mandatory to discuss about a well–designed lattice–based digital signature in [47, 48]. Especially in [47], the researchers designed a cryptosystem scheme whose private and public keys are created using Bonsai Tree [49].

A lattice–based digital signature in [48] introduces a security level of 100 bits for optimized embedded systems, which provides optimal size of keys (private key, 2,000 bits; public key, 12,000 bits; and digital signature, 9,000 bits). Due to its efficiency and simplicity, this schemes are nominated as digital signing algorithms for blockchain–associated works such as Qchain [50], which is post–quantum cryptosystem for maintaining public key encryptions in decentralized networks.

Table 6.4, shows different lattice–based digital signature schemes, which are passed into the second round of NIST call. In that comparison, this one shows that lattice–centred scheme needs the key size lesser than the multivariant–based digital signature schemes, but, actually, the created digital signatures are somewhat larger in size. In overall comparison, FALCON acts as best signature with less signature and key size. Some other signatures like qTESTA are faster in digital signature, but major downside is its bigger key size [74].

6.2.2.4   Super Singular Elliptic–Curve Isogeny Digital Signature

For producing post–quantum signature, some researchers also utilize super singular elliptic curves Isogeny procedure [75], but it has poor performance so there are less research works in this scheme. Especially in [76], for some schemes, the author analyzes some digital signatures relying on Unruh transform and Isogeny problems, which provide quite efficient verification and digital signature with less key size.

Another digital signature relying on Unruh transformation [77], which provides 128 bits of quantum security level, 48 bytes of private key, 336 bytes of public key, but it generates digital signature of 122,880 bytes even though some comparison techniques are used. Thus, it is compulsory to concentrate on size of key concerns while employing Isogeny centred digital signature, SIDH (Supersingular Isogeny Diffie–Hellman); especially, it is designed in the resource constrained systems. This scheme needs to utilize some key comparison techniques which often engage with computationally rigorous steps [78, 79].

6.2.2.5 Hash–Based Digital Signature

These types of digital signature rely on the defense system of hash functions as an alternative for mathematical rigidity problems. From late 1970s, these types of digital signatures were introduced. Based on one way function, Lamport designed a digital signature scheme [80]. Now, research perspective turned into variants of extensive Merkle digital signature (XMSS) [105] like SPHINCS and XMSS–T [106]. They are measured as potentially hash function–based on digital signature for post–quantum scheme which is derived from Merkle tree analyzed in [107].

Even though some researchers think that SPHINCS and XMSS are unfeasible for applications of blockchain because of its performance [108], other schemes need to be considered. For illustration, XMSS uses only certification path in its place of a tree, which is personalized for the blockchains. It uses restricted keys and one time keys for preserving minimum user tracking and obscurity [109].

Another researcher [108] analyzed eXtended Naor–Yung digital Signature Scheme (XNYSS), which is a digital signature technique combined with Naor–Yung chain and one time hash function–based digital signature that agrees on producing related digital signature chains [110].

6.3 Post–Quantum Blockchain Performance Comparison

6.3.1 Encryption Algorithm

Table 6.5 analyzes the encryption techniques of post–quantum schemes (public key cryptosystems), which are executed on both full blockchain and normal blockchains on hardware systems. Those systems vary for each cryptosystems, and results obtained are varied for different types of micro processor's performance.

In Table 6.5, it is clearly analyzed that the cycle is counted for every micro–processor for encryption/decryption and key generating techniques.

Table 6.5 Comparison on post-quantum encryption algorithms performance.

Reference	Cryptosystem	Claimed classical security (bits)	Performance evaluation hardware	Key generation (#Cycles)	Encapsulation (#Cycles)	Decapsulation (#Cycles)
[51]	BIKE–1 Level 1	128	Intel Core i5–6260U @ 1.80 GHz, 32 GB of RAM	730,025	689,193	2901,203
	BIKE–1 Level 3	192		1,709,921	1,850,425	7,666,855
	BIKE–1 Level 5	256		29,086,647	3,023,816	1,7483,906
	BIKE–2 Level 1	128		6,383,408	281,755	2,674,115
	BIKE–2 Level 3	192		22,205,901	710,970	7,114,241
	BIKE–2 Level 5	256		58,806,046	1,201,161	1,6385,956
	BIKE–3 Level 1	128		433,258	575,237	3,437,956
	BIKE–3 Level 3	192		1,100,372	1,460,866	7,732,167
	BIKE–3 Level 5	256		2,300,332	3,257,675	18,047,493
[58]	Classic McEliece (mceliece8192128)		Intel Xeon E3–1220v3 @ 3.10 GHz	~ 4675000000	~ 296000	~ 458,000

(Continued)

Table 6.5 Comparison on post-quantum encryption algorithms performance. (*Continued*)

Reference	Cryptosystem	Claimed classical security (bits)	Performance evaluation hardware	Key generation (#Cycles)	Encapsulation (#Cycles)	Decapsulation (#Cycles)
[81]	CRYSTALS Kyber–512	128	Intel Core i7–4770K @ 3.5 GHz	118,044	161,440	190,206 (~ 279,150)
	CRYSTALS Kyber–512 90s			232,368	285,336	313,452 (~ 436,088)
	CRYSTALS Kyber–768	192		217,728	272,254	315,976 (~ 469,008)
	CRYSTALS Kyber–768 90s			451,018	514,088	556,972 (~ 758,934)
	CRYSTALS Kyber–1024	256		331,418	396,928	451,098 (~ 6,675,596)
	CRYSTALS Kyber–1024 90s			735,382	810,398	860,272 (~ 1,148,394)

(*Continued*)

Table 6.5 Comparison on post-quantum encryption algorithms performance. (*Continued*)

Reference	Cryptosystem	Claimed classical security (bits)	Performance evaluation hardware	Key generation (#Cycles)	Encapsulation (#Cycles)	Decapsulation (#Cycles)
[85]	FrodoKEM-640 AES	128	Intel Core i7–6700 @ 3.4 GHz	1,384,000	1,858,000	1,749,000
	FrodoKEM-640 SHAKE			7,626,000	8,362,000	8,248,000
	FrodoKEM-976 AES	192		2,820,000	3,559,000	3,400,000
	FrodoKEM-976 SHAKE			16,841,000	18,077,000	17,925,000
	FrodoKEM-1344 AES	256		4,756,000	5,981,000	5,748,000
	FrodoKEM-1344 SHAKE			30,301,000	326,111,000	32,387,000
[62]	HQC Level 1 (hqc–128–1)	128	Intel Core i7 –7820X CPU @ 3.6 GHz, 16 GB of RAM	110,000	190,000	310,000
	HQC Level 3 (hqc–192–1)	192		190,000	330,000	510,000
	HQC Level 5 (hqc–256–1)	256		270,000	470,000	690,000

(*Continued*)

Table 6.5 Comparison on post–quantum encryption algorithms performance. (*Continued*)

Reference	Cryptosystem	Claimed classical security (bits)	Performance evaluation hardware	Key generation (#Cycles)	Encapsulation (#Cycles)	Decapsulation (#Cycles)
[88]	LAC–128 (CCA)	128	Intel Core i7–4770S @ 3.10 GHz, 7.6 GB of RAM	90,411	160,314	216,957
	LAC–192(CCA)	192		281,324	421,439	647,030
	LAC–256 (CCA)	256		267,831	526,915	874,742
[65]	LEDACrypt KEM Level 1 (for 2 circulant blocks)	128	Intel i5–6600 @ 3.6 GHz	–		
	LEDACrypt KEM Level 3 (for 2 circulant blocks)	192		–		
	LEDACrypt KEM Level 5 (for 2 circulant blocks)	256		–		

(*Continued*)

Table 6.5 Comparison on post–quantum encryption algorithms performance. (*Continued*)

Reference	Cryptosystem	Claimed classical security (bits)	Performance evaluation hardware	Key generation (#Cycles)	Encapsulation (#Cycles)	Decapsulation (#Cycles)
[89]	NewHope–512 (CCA)	128	Intel Core i7–4770K @ 3.5 GHz	117,128	180,648	206,244
	NewHope–1024 (CCA)	256		24,4944	377,092	437,056
[92]	NTRUEncrypt (ntruhrss701)	128/192		23,302,424	1,256,210	3,642,966
	NTRUEncrypt (ntruhps2048677)			21,833,048	1,313,454	3,399,726
	NTRUEncrypt (ntruhps4096821)	192/256		31,835,958	1,856,936	4,920,436
	NTRU Prime (sntrup4591761)	153–368	Intel Xeon E3–1275v3 @ 3.5 GHz	940,852	44,788	93,676
	NTRU Prime (ntrulpr4591761)	155–364		44,948	81,144	113,708

(Continued)

Table 6.5 Comparison on post–quantum encryption algorithms performance. (*Continued*)

Reference	Cryptosystem	Claimed classical security (bits)	Performance evaluation hardware	Key generation (#Cycles)	Encapsulation (#Cycles)	Decapsulation (#Cycles)
[68]	NTS–KEM Level 1	128	16–Core server with Intel Xeon E5–2667v2 @ 3.3 GHz, 256 GB of RAM	39,388,653	124,528	650,116
	NTS–KEM Level 3	192		125,672,723	396,513	1,181,373
	NTS–KEM Level 5	256		229,357,286	532,168	2,500,475
[70]	ROLLO–II 128	128	Intel Core i7 –7820X @ 3.6 GHz, 16 GB of RAM	9,620,000	1,520,000	4,960,000
	ROLLO–II 192	192		1,1040,000	2000000	6520000
	ROLLO–II 256	256		11,410,000	2,390,000	7,940,000
[97]	Round 5 KEM IoT	96–202	MacBook Pro 15.1 with Intel Core i7 @ 2.6 GHz	56,300	97,900	59,500

(*Continued*)

Table 6.5 Comparison on post-quantum encryption algorithms performance. (*Continued*)

Reference	Cryptosystem	Claimed classical security (bits)	Performance evaluation hardware	Key generation (#Cycles)	Encapsulation (#Cycles)	Decapsulation (#Cycles)
[72]	RQC I	128	Intel Core i7 -7820X @ 3.6 GHz, 16 GB of RAM	700,000	1,300,000	6,660,000
	RQC II	192		1,120,000	2,180,000	14,680,000
	RQC III	256		1,820,000	3,550,000	23,200,000
[99]	SABER KEM (LightSABERKEM)	125–169	Intel Core i5-7200U @ 2.50 GHz	85,474	108,927	119,868
	SABER KEM	203–244		163,333	196,705	215,733
	SABER KEM (FireSABERKEM)	283–338		259,504	308,277	341,654
[21]	SIKE (SIKEq434)	128	Intel Core i7-6700 @ 3.4 GHz	1,047,991,000	1,482,681,000	17,903,040,000
[101]	Three Bears (BabyBear CCA)	154–190	Intel Core i3-6100U @ 2.3 GHz	41,000	60,000	101,000
	Three Bears (MamaBear CCA)	235–241		79,000	96,000	156,000
	Three Bears (PapaBear CCA)	314–317		118,000	145,000	21,000

As the result of comparison, some lightest schemes like SABER, NTRU, and Three Bears are actually fast. In addition, it is necessary to concentrate on the part of processors that SABER and Three Bears are analyzed on less power microprocessors and the analysis of NTRU resulted on high power Intel Xeon microprocessor, which is used for servers.

In contrast, SIKE scheme is the slowest in the comparison, whereas some classic schemes like McEliece are affected by time consuming key creation techniques regardless of getting reduced encryption and decryption period. As a result, future researchers must design an optimized cryptosystem for blockchains with the intention of fast execution, less computational complication, and less execution time.

6.3.2   Digital Signatures

Different digital signature schemes such as post–quantum blockchains that handed to second level in NIST calls, which are compared in Table 6.6; the following attention is to be considered in the future researches:

- In Falcon scheme, performance is measured in unit of spent time as an alternative to cycles using the processor of vibrant frequency scaling that rely on temperature and load, which varies up to percentage of 15 [113].
- In Rainbow, some values mentioned inside the brackets shows key compressed style's performance observed and needs high computational complex systems comparing to normal systems because of process of decompressing.
- Dilithium's AVXs optimization seems to be more hopeful for post–quantum signatures, because the results are similar to ECDSA–256. Unluckily, size of key in dilithium remains bigger than key size of the ECDSA–256 key. Hence, future development should analyze and concentrate to reduce the key size.
- Some leisureliest cryptosystems seemed to be most encrypted schemes, which are SPHINCS, GeMSS, Rainbow, and PICNICS2:
  ➢ GeMSS, SPHINCS, and Rainbow schemes' execution time is affected because of the time dedicated for key generation.
  ➢ In the case of PICNIC2, digital signature speed reduces because of slow digital signature and verification processes.

Table 6.6 Evaluation of digital signature performance on post-quantum.

Algorithm	Evaluation platform	Performance (Reference Implementation)			Performance (Optimized AVX2 Implementation)		
		Key generation (#Cycles)	Digital signature (#Cycles)	Verification (#Cycles)	Key generation (#Cycles)	Digital signature (#Cycles)	Verification (#Cycles)
DILITHIUM 1280X1024 SHAKE (recommended)	Intel Core-i7 6600U (Skylake) CPU @2.6 GHz	371.083	1,562,215	375,708	156,777	437,638	155,784
DILITHIUM 1280X1024 AES (recommended)		–	–	–	99,907	350,465	109,782
FALCON-512	Intel Core i7–6567U @ 3.3 GHz	7.26 ms			–	–	–
FALCON-1024		21.63 ms					
GeMSS 128	Intel Core-i7 6600U CPU @2.6 GHz (Skylake)	–			36,800,000	529,000,000	84,600,000
GeMSS 192					167,000,000	1,720,000,000	233,000,000
GeMSS 256					508,000,000	2,830,000,000	550,000,000

(*Continued*)

Table 6.6 Evaluation of digital signature performance on post-quantum. (*Continued*)

Algorithm	Evaluation platform	Performance (Reference Implementation)			Performance (Optimized AVX2 Implementation)		
		Key generation (#Cycles)	Digital signature (#Cycles)	Verification (#Cycles)	Key generation (#Cycles)	Digital signature (#Cycles)	Verification (#Cycles)
LUOV Level 1 (Chacha8)	Intel Core i5–8250U CPU @ 1.60 GHz				1,100,000	224,000	49,000
LUOV Level 3 (Chacha8)					4,600,000	643,000	152,000
LUOV Level 5 (Chacha8)					9,700,000	1,100,000	331,000
MQDSS 31–48	Intel Core i7–4770K CPU @ 3.5 GHz	1,192,984	26,630,590	19,840,136	1,074,644	3,816,106	2,551,270
MQDSS 31–64		2,767,384	85268712	62,306,098	2,491,050	9,047,148	6,132,948
PICNIC2 L1–FS	Intel Core i7–4790 CPU @ 3.60 GHz	149,749	30,666,63719	1,957,340,295	21,026	229,947,918	100,546,772
PICNIC2 L3–FS		362,481	10,190,171,124	5,537,696,230	20,160	657,944,759	223,785,326
PICNIC2 L5–FS		691,790	25,488,037,138	12,943,455,830	35,716	1,346,724,260	387,637,876

(*Continued*)

Table 6.6 Evaluation of digital signature performance on post-quantum. (*Continued*)

Algorithm	Evaluation platform	Performance (Reference Implementation)			Performance (Optimized AVX2 Implementation)		
		Key generation (#Cycles)	Digital signature (#Cycles)	Verification (#Cycles)	Key generation (#Cycles)	Digital signature (#Cycles)	Verification (#Cycles)
qTESLA–p–I	Intel Core-i7 6700 (Skylake) @3.4 GHz	2,316,200	2,324,900	671,400	–	–	–
qTESLA–p–III		13,726,600	6,284,600	1,830,400			
Rainbow Ia	Reference: Intel Xeon CPU	35,000,000 (40,200,000)	402,000 (20,200,000)	155,000 (34,440)	8,290,000 (9,280,000)	67,700 (6,410,000)	21,700 (3,370,000)
Rainbow IIIc	E3–1225 v5 @3.30 GHz	340,000,000 (402,000,000)	1,700,000 (217,000,000)	16,440 (1,9400,000)	94,800,000 (110,000,000)	588,000 (61,800,000)	114,000 (17,800,000)
Rainbow Vc	(Skylake), AVX2: Intel Xeon CPU E3–1275 v5 @3.60 GHz (Skylake)	757,000,000 (879,000,000)	3,640,000 (469,000,000)	2,390,000 (45,400,000)	126,000,000 (137,000,000)	755,000 (87,200,000)	197,000 (43,000,000)
SPHINCS+ –SHAKE256– 128f-simple	Intel Core i7–4770K CPU @ 3.5 GHz	10,829,190	350,847,594	13,922,112	3,909,682	133,452,230	9,468,278

(*Continued*)

Table 6.6 Evaluation of digital signature performance on post-quantum. (*Continued*)

Algorithm	Evaluation platform	Performance (Reference Implementation)			Performance (Optimized AVX2 Implementation)		
		Key generation (#Cycles)	Digital signature (#Cycles)	Verification (#Cycles)	Key generation (#Cycles)	Digital signature (#Cycles)	Verification (#Cycles)
SPHINCS+ –SHAKE256– 192f-simple		15,192,014	645,965,282	21,943,196	6303,298	171,354,532	14,758,202
SPHINCS+ –SHAKE256– 256f-simple		74,279,484	902,307,648	21,261,734	16,898,344	416,398,690	15,383,888
SPHINCS+ –SHA 256–128f-simple		15,426,726	693,497,446	13,449,776	3,257,486	116,197,711	6,094,962
SPHINCS+ –SHA 256–192f-simple		21,274,744	464,737,100	20,803,660	2,280,172	140,223,132	9,723,976
SPHINCS+ –SHA 256–256f-simple		71620636	1,092,969,048	22,716,202	5,594,338	145,433,610	9,384,544
SPHINCS+ –Haraka 256–128f-simple		21,556,006	378,800,946	13,712,542	655,294	25,178,368	1,333,172

(*Continued*)

Table 6.6 Evaluation of digital signature performance on post–quantum. (*Continued*)

Algorithm	Evaluation platform	Performance (Reference Implementation)			Performance (Optimized AVX2 Implementation)		
		Key generation (#Cycles)	Digital signature (#Cycles)	Verification (#Cycles)	Key generation (#Cycles)	Digital signature (#Cycles)	Verification (#Cycles)
SPHINCS+ –Haraka 256–192f-simple		19,985,722	484,198,114	44,676,162	2,317,102	58,491,132	3,714,942
SPHINCS+ –Haraka 256–256f-simple		82,842,862	1,046,811,244	2,0879,946	2,510,894	65,870,866	1,949,510

6.4   Future Scopes of Post–Quantum Blockchain

Lot of analysis are going on the post–quantum blockchains to deal with the quantum system attacks. Many researchers recommend the safe implementation of quantum blockchains [104, 103].

In [103], author designed a safe quantum authentication transaction model, which relies on lattice–based cryptosystem with typical model for transactions to avoid the attacks by quantum systems. Correspondingly in [104], post–quantum cryptocurrency for blockchains based on lattice–based digital signature scheme design is proposed.

6.4.1   NIST Standardization

Future researchers can also concentrate on the most suitable post–quantum blockchains suggested by NIST. Before choosing the post–quantum blockchain, researchers should observe the current updated reports of NIST. In addition, it is advisable to choose the technique that suits for the hardware recourses with good computational speed and memory. For that, this chapter provides tables for more clarification on blockchain's levels of security.

6.4.2   Key and Signature Size

Even though many researches and analysis are going on, no specific algorithm is perfect for post–quantum blockchain when executed in less computation complex system resulting in high–speed execution with less key size and small digital signature or hash functions and consuming less energy. Such an effective algorithm is really challenging to design for resource controlled devices. Future researchers can focus on the post–quantum blockchain with an effective key size and smart digital signature for security.

6.4.3   Faster Evolution

Nowadays, many researchers are attracted by quantum computing attacks; there is a possibility for lot of new attacks to be developed in future adjacent to the post–quantum blockchains. Researchers need to have attention on the digital signature size and the resources for high speed schemes even in normal computational system.

6.4.4   Post–Quantum Blockchain From Pre–Quantum

Many researchers have different set up for converting post–quantum blockchain from the pre–quantum blockchain. One of those developments is to expand the life span of older blocks in blockchain, while the digital signature or security by hash function is negotiated. As the transaction of bitcoins in blockchain becomes harden to keep away from attacks, some mechanisms are developed. Another work implements a commit after release practice, which allows blockchain customers to transfer safely from versions of pre–quantum blockchains to post–quantum blockchains with signatures.

6.4.5   Generation of Keys

For the purpose of increasing security, few post–quantum cryptosystems have boundary for the count of transaction messages communicating by same signed keys. Hence, by an outcome, it is compulsory for creating newer signatures (keys) continually which need resources of high computational complexity and blockchain process becomes slower. Thus, future researchers are needed to analyze and implement effective key creation technique with efficient blockchain.

6.4.6   Computational Efficiency

As discussed in the chapter, few post–quantum cryptosystems require a considerable time for execution, resources, and memory for storage. Such requirements frequently result in augmented consumption of energy, so further proposals have to optimize the cryptosystem with the intention to increase the energy efficiency and computational efficiency, as a whole, overall efficiency of blockchains.

6.4.7   Choosing Hardware

Few computationally concentrated post–quantum schemes might not be appropriate for some hardware resources that are presently used in block-chain blocks (nodes). Hence, these schemes rely on some substitution among computational efficiency and security, which is not to limit the latent hardware that may act together with blockchains.

6.4.8   Overheads on Large Ciphertext

Some post–quantum cryptosystems produces large ciphertext, which is an overhead for blockchains and because of its performance may be affected. To deal with these problems, future proposals on post–quantum blockchain should have an objective to reduce the overheads on ciphertext by providing customized technique for compression.

6.5   Conclusion

The recent focus of developers and researchers are on the quantum computers growth with Distributed Ledger Technology (DLT) similar to blockchains as, in the same place, hash functions and public key encryptions are necessary. In this chapter, discussion is about attacks that quantum computers rely on Grover's and Shor's algorithm with the blockchains. In addition, here, in this chapter, analysis is done about how post–quantum schemes are applied to mitigate from such quantum attacks. Reviews and applications of most similar post–quantum cryptosystems for blockchain with their challenges are discussed here. Performance and characteristics of encryption cryptosystem and signature schemes are compared. For next generation of post–quantum blockchain, this chapter deeply provides a broad knowledge with reference to the quantum computer attacks.

References

1. Tiago, M. and Fernandez-Carames and Paula Fraga-Lamas, Towards Post-Quantum Blockchain: A Review on Blockchain Cryptography Resistant to Quantum Computing Attacks, in: *Centro de Investigación CITIC*, vol. 15071, pp. 21091–21116, Jan 2020, Universidade da Coruna, Coruna, Spain.
2. Li, C.-Y., Chen, X.-B., Chen, Y.-L., Hou, Y.-Y., Li, J., A New Lattice-Based Signature Scheme in Post-Quantum Blockchain Network, in: *Digital Object Identifier*, vol. 4, pp. 2026–2033, 10.1109/ACCESS, 2018.
3. Blomer, J. and Naewe, S., Sampling methods for shortest vectors, closest vectors and successive minima, in: *Proc. Int. Colloq. Automata, Lang. Program*, Springer-Verlag Berlin, Heidelberg, Poland, pp. 65–77, Jul. 2007.
4. Hoffstein, J., Pipher, J., Silverman, J.H., NTRU: A ring-based public key cryptosystem, in: *Proc. 3rd Int. Symp. Algorithmic Number Theory*, Springer, Berlin, Heidelberg, Germany, pp. 267–288, Jun. 1998.

5. Alkim, E., Ducas, L., Poppelmann, T., Schwabe, P., Post-quantum key exchanged A new hope, in: *Proc. USENIX Secur. Symp.* pp. 327–343, Aug. 2016, USENIX Association, United States.

6. Stehle, D. and Steinfeld, R., Making NTRU as secure as worst-case problems over ideal lattices, in: *Proc. Annu. Int. Conf. Theory Appl. Cryptograph. Techn.* pp. 27–47, May 2011, Springer-Verlag Berlin, Heidelberg, Tallinn Estonia.

7. Aujla, G.S., Chaudhary, R., Kaur, K., Garg, S., Kumar, N., Ranjan, R., SAFE: SDN-assisted framework for edgecloud interplay in secure healthcare eco-system. *IEEE Trans. Ind. Inf.*, 15, 1, 469–480, Jan. 2019.

8. Lindner, R. and Peikert, C., Better key sizes (and attacks) for LWE-based encryption, in: *Proc. Cryptographers' Track RSA Conf.* pp. 319–339, Feb. 2011, Springer, Berlin, Heidelberg, USA.

9. Lyubashevsky, V., Peikert, C., Regev, O., A toolkit for ring-LWEcryptography, in: *Proc. EUROCRYPT*, Athens, Greece, pp. 35–54, May 2013.

10. Bernstein, D.J., Buchman, J., Dahmen, E., *Post-Quantum Cryptography*, Springer-Verlag, Berlin, Germany, 2009.

11. Petzoldt, A., Bulygin, S., Buchmann, J., Selecting parameters for the rainbow signature scheme, in: *Proc. PQCrypto*, Darmstadt, Germany, pp. 218–240, May 2010.

12. Ding, J., Petzoldt, A., Wang, L.-C., The cubic simple matrix encryption scheme, in: *Proc. PQCrypto*, Waterloo, ON, Canada, pp. 76–87, Oct. 2014.

13. Ding, J. and Schmidt, D., Cryptanalysis of HFEv and internal perturbation of HFE, in: *Proc. Int. Workshop Public Key Cryptogr.* Les Diablerets, Switzerland, pp. 288–301, Jan. 2005.

14. McEliece, R.J., A public-key cryptosystem based on algebraic coding theory. *Deep Space Netw. Prog. Rep., Tech. Rep.*, DSN PR 42–44, 114–116, Jan./Feb. 1978.

15. Lee, W., No, J.-S., Kim, Y.-S., Punctured Reed-Muller code-based McEliece cryptosystems. *IET Commun.*, 11, 10, 1543–1548, Jul. 2017.

16. Rostovtsev, A. and Stolbunov, A., Public-key cryptosystem based on isogenies. *Cryptol. ePrint Arch., Tech. Rep.*, 2006/145, 2006.

17. Childs, A., Jao, D., Soukharev, V., Constructing elliptic curve isogenies in quantum subexponential time. *J. Math. Cryptol.*, 8, 1, 1–29, Jan. 2014.

18. Biasse, J.-F., Jao, D., Sankar, A., *A Quantum Algorithm for Computing Isogenies Between Supersingular Elliptic Curves (Lecture Notes in Computer Science)*, vol. 8885, pp. 428–442, Springer, Cham, Switzerland, 2014.

19. De Feo, L., Jao, D., Plût, J., Towards quantum-resistant cryptosystems from supersingular elliptic curve isogenies. *J. Math. Cryptol.*, 8, 3, 209247, Jun. 2014.

20. Costello, C., Longa, P., Naehrig, M., Efficient algorithms for supersingular isogeny Diffie Hellman. *Cryptol. ePrint Arch. Tech. Rep.*, 2016/413, 2016.

21. Sathya, K. and Kumar, D.R., Energy efficient clustering in sensor networks using Cluster Manager, in: *2012 International Conference on Computing, Communication and Applications (ICCCA)*, 2012, February, IEEE, Dindigul.

22. Dhanaraj, R.K., Krishnasamy, L., Geman, O., Izdrui, D.R., Black hole and sink hole attack detection in wireless body area networks. *Comput. Mater. Continua.* 68, 2, 1949–1965, 2021.

23. Courtois, N.T., Finiasz, M., Sendrier, N., How to achieve a McEliecebased digital signature scheme, in: *Proc. Int. Conf. Theory Appl. Cryptol. Inf. Secur.* Gold Coast, QLD, Australia, pp. 157–174, Dec. 2001.

24. Krishnamoorthi, S., Jayapaul, P., Dhanaraj, R.K. *et al.*, Design of pseudo-random number generator from turbulence padded chaotic map. *Nonlinear Dyn.*, 2021.

25. Ding, J. and Schmidt, D., Rainbow, a new multivariable polynomial signature scheme, in: *Proc. ACNS*, pp. 164–175, Jun. 2005, Springer, Berlin, Heidelberg, USA.

7

Post-Quantum Cryptosystems for Blockchain

K. Tamil Selvi[1]* and R. Thamilselvan[2]

[1]Department of CSE, Kongu Engineering College, Thoppupalayam, Erode, Tamil Nadu, India
[2]Department of IT, Kongu Engineering College, Thoppupalayam, Erode, Tamil Nadu, India

Abstract

Blockchain with its inherent characteristics like transparency, accountability, and reliability finds its place in numerous applications. These characteristics are enabled through hash functions and public key cryptography. However, these hash functions and public key cryptography are non-resistance to quantum attacks. This leads to the rise of post-quantum cryptosystem for distributed ledger technologies like blockchain. The post-quantum cryptosystem can be modeled through public key post-quantum cryptosystems and post-quantum signing algorithms. Many variants of public key–based systems are code-based, multivariate-based, and lattice-based cryptosystems. Signing algorithms can be implemented as code-based or hash-based. Post-quantum blockchains are derived from quantum-resistant blockchain cryptography which are immune to Grover's and Shor's algorithm-based security attacks. Further secured blockchain transaction can be implemented using quantum key distribution (QKD) through secured key exchange. QKD can support one-time pad (OTP) generation, which is a large single key pre-shared between sender and receiver. This OTP can be generated using quantum random number generation. Hybrid post-cryptosystem that combines pre-quantum and post-quantum cryptosystem aims to protect the transactions of blockchain from quantum attacks. Although this system is secure, there is a complementation between security, resource consumption, and high complex of computation. The compression mechanisms can be employed to reduce the data transmission overhead. Thus, most relevant post-quantum blockchain system can be built based on applications requirements and security constraints.

*Corresponding author: ktamilselvikec@gmail.com

Rajesh Kumar Dhanaraj, Vani Rajasekar, SK Hafizul Islam, Balamurugan Balusamy and Ching-Hsien Hsu (eds.) Quantum Blockchain: An Emerging Cryptographic Paradigm, (173–200)
© 2022 Scrivener Publishing LLC

Keywords: Blockchain, post-quantum cryptography, one-time pad, quantum key distribution

7.1   Introduction

In the age of digital world, data security is the topmost concern for many business and applications in organization [1]. Most of the security aspects are based on cryptographic algorithms. These algorithms are under-pinned with confidentiality, data integrity, and availability of transactions of business. The services can business to business (B2B), business to consumer (B2C), and digitalized services [2]. Public key cryptography is the enabling technology for the security of the emerging public internet and E-commerce. With public key cryptosystem, secure and private data communication can be performed in the public internet. Blockchain [3] explores the decentralized security with distributed ledger among the multiple users. It consists of data block chains that are hashed for sharing information among multiple parties without central authority. This attractive feature of blockchain find its place in many domains like smart health, smart factories, logistics, and many more application domains based on need and application design requirements.

The users of blockchain interact securely using public key or asymmetric cryptography. It is needed for the authentication of the transactions. Hash functions find its place in blockchain to generate digital signature for the linkage of blocks and secure operations of the blockchain systems [4]. The evolution of quantum computing posed a threat to the block chain systems. The powerful quantum computers are capable of breaking cryptographic algorithms: RSA (Rivest, Shamir, Adleman), certain hash-based algorithms, and Elliptic Curve Cryptosystem (ECC) using Shor's algorithm [5] within time scale of polynomial. Most of the quantum computing systems used Grover's algorithm [6]. It generates the hashes for the recreation of blockchain. It is also used for detection of hash collision, which can provide integrity with block replacement. Post-quantum blockchains explores the resistance mechanism for the quantum attacks based on Shor's and Grover's algorithms.

7.2   Basics of Blockchain

Blockchain originated its component from Bitcoin [7]. It is a ledger publicly available, stores the information about the transaction and sharing with multiple parties that are independent of each other. The consensus protocol takes care of storage and verification of the transaction. Removal of transaction from the blockchain needs more computational efforts. The immutability of the transaction is provided by consensus protocol. The other salient features of blockchain are irreversibility, anonymity, decentralization, and persistence. It consists of three core components, namely, blocks, nodes, and miners. The blockchain consists of sequence of blocks and block encompasses data, nonce, and value of hash. The unique hash and nonce also references the hash of the previous block for the current block. The miners create the next unique block by a process known as mining. Miners have the responsibility of finding the nonce that generates the hash value accepted by all parties. Nonce is 32-bit, whereas hash is 256-bit entities. Node in the blockchain system has its own copy of chain of blocks and update the newly added block to it upon the algorithmic approval thus trusted and verified actions.

The sharing of information among the nodes in blockchain environment is peer-to-peer (P2P) mechanisms. The block is broadcasted in the network to all the nodes for validation. To solve the security issues, consensus mechanism can be regulated for common updates.

A computing node initiates the transaction request. Broadcasting of the requested transaction to computing nodes in P2P network. The current node state is given by the transaction and aggregated to form a block. All nodes in the network monitor the current state of the network and maintain the logs. Public key cryptography is employed for transaction validation by monitoring the status of transaction of the requested user. Once the transaction is verified, it becomes contracts and aggregated from a block. The consensus mechanism is used for block validation among the participating nodes. Only the validated blocks are added to the existing ledger to form the blockchain which is unaltered. Thus, the security mechanisms are applied for the given data and the transaction is completed. The whole workflow is depicted in Figure 7.1.

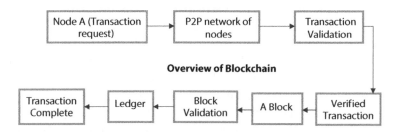

Figure 7.1 Overview of blockchain.

The important components of blockchain are as follows:

- Asymmetric cryptography for creation of secured digital blocks
- Blocks with group of transaction for conservation of states
- Consensus mechanism for validation of blocks based on common agreement protocol
- Secured distributed ledger which forms the blockchain

In the connected network with nodes, each node is aware of the other nodes before the initiation of any transaction. During the initiation of new transaction, the input data is embedded into it. In depth, the input is the hash of the data with source and destination entities. The transaction identity uniquely identifies each transaction composed of hashing of the input data using SHA-256 and recipient of the public key. The private key of the sender is used for encryption, thus results in digital signature which aids in identification of source uniquely. The transaction will be discarded when there is any change in content of the block that affect the signature and the identity of the transaction.

The transaction can be confirmed only if valid blocks are present in ledger. The confirmed transactions are committed with the signature and the ledger entry is the input for next transaction. Every transaction in the public key hash system produces a redeemable output for the receiver node with authorization. This ensures the privacy preservation and unique identification. Only those nodes that can produce valid signature with the private key can claim the ownership. The trusted mode is embedded with consensus mechanism among the participating nodes which is proof of work. Each block consisting of nonce, the previous block hash value, and the list of transaction of the blockchain are hashed using Merkle root. In addition, it also embeds timestamp and block version.

The consensus algorithm is the decentralized and distributed technique used for the shared update of the next state sequences. This ensures the common agreement among the participating nodes on the present state of the distributed ledger. The various approaches that can be used to achieve consensus are Proof of Work (PoW), Practical Byzantine Fault Tolerance (PBFT) algorithm, Proof of Stake (PoS), Proof of Burn (PoB), Proof of Capacity, Proof of Authority (PoA), and Proof of Elapsed Time (PoET).

For block to be validated, each transaction of the current block is verified with the ownership claim and conforming to the chronological ordering to the occurrences and confirmation of references. The timestamp accuracy is verified with the genesis block and by proof of work, the current block is verified. Any node accepts the block only if all the transaction in the block is valid and added to its current block and proceed to the next block. The longest block chain is valid to solve the dispute among the miners for the validity of the block.

7.3   Quantum and Post-Quantum Cryptography

Quantum computing harnesses the quantum mechanism to perform the computational operations. Instead of binary functions, quantum probabilities are used as function for the computation. The entity that has physical existence in a quantum environment with two states being superpositioned among themselves that can be inferred by dual states simultaneously is the principle behind which quantum computers work, which is termed as quantum bits (qubits). The key principle of quantum computing is the transformation of data into quantum probabilities. Qubits are the hardware aspects and software is the quantum algorithm. Amplitudes are the probabilities of the quantum states with complex numbers. Generally, it is represented as $\alpha|0 + \beta|1$, with α and β are amplitudes. During synthesis, probability $|\alpha|^2$ is for 0 and probability $|\beta|^2$ for 1, then $|\alpha|^2 + |\beta|^2 = 1$.

Quantum algorithm is a transformed set of complex numbers through quantum gates. After transformation, similar the quantum gates are grouped based on amplitudes with the amplitude moduli added to 1. It is represented as reversible unitary matrix. Consider a sample ubiquitous quantum gate; Hadamard gate can be represented as in Equation (7.1).

$$H = \begin{pmatrix} \dfrac{1}{\sqrt{2}} & \dfrac{1}{\sqrt{2}} \\ \dfrac{1}{\sqrt{2}} & -\dfrac{1}{\sqrt{2}} \end{pmatrix} \qquad (7.1)$$

The most important quantum cryptographic algorithm is Shor's algorithm. This algorithm speeds up the factoring using discrete logarithms and elliptic curve discrete algorithms. It breaks all the symmetric key encryption algorithms employed in the Internet. It solves the group of problems, for example, Abelian hidden subgroup problem by exploiting the periodicity in the functions. Quantum Fourier Transform (QFT) is a unitary transform that acts on the quantum states that can be constructed in polynomial time. Consider an integer x, with $0 \leq x < y$ for some y. The QFT(x) is represented as in Equation (7.2) with the form $|x\rangle$ to

$$\frac{1}{\sqrt{y}} \sum_{n=0}^{y-1} |n\rangle e^{\frac{2\pi i n x}{y}} \qquad (7.2)$$

This sends

$$\sum_{j=0}^{y-1} x_j |j\rangle \rightarrow \sum_{n=0}^{y-1} a_k |k\rangle \qquad (7.3)$$

Grover's algorithm provides solution to the problem of finding the pre-calculated value of the function which is hard to revert. Consider the hash value of date is given, $y = H(x)$ and the function $H(x)$ can be implemented in quantum computations. Grover's algorithm aims to find x for the given hash function y within the time of $O(\sqrt{n})$ with n that represents the size of the valid hashes of the data. It works more efficiently than the brute force approach.

Post-quantum cryptography refers to public key crypto-algorithms to secure against quantum attacks. Most of the existing security algorithms are based on the mathematical operations like factorization, discrete logarithms and elliptic curve logarithms. These algorithms can be resolved using Shor's and Grover's algorithms. Various approaches have been proposed for post-quantum cryptography like multivariate, code-based, hash-based, supersingular elliptic curve isogency, lattice-based, and quantum resistance with symmetric key.

The recent advancement in the area of quantum-based cryptography is revolved around the concept of quantum key distribution (QKD), which is a random bit stream generated between the communicating parties. After communication establishment, the random message is taken as one-time pad (OTP) for encryption of the message. The secret key distribution is governed with quantum no-cloning theorem. With this randomized protocol, the encrypted message is cryptographically secure. QKD technique encompasses rectilinear and orthogonal bases [8] to avoid the redundancy of the qubits. Two channels, namely, the quantum and classical channels, are utilized for efficient data transmission with Huffman encoding. The secret key is generated using quantum channel and bit verification by classical channel. Trusted center is used for key generation and storage.

However, QKD suffers from technical limitations and barrier for acceptance. In OTP encryption, QKD must follow the key requirement that it should be in the message form to be encrypted with no reuse and randomness. It is a point-to-point key generation with slow rate. The QKD with OTP is a proven future proof of solution for post-quantum cryptography. The ideal characteristics for post-quantum in blockchain application are summarized as follows.

- Minimal key size
- Short sized signature and its hash value
- Faster computation
- Nominal computational complexity
- Minimal energy consumption

Hash functions are established as secure and cope to withstand quantum attacks compared to public key cryptosystem. Grover's algorithm accelerates the quantum attacks in two ways in the blockchain environment. The hash collision can be detected and replaced it with the entire block is not suitable for post-quantum computing. The integrity of the blockchain is undermined in which the entire block can be recreated fastly by Grover's algorithm. Shor's algorithm also has the impact on the hash function of the blockchain. If the hash function in the blockchain is broken, then digital signature can be forged with quantum computing and digital data will be stolen. NIST provides the classification of security levels for post-quantum cryptography, which is depicted in Table 7.1.

Table 7.1 NIST security levels.

NIST security levels	Equivalent symmetric key security
Category 1	128-bit key with search for key on block cipher
Category 2	256- bit hash function for collision search
Category 3	192-bit key with search for key on block cipher
Category 4	384- bit hash function for collision search
Category 5	256-bit key with search for key on block cipher

7.4 Post-Quantum Cryptosystems for Blockchain

The public key encryption along with digital signatures is superimposed to provide post-quantum cryptosystems for blockchain. It is mostly used for implementation of encryption and decryption mechanism and for signature of the transactions of the blockchain. The taxonomy of post-quantum cryptosystem for blockchain is depicted in Figure 7.2.

7.4.1 Public Key Post-Quantum Cryptosystems

7.4.1.1 Code-Based Cryptosystems

The error correction code is used in code-based cryptography. These algorithms explore the features of decoding linear codes and found to be robust against the quantum attacks with the increased factor of key size by 4. The best way to decode the data is to transform into low weight code world problem [9]. The general flow of code-based cryptosystem is depicted in Figure 7.2. The noise code is the cipher text and can be recovered to original data only by the genuine user. It is infeasible to solve the larger dimension of such problems. The most popular code-based cryptosystem is proposed by McEliece. It combines error checking with security measures against unauthorized access with high speed transformation [10]. In McEliece scheme, open key is represented as matrix $G_X = XMPD$, with generating matrix of X on algebraic code over the finite field. P and D are (nxn) permutation and diagonal matrix. Matrices X, P, and D are secret keys, which masks the algebraic code using random code. The attacker is represented

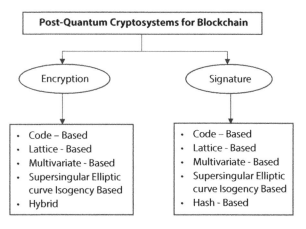

Figure 7.2 Post-quantum cryptosystems for blockchain.

Table 7.2 McEliece cryptosystem.

Parameters	The set of error correcting codes in linear binary form [n, k]
Generation of Key	(Key, value)-(G,Φ) Public Key: Matrix $M \in \{0,1\}^{kxn}$, spans over <G> Private Key: Decoder - Φ is a bounded factor for <G>
Encryption	$\{0,1\}^k, \rightarrow \{0,1\}^n$, with $X \rightarrow XG+e, e \in \{0,1\}^n$, Hamming weight in random
Decryption	$\{0,1\}^n, \rightarrow \{0,1\}^k$, G^* is the right reverse of G

by random formation of the linear code in the form of generating matrix with security of unknown efficient decoding algorithm. The approved user can remove the mask code with fast decoding algorithm using secret keys. The parameters used in McEliece cryptosystem is given in Table 7.2

The vector of length n is termed as cryptogram, which is calculated using the formulation, IG_x+e, where I is an information vector over finite field and e is secret key vector of weighted error, $W_h(e) \leq t, d = 2t+1$. The secret key vector e is per session-based and linked weight regulates the hardness of the decoded noise code. The attacker needs the coded data using the generating matrix. However, decoding with random code is unattainable and hence more secure without the secret keys. The process of code-based cryptosystem is shown in Figure 7.3.

Niederreiter cryptosystem [11] using binary Goppa codes speeds up the transformation process. The secret or open key is represented as $H_x = XHPD$ with validation matrix H of the algebraic code over the finite fields. The $(n–k) \times (n–k)$ is a degenerate matrix with P and D being permutation and diagonal matrix, respectively. Matrices X, P, and D are secret keys, which masks the algebraic code using random code. The authorized and unknown users have the same view as in McEliece cryptosystem. The data is first transformed in static environment of weights and validation matrix.

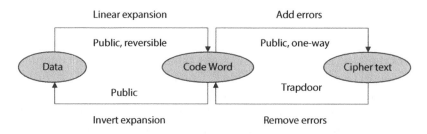

Figure 7.3 Code-based cryptosystem.

The maximum number of bits in data can be encrypted using Niederreiter cryptosystem is given by Equation (7.4). Let $w(e)=t$ be the weight with binary code (n, k, d) and the bits are transmitted.

$$S_{inf} = \left[\log_2 C_n^t \right] = \left[\log_2 \left(\frac{n!}{t!(n-t)!} \right) \right] \quad (7.4)$$

The major differences between McEliece and Niederreiter cryptosystems are generalized as follow.

- The information is placed in masked code word in McEliece cryptosystem, whereas, in Niederreiter cryptosystems, the information is placed by equilibrium encoding in the error vector code.
- Decoding in McEliece cryptosystem is removal of random error code vector, and, in Niederreiter cryptosystems, syndromic vector from masked vector and error vector code.

The main pitfall in the above cryptosystems is due to the large size of the matrices and need compression mechanism and use of different code blocks. Some of the coding mechanisms employed are Quasi-Cyclic Low Rank Parity Check (QCLRPC), Low Density Parity Check (LDPC), and other advanced coding mechanisms. ROLLO (Rank-Ouroboros, Lake, and Locker) is a code-based cryptosystem provide security against quantum and classical systems. ROLLO-II [12] is used as encryption scheme based on public key which is defined by three modules, namely, key generation, encryption, and decryption. λ is a security parameter used for key generation, and key public and private entities are given as output (p_k, s_k). Encryption provides cipher text for the given data, and decryption provides the plain text. P is irreducible polynomial over the finite field $\mathbb{P}_q [X]$ of power n which constitute the parameter for cryptosystems.

Key Generation: Pick (x, y) in the finite field, $\mathbb{P}_q [X]$. Sets $h = x^{-1} y \bmod P$ which returns the keys, $(p_k, s_k) = (h, (x, y))$.

Encryption (D, p_k): Pick (e_1, e_2) over the finite field and set support as $E = \text{Support} (e_1, e_2)$ $c = e_1 + e_2 h \bmod P$. Compute cipher text, $D \oplus Hash(E)$ and returns cipher text $C = (c, \text{cipher})$

Decryption (C, s_k): Sets $s = xc \bmod P$ with $F = \text{Support} (x, y)$ and $E = $ Rank Support Recover (F, s, r) and returns $D = cipher \oplus Hash(E)$

The proper family of codes provides restriction on the generation matrix G, and block circulant matrices are used for minimal storage of the required keys. The quasi-cyclic code is the code spanned by the block-circulant matrix. Each row in square matrix is the rotation of single item to the right of the previous row is the circulant matrix. When the index is small, the number of unknown decreases with quasi-cyclic code. The main advantage is the generator matrix and parity matrix can be represented as array of circulant which is dependent on first row. The other striking property is the isomorphism between the polynomial ring mod $x^n - 1$ and the circulant ring of $n \times n$. With these properties, efficient computations can be made with polynomial than with matrices.

Low-Density Parity Check is a linear code that consists of rows with constant Hamming codes below 10. Another class of code, Moderate density Parity Check (MDPC), consists of rows with larger weights in $O\left(n^{0.5} \log^{0.5} n\right)$ with the code word of length n. Quasi-cyclic MDPC McEliece cryptosystem consists of key pair generation with quasi-cycle of MDPC code $(n, n-r)$. The pair of generation matrix and error correction capability code forms the public key. The parity check matrix forms the private key. Encryption involves encoding data with error code to obtain code word. The ciphertext is obtained by generator matrix with error vector with weight t. Decryption is decoded by bit-oriented flipping algorithm.

Hamming quasi-cyclic cryptosystem (HQC) is based on Hamming metrics. The linear code for code word is denoted as [n, k] with generator matrix (G) for which the parity-check matrix (H) and the minimum distance for the code word is given by Equation (7.5).

$$d = \min_{u,v \in C,\ u \neq v} \omega(u-v) \tag{7.5}$$

ω is the norm over the code word (C), and u and v belong to G and H, respectively. Syndrome decoding is a decoding problem in which, for decoding, syndrome of the received vector is given rather than the received vector. The syndrome is a word selected from parity-check matrix with constraints. HQC encryption has four tuple polynomials, namely, setup, key generation, encrypt, and decrypt.

Setup: Provides the global parameters – $(n, k, \delta, \omega, \omega_r, \omega_e)$.

Key Generation: The generator matrix (G) based on code word and $s_k = (x, y) \in R$ such that $\omega(x) = \omega(y) = \omega$ and $p_k = (Sample, s = x + sample.y)$ and returns (s_k, p_k).

Encryption (p_k, D): Generates over the finite field of data with the $r = (r_1, r_2)$ and so the satisfied property of $\omega(r_1) = \omega(r_2) = w_r$ and provides (u, v). $u = r_1 + sample.r_2$ and $v = DG + s.r_2 + e$ and returns $c = (u, v)$.

Decryption (s_k, c): Returns the decoded word with syndrome of $(v - u.y)$.

7.4.1.2 Lattice-Based Cryptosystems

A periodic structural arrangement of points in a n-dimensional space is the lattice. The Lattice-Based Cryptosystem (LBC) is grounded on either the nearest vector formulation or the shortest vector formulation. LBC uses two-dimensional constructs based on linear algebra termed as lattice which is resistance to quantum attacks. Most of the LBC schemes uses shortest vector problem which requires the mechanism of finding a point in the grid that is close to the origin in the given space. With the increase in dimensions, quantum attacks are impossible. Lattice problems are NP-hard that is non-deterministic polynomial time problems. A lattice basis (B) with full rank is denoted as set of non-linear, independent vectors in the n-dimension vector space.

$$B = \{b_1, \ldots, b_n\}, b_k \in \mathbb{R}^n \tag{7.6}$$

The lattice L_B is a set of amalgamations of B, basis which is the linear combination of vectors across n-dimension space composed of vectors. The basis in the cryptography is the set of vectors that constitute the lattice to produce any point in the given grid. Based on the hidden hyper plane problem, post-quantum cryptosystem is formulated. The various LBC schemes available are Ajtai-Dwork cryptosystem, N-th degree Truncated (NTRU) and Learning with Errors (LWE) cryptosystem. Key generation embedded with encryption and decryption is also a component of these systems.

Key Generation
- Creation of optimal basis $\mathbb{R}$
- Use unimodular transformation, convert optimal basis $\mathbb{R}$ to noise basis $\mathbb{Q}$.
- The public basis is noise basis $\mathbb{Q}$, and $\mathbb{R}$ is private basis.

Encryption
- A lattice-based vector ω is chosen from $\mathbb{Q}$ and p, a plain text vector is added together.

- The cipher text, $c = \omega + p$ is sent as vector

Decryption
- Explore the closest lattice ω to c, the cipher text using R.
- Generate the plain text, $p = c - \omega$.

Ajtai-Dwork Cryptosystem [13] provides worst-case analysis of security attacks. This proposed work explores the correlation complexity analysis of average and worst case on the shortest vector problem. The lattice u is the non-zero shortest element that is unique, which becomes the approximation problem. Table 7.3 provides the security parameters, encryption, and decryption mechanisms.

The optimal selection of parameters is crucial for the precision level of the protocol used in cryptosystems. LWE [14] is closely related as sub-problems like search LWE and decision LWE. It is very hard to solve the lattice problem. The cryptosystem is parameterized by security parameter (n), noise parameter ($\alpha > 0$), modulus (q), and number of equations (m). The choice of parameters that guarantees correctness and security is given as follows. The modulus value is chosen as prime number between the range n^2 and $2n^2$. The number of equations is defined as $m = 1.1\ nlogq$ and noise parameter is $a = 1/\left(\sqrt{n}\log n\right)$.

Private key: Uniform vector s chosen from $\mathbb{P}_q^n$.
Public key: It consist of m samples $(u_i, v_i)_{i=1}^m$ obtained from LWE distribution using the parameters q, s, and α.

Table 7.3 Ajtai-Dwork cryptosystems.

Parameters	Integer n, m
Private keys	$s \in \mathbb{R}^n$
Public keys	A set of m random points, $\{a_i\}$ with i ranges from 1 to m and s, $a_i \approx 0\ mod\ 1$
Encryption	$0 \Rightarrow$ Generate a random point x in lattice vector $\mathbb{R}^n$, $1 \Rightarrow$ Consider a point y such that $\sum_{l \in y} y_l$
Decryption	Evaluate $\langle s, a_i \rangle$. By linearity, $r \approx 0$, decrypt the cipher text as 1, otherwise 0.

Encryption: Perform the following operation for each bit of the data. Let S be random set of samples chosen from the subsets of 2^m. Encryption for bit 0 is given by $(\sum_{i \in S} u_i, \sum_{i \in S} v_i,)$ and for bit 1 is given by $\left(\sum_{i \in S} u_i, \left\lfloor \frac{q}{2} \right\rfloor \sum_{i \in S} v_i, \right)$.

Decryption: For bit 0, the pair (u, v) if b is $\langle u,s \rangle$ chosen to 0 than to $\left\lfloor \frac{q}{2} \right\rfloor$ mod q, otherwise 0.

Polynomial rings can be used with the lattice for ideal lattice cryptosystems. In terms of key size and run times, NTRU method is more efficient. It provides protection against quantum attacks and used as substitute for other cryptosystems like RSA and elliptic curve systems. Lattice reduction algorithm can be used in place for basis reduction and keys.

7.4.1.3 Multivariate-Based Cryptosystem

This scheme relies on providing solution to the systems of multivariate equations which are NP-hard or NP-complete. Initial systems provide solving quadratic equations in the finite field and also use Frobenius automorphisms to achieve higher power consumption with the ease of generating public keys. Consider the polynomial $p(a)$ of degree n is irreducible over $\mathbb{H}_q$, the finite field. The n degree field extension is Q and can be defined as $\mathbb{H}_q(a)/p(a) \cong \mathbb{Q}$. The vector space isomorphism mapped as $\varphi : \mathbb{Q} \to \mathbb{H}_q^n$, defined as $\varphi(a_0 + a_1 x + \ldots + a_{n-1} x^{n-1}) = (a_0, a_1, \ldots, a_{n-1})$. The core map, $f \in \mathbb{Q}$, is proposed as $f(X) = X^{q+1}$. The generalized cryptosystem attributes are given in the following.

Private key: The affine transformations T and U defined as $H_q^n \to H_q^n$.
Public key: Defined by function $P = T \cdot \varphi^{-1} \cdot f \cdot \varphi \cdot U$ with $P_i \in \mathbb{H}_q[X] = \mathbb{H}_q[x_1, x_2, \ldots, x_n]$.
Encryption: The ciphertext, $y_i = P_i(x_1, x_2, \ldots, x_n)$ is obtained by plugging the plain text $(x_1, x_2, \ldots, x_n)$ in the public key equations
Decryption: With ciphertext, $(y_1, y_2, \ldots, y_n)$, the holder of private key can recover the plain text using the computations given in the following.

- Compute $(u_1, u_2, \ldots, u_n) = U^{-1}(y_1, y_2, \ldots, y_n)$
- Compute $(u_1', u_2', \ldots, u_n') = \varphi^{-1} \cdot f \cdot \varphi(u_1, u_2, \ldots, u_n)$
- Compute $(x_1, x_2, \ldots, x_n) = T^{-1}(u_1', u_2', \ldots, u_n')$

Hidden Field Equation (HFE) is a new multivariate scheme that aims to provide resistance against security attacks by new algorithms [15]. HFE uses the general polynomial with bounded degree D. The function can be described as shown in Equation (7.7).

$$f(x) = \sum_{\substack{q^i + q^j \leq D}}^{i \leq j} \alpha_{i,j} x^{q^i + q^j} + \sum_{q^i \leq D} \beta_i x^{q^i} + \gamma_i \qquad (7.7)$$

The new multivariate cryptosystem is EFLASH [16], which is based on big field scheme. This scheme is dependent on the multiplicative structure of the degree with the extension over the finite fields. Mostly, the function is quadratic in nature and can be expressed as in Equation (7.8). The various cryptanalysis techniques associated with this scheme are min rank, differential techniques, and algebraic formations.

$$\sum_{0 \leq i,\ j < d} \alpha_{i,j} x^{q^i + q^j} \qquad (7.8)$$

7.4.1.4   Supersingular Elliptic Curve Isogeny-Based Cryptosystems

In supersingular elliptic curves, the difficulty in finding the isogenies provides a new candidate public key cryptosystems in post-quantum arenas. The intuition behind it is the transmission of data of torsion bases under isogency, which allows the communicating parties to construct the shared commutative square under the assumption of non-commutativity of the ring structure with endomorphic identity. Consider the ECC E_1 and E_2 defined over $\mathbb{H}_q$. An isogeny is mapped as $\varphi : E_1 \to E_2$ over the field $\mathbb{H}_q$. It is a group homomorphism with $E_1(\mathbb{H}_q)$ to $E_2(\mathbb{H}_q)$ that is non-constant rational map defined over $\mathbb{H}_q$. A ring is formed by set of endomorphisms with the zero map with point-wise addition and composition and denoted as $End(e)$. A graph in which all nodes consist of all elliptic curve in $\mathbb{H}_q$ that belong to the class of fixed isogeny is termed as isogeny graph.

Supersingular Isogeny Key Encapsulation (SIKE) [17] provides secure scheme for asymmetric encryption. It comprises of triple KEM (key generation, encapsulation, and decapsulation). During generation of key, the input public parameters are concatenated with n-random bit integers (s) and a random integer (s3) with (p_k), the public key. The output is the private key (s_k). With public parameters and public keys as input, encapsulation outputs ciphertext (c_t) and the shared secret key (K). Decapsulation outputs the shared secret key with valid verification of ciphertext or random value with the failure. The main difference between the elliptic curve and SIKE is based on key exchange protocol, Diffie-Hellman mechanism [18]. The security of the system is enhanced with the complexity in finding a particular isogency between the two elliptic curves of finding the path between the elliptic curves in isogency graph.

The public key encryption based on SIKE is given as follow with the following phases: setup, key generation, and encryption followed by decryption. The secret parameter is E, the supersingular curve defined over $\mathbb{H}_q$, and the torsion point S is denoted as ℓ_A, that defines isogeny $\varphi : E \rightarrow E / \langle S \rangle$. The public parameters are $E / \langle S \rangle$ and E. The generators are P, Q, and their images $\varnothing(P), \varnothing(Q)$.

Setup: Choose a parameter $x = \ell_A \ell_B . f \pm 1, E_0, \{P_A, Q_A\}, \{P_B, Q_B\}$ with the hash function H for the data points

Key Generation: u_A, v_A are random elements not divisible by ℓ_A. Compute $E_A, \varnothing_A(P_B), \varnothing_A(Q_B)$ and choose a random number k. The public key is $(E_A, \varnothing_A(P_B), \varnothing_A(Q_B), k)$ and the private key is (u_A, v_A, k).

Encryption: Use public key $(E_A, \varnothing_A(P_B), \varnothing_A(Q_B), k)$ and data $y \in \{0,1\}^n$ $y \in \{0,1\}^n$ with two random numbers p_B, q_B not divisible by ℓ_B and compute

$$h = H_k\left(j(E_{AB})\right)$$

$$c = h \oplus y$$

The ciphertext is $(E_B, \varnothing_B(P_A), \varnothing_B(Q_A), c)$

Decryption: With ciphertext and private key (u_A, v_A, k), find the plain text or data as follows:

$$h = H_k\left(j(E_{AB})\right)$$

$$y = h \oplus c$$

Other scheme for Transport Layer Security (TLS) using handshake time is given by HRSS-SXY (Hulsing-Rijneveld-Schanck-Schwabe–Tsunekazu Saito–Keita Xagawa–Takashi Yamakawa) system. It is based on supersingular isogeny-based encapsulation of key. The difference in key size affects

Table 7.4 HRSS-SXY and SIKE.

KEM	Public key size (Bytes)	Ciphertext (Bytes)	Secret size (Bytes)	Key gen (op/s)	Encaps (op/s)	Decaps (op/s)
HRSS-SXY	1,138	1,138	32	3,952.3	7,6034.7	2,1905.8
SIKE	330	346	16	367.1	228.0	209.3

the handshake time and hence increases the complexity of the scheme for cryptography. Table 7.4 provides the different key sizes of HRSS-SXY and SIKE.

7.4.1.5   Hybrid Cryptosystems

Curve25519 [19] is based on elliptic curve with 128 bits of security and used for ECC and Diffie-Hellman key exchange mechanisms. X25519 is the function used for Diffie-Hellman key agreement. It is a key exchange or agreement scheme used in cryptographic protocols based on Montgomery curve. This is a safe curve and have many advantages over the other existing protocols based on secure elliptic curve. The public and private keys are represented by 32-bit strings. It requires masking for private keys and the public keys are derived from the secret key cannot be interchanged.

Combined ECC and Post-Quantum-2 (CECPQ2) [20] is the TLS-based quantum security developed by Google. It aggregates two mechanisms HRSS-SXY and X25519 for key exchange. CECPQ2 uses shared secret key of 32 bytes from HRSS and shared secret content from X25519 of 32 bytes. These keys are concatenated and form a secret key. The striking feature of the post-quantum key exchange mechanism is the larger public key size. This affects the duration of handshake duration in TLS connectivity. HRSS overcomes this faster execution order with larger key size. The improved version is CECPQ2b which combines SIKE and X25519. For TLS process, chrome canary acts as client side and Cloudflare acts as server side. With some experimental results conducted with the benchmark data, it is noticed that HRSS is more computational efficient thanX25519 on the server side and less on client side. The experimental results are shown in Table 7.5.

All the proposed hybrid systems seem soundful, and it requires more computational resources and energy consumption. Hence, there is a

Table 7.5 Performance of HRSS and X25519.

Operation area	HRSS-SXY (ops/s)	X25519 (ops/s)
Client side	3,099.6	11,707.2
Server side	69,437.9	11,707.2

trade-off between the complexity of the system and the resource requirements. When TLS is being used, size of the payload is also an influencing factor and plays a critical role. Based on the payload size, the security parameters and key sizes are also dependent on the communication attributes.

7.4.2   Post-Quantum Signing Algorithms

The main drawback with the public key cryptosystem is the compromised keys with the non-authentication of data. In the blockchain environment, to sign the transaction during transmission, public key cryptography is used and may have the vulnerable quantum attacks. The additional layer of security is provided in the blockchain environment with the hashed addresses. The various post-quantum attacks possible in the blockchain systems are given as follows.

- **Address reuse:** After signing of the transaction with the public key, which is revealed, it should not be reused for security purpose. However, some mining and pooling client reuse the address, which results in security pitfalls and exposure of the transaction.
- **In-flight transactions:** The broadcast of the transaction in the network and yet to be added in the blockchain is vulnerable to attacks. The private key of the attackers is used to sign the legitimate transaction and hence impossible to recover the transaction.
- **Failure/rejected transactions:** When a particular transaction is rejected or failed due to the malicious users or underfitting of the security constraints, there is a possibility of security attacks on keys.
- **Transaction mixing/multisign transaction:** With the advanced join protocols of blockchain, the keys will be revealed before the transaction is finalized by other communicating parties of the network.

7.4.2.1   Code-Based Cryptosystems

One of the code-based cryptosystems that is quantum secure is Fiat-Shamir signatures. It is based on zero knowledge proof of knowledge with sigma protocol. It uses transformation of identification schemes to signatures. It also allows the formation of group signature from the public and private key revealing and construction of more advanced signatures. The identification scheme is the sigma protocol which is a three-message protocol. The message, *com* called commitment, is sent to the verifier for authentication by the prover. The random challenge, *ch*, is sent to the prover as response by the verifier. The prover sends his response, resp and is checked by verifier (*com,ch,resp*) for valid interactions. The hash function is used for creating the challenge as $ch = H(x \| com)$ for the data x. This results in the production of the code for the verifier rather than that of random challenges.

Based on Goppa codes, small quantum machines can be assisted in generating Courtois-Finiasz-Sendrier (CFS) signatures [21]. This scheme brings the code-based cryptosystems based on signatures based on syndrome decoding. To sign a data, error vector is created using the hash function. This decodable error vector is not approved by the hash function. The decodable vector is obtained by appending counter with the data with the counter is increment till the vector is valid. The computational complexity lies in finding a decodable hash from the counter value. For the error vector of n-bits with 1-bit t, the decodable syndromes are given as $\binom{n}{t}$ for the aggregation with the error vector in total of 2^m with the assumption of $n \approx 2^m$. The decodable syndrome density is given by Equation (7.9).

$$\frac{\binom{n}{t}}{2^{mt}} \approx \frac{\frac{n^t}{t!}}{2^{mt}} \approx \frac{\frac{n^t}{t!}}{n^t} \approx \frac{1}{t!} \tag{7.9}$$

7.4.2.2   Lattice-Based Cryptosystems

Short Integer Solution (SIS) used in lattice-based cryptosystems based on Gaussian Elimination technique. The collision resistance hash function can be obtained using SIS. SIS problem is similar to finding the small vector in the lattice for the solution of integers which is a hard problem. The m random vectors are given, $x_i \in \mathbb{Z}$, the aim is to find the non-zero solutions of system of linear equations. Consider $A \in \mathbb{Z}$ is an *nxn* matrix consist of uniform random vectors. The small non-zero vector (x) can be found in the dimension of lattice space; the following constraints have to be satisfied.

$$\|x\| \le \beta$$

$$f_A(x) = Ax = 0 \in \mathbb{Z}$$

Bimodal Lattice Signature Scheme (BLISS) is based on modified rejection sampling algorithm and other lattice primitives. The rejection sampling algorithm that samples the bimodal Gaussian distribution with modified instantiation results in reduced standard deviation of the obtained signatures which is asymptotically equal to square root of security parameters. The striking features of BLISS are low rejection rate, memory-efficient Gaussian sampling and signature compression. According to discrete Gaussian scheme, the coefficients of the signature polynomials are distributed, the final signature can be compressed using Huffman coding.

Secret key: S
Public key: A such that $qI = AS \bmod 2q$
Sign(μ):
Pick a random y
Compute $c = H(Ay \bmod 2q, \mu)$
Choose random x in $\{-1,1\}$
$z = xSc + y$
Output (z,c)
Verify (z, c)
Check z is small and $c = H(Ax - qc \bmod 2q, \mu)$

Blind Signature (BS) is a privacy-oriented cryptography using hard lattice problem and have merits over discrete logarithms and factoring problems. BS allows the signer to sign the information without exposing it with constraint on number of signed signatures. The receiver of the signature provides anonymity with their closed transaction. Three procedures used are key generation, signature protocol, and signature verification. The interactive protocol between the signer (S) and verifier (U) is the signature protocol.

Key generation $Kg(1^n)$: The signing key (S_k) is private and verification key (p_k) which is public are output of this phase
Signature protocol $Sign(s_k, D)$: It is described by joint execution of the signer and the verifier. The output is view (V), private of output of signer.

The signature d on the information D under (S_k) is the private output of verifier. It is represented as $(V,d) \leftarrow \langle S(s_k), U(p_k, D) \rangle$

Signature verification: Depends on validness of signature for information D under p_k, outputs 1, otherwise 0.

7.4.2.3 Multivariate Based Cryptosystem

In multivariate cryptosystem, the generation of public key is done using trap door function. This function acts as private key and hence large number of public keys with lesser signatures. Identity-based signature (IBS) consists of tuple of polynomial, namely, setup, key derivation, sign, and V_f. The setup procedure is executed by the trusted key distribution center to generate master mp_k, which is public, while the private key is ms_k. The key derivation algorithm acts on input ms_k and user identity id to generate secret signing key us_k. With the input of (us_k, M), the signing algorithm returns the signature σ for the message M. The verification algorithm V_f with the input (mp_k, id, M, σ) returns 1 if valid signature is valid for user identity and message, otherwise return 0.

The first signature scheme with security reduction is MQDSS, based on providing solutions for quadratic equations of multivariate systems. It achieves post-quantum security of 128 bits. The parameters of MQDSS are security parameter k and m, n that provides security levels. The hash function for cryptography is given by $H : \{0,1\}^* \rightarrow \{0,1\}^k$. The algorithm that generate signature takes the input of secret key and message provides message digest. A Great Multivariate Short Signature (GeMSS) results in production of small signatures. It has large/medium public key with fast verification process. It requires the spanning over the two finite fields to extract the roots of the polynomial. The secret key is given by (F, S, T) with polynomial F and degree S and T. The polynomial is of the form as expressed in Equation (7.10).

$$F = \sum A_{ij} \cdot X^{2^i + 2^j} + \sum \beta_i (v_1, \dots v_v) \cdot X^{2^i} + \gamma(v_1, \dots v_v) \quad (7.10)$$

7.4.2.4 Supersingular Elliptic Curve Isogency-Based Cryptosystem

Supersingular elliptic curve isogenies can also be used for creation of post-quantum digital signature. The Unruh transformation is used for producing smaller key size and with 128-bit level of security, 336 bytes of public key, 48 bytes of private key, and 122,880 bytes of signature. Key size is an issue with implementation isogency-based systems. Consider Σ as the isogency-based zero-knowledge proof of identity and apply Unruh's transformation to obtain the (P_{OE}, V_{OE}), proof identity which is non-interactive (P_{OE}, V_{OE}) and is used to generate digital signature.

Security parameters: Prime number $P = \ell_A^{eA} \ell_B^{eB} f \pm 1$ with supersingular curve E, generator (P_B, Q_B) of the torsion group $E[\ell_B^{eB}]$.

Key generation: Select a random point S and compute isogency $\varphi: E \to E/\langle S \rangle$ with the output of key pair (p_k, s_k).

Signing: Message m is signed as $Sign(s_k, m) = P_{OE}((p_k, m), s_k)$.

Verification: The signature σ is verified for the message as $Verify(p_k, m, \sigma) = V_{OE}(((p_k, m), \sigma))$.

7.4.2.5   Hash-Based Cryptosystem

Lamport One-Time Signature Scheme (LOTSS) has the public key that can be used only one time to sign a particular message. Its security features depend on the complexity of the hash function. The three phases of the scheme are key generation, signing and verification.

Key generation: Choose random number R_{ij}, $1 \leq i \leq k$ and $j = \{0, 1\}$. Compute $S_{ij} = Hash(R_{ij})$. The private key is R_{ij} and the public key is S_{ij}.

Signing: The message M is converted into bits $M = (m_1, \ldots m_k)$ of 0 and 1 bits. For 0 bit in M, $sig_i = X_{i0}$ and for bit 1, $sig_i = X_{i1}$. The final signature is given by $sig = sig_1 \ldots .. sig_k)$.

Verification: For each i, compute the hash value $H(Sig_i)$. For message with bit 0, hash value must be $H(Sig_i) = S_{i0}$; otherwise, $H(Sig_i) = S_{i1}$

Merkle tree Signature Scheme (MSS) uses LOTSS to generate multiple keys for signing multiple messages simultaneously. It uses binary hash tree with leaf nodes consist of hash value of LOTSS public key. The value in the internal node is obtained by the hash of its two children. The authentication of the leaf node is provided by the root node. The level of the tree is given by H. The one-time key pair is (U_i, V_i), $0 \leq i \leq 2^H)$. The signature key is U_i and the verification key is V_i. The public key is the root of MSS tree. The message M is signed using one of the key pairs. The signature is defined as $SIG = (sig, LOTSS_i, A_i)$ with the authentication path A_i. The verification is done with on the message M. If the leaf node produces the hash value $LOTSS_i$ matches with the value computed by the root, then the signature is accepted, otherwise rejected.

The other hash-based method is SPHINCS which signs message using Winternitz one-time signature and authenticated using FORS tree. The security parameter is n, signature parameter is w, height of the hypertree is h, d is the layers in hypertree with tree count in FORS; and k and t are the count of leaves in FORS tree. It uses four hash functions for signing and verification. This is a stateless hash-based post-quantum cryptosystem and can sign more than hundreds of messages per second.

7.5   Other Cryptosystems for Post-Quantum Blockchain

QChain is an infrastructure based on public key that uses blockchain that is resistant to quantum attacks. The quantum-resistant primitive is LWE as shown in Figure 7.4. The ring-LWE and the polynomial ring are defined with polynomial degree with irreducible degree of n−1 is used for encryption with public key. The standard deviation σ in Discrete Gaussian distribution is used for error distribution. Number Theoretic Transformation (NTT) is employed for efficient encryption time and denoted as $\tilde{z} = NTT(z)$. For cryptography, nonce is defined from $nonce \leftarrow \{0,1\}^n$ and random number is given by $rand \leftarrow \{0,1\}^n$. Table 7.6 provides post quantum cryptosystem provided by NIST. Further comparative analysis of different cryptographic techniques are explored in Table 7.7

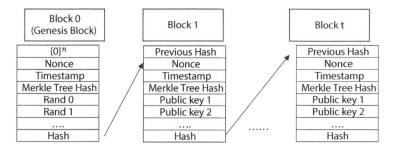

Figure 7.4 Structure of QChain.

Table 7.6 Summary of post-quantum cryptosystems and key encapsulation for Round 1 and Round 2 by NIST.

PCS	Hard problems	Sign	KEM	Total
Lattice	Find shortest and closest vector	5(3)	23(9)	28(12)
Code	Decoding of linear code with randomness	3(0)	17(7)	20(7)
Multivariate	Solution of multivariate quadratic equations	8(4)	2(0)	10(4)
Hash	Resistance of hash function to second pre image	3(2)	0(0)	3(2)
Others	-	0(0)	1(1)	1(1)
Total	-	**21(9)**	**48(17)**	**69(26)**

7.6 Conclusion

The recent advancement in post-quantum cryptosystems for blockchain has sparked the real-time applications and research interests. The hash function and public keys in distributed ledger scheme is important and hence scope for quantum attacks. These attacks can be mitigated by post-quantum cryptosystems based on public key encryption and digital signatures. This article provides the broader view on the existing literature and comparative analysis on the recent advancement in the field of blockchain and post-quantum cryptosystems.

Table 7.7 Comparative Analysis of different post-quantum cryptosystems.

	Hash-based signatures	Multivariate cryptography	Code-based cryptography	Lattice-based cryptography
General Point of Interest	Building block is one-time signature mechanism. A single message is signed securely with one-time signature.	It depends on the complexity of solution of system with multivariate polynomial security equations.	Private key is associated with error-correcting code and public key error and scrambled version of the code. The complexity of the generated linear codes provides the security.	Security is provided by complexity in finding the closest point in a lattice in the given dimension with the given arbitrary point in the space.
Schemes	Sign	Sign encryption and hash	Sign encryption	Sign, Encryption, and Hash with identity and encryption with homomorphism
Security Reduction	Collision resistant	Invertible code	Solution of multivariate polynomial equations	Good basis in the multidimensional space of points for lattice

(Continued)

Table 7.7 Comparative Analysis of different post-quantum cryptosystems. (*Continued*)

	Hash-based signatures	Multivariate cryptography	Code-based cryptography	Lattice-based cryptography
Theoretical speeds	Hash function dependent	Hardware oriented	Hardware oriented	Software oriented
Practical speeds	Extremely fast	Good	Good	Good
Advantages	The fastest method and modular approach	Secured mechanism with well-defined modules	Key size is smaller with faster computation	Highly secure with more flexibility
Disadvantages	Works with sign, need larger footprint	Memory intensive with less security	Insecure	Low Security

References

1. Gao, Y.-L. *et al.*, A secure cryptocurrency scheme based on post-quantum blockchain. *IEEE Access*, 6, 27205–27213, 2018.

2. Suhail, S., Hussain, R., Khan, A., & Hong, C. S., On the role of hash-based signatures in quantum-safe internet of things: Current solutions and future directions. *IEEE Internet Things J.*, 8, 1, 1–17, 2020.

3. Fernández-Caramés, T.M. and Fraga-Lamas, P., Towards post-quantum blockchain: A review on blockchain cryptography resistant to quantum computing attacks. *IEEE Access*, 8, 21091–21116, 2020.

4. Ali, I. *et al.*, A blockchain-based certificateless public key signature scheme for vehicle-to-infrastructure communication in VANETs. *J. Syst. Archit.*, 99, 101636, 2019.

5. Aumasson, J.-P., The impact of quantum computing on cryptography. *Comput. Fraud Secur.*, 2017, 6, 8–11, 2017.

6. Gilliam, A., Pistoia, M., Gonciulea, C., Optimizing quantum search using a generalized version of Grover's algorithm. 06468, 2020. arXiv preprint arXiv:2005.

7. Martínez, V.G., Hernández-Álvarez, L., Encinas, L.H., Analysis of the Cryptographic Tools for Blockchain and Bitcoin. *Mathematics*, 8, 1, 131, 2020.

8. Xu, F. *et al.*, Secure quantum key distribution with realistic devices. *Rev. Modern Phys.*, 92, 2, 025002, 2020.

9. Bernstein, D.J., Introduction to post-quantum cryptography, in: *Post-quantum cryptography*, pp. 1–14, Springer, Berlin, Heidelberg, 2009.

10. Baldi, M. *et al.*, Enhanced public key security for the McEliece cryptosystem. *J. Cryptol.*, 29, 1, 1–27, 2016, Fort Lauderdale, USA.

11. Wang, W., Szefer, J., Niederhagen, R., *FPGA-based Niederreiter cryptosystem using binary Goppa codes. in International Conference on Post-Quantum Cryptography.* pp. 77–98, Springer, Cham, 2018.

12. Lablanche, J. *et al.*, Optimized implementation of the NIST PQC submission ROLLO on microcontroller. *IACR Cryptol. ePrint Arch.*, 2019, 787, 2019.

13. Asif, R., Post-quantum cryptosystems for Internet-of-Things: a survey on lattice-based algorithms. *IoT*, 2, 1, 71–91, 2021.

14. Grilo, A.B., Kerenidis, I., Zijlstra, T., Learning-with-errors problem is easy with quantum samples. *Phys. Rev. A*, 99, 3, 032314, 2019.

15. Ping, Y. *et al.*, Building Secure Public Key Encryption Scheme from Hidden Field Equations. *Secur. Commun. Netw.*, 2017, 2017.

16. Cartor, R. and Smith-Tone, D., EFLASH: a new multivariate encryption scheme, in: *International Conference on Selected Areas in Cryptography*, Springer, 2018.

17. Azarderakhsh, R. *et al.*, *Supersingular isogeny key encapsulation*, Submission to the NIST Post-Quantum Standardization project, 2017.

18. Campagna, M. *et al.*, Supersingular isogeny key encapsulation, 2019.

19. Salarifard, R. and Bayat-Sarmadi, S., An efficient low-latency point-multiplication over curve25519. *IEEE Trans. Circuits Syst. I: Regul. Pap.*, 66, 10, 3854–3862, 2019.
20. Kwiatkowski, K. *et al.*, Measuring TLS key exchange with post-quantum KEM. *Workshop Record of the Second PQC Standardization Conference*, 2019, https://csrc. nist. gov/CSRC/media/Events/Second-PQC-Standardization-Conference/documents/accepted-papers/kwiatkowski-measuring-tls.pdf.
21. Possignolo, R.T., Margi, C.B., Barreto, P.S., Quantum-assisted QD-CFS signatures. *J. Comput. Syst. Sci.*, 81, 2, 458–467, 2015.

8

Post-Quantum Confidential Transaction Protocols

R. Manjula Devi[1]*, P. Keerthika[1], P. Suresh[2], R. Venkatesan[3], M. Sangeetha[1], C. Sagana[1] and K. Devendran[1]

[1]Department of Computer Science and Engineering, Kongu Engineering College, Perundurai, Erode, India
[2]Department of Information Technology, Kongu Engineering College, Perundurai, Erode, India
[3]Department of Computer Science and Engineering, Karunya Institute of Technology and Sciences, Coimbatore, India

Abstract

In recent years, much extraordinary progress has been achieved in the advancement of Quantum computers due to tremendous speed up in processing. However, the threat of large-scale impact on society has led to widespread initiatives to develop new cryptographic algorithms, standards, and migration paths, which are collectively referred to as "post-quantum cryptography". The concept of a Zero-Knowledge Protocol (ZKP) along with its noninteractive variants has been surveyed and well explained. Providing the deep insight of the protocols adapted for confidential transaction in post-quantum cryptography by applying zero-knowledge proof is the major purpose of this chapter.

Keywords: Quantum computers, zero-knowledge protocol, zero knowledge proof, post-quantum cryptography, confidential transactions, interactive ZKP, non-interactive ZKP, quantum blockchain

8.1 Introduction

In recent years, much extraordinary progress has been achieved in the advancement of quantum computers due to tremendous speed up in

---

*Corresponding author: rmanjuladevi.gem@gmail.com

Rajesh Kumar Dhanaraj, Vani Rajasekar, SK Hafizul Islam, Balamurugan Balusamy and Ching-Hsien Hsu (eds.) Quantum Blockchain: An Emerging Cryptographic Paradigm, (201–220)

processing. Quantum computers are the computers that perform quantum computations. Simply put, quantum computers are extremely advanced devices that make use of quantum mechanics to find solutions for complex mathematical problems that are almost impossible to solve for regular computers. Quantum computers provide unprecedented computational powers, such that almost all current public key cryptosystems will be cracked. As a result, the development of a fully functional quantum computer will significantly compromise the confidentiality and integrity of the digital communications and transactions that happens on the internet and elsewhere. It offers significant potential for science and society as a result of technological advancement in large-scale quantum computing, but it also poses a challenge to the current state of standardized public key cryptosystems. The impact extends across security for the internet, IoT devices, and legal infrastructure based on the currently used cryptographic systems and everything from our financial transactions to our private email messages. Systems and solutions that are regarded as reasonably secure today may become weakened or broken, and the data contained in these systems may suddenly be compromised if sufficiently powerful quantum computers become available in the future. Quantum computing devices that exist today are limited, and innovation progress is rapid. However, the threat of large-scale impact on society has led to widespread initiatives to develop new cryptographic algorithms, standards, and migration paths, which are collectively referred to as "post-quantum cryptography".

The following terms such as quantum-resistant, quantum-proof, or quantum-safe cryptography are used as the equivalent term of "post-quantum cryptography". The fore-mentioned term is a cryptographic algorithm, which has been developed to secure against an attack from both quantum and classical computers [1]. It is the encryption systems that are not easily cracked through the use of quantum computers. Even after a large-scale quantum computer is installed, it yearns to keep the communications, business processes, transactions, and information safe and secure. The goal is to update existing mathematical-based algorithms and standards in order to prepare for the quantum computing age.

8.2   Confidential Transactions

"Confidential transactions" is abbreviated as CTs. The general idea of CTs was proposed first by Adam Back who is CEO of Blockstream on BitcoinTalk in 2013, which aims to make the content of a transaction private. It was built in order to improve the blockchain's cryptosystem mechanism. CTs facilitate this by allowing specific information to be written in a format that both parties can understand easily. External actors, on the other hand, would only see encoded, unintelligible data.

Definition 1 (Confidential Transaction). The following data constitutes a CT:

- Input: A list of references, which is extremely clear, to other transactions' outputs, as well as signatures based on such outputs' authentication keys.
- Output: A list that contains Pedersen commitment to an amount, a verification key, and Back-Maxwell range proof whose value lies in $[0, 2^n - 1]$. Here, the value of n is significantly smaller than the committed-value group's bit length.
- A fee f, which is listed explicitly

8.2.1 Confidential Transaction Protocol

A CT protocol is a cryptographic protocol that encrypts the value of amount of a transaction. It is represented as a Zero-Knowledge Protocol (ZKP), which is cryptographic protocol designed to enhance security and anonymity in the cryptocurrency transactions on a private blockchain. This protocol is used in the application that allows transactions to be encrypted or encrypted within a network. The actual amounts of each transaction carried out cannot be viewed, even if they may be checked and validated within the network. It is also concealed from the issuers and recipients of such transactions. The encryption is unique in that it allows you to check that no bitcoins were generated or lost during a transaction while keeping the transaction amounts private. CTs keep the amount and type of assets transferred visible only to participants in the transaction.

8.3 Zero-Knowledge Protocol

Zero-knowledge proof is another name for ZKP. Based on the fact that "there is no ("zero") knowledge revealed about the secret", the term "zero knowledge" has been originated. During 1980s, Shafi Goldwasser, Silvio Micali, and Charles Rackoff who are researchers at MIT have suggested an encryption scheme. It is unique mathematical methods that will verify the data without unveiling or sharing that underlying data in a transaction. A "prover" and a "verifier" are the two entities involved each transaction. During the transaction, the prover tries to persuade and show that a particular statement is valid to the verifier. In this transaction, only the validity of the statement is revealed details to the verifier. The prover shows that they can compute anything without disclosing the input or the computational method by supplying the final result. The verifier, on the other hand, only learns about the output.

8.3.1   Properties

A language, L, is a collection of strings which is made up of binary alphabet $\Sigma = \{0,1\}$ that have meaning of $L \subseteq \{0, 1\}^*$. Then, the tuple (x, L) or more intuitively, $x \in L$ makes up the statement.

A zero-knowledge proof must satisfy the following three properties: completeness, soundness, and zero-knowledge.

1. **Completeness:**
   The verifier would "always" agree without the need for external assistance if the assertion is true and everyone follows the rules.
2. **Soundness**
   If the statement is false, then the verifier will "always" reject it. That means, the verifier cannot be convinced by cheating prover in any scenario that the prover's knowledge is correct, but it has a lower chance of being correct.
3. **Zero-Knowledge**
   In both cases, no additional details is provided by the prover to the verifier other than whether the argument is true or false, i.e., it shows nothing more to the verifier.

8.3.2   Types

The two different kinds of zero-knowledge proof: interactive and non-interactive.

8.3.2.1   Interactive Zero-Knowledge Proof

An interactive zero-knowledge proof uses statistical probability to persuade the verifier by the prover about the specific fact through a sequence of acts. It necessitates the verifier continuously asking a series of questions about the prover's "knowledge". Both the verifier and the prover have to be online at the same time for the "interactive" method to work, making it difficult to scale up on the real world application.

Definition 1 (Zero-Knowledge Interactive Proof). Let language L ∈ NP and ⟨P, V⟩ denote a protocol between a (possibly unbounded computational power) prover P and a [Probabilistic Polynomial Time (PPT)] verifier V. Let p(.) be polynomial. Whenever the succeeding three properties are fulfilled, ⟨P, V⟩ is s said to be interactive proof method for L.

- **Completeness:**
  If $x \in L$, then Verifier, V, should be persuaded by an honest prover, P, by simply following the protocol specifications.

  $\forall x \in L,$

  $$Pr[\langle P(x,w), V(x) \rangle = 1] \geq 1 - \frac{1}{p(|x|)}$$

  Let P(x, w) be a prover P who is honest and unbounded with input (x, w).
  Let P(x,w) be an unbounded honest prover P whose input is (x, w) and NP witness, w of x.

- **Soundness:**
  If $x \notin L$, then verifier, V, should not be persuaded by any prover, P, if he or she would actually cheat by deviating from the protocol specification.

  $\forall x \notin L, \forall P^*$

  $$Pr\left[\langle P'(x,w), V(x) \rangle = 1\right] < 1 - \frac{1}{p(|x|)}$$

- **(Computational) Zero-Knowledge:** $\forall V^*, \exists (PPT) Sim_{V^*}$ s.t $\forall x \in L,$

  $$View[\langle P(x, w) \leftrightarrow V^*(x) \rangle] \approx_c Sim_{V^*}(x)]$$

  Let $V^*(x)$ be a PPT verifier V^* who is dishonest with x as an input.
  where *Sim* is represented as simulator.

8.3.2.2 Non-Interactive Zero-Knowledge Proof (NIZKP)

As the name implies, NIZKP is a zero-knowledge proof in which there is no need of the interaction between the prover and the verifier [2]. It avoids the possibility of collusion because the verifier and the prover need not to be online at the same time. Instead, the prover will issue all of the challenges at once, with the verifier(s) responding later. It does, however, necessitate some additional structure: a string (σ) which is a random and publicly trusted by both Prover and Verifier.

Definition 2 (Non-Interactive Zero-Knowledge Proof). Let $L \in NP$. Let $\langle P, V \rangle$ be a protocol specification between a (possibly unbounded computational power) prover P and a (PPT) verifier V. Let p(.) be polynomial. Then, $\langle P, V \rangle$ is said to be a non-interactive proof system for L if the following three properties are satisfied:

- **Completeness:**

$$\forall x \in L,$$

$$Pr[\langle P(\sigma, x, w), V(\sigma, x) \rangle = 1] \geq 1 - \frac{1}{p(|x|)}$$

- **Soundness:** $\forall x \notin L, \forall P^{\star}$

$$Pr[\langle P'(\sigma, x, w), V(\sigma, x) \rangle = 1] < 1 - \frac{1}{p(|x|)}$$

- **(Computational) Zero-Knowledge:** $\forall V^{\star}, \exists (PPT) Sim_{V^{\star}}$ s.t $\forall x \in L,$

$$View[\langle P(\sigma, x, w) \leftrightarrow V^{\star}(\sigma, x) \rangle] \approx_{c} Sim_{V^{\star}}(x)$$

where *Sim* is represented as simulator

8.3.2.2.1   NIZKP for Authentication

Authentication protocols that are currently in use strive for creating authenticated sessions which are insecure during the consumption of minimal energy and incurring minimal computational overheads. Traditional authentication schemes require the devices to store some type of authentication data with risk basis. Approaches that rely solely on private/public key infrastructure with additional have costs for computing and maintenance. A new scheme has been proposed in order to exchange the information that is confidential in an insecure environment based on NIZKPs within IoT. Here, relevant data can be inferred from a single communication to verify the sender's legitimacy [3]. Since the topology in Mobile Ad hoc Networks (MANETs) is getting changed in a very frequent manner, Authentication is difficult and challenging task. In central authority–based authentication schemes, central authority requires re-authentication of nodes for every movement of a node beyond the network and before the node rejoins the network. To achieve re-authentication, a new NIZKP has been proposed, which performs neighborhood authentication on the node that are ready to rejoin the network. This reduces reliance on the central authority for re-authentication, reducing the risk of re-authentication-related attacks [4]. To provide authentication in resource-constrained IoT settings, a new authentication protocol using the idea of NIZKP has been proposed [5]. It takes into account the limitations of devices and sensors used for IoT communication. For the development of the authentication issue, our protocol takes into account about the instability of the inherent network and replaces NP-hard problem with the Merkle tree structure. Using graph isomorphism, NIZKP's performance was compared to that of conventional ZKP approaches. The DS-NIZKP scheme (expanded as an NIZKP-based solution with digital signature) is used to perform node authentication [6]. To provide zero-knowledge and authentication of both the sender and the message, this method uses a digital signature with a hash function. In a static deployment of Wireless Sensor Networks (WSNs) with an index-based data dissemination scheme, a protection scheme has been implemented to provide confidentiality, integrity of data, and authentication at end-entity among peers. It has two distinct features: mutual authentication via a digital signature scheme and hash function during the integration of public key transport mechanism with complementary key negotiation protocol [7].

8.3.3   Zero-Knowledge Proof for Graph Isomorphism

Assume that the prover wants to show that two graphs G1 and G2 are isomorphic and that the prover does indeed know an isomorphism. Now, the definition of graph isomorphism is given below.

Definition 3 (Graph Isomorphism). Let $G = (V_1, E_1)$ and $H = (V_2, E_2)$ be two graphs with $|V_1| = |V_2| = n$. G and H are said to be isomorphic if and only if a permutation $\pi \in S_n$ occurs between them such that $\{u, v\} \in E_1$ iff $\{\pi(u), \pi(v)\} \in E_2$.

Algorithm

Let $G_1 = (V_1, E_1)$, $G_2 = (V_2, E_2)$ represent two graphs as the protocol's input. The prover knows the permutation π^* that results in $\pi^*(G_1) = G_2$. Without showing the permutation π^*, the prover needs to persuade the verifier that the graphs are isomorphic.

- The prover chooses a permutation $\pi_R : V \rightarrow V$ at random and sends the graph.
- The prover receives b from the verifier, who chooses a random $b \in \{1, 2\}$.
- If $b = 1$, and $\pi_R \circ (\pi^*)^{-1}$, then the prover sends back π_R.
- Otherwise, if the previous round's permutation π is such that $(Gb) = G$ after checking, then the verifier accepts it.

Theorem 1. Let the prover algorithm be represented as P and the verifier algorithm is represented as V in the above protocol. Then,

- Completeness: The interaction ends when the verifier accepts with probability 1 if G_1 and G_2 are not isomorphic.
- Soundness: The interaction ends when the verifier accepts with probability ½ if G_1 and G_2 are isomorphic for every alternative prover strategy P* of arbitrary complexity.

8.3.4   Zero-Knowledge Proof for Graph Non-Isomorphism

The graph non-isomorphism (GNI) problem has been solved using a zero-knowledge proof system.

Algorithm

Let $G_1 = (V_1, E_1)$, $G_2 = (V_2, E_2)$ be two graphs that are used as inputs in a game with two players exchanging information. The prover's aim is to persuade the verifier that these two graphs G1 and G2 are not isomorphic. Herewith, the list of the steps involved in the ZKP is shown in the following:

- Common input: $G_1 = (V_1, E_1)$, $G_2 = (V_2, E_2)$ be two graphs that are used as an input of a game
- The prover is attempting to persuade the verifier that they are not isomorphic.

- The prover receives $G=\pi(G_b)$ from the verifier, who chooses a random $b \in \{1, 2\}$ and a permutation $\pi : V \rightarrow V$.
- Prover determined the bit $a \in \{1, 2\}$ and send that bit a to the verifier which leads G_a and G are isomorphic
- If a = b, then the verifier accepts the result.

Theorem 1. Let the prover algorithm be represented as P and the verifier algorithm is represented as V in the above protocol. Then,

- Completeness: The interaction ends when the verifier accepts with probability 1 if G_1 and G_2 are not isomorphic.
- Soundness: The interaction ends when the verifier accepts with probability ½ if G_1 and G_2 are isomorphic for every alternative prover strategy P* of arbitrary complexity.

8.3.5   Zero-Knowledge Proof for NP-Complete Problems

All problems belonging to the class of non-deterministic polynomial time (NP) decision problems have interactive zero-knowledge proofs if there is a stable encryption scheme that is secure [8]. NIZKP systems have been announced, and it was shown that they exist in NP for all languages [9]. Kilian developed the first scheme for NP that attains poly-logarithmic communication based on interactive zero-knowledge proof [10].

8.3.5.1   *Three-Coloring Problem*

Graph Three-Coloring is NP-complete problem. A graph G is three-colorable if its vertices may be colored with only three colors and no two vertices of the same color are connected by an edge. The definition of three-coloring problem is given below:

Definition 4 (Three-Coloring Problem). Let an n-verticed graph be symbolized as G = (V, E), and the vertex set is symbolized as V={1,…, n}. The three-coloring problem entails determining whether or not there is a coloring function $\phi:V \mapsto \{1, 2, 3\}$ as a result $\phi(u) \neq \phi(v)$ for any edge {u, v} $\in$ E.

Algorithm
Let G = (V, E) represent the graph as an input to the protocol. The graph, G, is known by the verifier as well as the prover. In the protocol, the prover is given a private input called the witness, which is a three-coloring of

the graph G. For three-coloring problem, below is the sequence of step involved in the zero-knowledge proof.

1. Prover chooses a permutation π over the set $\{1, 2, 3\}$ in a uniform manner. Randomly permute the three colors to obtain a new coloring. Utilize a commitment scheme to commit the color of all vertices.

$$\text{For } i = 1 \text{ to n, } \forall i \in [n]$$

send a commitment, c_i, assigned with the value $\pi(\varphi(i))$ to the verifier.

$$c_i = \pi(\varphi(i))$$

2. Verifier will select an edge, $e = \{i, j\} \in E$, and send that edge $e = \{i, j\}$ to the prover uniformly.
3. When the prover receives that edge $e = \{i, j\} \in E$, the ith and j^{th} values, c_i and c_j are decommitted by the prover.
4. The decommitted values, c_i and c_j of $\{1, 2, 3\}$, are checked by the Verifier to see whether they are different.

Return Accept if $c_i \neq c_j$. Reject otherwise.

8.3.6   Zero-Knowledge Proofs for Specific Lattice Problems

For standard approximation problems on lattices, a protocol named as non-interactive statistical zero-knowledge (NISZK) has been developed by Peikert and Vaikuntanathan. A lattice is a collection of problems with a function, $\varepsilon(n)$, as a parameter [11]. SOS, which is expanded as "smooth-or-separated", is an intermediate lattice problem that has been implemented. The two properties, which are captured perfectly the SOS problem, needed for the basic NISZK proof system: in YES cases, A Gaussian smoother with parameter 1 can absolutely smooth the lattice, and in NO cases, with a rational chance, at least n points away from the lattice is a random point.

8.3.7   Zero-Knowledge Proof for Blockchain

On the blockchain, the most important building blocks for a variety of privacy-focused applications are NIZKPs. It allows the statement truth to be proved without disclosing the extra details. The examples are digital signature systems, verifiable computation, user authentication protocols, and electronic voting. Non-interactive zero-knowledge assertion systems that are currently in use have been examined as well as their implementations in private smart contracts and CTs on the blockchain.

8.3.7.1   Messaging

End-to-end encryption is required in messaging to ensure that only the person with whom you are communicating can read your private message. Users are asked to check for their identity with the server to ensure protection. However, with the implementation of ZKP, end-to-end trust in the messaging environment can be established without revealing any additional data.

8.3.7.2   Authentication

Zero-knowledge proof can also help secure the transmission of sensitive data such as authentication information. It will provide users with a secure channel from which they can use their data without exposing it. Data leakage is avoided in this way for the worst-case scenario.

8.3.7.3   Storage Protection

The area of storage usefulness is another potential application for zero-knowledge proofs. To protect both the storage unit as well as the data contained inside it, the above task is accompanied by a protocol. To provide a smooth and safe experience, the access channels are, of course, secured.

8.3.7.4   Sending Private Blockchain Transactions

Blockchain transactions that are private have to be kept out of the hands for third parties when sending them. Although conventional approaches are somewhat defensive, they do contain some flaws. Another field where ZKP comes into play is here. When implemented correctly, the idea aids in making private blockchain transactions virtually impossible to hack or intercept.

8.3.7.5   Complex Documentation

Since zero-knowledge proof can encrypt data in chunks, it can be used to monitor which blocks are accessible to a specific user at the same time access to others is denied. The complicated documents are protected from the person who is rejected to view it.

8.3.7.6 File System Control

The file system is another example of an efficient zero-knowledge proof implementation. The idea applies several layers of protection to users, files, and even logins, making data hacking and manipulation extremely difficult.

8.3.7.7 Security for Sensitive Information

Finally, zero-knowledge proof improves the approach followed by blockchain technology for changing the way people transact. When user requests information, ZKP applies a security level at high-end to any block that contains information about banking which is sensitive. That sensitive information includes the details and history of credit card and requires banks to perform manipulation only on the appropriate blocks. Other blocks are unaffected and thus secure.

8.3.8 Zero-Knowledge Proof for High Level Compilers

Developers can easily convert a computation into a circuit using high-level compilers. Code produced in a high-level language is accepted by these compilers. As a result, both old and new algorithms can be converted with ease. Pinocchio is a software package which is used to create zero-knowledge arguments of non-interactive type [12]. A high-level compiler is included for translating C code to Boolean or arithmetic circuit representation which is further converted into a quadratic arithmetic program (QAP) by the compiler, which then executes the zero-knowledge statement protocol. On the Ethereum network, ZoKrates is a toolbox used for computations in offchain zero-knowledge. Rank-1 Constraint System (R1CS) has been adopted to compile the customized code which is written using high-level imperative language [13].

8.4 Zero-Knowledge Protocols

8.4.1 Schnorr Protocol

The most basic and widely used proof of knowledge protocol is the Schnorr protocol. It works by applying discrete logarithm knowledge without giving any information about its value.

The Fiat-Shamir transformation renders it as non-interactive [14]. The Schnorr protocol is HVZK protocol. HVZK is expanded as "honest verifier zero knowledge". In HVZK, verifier chooses his challenge randomly, then he learns nothing about the log.

Let G_q be the cyclic group for which the Schnorr protocol is defined. The elements in G_q, are generator g and prime order q. The parameters, generator g and group, are considered to be public. Suppose that the knowledge of discrete logarithm $x = \log_g y$ has to be proved by a prover for some group element $y = g^x$, then the prover and the verifier communicate as follows:

1. The first message, $t = g^r$, is generated by the prover (P). This message is computed using a random number (r).
2. Again, by prover (P), the computed message t is sent to the verifier (V).
3. In turn, random challenge (c) is responded from verifier (V).
4. After receiving c, the response, $s = r + cx$, is computed by prover, P.
5. The computed response(s) is send to the verifier (V).
6. The response is accepted by verifier (V) if $g^s = ty^c$.

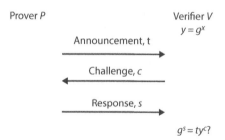

Completeness:

$$\text{if } s = r + cx, \text{ then } g^s = g^{r+cx} = g^r \cdot g^{cx} = g^r \cdot (g^x)^c = t.y^c.$$

Proof of knowledge:
Let P* be a prover (possibly malicious) who, with probability δ, persuades the honest verifier. The extractor is constructed as follows:

1. Assume that the prover (P) is available in state Q. Prover (P) computes output $t = g^r$.
2. A random value (c_1) is generated and given as input to the prover (P). Based on c_1, $s_1 = r + c_1 x$ is computed

3. Then, the prover (P) is rewind back to state Q
4. Now, another random value c_2 is generated and given as input to the prover (P). Based on c_2, $s_2 = r + c_2 x$ is computed.
5. Determine $\dfrac{s_1 - s_2}{c_1 - c_2}$ using c1, c2, s1 and s2.

Since P^* succeeds with probability 1, we know that

$$g^{s_1} = t.y^{c_1} \text{ and } g^{s_2} = t.y^{c_2}$$

From the above equation,

$$t = \frac{g^{s_1}}{y^{c_1}} \text{ and } t = \frac{g^{s_2}}{y^{c_2}}$$

Therefore,

$$\frac{g^{s_1}}{y^{c_1}} = \frac{g^{s_2}}{y^{c_2}}$$

$$\frac{g^{s_1}}{y^{s_2}} = \frac{y^{c_1}}{y^{c_2}}$$

$$g^{s_1 - s_2} = y^{c_1 - c_2}$$

$$y = g^{\frac{s_1 - s_2}{c_1 - c_2}}$$

From this equation, $y = g^x$

$$x = \frac{s_1 - s_2}{c_1 - c_2}$$

Note: the extraction fails if $c_1 = c_2$ with the probability 1/q. Therefore, the knowledge error here is e = 1/q.

8.4.2   Σ-Protocols

Σ-protocols (sigma protocols) are the protocols that form the fundamental component of Zero-Knowledge Proofs. It is actually expected to be special honest-verifier zero knowledge, in which an additional input, such as a challenge c, can be accepted by the simulator and then generate conversations with that challenge c.

Assume $x \in V$ represents the input that act as a common source of information for both the verifier and the prover, and $w \in W$ represents the witness that act as input for prover which is kept as private. Let a binary relation be represented as $R = \{(x;w)\} \subseteq V \times W$. Let the language corresponding to binary relation R be represented as $L_R = \{x \in V: \exists_{w \in W}(x;w) \in R\}$.

A sigma protocol is a three-phase protocol that comprised of the following:

- Let **a** be the first message which is send by prover, P, to the verifier, V.
- Let **e** be the random t-bit string which is send by verifier, V, which is a random challenge
- Let **z** be the response message which is send by prover, P

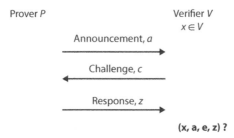

The following three properties are satisfied when verifier, V, accepts the conversation (a; e; z) based solely on (x, a, e, z):

1. **Completeness.** V always accepts if the protocol is followed by P and V.
2. **Special soundness.** A PPT algorithm E (**extractor**) exists that computes witness w that satisfies $(x;w) \in R$, given any input $x \in V$ and any pair of conversations (a;e;z) and (a;e';z') that is accepted with $c \neq c'$.
3. **Special honest-verifier zero-knowledgeness.** Given any $x \in L_R$ and any challenge $c \in C$, a PPT algorithm S (simulator) exists that produces conversations (a; e; z). The produced conversation's probability distribution is same as the conversations that take place between P and V with challenge c and input x which

is common. The Σ-protocol is said to be trivial if C consists of a single element. Here, any witness w used by P should satisfies (x;w) ∈ R. Furthermore, given any x ∈ V\L$_R$ and any given challenge, c ∈ C, Simulator S just needs to generate random accepting conversations (a; e; z).

8.4.2.1 Three-Move Structure

Sigma protocols are three-phase protocols for proving knowledge of values in some relation without disclosing the values themselves. Sigma protocols follow the following three-move structure (commitment, challenge, and response)

1. **Commitment:**
   The prover generates a random number, creates a commitment to that randomness, and sends the commitment to the verifier.
2. **Challenge:**
   After getting the commitment, as a challenge, the verifier produces and provides a random number to the prover. It is important that the verifier does not send the challenge before getting the commitment or else the prover can cheat.
3. **Response:**
   The prover takes the challenge and creates a response using the random number chosen in step 1, the challenge and the witness. The prover will then send the response to the verifier who will do some computation and will or will not be convinced of the knowledge of the witness.

8.5 Transformation Methods

In order to convert from interactive ZKP to noninteractive ZKP, the following are some of the most commonly used methods:

- CRS model
- Fiat-Shamir heuristic
- Unruh transformation

8.5.1 CRS Model

CRS is expanded as Common Reference String, which is introduced by Blum, Feldman, and Micali. For any problem in NP, CRS model is the first NIZKP based on the string, which is shared by the participants [15]. Whenever all participants are having access to the same string, a secure setup is required by the CRS model. Any scheme based on this model has to be considered stable if and only if the generated CRS was secure and correct. The development of a CRS for a large group of people is very complicated and time-consumption method. As a result, schemes based on CRS model are difficult to set up. However, they are typically fast to run and produce small proofs.

8.5.2   Fiat-Shamir Heuristic

In order to make the interactive ZKPs as non-interactive, Fiat-Shamir heuristic transformation is developed. It is a transformation by removing the role of the verifier who provides a random challenge value, with a hash function that uses the prover's encrypted nonce as input [14]. To generate a digital signature scheme from a public randomness-based interactive proof of information protocol, the Fiat-Shamir heuristic is used. The Fiat-Shamir transform employs a hash function for computation, the outputs of which can in some ways be regarded as the CRS, to replace interaction and (part of) randomness. Since the hash function output is independent of the inputs [16] and uniformly random, it secures the random oracle model (ROM) [14]. All zero-knowledge security features [17] is not maintained by ROM even though it is more secure compare to regular mode. There is, however, no need for a complicated setup.

8.5.3   Unruh Transformation

With quantum computing, Fiat-Shamir technique is not compatible and not providing secure schemes for specific protocols [19]. In order to overcome from the above drawback, the Unruh transformation technique is developed as an alternative to the Fiat-Shamir heuristic [18]. For every interactive one in the ROM against quantum opponents, the Unruh transformation provides a NIZK proof that is provable and secure. No setup is needed, as it is with Fiat-Shamir.

8.6   Conclusion

Over the past few years, extraordinary developments have been brought regarding the quantum computers. However, the threat of large-scale impact on society has led to widespread initiatives to develop new cryptographic algorithms, standards, and migration paths, which are collectively referred to as "post-quantum cryptography". The concept of a ZKP along with its noninteractive variants has been surveyed and well explained. An overview of the protocols for CT in post-quantum cryptography by applying zero-knowledge proof has been provided.

References

1. Bernstein, D.J., Introduction to post-quantum cryptography, in: *Post-Quantum Cryptography*, pp. 1–14, Springer Berlin Heidelberg, Berlin, Heidelberg, 2009.
2. Wu, H. and Wang, F., A Survey of Noninteractive Zero Knowledge Proof System and Its Applications. *Sci. World J.*, 2014, 1–7, 2014.
3. Martín-Fernández, F., Caballero-Gil, P., Caballero-Gil, C., Authentication Based on Non-Interactive Zero-Knowledge Proofs for the Internet of Things. *Sensors*, 16, 1, 75, Jan. 2016.
4. Samundeesw, S. and Sriram, V.S.S., NIZKP to Achieve Authentication in Ad-hoc Networks. *Res. J. Inf. Technol.*, 5, 3, 402–410, Mar. 2013.
5. Walshe, M., Epiphaniou, G., Al-Khateeb, H., Hammoudeh, M., Katos, V., Dehghantanha, A., Non-interactive zero knowledge proofs for the authentication of IoT devices in reduced connectivity environments. *Ad Hoc Networks*, 95, 101988, Dec. 2019.
6. Tsague, A.Z., Fute, E.T., Amraoui, A.E.L., Tonye, E., DS-NIZKP : A ZKP-based Strong Authentication using Digital Signature for Distributed Systems. *Int. J. Comput. Sci. Inf. Secur. (IJCSIS)*, 16, 6, April 2019, 2018.
7. Tsague, A.Z., Fute, E.T., Tonye, E., Amraoui, A.E.L., Peer to Peer Authentication for Index-based Distributed Data Collection: A Zero-Knowledge-based Scheme to Security for Wireless Sensor Networks Peer to Peer Authentication for Index-based Distributed Data Collection: A Zero-Knowledge-based Scheme to Sec. *Am. J. Adv. Res.*, 3–2, 1–6, 2019 January, 2019.
8. Goldreich, O., Micali, S., Wigderson, A., Proofs that yield nothing but their validity or all languages in NP have zero-knowledge proof systems. *J. ACM*, 38, 3, 690–728, Jul. 1991.
9. Blum, M., De Santis, A., Micali, S., Persiano, G., Noninteractive Zero-Knowledge. *SIAM J. Comput.*, 20, 6, 1084–1118, Dec. 1991.
10. Kilian, J., A note on efficient zero-knowledge proofs and arguments (extended abstract), in: *Proceedings of the twenty-fourth annual ACM symposium on Theory of computing - STOC '92*, pp. 723–732, 1992.
11. Peikert, C. and Vaikuntanathan, V., Noninteractive Statistical Zero-Knowledge Proofs for Lattice Problems, in: *Advances in Cryptology – CRYPTO 2008*, pp. 536–553, Springer Berlin Heidelberg, Berlin, Heidelberg, 2008.

12. Parno, B., Howell, J., Gentry, C., Raykova, M., Pinocchio: Nearly Practical Verifiable Computation, in: *2013 IEEE Symposium on Security and Privacy*, May 2013, pp. 238–252.

13. Eberhardt, J. and Tai, S., ZoKrates - Scalable Privacy-Preserving Off-Chain Computations, in: *2018 IEEE International Conference on Internet of Things (iThings) and IEEE Green Computing and Communications (GreenCom) and IEEE Cyber, Physical and Social Computing (CPSCom) and IEEE Smart Data (SmartData)*, Jul. 2018, pp. 1084–1091.

14. Fiat, A. and Shamir, A., How To Prove Yourself: Practical Solutions to Identification and Signature Problems, in: *Advances in Cryptology — CRYPTO' 86*, pp. 186–194, Springer Berlin Heidelberg, Berlin, Heidelberg, 1986.

15. Blum, M., Feldman, P., Micali, S., Non-interactive zero-knowledge and its applications, in: *Proceedings of the twentieth annual ACM symposium on Theory of computing - STOC '88*, pp. 103–112, 1988.

16. Pointcheval, D. and Stern, J., Security Proofs for Signature Schemes. *Int. Conf. Theory Appl. Cryptogr. Tech.*, 387–398, 1996.

17. Pass, R., On Deniability in the Common Reference String and Random Oracle Model. *Annu. Int. Cryptol. Conf.*, 316–337, 2003.

18. Unruh, D., Non-Interactive Zero-Knowledge Proofs in the Quantum Random Oracle Model. *Annu. Int. Conf. Theory Appl. Cryptogr. Tech.*, 755–784, 2015.

19. Ambainis, A., Rosmanis, A., Unruh, D., Quantum Attacks on Classical Proof Systems: The Hardness of Quantum Rewinding, in: *2014 IEEE 55th Annual Symposium on Foundations of Computer Science*, Oct. 2014, pp. 474–483.

9

A Study on Post-Quantum Blockchain: The Next Innovation for Smarter and Safer Cities

G.K. Kamalam[1*] and R.S. Shudapreyaa[2]

¹Department of Information Technology, Perundurai, Erode, Tamilnadu, India
²Department of Computer Science and Engineering, Kongu Engineering College, Perundurai, Erode, Tamil Nadu, India

Abstract

The populace is proliferating; however, the resources are not growing. To scatter to wishes to humans and to improve their standard of dwelling, the smart city concept is bought. Smart metropolis aims to make most desirable and sustainable use of all resources while keeping an appropriate balance between social, environmental, and economic fees. Smart cities have diverse businesses, markets, and sectors. The application for a smart city benefits from the data obtained by a large number of sensors to establish an exact decision made. The relationship between various components and the introduction of a smart city, however, urges protection interventions when they face vital security threats and concerns with credibility. The blockchain is a dispensed ledger between peers; this is append-only, immutable, updateable by consensus, and cryptographically secure because of its good properties such as decentralization, auditability, immutability, and accountability. Blockchain has the power to facilitate the growth of smart cities. In order to establish a stable, validated, and unalterable knowledge ledger, blockchain operates by validating transactions through a distributed network. Research teams have used blockchain's assistant to protect smart cities and increase the precision of their decisions to fix this dilemma. Quantum computers, which are machines that use quantum physics to solve mathematical problems that are difficult or impossible to solve with regular computer hardware, have gotten a lot of attention in recent years. When

*Corresponding author: kamalamparames@gmail.com

Rajesh Kumar Dhanaraj, Vani Rajasekar, SK Hafizul Islam, Balamurugan Balusamy and Ching-Hsien Hsu (eds.) Quantum Blockchain: An Emerging Cryptographic Paradigm, (221–240)
© 2022 Scrivener Publishing LLC

quantum computers become widely available, all present public key cryptosystems will be able to break them, resulting in the creation of large-scale quantum computers. The secrecy and security of digital correspondence on the Internet and elsewhere will be severely undermined by this. Post-quantum cryptography strives to provide cryptographic architecture that can work with existing protocols and networks while remaining secure against conventional and quantum computers. However, with the latest emergence of quantum computers, along with blockchain itself, quantum-based algorithms definitely challenge the reliability of classical encryption, angering blockchain-based application insurance, including vital applications like the smart cities. In this chapter, we reveal the architecture of blockchain-based smart cities and provide an outline of understanding that involves the risks of a quantum machine on blockchain and ultimately smart citybased blockchain implementations.

Keywords: Smart city, blockchain, cryptosystems, quantum computers, post-quantum cryptography

9.1   Blockchain: The Next Big Thing in Smart City Technology

9.1.1   What is Blockchain, and How Does It Work?

The blockchain technology is digital and peer-to-peer in nature. It is protected by a cryptographic mechanism, and the new information can only be appended, no modification can be carried out in the existing information, and updating is possible only through consensus between the peers. It is a system of recording information of all the transactions occurred in a P2P network [1]. The decentralized ledger of transactions is duplicated and available in the distributed network, which makes it highly secured and not possible to hack the information or modify the information in the ledger. Blockchain is interconnected list of transactions. It is stored in a distributed network of systems, eliminating the potential of a system failure or insecurity in the distributed ledger of transactions. Using digital signatures, every block gets linked together in a unique way. This makes the system to be tamper-proof that is the modification in one block is not possible without altering the content in the previous one. The item can be safely delivered without the intervention of a third party, which is a unique feature of blockchain technology. Bitcoin is a term that refers to technology in addition to cryptocurrency. To create algorithms, the bit-coin protocol relied on ledgers and consensus. Blockchain is ready to be revolutionizing in performing transaction in all domains such as banking sector, electricity, educational fields, and healthcare domain. The government and public sector requires a system that satisfies the secure, authenticated, and reliable trustworthy information interchange across distributed environment. Blockchain is the one that satisfies the need of government to define a structure using the information that supports the transactional needs [12]. Applications like voting, supply chain management, and citizen registration face systemic problems like inefficiency, data integrity problem, lack in transparency, and leading to corruption. Blockchain brings a very strong impact on these applications, in which data security is satisfied, transparency is achieved, and no corruption exists.

Across the globe, the most important domain focused by all the governments is smart city. Most of the countries made use of the opportunities penetrating form urbanization and have generated methodologies to transform the city into smart city. Most of the features defined by the government for smart city can be implemented using blockchain such as security and transparency.

9.1.1.1   The Blockchain Advantage

The features that make blockchain technology unique are as follows (as shown in Figure 9.1).

> **Shared Ledger:** It is a distributed system which is append-only, cannot modify the existing information, and shared among the network of business. The system remains resilient, and there is no case of single point failure.
> **Consensus:** It can commit a transaction if all parties involved in the transaction agree to a network of transactions that are verified.
> **Provenance:** Complete detail of an asset is present in a blockchain.
> **Immutability:** Information committed in a shared ledger is trustworthy, and it is tamper-proof which means that the records cannot be modified.
> **Finality:** The completed transaction over a blockchain cannot be reverted.

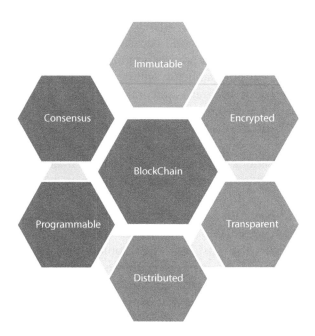

Figure 9.1 The blockchain advantage.

> **Smart contracts:** Code implemented over a blockchain executes in the sequence of triggering event.

Figure 9.2 illustrates the way the blockchain technology resolves the problems that arise during information regarding transactions. Left side of the figure illustrates the key issues and right side shows how it is overcome by using blockchain technology.

9.1.1.2   What is the Mechanism Behind Blockchain?

It works by verifying transactions over a network of computers and generates a unalterable, permanent, and trusted ledger comprising the transactions occurred over a blockchain [19].

9.1.2   The Requirements for a Blockchain System

For problems that emerge out of transactions comprising data and assets, blockchain does not provide a single-step solution [1]. To know whether the blockchain will provide a feasible solution is determined by the important prerequisites. Figure 9.3 signifies the factors that necessitate the ability of blockchain as a solution.

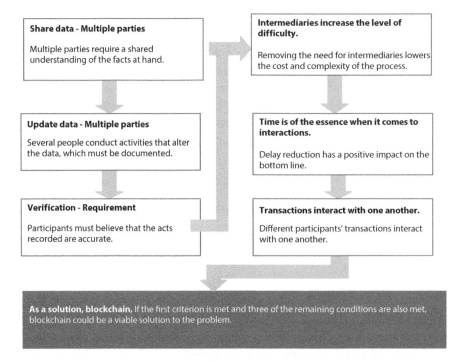

Figure 9.2 Essential prerequisites for a blockchain solution.

9.1.3   Using the Blockchain to Improve Smart City Efforts

The term smart city is referred as a framework implements a vision for modernization and advanced urban area. To improve resident's quality of living, resource utilization maximization, promising investment environment for business, and transparency for government are achieved by leveraging

Figure 9.3 Blockchain technology's impact on smart cities.

technology and utilizing existing infrastructure to build smart city. IT, physical, business, and social infrastructure are all regarded to be part of it [13]. These systems all work together to produce data. that is intelligent and actionable for decision-making. The objective of blockchain technology is to provide decent life for residents, giving smart, secure, and transparent solutions for problems, bringing out an environment that is sustainable and clean. Blockchain technology's impact on smart cities is shown in Figure 9.3. Areas in smart cities where blockchain can contribute are shown in Figure 9.4.

9.2   Application of Blockchain Technology in Smart Cities

9.2.1   Big Data

9.2.1.1   Role of Big Data

An environment contains a broad range of data types, which are classified into three categories based on their structure semi-structured, structured, and unstructured. For example, a map including traffic data, LBS position data, environmental and meteorological data, mobile phones, video tracking, GPS data, and point-of-interest data is extensively utilized. Intelligent traffic systems, political knowledge, wellness, intelligence communities, and people's wisdom all employ big data [2]. Tourism is frequently employed in sectors such as city infrastructure, complicated data collected by major cities, and how to make use of so much data to make the city more intelligent; big data analysis plays a significant part in this.

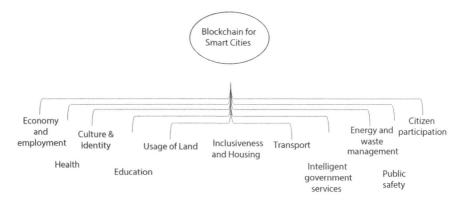

Figure 9.4 Areas in smart cities where blockchain can contribute.

9.2.1.2   *Problems of Big Data*

Big data has the challenge of continuously growing, and companies often struggle to capitalize on opportunities and generate relevant insight [14]. Inadequate interpretation of big data and insufficient awareness causes companies to fail with their big data projects, which are the major problems in big data.

9.2.2   Energy Internet

9.2.2.1   *Role of Energy Internet*

Energy demand rises as the world becomes more urbanized. For the energy's purpose, the goal of the internet's creation is to establish an ecologically friendly, long-term, low-carbon, cost-effective, and energy-efficient smart energy system [2]. It will actualize the connectivity of distributed boost energy consumption ratio and considerably reduce the burden of non-renewable energy and renewable energy on the basis of satisfying the need for urban environmental sustainability. For starters, energy internet growth will successfully aid energy consumption and supply difficulties by utilizing distributed energy and energy scheduling through information sharing. Allow for the integration of conventional and renewable energy development in order to accomplish free energy point-to-point exchange and address the distributed renewable energy challenge as well as increasing the share of renewable energy in the energy grid. As a result of distribution and consumption, technical assistance, and energy transmission and conversion for various types of distributed energy storage, electric cars, energy unit loads, and related equipment over the internet are provided. Second, with the participation of the market's main body—transmission, it helps in building energy on the internet for energy distribution, conversion, and utilization; providing technical support for various types of distributed energy storage and energy unit load; and providing an interconnection interface and electric vehicles. Usual top innovation has resulted in a flattened new business paradigm in the energy industry.

9.2.2.2   *Problems of Energy Internet*

Data protection is an issue that businesses face when using Internet of Things (IoT) devices in energy systems and rising international energy demand, as well as issues of scarcity and environmental impact associated with traditional sources of energy [15].

9.2.3   Internet of Things

9.2.3.1   Role of IoT

The IoT, which links items and communicates with them through information sensing devices, saves time, boosts resource efficiency, and improves data collecting accuracy and coverage [2]. IoT sensing devices in cities are a critical component of linking communication and network connections in smart cities, and the IoT is a crucial component of connecting communication and network connections in smart cities. The sensing devices follow and monitor the operation of numerous scenarios in the city in real time.

In future objects, household appliances, workplaces, computers, industries, and individuals are projected to be able to analyze, interact, and perceive data everywhere. Fortunately, building a smart city system that combines and fully optimizes diverse technologies will be a considerable task. Furthermore, smart city initiatives must protect both the resources of the users and the resources of the environment.

9.2.3.2   Problems of IoT

There seem to be no protocols for IoT edge interface authentication and authorization [2]. For IoT-based incident management operations, there are no best practices. IoT components, no auditing or logging standards have been developed. IoT devices with restricted interfaces can communicate with security systems and platforms.

9.3   Using Blockchain to Secure Smart Cities

9.3.1   Blockchain Technology

Blockchain technology is a self-contained ledger that records all transactions, trades, sales, and contracts. Blockchain was originally designed to serve crypto-currencies, but it can now be used to conduct any type of transaction without the need for a middleman. The advantage of blockchain is that an attacker just has to corrupt 51% of the networks to outwit the hashing capabilities of the target network [16]. As a result, attacking the blockchain network would be computationally impractical. The sample below demonstrates how blockchain technology works. Assume A and B are two users in a blockchain-based parking system, with A paying parking fees to B, the system's administrator. The transaction is represented online as a block, which comprises information like as the previous block, block number, transaction data, and proof of work that is broadcast to all network entities. The transaction is confirmed and put to the blockchain after the block is examined by the other entities. If more than half of them approve it, then the transaction is confirmed and put to the blockchain [17]. The charge is subsequently sent from entity A to authority B's account.

9.3.2   Framework for Security

9.3.2.1   Physical Layer

The smart city system is shown in Figure 9.5. Sensors and actuators are installed in smart cities to gather and send data to higher levels. Because of insufficient encryption and access control techniques, several of these devices, such as the Nest thermostat and the Acer Fitbit, are subject to security risks [3]. Furthermore, no widely approved standard for smart devices

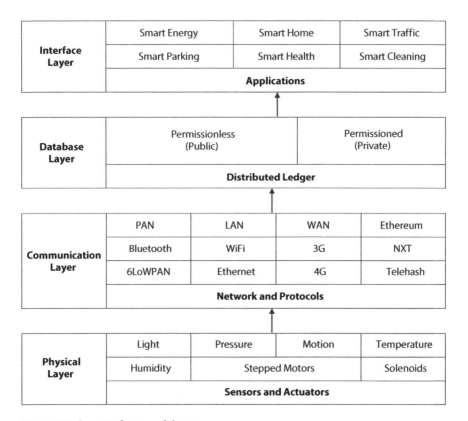

Interface Layer	Smart Energy	Smart Home	Smart Traffic
	Smart Parking	Smart Health	Smart Cleaning
	Applications		

| Database Layer | Permissionless (Public) | Permissioned (Private) |
| | **Distributed Ledger** | |

Communication Layer	PAN	LAN	WAN	Ethereum
	Bluetooth	WiFi	3G	NXT
	6LoWPAN	Ethernet	4G	Telehash
	Network and Protocols			

Physical Layer	Light	Pressure	Motion	Temperature
	Humidity	Stepped Motors		Solenoids
	Sensors and Actuators			

Figure 9.5 Security framework layers.

exists that permits data produced by them to be transferred for cross-functionality and incorporated. To solve these issues in smart devices, vendors need to agree on implementation and communication standards.

9.3.2.2 Communication Layer

At this layer, smart city networks employ many communication protocols to transfer information across various systems like Bluetooth, 6LoWPAN, 3G, 4G, WiFi, and Ethernet. It provides protection and privacy of transmitted data, and blockchain protocols must be incorporated with this layer. Transaction records, for example, can be converted into blocks and broadcast over the network using telehash. Peer-to-peer networking can be accomplished with protocols like BitTorrent, while smart contract functionality can be achieved with Ethereum. Conversely, since the specifications differ from application to application. It is a huge difficulty to integrate conventional communication methods with blockchain. A possible solution might be to use several blockchains and a blockchain access layer to provide application-specific features.

9.3.2.3 Database Layer

A distributed ledger is a form of decentralized database in blockchain that stores records one by one. Each record in the ledger includes a unique cryptographic signature and a time stamp. Any legal consumer has access to the ledger's entire transaction history, which can be verified and audited. In practice, there are two types of distributed ledgers: permission less and permissioned. The key benefits of a permissionless ledger are its censorship resistance and transparency. In contrast to the private ledger, the public ledger must maintain complicated shared records and takes longer to reach consensus. Furthermore, public ledgers are vulnerable to anonymous threats. As a result, for real-time applications such as traffic systems in a smart city, private ledgers are advised to assure scalability, efficiency, and security.

9.3.2.4 Interface Layer

The framework includes a number of smart applications that work together to make intelligent choices. A smart phone application, for example, may send location data to a smart home device, prompting the air conditioner to switch on 5 min before you arrive home. Nonetheless, the apps must be properly connected, as flaws in one program may provide hackers access to other operations that rely on it.

9.4   Blockchain Public Key Security

The power of resisting classical computing attacks of symmetric, asymmetric cryptosystems is estimated using bits-of-security level. Bits-of-security level represents the estimate of the computational efficiency needed to crack a cryptosystem with brute-force technique through classical computers [4]. In the era of post-quantum, pre-quantum crypto-algorithms and hash functions are still applicable, and it just needs to increase the size of the key/output. In public key system of cryptography, it includes two keys—public and private. These key are related together mathematically; the power of cracking private key from the paired public key is based on the computational skill needed to enforce a brute-force attack in searching the key. Public key system of cryptography depends on mathematical problems such as factorization of integer or elliptic curves which provides no efficient solution. Asymmetric key system of cryptography eliminates the problem of key distribution and well suits to insecure network. It does not require exchanging the keys between the sender and receiver and provides increased security. Symmetric key system of cryptography needs a secure process to pool and distribute keys among the sender and receiver involved in information exchange. To make it secure distribution, it requires a special format for keys such as large prime and random generation of strings with k-bits. In spite of the efficient key distribution technique, quantum computing brings endanger to the public key systems of encryption. Quantum attacks with the help of fast Shor's algorithm affects the public key techniques based on factorization of integer problem such as RSA, DSA, and elliptic-curve technique which is based on discrete logarithmic problem. Shor's algorithm solves the public key techniques at a faster rate on well-built quantum computer. Similarly, quantum attack uses Grover's algorithm to solve brute force attack on symmetric key system of cryptography dramatically within a quadratic factor. Cost for cracking 80-bit security level is in the range of tens of thousands to hundreds of million dollars. For next 30 to 40 years, the bit security level that is secure is 112-bit security level. Quantum computer to crack 160-bit elliptic curve requires nearly 1,000 qubits, and 1,024-bit RSA can be cracked using 2000 qubits, but, currently, available quantum computers provide only 79 qubits; therefore, it is best to transit to post-quantum cryptosystems [18]. Even these quantum computers can easily crack the current efficient public key cryptosystems. Hence, it is advisable to develop blockchains to cater to needs of the era of post-quantum.

9.4.1   Hash Function Security

The conventional hash functions resist the effect of quantum attacks because it looks improbable to design quantum techniques to solve problems of NP-hard nature. Designing new function for hash requires magnifying the size of the output. Grover's algorithm attacks blockchain in two methods. One method is to identify any hash collisions has occurred and replaces complete blockchain blocks [4]. Hash function should provide an output consisting of 3*n bits, so that an n-bit level of security can be achieved. Second method, the Grover's algorithm accelerates blockchains mining such as Bitcoin leading to faster pace in the creation of nonces which ultimately results in recreating the complete bockchains at a faster rate, thus less likely to satisfy the integrity. Moreover, quantum attacks by Shor's algorithm crashes the functions of hashing. Suppose the hash function of a blockchain is crashed, digital signature can be forged easily by Shor's algorithm. It is used to spoof the users of blockchain and pilfer their assets that are digital.

9.4.2   Characteristics and Post-Quantum Schemes of Blockchain

Post-quantum cryptosystem effectiveness lies in bringing out a blockchain encompassing the important features as follows:

- **Smaller key size:** Devices that are interacting with blockchain require using public and private key size smaller to lessen the space of storage [4]. In addition, smaller key size requires lesser complex computational nature of operations for processing. This characteristic becomes essential for the blockchains that brings out the interaction of IoT devices, which usually requires lesser storage and computational power. IoT emerges widespread with blockchain to overcome the limitations of security challenges faced.
- **Smaller signature and hash length:** Blockchain stores detail of transactions which comprises signature of the user, data hashes and block hashes. Increase in size of signature and length of the hash ultimately leads to increase in the size of the blockchain.
- **Fast execution:** To make blockchain to handle huge transactions every second, post-quantum schemes are needed, and also it requires to be completed at a faster rate. The fast

execution leads to efficient time complexity so that the blockchain transactions can be carried out in resource constrained devices also.

o **Low computational complexity:** Fast execution alone does not lead the post-quantum cryptosystem [19] to be simple in computational complexity. For example, some schemes may be faster in Intel microprocessors may not be faster in ARM-based microcontrollers. Hence, it is required to bring out a balance between execution, computational complexity, and hardware devices.

o **Low energy consumption:** Bitcoin is said to be power hungry because it requires high energy to execute consensus protocol. Energy consumption also depends on the hardware used, number of transactions performed, and the scheme used for achieving secured transactions.

9.5   Quantum Threats on Blockchain Enabled Smart City

9.5.1   Shor's Algorithm

Shor's algorithm for factoring integers in polynomial time is well-known. Because the best-known classical technique takes super polynomial time to factor the product of two primes, which addresses the period-finding issue, the commonly used cryptosystem, RSA, relies on factoring being difficult for big enough numbers. An efficient period finding approach may be used to factor integers since a factoring problem can be turned to a period finding problem in polynomial time [5]. For the time being, sufficient enough to state that if we can efficiently compute $p^y \mod n$ period, we can also factor efficiently.

Consider the periodic function: $G(y) = p^y \mod n$ where p and n are both positive integers, p is smaller than n, and they do not share any factors.

9.5.1.1   *Modular Exponentiation*

You may have observed that producing U^{2j} gates by repeating U increases exponentially with j and does not result in a polynomial time process [6].

$$U^{2j}(y) = (a^{2j}y \bmod N)$$

This grows polynomially with j; fortunately, calculating a 2j mod N efficiently is possible [7]. To calculate exponential, traditional computers might utilize a method called as repeated squaring. The repeated squaring procedure becomes quite straightforward in our instance since we are just working with exponentials of the type 2j.

9.5.1.2   Factoring

Although there are specific criteria for choosing difficult-to-factor numbers, the basic idea is choosing the product of two big prime integers [8]. The first step in a normal factoring approach is to examine whether there is a faster way to factor the integer (is really the value even?). Before using Shor's worst-case scenario period discovery, is there a number that has the form N = a b? Because we want to concentrate on the quantum section of the method, we will start with the scenario when N is the product of two prime numbers.

9.5.2   Grover's Algorithm

As you have surely heard, one of the many advantages of a quantum computer over a regular computer is its increased speed in searching databases [9]. Grover's algorithm is used to show this. This method can quadratically speed up an unstructured search problem, but it may also be used as a general technique or subroutine to speed up a variety of different ways.

Grover's approach uses O(logN) storage space and O(N1/2) time to search an unsorted database with N items. While Grover's method is often referred to as "searching a database," "inverting a function" may be a better description. Grover's methodology allows us to calculate x given y if we have a function y = f(x) that can be evaluated on a quantum computer. Because we may build a function that generates one value of y if x matches a desired item in a database, and another value of y for other values of x, inverting a function is tied to database searching.

Procedure
Step 1: Set the system to the initial condition

$$| s \ ranglete = \frac(1)(\sqrt(n)) \sum\_x | x \ranglele$$

Step 2: Repeat the "Grover iteration" steps r(n) times. The function r(n) is discussed in the next section.

a. Use the operator Uω.
b. Use the operator Us = 2 | s > le < les | -1.

Step 3: Execute the measurement Ω. The measurement result for n >> 1 will have a probability approaching 1. From λω, ω may be obtained.

By combining phase kickback and computing [10], Grover's technique creates a reversible classical circuit that determines the correct answer and transforms it into an oracle.

9.6   Post-Quantum Blockchain–Based Smart City Solutions

9.6.1   Lattice-Based Cryptography

In this section, we utilize as a set of all reals and as a set of positive integers to define the lattice. m is the m-dimensional Euclidean vector space, where m, n, and m n are all positive integers. Numerous studies have now embraced lattice-based cryptography, which is thought to be safe against quantum computers. Usually, it is used to protect blockchain from quantum assaults that might compromise elliptic curve cryptography (ECC). Using the Ring Short Integer Solution lattice hardness assumption, the public will be able to verify if two or more signatures were created by the same signatory while maintaining anonymity and security. The suggested technique generates sub-public and sub-private keys using Bonsai Tree technology, which aids in the creation of a lightweight wallet. The lattice-based signature method is safe against the adaptively generated message attack in the random oracle model, according to this proposal's security proof, making it more suited for transaction implementation in the post-quantum blockchain (PQB) network. When this signature technique is applied to a blockchain, a PQB is created [9]. The suggested cryptocurrency system can withstand quantum computer attacks, according to the research.

9.6.2   Quantum Distributed Key

Using a Quantum Distributed Key (QDK) is another way to develop a solution that is resistant to quantum assaults. Individual photons are used by QDK to exchange cryptographic key data between users. Each photon corresponds to a single bit of data, which can be either 1 or 0. The value of each bit is determined by the state of the photon, according to quantum physics theory (the spin and polarization). A laser is utilized at the transmitter end of the QDK to generate a stream of single photons. The photon should be in one of two polarization states: horizontal or vertical, which will be measured at the receiver end. Based on quantum physics rules, QKD ensures information-theoretic and unconditional security. The QKD network layer was blended into the existing blockchain system to safeguard the relevant sub algorithm against quantum assaults, according to the research [9]. As a result, the technology that enables QKD networks has been shown in a number of tests and is currently available from a number of commercial vendors. Critical infrastructures, such as smart grids, financial institutions, and national military, might all benefit from QKD. Unfortunately, because the block formation technique requires more computer power, QKD may not be suitable for protecting a full-scale cryptocurrency system, but it can still be beneficial for protecting smaller access to information.

9.6.3   Quantum Entanglement in Time

According to the research, there is a "spooky effect at a distance" in spatially distant quantum systems, as Einstein characterized it. The strange activity incorporates non-classical correlations, which have been used to develop a quantum blockchain. Blockchain is encoded into a temporal Greenberger-Horne-Zeilinger (GHZ) state of photons that cannot overlap at the same moment in this manner [9]. This study employs a super-dense coding method to leverage the quantum blockchain and convert the classical information into spatially entangled Bell states, replacing the components of a classical blockchain with a quantum system. The authors used this information to turn each block in the chain into a temporal Bell state and record the time of block generation, such as the first block being generated at time t = 0: Entanglement is generated between the two later photons absorbed consecutively at time t = τ and t = 2τ by projecting the temporal Bell state on two photons at time t = τ. Quantum blockchain–based temporal entanglement is a powerful way to protect blockchain-based smart cities. The records are still present and may be read using this approach, but they cannot be touched since the photons that carry them are no longer there which will ensure the security and privacy of blockchain-based smart cities.

9.7   Quantum Computing Fast Evolution

The recent trend that has a vast scope for research, academic, and industry is the quantum computing. Hackers may design and execute possible attacks toward the post-quantum system for cryptography. To resist the new attack designed against post-quantum cryptosystem, the researchers have to give attention on developing the techniques.

9.7.1   Transition—Pre-Quantum Blockchain to Post-Quantum Blockchain

Methods have been developed to make a change from pre- to post-quantum blockchains. In [10], author devised a technique that, if hash function or the digital signature is revealed, the technique extends the validity of blocks of past blockchains. In [11], author devised a protocol for commit-delay-reveal. The protocol makes the users of blockchain to transfer funds in a secured manner from pre-quantum version of Bitcoin to post-quantum version of scheme comprising digital signature.

9.7.2   Large Scale and Signature Size

Compared to traditional public key cryptosystems, cryptosystems concerning post-quantum need larger key size. In public key cryptosystem, the key size ranges between 2^7 bits and 2^{12} bits. Considering the cryptosystems involving digital signature, larger signatures resultin poor performance.

9.7.3   Slow Key Generation

To improvise the security mechanism in post-quantum techniques, restrictions have been imposed on the number of massages to be signed using same key. In this regard, it makes essential to bring out new keys, which leads to slow down the process of blockchain and increases the computational complexity of the resources. The developers have to concentrate on devising a methodology to make a balance between the key generation and efficiency optimization of blockchain process.

9.7.4   Computational and Energy Efficiency

From Sections 9.4 and 9.5, it is concluded that to achieve efficiency in post-quantum cryptosystem, post-quantum techniques need increase in execution time, storage requirement, and the computational complexity of the resources. These needs ultimately lead to the increase in the consumption of energy of devices. The researchers have to focus on bringing out a novel technique that optimizes cryptosystems to increase the efficiency of energy and computation ultimately leads to overall blockchain efficiency.

9.7.5   Blockchain Hardware Unusability

Post-quantum cryptosystems that are computationally intensive does not support certain hardware, which plays an essential role in the implementation of nodes of blockchain. Hence, it requires for the post-quantum techniques to have a balance among security, computational complexity, and need not confine on hardware essential for the blockchain interaction.

9.7.6   Overheads Due to Large Ciphertext

Cryptosystems indulged with more overhead, which lead to an impact in the overall blockchain performance. To address this, developers of post-quantum reduce overhead induced by the ciphertext incorporating efficient inherent compression techniques in cryptosystems.

9.7.7   Quantum Blockchain

In addition to the cryptosystems in changing toward post-quantum, researchers introduced blockchains in quantum-computing. Authors [10, 11] introduced migration of Bitcoin toward quantum computers; other researchers have identified the ways of accelerating the mining process by bringing some modification in the Grover's methods. Quantum cryptography implements smart contracts. Research opportunity available in plenty in key-establishment physics-based domains collectively termed Quantum Key Distribution (QKD).

9.8   Conclusion

Classical encryption and security protocols, such as blockchain, are put in danger by quantum computers and quantum-based cryptography. Because it houses sensitive information and data about users and their many components, blockchain-based smart cities are a key application that must be protected from future quantum assaults. In this article, we provide a broad overview of the potential future hazards associated with blockchain-based smart cities. The traditional blockchain-based smart city framework is also examined, and some of the most promising post-quantum solutions, including lattice-based cryptography, QKD, and entanglement in time-based quantum blockchain, are presented. These systems have been shown to be vulnerable to quantum assaults in the laboratory, and they are ideal for use in a PQB-based smart city before quantum computers reach their full potential.

References

1. Monrat, A.A., Schelén, O., Andersson, K., A survey of blockchain from the perspectives of applications, challenges, and opportunities. *IEEE Access, 7*, 117134–117151, 2019.

2. Bodkhe, U., Tanwar, S., Parekh, K., Khanpara, P., Tyagi, S., Kumar, N., Alazab, M., Blockchain for industry 4.0: A comprehensive review. *IEEE Access, 8*, 79764–79800, 2020.

3. Zheng, W., Zheng, Z., Chen, X., Dai, K., Li, P., Chen, R., Nutbaas: A blockchain-as-a-service platform. *IEEE Access, 7*, 134422–134433, 2019.

4. Tanwar, S., Parekh, K., Evans, R., Blockchain-based electronic healthcare record system for healthcare 4.0 applications. *J. Inf. Secur. Appl., 50*, 102407, 2020.

5. Beck, R., Müller-Bloch, C., King, J.L., Governance in the blockchain economy: A framework and research agenda. *J. Assoc. Inf. Syst., 19*, 10, 1, 2018.

6. Velliangiri, S., Manoharn, R., Ramachandran, S., Rajasekar, V.R., Blockchain Based Privacy Preserving Framework for Emerging 6G Wireless Communications. *IEEE Trans. Ind. Inf.*, 2021.

7. Hou, H., The application of blockchain technology in E-government in China, in: *2017 26th International Conference on Computer Communication and Networks (ICCCN)*, 2017, July, IEEE, pp. 1–4.

8. Chandraprabha, M. and Dhanaraj, R.K., Machine learning based Pedantic Analysis of Predictive Algorithms in Crop Yield Management. *2020 4th International Conference on Electronics, Communication and Aerospace Technology (ICECA). 2020 4th International Conference on Electronics, Communication and Aerospace Technology (ICECA)*, 2020, November 5.

9. Ali, O., Ally, M., Dwivedi, Y., The state of play of blockchain technology in the financial services sector: A systematic literature review. *Int. J. Inf. Manage., 54*, 102199, 2020.

10. Berdik, D., Otoum, S., Schmidt, N., Porter, D., Jararweh, Y., A survey on blockchain for information systems management and security. *Inf. Process. Manage., 58*, 1, 102397, 2021.

11. Namasudra, S., Deka, G.C., Johri, P., Hosseinpour, M., Gandomi, A.H., The revolution of blockchain: State-of-the-art and research challenges. *Arch. Comput. Methods Eng., 28*, 3, 1497–1515, 2021.

12. Rajasekar, V., Premalatha, J., Sathya, K., Enhanced Biometric Recognition for Secure Authentication Using Iris Preprocessing and Hyperelliptic Curve Cryptography. *Wireless Commun. Mobile Comput., 2020*, 8841021, 1–15, 2020. https://doi.org/10.1155/2020/8841021.

13. Chen, J., Gan, W., Hu, M., Chen, C.M., On the construction of a post-quantum blockchain for smart city. *J. Inf. Secur. Appl., 58*, 102780, 2021.

14. Saha, R., Kumar, G., Devgun, T., Buchanan, W., Thomas, R., Alazab, M., Rodrigues, J., A Blockchain Framework in Post-Quantum Decentralization. *IEEE Trans. Serv. Comput.*, 1–12, 2021.

15. Li, Z., Tan, T.G., Szalachowski, P., Sharma, V., Zhou, J., Post-Quantum VRF and its Applications in Future-Proof Blockchain System. *arXiv preprint arXiv:2109.02012*, 2021.
16. Buser, M., Dowsley, R., Esgin, M.F., Kermanshahi, S.K., Kuchta, V., Liu, J.K., Zhang, Z., Post-Quantum Verifiable Random Function from Symmetric Primitives in PoS Blockchain. *IACR Cryptol. ePrint Arch*, vol. *2021*, p. 302, 2021.
17. Fernández-Carames, T.M. and Fraga-Lamas, P., Towards post-quantum blockchain: A review on blockchain cryptography resistant to quantum computing attacks. *IEEE Access*, 8, 21091–21116, 2020.
18. Campbell Sr., R., Evaluation of post-quantum distributed ledger cryptography. *J. Br. Blockchain Assoc.*, 2, 1, 7679, 2019.
19. Torres, W.A., Steinfeld, R., Sakzad, A., Kuchta, V., Post-quantum linkable ring signature enabling distribut ed authorised ring confidential transactions in blockchain, in: *Cryptology ePrint Archive*, 2020.

10

Quantum Protocols for Hash-Based Blockchain

Sathya K.[1]*, Premalatha J.[2], Balamurugan Balusamy[3] and Sarumathi Murali[4]

[1]*Department of CT/UG, Kongu Engineering College, Tamil Nadu, India*
[2]*Department of IT, Kongu Engineering College, Tamil Nadu, India*
[3]*School of Computing Science and Engineering, Galgotias University,
Greater Noida, India*
[4]*University of Sydney, NSW, Darlington, Australia*

Abstract

Protocols are predefined rules established to allow data communication across computing systems. Protocols enforce the structuring and encoding of data for safe and secure transmission. They must protect data from malicious hands and reach the destination in an intended way. Blockchain being a decentralized network with peers, protocol is a crucial factor required to ensure trust among peers, secure transmission of data, achieve consensus among peers, and so on. Many protocols were put into use for the abovementioned purposes decades ago. However, with the advent future of quantum computers and their ability to compute very complex problems in shorter time periods, a threat to break these protocols arises. Blockchain protocols must be chosen based on several factors like network bandwidth, size of peers, and type of the network. This chapter explores the modern protocols introduced into Blockchain and can withstand the attacks constituted by quantum computers.

Keywords: Quantum voting, commitment protocol, byzantine agreement, proof of stake, quantum blockchain, MatRict, code-based cryptography, certificateless signature

---

**Corresponding author*: pearlhoods@gmail.com

Rajesh Kumar Dhanaraj, Vani Rajasekar, SK Hafizul Islam, Balamurugan Balusamy and Ching-Hsien Hsu (eds.) Quantum Blockchain: An Emerging Cryptographic Paradigm, (241–262)
© 2022 Scrivener Publishing LLC

10.1   Introduction

Internet communication uses various protocols like HTTPS, FTP, SSH, and SSL. Blockchain protocols work in different way in a blockchain network. They aim at achieving consensus among peers, mining of blocks, secure transactions, user authentication, and so on. Blockchain technology is a decentralized network of peers with no central entity to keep track of transactions happening in the network. Instead, all transactions in the network are recorded in the ledger and distributed to all peers in the form of blocks. This kind of ledger is now known as public ledger [1]. The transactions in the block are verified by the cryptographic hash functions. Cryptographic hash functions are also known as one-way functions that take variable size input and produce a fixed size unique output always. Every unique input when fed to a hash function would produce a unique output and they are said to have one-to-one mapping.

Blockchain holds its strength in the consensus of distributed ledger among its peers. Distributed ledger holds the history of all secure transactions that occurred in the network and all peers in the network are aware of it. In practice, some peer nodes may go down for some time due to various reasons like network failure and system failure. When the failed nodes come back alive in the network, they must be provided with the recent copy of distributed ledger so that all nodes are consistent in their ledger copy.

10.2   Consensus Protocols

Consensus protocols play a crucial role in maintaining the consensus of distributed ledger across the peers of the blockchain network. They must not only aim at achieving consensus, besides they must focus on achieving trade-off between consistency, availability, and partition fault tolerance [2]. In general, blockchain networks also face yet another problem of Byzantine Generals problem. This problem arises when some malicious nodes intentionally disseminate false information in the process of overcoming any failure. Some of the common consensus protocols used in blockchain networks are as follows:

- Proof of Work (PoW)
- Proof of Stake (PoS)
- Delegated Proof of Stake (DPoS)

- Practical Byzantine Fault Tolerance (PBFT)
- Proof of Capacity
- Proof of Elapsed Time

10.2.1   Proof of Work (PoW)

It is the oldest protocol to be used in blockchain network. This protocol aims to generate a hash value for a valid transaction with predefined set of trailing zeros. Not any random value added to the transaction would result in such perfect hash value. It is the job of miners to mine for a good random value known as nonce to be added to the transaction to achieve the perfect hash value with predefined trailing zeros. In this process of mining, miners compete to find the random number that fits the puzzle and are rewarded for the computation power spent as shown in Figure 10.1. PoW protocol is suitable for permissionless blockchain networks with linear structure of blocks. The major drawback of this protocol is huge energy consumption by all miners in mining the nonce value.

10.2.2   Proof of Stake (PoS)

PoS protocol came into existence to overcome the power demanding PoW. Instead of all miners competing to mine the nonce value, a miner is picked in some fashion. The miner, before starting to validate the transaction, puts some amount of his cryptocurrency at stake in case the validation goes wrong. Once the miners succeed, his stake amount and a reward are returned to the miner as shown in Figure 10.2. This reduces the competition among miners, wastage of power, and no miners will turn malicious in validating wrong transactions as their money is at stake. Selection of

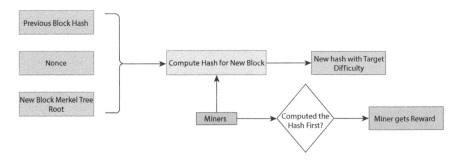

Figure 10.1 Proof of work protocol.

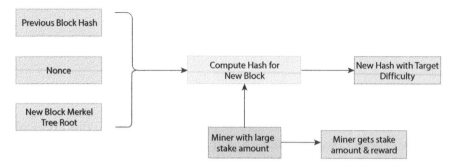

Figure 10.2 Proof of stake protocol.

miners can be based on any one of reasons like high stake amount, high success rate, and linear order [3]. This protocol eliminates the chances of single miner getting hold of the consensus protocol as in PoS protocol.

10.2.3   Delegated Proof of Stake (DPoS)

DPoS is an extended form of PoS. The miners are now known as delegates. The participants of the blockchain network vote their delegate. The delegate with most voting will now perform the transaction validation as shown in Figure 10.3. This protocol is more reliable as compared to PoS since the delegate's reputation is a crucial factor in the voting process. The

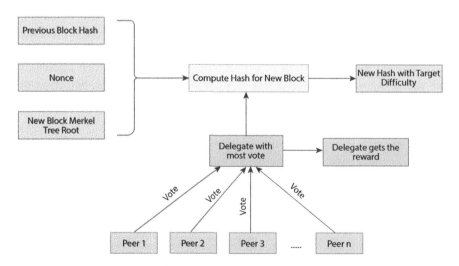

Figure 10.3 Delegated proof of stake protocol.

electors choose their delegates and when the delegates are rewarded for their validation, the reward is shared among the delegate and electors.

10.2.4   Practical Byzantine Fault Tolerance (PBFT)

PBFT protocols were designed to tolerate Byzantine Generals problem. When one or more nodes in the network turn malicious and respond wrong information to other peers or do not respond to peers at all, achievement of consensus is a difficult task. PBFT protocols can withstand such scenario. This protocol works by reaching an agreed value for their messages by all the non-faulty nodes [4, 5]. If malicious nodes do not respond, then some default vote value can be assigned and added to the total value. If any message is not received in stipulated time, then the node is considered by peers as faulty. This protocol works only when number of non-faulty nodes in the network is more than two-thirds of the total nodes.

10.2.5   Proof of Capacity

Proof of capacity is a protocol that uses the hard drive space of miners as a key aspect in choosing the next miner as shown in Figure 10.4. Miners need not invest much in their computation resources as in PoS. Miners are chosen with more hard drive space to validate and create a block in the network.

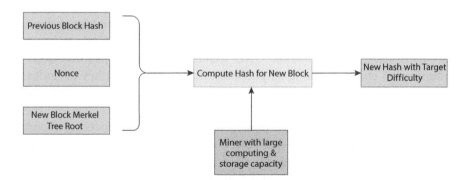

Figure 10.4 Proof of capacity protocol.

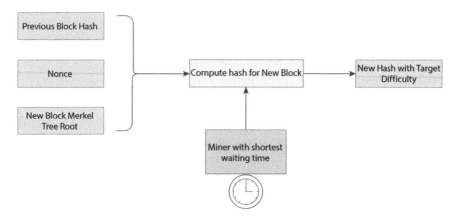

Figure 10.5 Proof of elapsed time protocol.

10.2.6   Proof of Elapsed Time

This is one of the fair protocols to choose the miners in fair process. Miners wait for their turn to create blocks. They wait for random periods and create a new block with their transaction, and the amount of time waited is also included. The block is broadcasted into the network. Peers choose the block with minimum waiting time and get appended to the existing chain of blocks as shown in Figure 10.5. Proper checks must be made to ensure all nodes get a chance to build blocks by having lowest timer value at least once.

10.3   Quantum Blockchain

Blockchain nodes would have two layers of network as shown in Figure 10.6. One layer is for Quantum Key Distribution (QKD) used for authentication, and other layer is used for sharing transaction messages once authentication has been done. QKD establishes a secure pairwise communication channel among all peers to establish the secret key of nodes. In a network of n nodes, when a node decides to create a transaction, it is sent to remaining n − 1 nodes through an authenticated channel. The unconfirmed transactions are pooled together. Mining process is found to be extremely attacked by quantum computers in two ways, namely, no rigid digital signatures included in the transaction and a miner with quantum computer can have centralized control of the mining process [6]. To overcome these issues, quantum blockchain creates blocks in decentralized

Figure 10.6 Quantum blockchain.

manner. The broadcasting protocol is securely used to achieve Byzantine agreement among nodes using the authenticated channel with only presence of fault nodes less than n/3. At regular interval, the network verifies the unconfirmed transactions and obtains consensus of all nodes whether to accept or deny the transaction. All the accepted transactions are bundled up into a block and ordered based on their timestamp. The block is then added to the database.

The broadcast protocol need not use the quantum channel as it consumes more energy for data transmission. Data transmission can be done through normal communication channel and sharing of secret key is only done through the quantum channel.

10.3.1   Quantum Protocols in Blockchain

Most of the cryptographic algorithms build their strength from the use of complex computational algorithms. Attackers spend their resources in factorizing the large numbers used in cryptography to break the cryptosystem. Factorization of large numbers was a big deal with limited computation resources. With the introduction of quantum computers, any complex computational algorithms are done within a matter of minutes. This led to breakage of cryptosystems at quicker rates. To withstand the breaking capability of quantum computers, various quantum protocols were introduced. Quantum protocols can be applied in walk of security like encryption, commitment of transactions, voting protocols, and so on. This section will introduce some of the quantum protocols introduced in the blockchain network.

10.3.1.1   Quantum Bit Commitment Protocols

Bit commitment protocol is used to achieve a commitment of a bit value between two untrusted parties A and B. The two parties make a commitment with zero knowledge of the bit value by the other party. This protocol will consist of two phases, namely, commitment phase and opening phase. Let A and B be the two parties involved in the commitment protocol.

10.3.1.1.1   Commitment Phase

In the commitment phase, the sender A will choose a bit value (0 or 1) for the bit "x". The sender will not reveal the bit value of "x" to other party. Instead, the sender will provide some evidence related to the chosen value of "x". The receiver party has zero knowledge about the bit value of "x".

10.3.1.1.2   Opening Phase

In the opening phase, sender A will provide some information needed to reconstruct the bit value of "x" to the receiver. The receiver B will now reconstruct the new bit value "x" based on the evidence and information provided by the party A.

The commitment protocol must have the two requirements, namely, concealing and binding. Concealing ensures the party B will not know the original bit value "x" determined by A before the opening phase [7]. Binding property ensures the party A will not be able to change the value of "x" once committed after the commitment phase. The protocol must aim to achieve x = x' as shown in Figure 10.7.

Quantum Bit Commitment (QBC) protocols are deigned to be unconditionally secure irrespective of any given scenario. The probability of sensing any cheat actions is as high as 1. Party A is said to be cheating if it

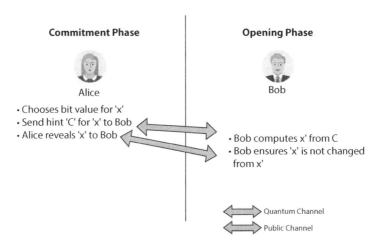

Figure 10.7 Quantum bit commitment protocol.

violates the binding property and part B is said to be cheating if violates the concealing property. Some of the QBC protocols are as follows.

10.3.1.2   Quantum Voting Protocols

Voting protocols finds applications in many fields. This chapter will focus on the use of voting protocols involved in blockchain network [8, 9]. Whenever a new voting protocol is introduced in the blockchain, it is expected to have the following features:

- Anonymous rights of voters
- Integrity of the vote after being cast
- Strict single submission of vote
- Verifiability of their vote being counted by voters
- Eligibility of voters
- Fairness in the voting system

10.3.1.2.1   Simple Quantum Voting Protocol

The voting protocol is applied in a network of nodes where nodes vote to solve a specific issue. The voters have the rights to support or oppose an issue. Their opinion is recorded by a binary value "x" which can have either 0 (opposing the issue) or 1 (supporting the issue). Thus, $x \in (1, 0)$. Consider a blockchain network with n nodes, the voting protocol would construct an $n \times n$ matrix where every row of the matrix is the value provided by a voter. The voting protocol has two phases, namely, Ballot commitment phase and Ballot tallying phase, as depicted in Figure 10.8.

10.3.1.2.1.1   BALLOT COMMITMENT PHASE

1. Let V_i be the voter from the n nodes such that $i = 1, 2,\ldots, n$. The voter V_i will provide the values for the ith row of $n \times n$ matrix. The values provided by V_i are represented as m_{i1}, m_{i2}, $\ldots$, m_{in}. The values are chosen such that sum of their values and 0 are congruent to (mod n + 1).

2. In the next step, the node V_i from its row values m_{i1}, $m_{i2},\ldots$, m_{in} (generally represented as m_{ij}) will send the value m_{ij} to the node V_j through the secure quantum channel.

3. With the repetition of steps 1 and 2, every node V_i will now know the ith column values from all other peer nodes. With the ith column values $c_{1i}, c_{2i},\ldots, c_{ni}$, the node V_i will calculate

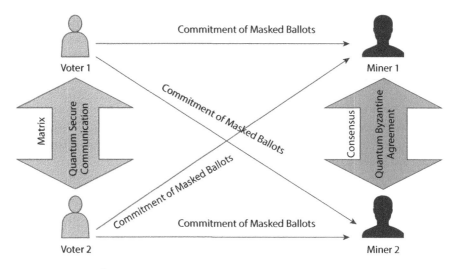

Figure 10.8 Simple quantum voting.

the masked ballot $\tilde{v}_i = v_i + \sum_j c_{ji}(\bmod\ n+1)$ and broadcasts the $\tilde{v}_i$ to the miners in the network using the QBC protocol.

10.3.1.2.1.2   BALLOT TALLYING PHASE

In the ballot tallying phase, the miners play the key role in verifying the ballot values $\tilde{v}_i$ received from all voters.

1. All voters Vi send their masked ballot $\tilde{v}_i$ where i = 1, 2,..., n to the miners.
2. Miners in the network try to achieve a consensus on the masked ballot values $\tilde{v}_i, \tilde{v}_2, ... \tilde{v}_n$
3. The final result of voting is calculated by summing all the masked ballot values which must be equal to the ballot values chosen by the voters in step 1 of ballot commitment phase. Therefore, $\sum_i \tilde{v}_i \equiv \sum_i (v_i + \sum_j c_{ji}(\bmod\ n+1)) \equiv \sum_i v_i$.

10.3.1.2.2   Anti-Quantum Voting Protocol

Various voting protocols in blockchain aimed to achieve anonymity and transparency in the voting process. However, these protocols were found to be non-resistance against quantum attacks. To provide the resistance to quantum attacks, a voting protocol with auditing function and anti-quantum functions were introduced in the blockchain [10]. In general, voting algorithms uses public key cryptosystem which requires time consuming certificate verification process. In addition, the public key cryptosystem ensures the privacy of the voters and have no mechanism to deal with the violators. To make the voting protocol resistant to quantum attacks and audit the accountability of vote violators, code-based cryptography and certificateless signature cryptography are needed.

10.3.1.2.2.1   Code-Based Cryptography

Code-based cryptography is one of the mathematical techniques based on which a public key cryptosystem can be constructed. The code-based technique constructs cipher text from a linear error correcting code like binary Goppa code. To the binary code, a random error is added and encrypted using a public key matrix. The receiver has to decode the ciphertext in polynomial time by removing the random errors added to obtain the original plain text. Figure 10.9 depicts the code-based cryptography. If the receiver is not able to decode with corresponding private key, then quantum attacks are not possible on code-based cryptography as they are

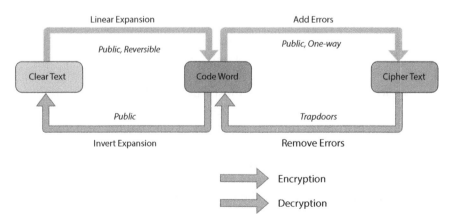

Figure 10.9 Code-based cryptography.

regarded as NP-complete problems that cannot be solved in polynomial time.

10.3.1.2.2.2   CERTIFICATELESS DIGITAL SIGNATURE
The creation of digital signature involves computational Diffie-Hellman Problem and bilinear pairings [11].

Bilinear Pairing: Let C1 and C2 be an additive and multiplicate cyclic groups produced by the number P of order q, respectively. Let three random numbers x, y, and z be chosen from the field Z_q. A bilinear mapping f: C1 X C1$\square$C2 will be obtained with the properties of bilinearity, non-degeneration, and computability.

- The mapping f is said to be bilinear if $f(xM, yN) = f(M, N)^{xy}$ for all M, N ϵ C1 and x, y ϵ Z_q.
- The mapping f is said to be non-degenerate if there exists two values M, Nϵ C1 such that $f(M, N) \neq 1$.
- The mapping f is said to be computable if there exists an efficient algorithm that can compute $f(M, N)$ for all M, Nϵ C1 in polynomial time.

Computational Diffie-Hellman Problem: From an additive cyclic group C generated by q, it is computationally difficult to calculate the third element $q_3 = xyq$ from the two known group elements $q_1 = xq$ and $q_2 = yq$ given x and y are unknown. The voting system with certificateless code-based technique is shown in Figure 10.10.

The system model of anti-quantum voting protocol requires four types of entities, namely, regulator, voting initiator, voter, and candidate.

- **Regulator:** Regulator is a most trusted entity in the network and has the responsibility of generating partial private keys and distributes them to the voters. It also has the responsibility of identity recovery of voters in the final audit phase. To manage any dispute in vote auditing, regulator is able to trace back the anonymity of votes to the ID of voter. This helps them to identify the voters who did not comply in the voting phase and can be complained. To help in this process, regulators tie up the PSK of a voter with its ID and archive them for audit purpose [12]. Regulator plays role only in

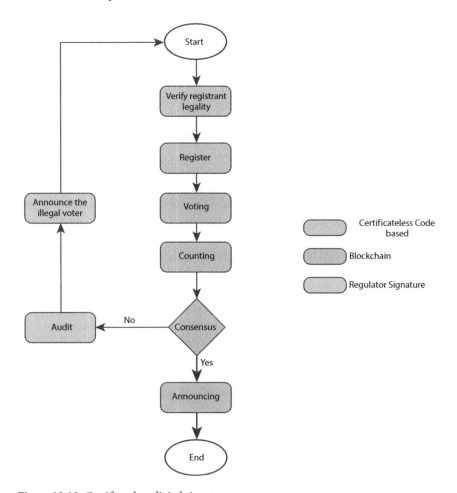

Figure 10.10 Certificateless digital signature.

managing the voter entities and do not participate in the voting process.

- **Voting initiator:** Voting initiator is the entity responsible for generating the list of candidates going to participate in voting. To initiate the voting, he enlists the details of candidates in the blockchain contract using name and their corresponding public key address.

- **Voter:** Voters are the participants in the network. They register with the regulator are provided with the partial private keys and ID. From the partial key, they compute their complete private and public key by choosing a random value. With the keys generated, voters participate in the voting process.

- **Candidate:** Candidate is any node willing to take part in voting. The candidates are listed down by the initiator with their public key addresses in the smart contract. Candidates must be one of the nodes in the blockchain network.

The Voting Process: The voting process involves voters signing their ballots. Ballot is considered to be a blockchain transaction and includes the details like name and public key address of the chosen candidate. During the voting process, voters sign their ballot by including the public key address of their chosen candidate and the signed ballot and its hash value is broadcasted in the blockchain network [13]. The steps involved in the voting process are listed as follows.

1. The voters are registered with the regulator and are provided with the partial private keys. Voters then generate their own public key and private key pairs. The security parameters for the network are set based on the requirements.
2. Initiator posts the candidates list in the smart contract.
3. Voters involve in the voting process by choosing their candidate and output a signed ballot.
4. All signed ballots are broadcasted in the network along with their hash values. Once they are verified, a block of all ballots is created and is now accessible by every node in the network.
5. All nodes run a consensus algorithm to achieve the voting result. If any discrepancy is raised in the consensus achievement phase, then an audit algorithm is performed by the regulator.
6. In the auditing phase, the regulator tracks down the voter who created the defective ballot. The voter is penalized.

Security Analyses of Anti-Quantum Voting Protocol:
The anti-quantum voting protocol has the following security features.

1. The anti-quantum voting protocol with certificateless signature is unforgeable.
2. It has the salient feature of conditional anonymity.

3. The voting protocol allows verifiability of votes in case of any discrepancy during an audit.
4. The voting protocol has the feature of auditability and can be done by the regulator.
5. The voting protocol is resistant to various security attacks like replay attack, man-in-the middle attack, modification attack, counterfeiting attack, and quantum attacks.

10.4 Quantum Honest-Success Byzantine Agreement (QHBA) Protocol

QHBA is a replacement protocol for classical Byzantine Agreement Protocol to improve the efficiency of the blockchain network. To improve the efficiency of blockchain transactions and secure against quantum attacks, quantum certificates are embedded into its transactions. QHBA is applied in a network of "n" agents to commonly agree upon a value. A node chooses an input value a_s from the set of possible values S, $a_s \in S$. The QHBA protocol aims to achieve honest agreement among all the nodes on the value of the input chosen by a distinct node [14]. The protocol is said to have achieved honest-success Byzantine agreement if the following conditions are met:

    i.   If the node (sender) that chooses a_s is honest, then all other agents must agree upon the same value b, such that $b = a_s$.

    ii.   If the sender node is dishonest, then all other honest agents can either terminate the agreement protocol or agree upon a common value b from the set S, $b \in S$.

When in a network, number of dishonest agents n_d is less than a fraction of k where $0 < k < 1$, the network is said to be k-resilient. QHBA can achieve resilient up to $\dfrac{n_d - 2}{n_d}$ where n_d is the number of dishonest agents. This protocol works in three stages, namely:

    i.   Distribution of list using quantum communication
    ii.   Formation of list by composition
    iii. Consensus achievement among agents

Stage 1: Distribution of list using quantum communication

To distribute the correlated lists among agents, quantum three-pass protocol is used. The quantum three-pass protocol uses bit encryption. The sequence of bits is exchanged by encrypting them twice sequentially by the sender and receiver using their respective private encryption keys. Then, the encrypted bits are decrypted twice by the sender and receiver using their respective private decryption keys.

Among the set of "n" agents $\{A_1, A_2, \ldots, A_n\}$, let A_1 be the sender of correlated list and the remaining nodes $A_2, \ldots A_n$ be the receivers of the list. There exist "d" distributing agents $\{A_{n+1}, A_{n+2}, \ldots, A_{n+d}\}$ responsible for distributing the correlated list. The distributing agents use quantum three-pass protocol to distribute the correlated list $List_k$ to the agent $A_k \epsilon \{A_1, A_2, \ldots, A_n\}$. The distribution of list must follow the below conditions:

    i.   When k = 1, 2, …, n, $|List_k|$ must be equal to "x" such that "x" is a multiple of 6.

    ii. $|List_k| \epsilon \{0, 1, 2\}^x$, where $x/3$ numbers are 0, $x/3$ numbers are 1 and $x/3$ numbers are 2.

    iii.   For $k = 2, 3, \ldots, n$, $|List_k| \epsilon \{0, 1\}^x$

    iv.   For $j = 1, 2, \ldots, x$, if $List_1[j] = 0$, then $List_2[j] = \ldots = List_n[j] = 0$.

    v.   For $j = 1, 2, \ldots, x$, if $List_1[j] = 1$, then $List_2[j] = \ldots = List_n[j] = 1$.

After the completion of distribution process, the remaining agents A_2, $A_3, \ldots, A_n$ communicate with the sender A_1 to check if the above conditions are met for the distributed list. When Θn agents disagree with the received list distributed by the distributor A_i that it does not satisfy the above conditions, where $0 \leq \Theta \leq 0.5$ and then the sender agent A_i is considered dishonest distributor. Rewards to the distributors are allowed only when they are accepted as honest distributor and no rewards are given to the dishonest distributor.

Stage 2: Formation of list by composition

Once stage 1 completes successfully with the distribution of correlated list, every agent in the network will sequentially compose a unique list required for the consensus achievement stage. Let "h" distributor among "d" distributors be classified as honest distributors in stage 1. Then, the lists distributed by the distributors $\{A_{n+1}, A_{n+2}, \ldots, A_{n+h}\}$ be denoted by $\{\varepsilon_{n+1}, \ldots \varepsilon_{n+h}\}$ where $\varepsilon_{n+1} = \{List_i^{n+1}, \ldots List_n^{n+1}\} \ldots \varepsilon_{n+h} = \{List_i^{n+h}, \ldots List_n^{n+h}\}$. The new unique list $\varepsilon = \{List_1, \ldots List_n\}$ is constructed by sequentially composing it as

$List_1 = \{List_1^{n+1}, \ldots List_1^{n+h}\}, \ldots\ List_n = \{List_n^{n+1}, \ldots List_n^{n+h}\}$. This procedure of composition guarantees $(1/n)^{th}$ contribution of every honest distributor to the unique list ε.

Stage 3: Consensus achievement among agents

After the unique list ε is formed in stage 2, the agents $\{A_1, A_2, \ldots, A_n\}$ follow the below given steps to achieve consensus. This protocol works with the assumption of at least half of the total "n" agents are honest.

    i.   The sender A_1 picks a random binary number $b_{1,i}$ and list of positions of $b_{1,i}$ in the list $List_1$ represented by $pos_{1,i}$ to all other agents A_i such that $i = 2, 3, \ldots, n$. The number of positions of $b_{1,i}$ must be $x/3$ where "x" is the length of $List_1$. When all the messages containing the binary number and list of positions sent to remaining agents by A_1 is same $(b_{1,2}, pos_{1,2}) = (b_{1,3}, pos_{1,3}) = \ldots = (b_{1,n}, pos_{1,n})$, the agent A_1 is said to be honest. If the messages received by any two agents, namely, A_k and A_j are different $(b_{1,k}, pos_{1,k}) \neq (b_{1,j}, pos_{1,j})$, then the agent A_1 is dishonest. A honest agent will choose only the $b_{1,k}$ as its output value and a dishonest agent may choose any value (either 0 or 1) as its output value irrespective of $b_{1,k}$.

    ii.   Agent $A_k \in \{A_2, A_3, \ldots, A_n\}$ after receiving the message $(b_{1,k}, pos_{1,k})$ from A_1 will then perform the consistency check. During the consistency check, A_k will check whether indices of $b_{1,k}$ in $List_k$ is same as $pos_{1,k}$. When the message is consistent and the agent A_k is also honest, it distributes the message $(b_{1,k}, pos_{1,k})$ to other agents except itself and A_1. In case the message is inconsistent with the $List_k$, agent A_1 is considered to be dishonest and transmits a signal $\overline{\tau}$ denoting "An inconsistent message is received from A_1" to all other agents. There might be a situation where the agent A_k itself dishonest, and it may choose to send $b_{1,k}$ or $\overline{b}_{1,k}$ with a list of randomly chosen indices. The message sent by A_k will now be denoted by $(b_{k,j}, pos_{k,j})$ where $j \neq 1$ and k.

    iii. Every agent continues the above step until all agents exchanged messages with each other after a consistency check. Each honest agent A_k will now determine the output value depending on the given below conditions.

        a.   Let C denote the number of agents consistent with A_k such that $|C| \geq 2$.

- All messages from agents in C $\forall j \in C, (b_{j,k}, pos_{j,k})$ are consistent with $List_k$.
- There are some agents $\exists i, j \in C, b_{i,k} \neq b_{j,k}$.
- The agent A_k will set its output value to be $\dagger$ denoting no consistent value is obtained in the process.

b. Let C denote the number of agents consistent with A_k such that $|C| \geq 2$.

- All messages from agents in C $\forall j \in C, (b_{j,k}, pos_{j,k})$ are consistent with $List_k$.
- $\forall i \notin C, (b_{i,k}, pos_{i,k})$ are inconsistent with $List_k$.
- All agents in C are honest and agent A_k will set its output value O_k as $b_{j,k}$.

c. Let C denote the number of agents consistent with A_k such that $|C| \geq 2$.

- All messages from agents in C $\forall j \in C, (b_{j,k}, pos_{j,k})$ are consistent with $List_k$.
- $\forall i \notin C$, the messages received from A_i are $\dagger$.
- All agents in C are honest and agent A_k will set its output value O_k as $b_{j,k}$.

d. If none of the above conditions are met, agent A_k will set its output value O_k as $\dagger$.

iv. In a network of "n" agents, when at least half of the agents $(n/2)$ choose the same output bit value $O \in \{0, 1\}$, the protocol is said to have achieved consensus on the output bit value O. The agents that achieved the output value same as O are considered to be honest and are rewarded.

10.5   MatRiCT Protocol

Before the introduction of MatRiCT, RingCT protocol was the classical protocol used for securing confidential transactions in a blockchain network. RingCT aims to hide the identity of the sender and the information of the transaction from other peers in the network. To make the confidential transactions efficient and secure against quantum attacks, MatRiCT protocol is introduced. This protocol focuses on the functionality of two entities in a blockchain network namely, the sender and the verifier. Sender is the entity that initiates a transaction and creates necessary proof to validate it. Verifiers are the entities that validate the transaction using the proof. Recipient is the entity receiving the transaction [15].

MatRiCT is a post-quantum protocol based on RingCT to work efficiently, scale for large blockchain networks, and has the feature of auditability to trace back to the spender in later stages when required. The MatRiCT protocol has six phases of implementation as follows:

i. Setting up the system parameters
ii. Generation of public-private key pairs
iii. Generation of serial number for the given secret key
iv. Creation of coins
v. Spending the coins in transaction
vi. Verifying the transaction

10.5.1 Setting Up the System Parameters

Implementation of MatRiCT begins with the generation of random matrix G from a given initial seed value and an optional string argument. The optional argument helps in generating different random matrix every time if same seed is used. The size of ring to be used be set to N. the challenge space for the hash function to be used is defined as $C_{w,p}^d = x \in \mathbb{Z}[X]$ where x must satisfy any one of the following conditions.

a. Degree of x must be $d - 1$
b. Hamming Weight of x, $HW(x) = w$
c. $\|x\|_\infty = p$

When the parameter d is provided, this step will determine the values of w and p such that, $|C_{w,p}^d| > 2^{256}$. Then, a hash function $\mathfrak{f}$ is chosen that satisfies the challenge space $|C_{w,p}^d|$.

10.5.2 Generation of Public-Private Key Pairs

The cyclometric ring R_b of degree b is defined as $R_b = \dfrac{\mathbb{Z}_b[X]}{X^b + 1}$. This phase generates a secret key vector which is a random vector defined over R_b that has a maximum absolute coefficient of initial randomness, B_{max}. The public key is generated from the secret key vector with commitment to zero.

10.5.3   Generation of Serial Number for the Given Secret Key

The serial number is generated such that it is a commitment to zero under the secret key as randomness. To achieve the successful generation of serial number, the commitment matrix is set to a height of n_s.

10.5.4   Creation of Coins

The process of generating coins for the purpose of transactions is known as minting. The coins are minted as computed as commitments to the input transaction amount. The commitment key used in this process is same as the one used in generation of secret key.

10.5.5   Spending the Coins in Transaction

It begins with the computation of corrector values c_v that are exactly divisible by 2. With the corrector values c_v, the spender then mints the output coins depending on the amount to be transferred. The spender then runs an aggregated binary proof algorithm that involves rejection sampling technique. The rejection sampling technique is applied to binary secrets having the same Hamming weight. Finally, the spender performs the ring signature to denote his/her ownership of the account from which the amount is being transferred. Additional ring signature is added to prove the integrity of the amount being transferred.

10.5.6   Verifying the Transaction

The transaction is verified by validating the proof generated by the sender. The verification process by the verifier involves the generation of missing components that were not generated by the spender and the whole components are put together to verify their hash value. When their hash value matches, the transaction is verified. The missing components can be generated from the proof components and hence need not be transmitted to the verifier.

10.6   Conclusion

Protocols enforce the structuring and encoding of data for safe and secure transmission. They must protect data from malicious hands and reach the destination in an intended way. Blockchain being a decentralized network with peers, protocol is a crucial factor required to ensure trust among peers, secure transmission of data, and achieve consensus among peers. PoS protocol came into existence to overcome the power demanding PoW. Bit commitment protocol is used to achieve a commitment of a bit value between two untrusted parties. Proof of capacity is a protocol that uses the hard drive space of miners as a key aspect in choosing the next miner.

References

1. Sutradhar, K. and Om, H., Hybrid quantum protocols for secure multiparty summation and multiplication. *Sci. Rep.*, 10, 1, 1–9, 2020.
2. Brady, L.T., Baldwin, C.L., Bapat, A., Kharkov, Y., Gorshkov, A.V., Optimal protocols in quantum annealing and quantum approximate optimization algorithm problems. *Phys. Rev. Lett.*, 126, 7, 070505, 2021.
3. Unruh, D., Quantum relational Hoare logic. *Proc. ACM Program. Lang.*, 3, POPL, 1–31, 2019.
4. Krishnamoorthi, S., Jayapaul, P., Dhanaraj, R.K., Rajasekar, V., Balusamy, B., Hafizul Islam, S.K., Design of pseudo-random number generator from turbulence padded chaotic map. *Nonlinear Dyn.*, 104, 2, 1627–1643, 2021.
5. Hosseinidehaj, N., Babar, Z., Malaney, R., Ng, S.X., Hanzo, L., Satellite-based continuous-variable quantum communications: State-of-the-art and a predictive outlook. *IEEE Commun. Surv. Tutorials*, 21, 1, 881–919, 2018.
6. Brady, L.T., Baldwin, C.L., Bapat, A., Kharkov, Y., Gorshkov, A.V., Optimal protocols in quantum annealing and quantum approximate optimization algorithm problems. *Phys. Rev. Lett.*, 126, 7, 070505, 2021.
7. Abd EL-Latif, A.A., Abd-El-Atty, B., Venegas-Andraca, S.E., Mazurczyk, W., Efficient quantum-based security protocols for information sharing and data protection in 5G networks. *Future Gener. Comput. Syst.*, 100, 893–906, 2019.
8. Krishnamoorthi, S., Jayapaul, P., Rajasekar, V., A modernistic approach for chaotic based pseudo random number generator secured with gene dominance. *Sādhanā*, 46, 1, 1–12, 2021.
9. Kumar, A., Dadheech, P., Singh, V., Poonia, R.C., Raja, L., An improved quantum key distribution protocol for verification. *J. Discrete Math. Sci. Cryptogr.*, 22, 4, 491–498, 2019.

10. Zhukov, A.A., Kiktenko, E.O., Elistratov, A.A., Pogosov, W.V., Lozovik, Y.E., Quantum communication protocols as a benchmark for programmable quantum computers. *Quantum Inf. Process.*, 18, 1, 1–23, 2019.

11. Rajasekar, V., Premalatha, J., Sathya, K., Dhanesh Raakul, S., Saracevic, M., An Enhanced Anti-phishing Scheme to Detect Phishing Website, in: *IOP Conference Series: Materials Science and Engineering*, vol. 1055, no. 1, p. 012077, IOP Publishing, Chennai, 2021.

12. Yan, L., Sun, Y., Chang, Y., Zhang, S., Wan, G., Sheng, Z., Semi-quantum protocol for deterministic secure quantum communication using Bell states. *Quantum Inf. Process.*, 17, 11, 1–12, 2018.

13. Kumar, R.N., Chandran, V., Valarmathi, R.S., Kumar, D.R., Bitstream Compression for High Speed Embedded Systems Using Separated Split Look Up Tables (LUTs). *J. Comput. Theor. Nanosci.*, 15, 5, 1719–1727, 2018.

14. Rajasekar, V., Jayapaul, P., Krishnamoorthi, S., Saracevic, M., Elhoseny, M., Al-Akaidi, M., Enhanced WSN Routing Protocol for Internet of Things to Process Multimedia Big Data, 2021.

15. Upadhyaya, T., van Himbeeck, T., Lin, J., Lütkenhaus, N., Dimension reduction in quantum key distribution for continuous-and discrete-variable protocols. *PRX Quantum*, 2, 2, 020325, 2021.

11

Post-Quantum Blockchain–Enabled Services in Scalable Smart Cities

Kumar Prateek* and Soumyadev Maity

Department of Information Technology, Indian Institute of Information Technology Allahabad, Prayagraj, India

Abstract

The mass migration of rural citizens toward urban areas in search of better employment opportunities, better education erupts a new threat for urban citizens. The increased population due to migration contributes in increasing traffic jams, green house gas emissions, waste disposal. To provide better day-to-day services to citizens, common issues such as fair broadband distribution and connectivity, digital and knowledge inclusion needs to be respected with possible integration and smooth management of various social, physical, and business infrastructure. Furthermore, the rapid development of digital society opens up vast of opportunities in smart cities thus implementing goals of education and healthcare for all, green society, green city. However, the continued adoption of new technologies such as internet of things (IoT) and cloud technologies for various applications in smart cities suffers from issues such as high latency, bandwidth bottlenecks, scalability, security, and privacy. The smart cities are usually autonomous in nature, which relies on distributed infrastructure and features applications such as intelligent information processing, heterogeneous network infrastructure, ubiquitous sensing, and intelligent control systems implemented in areas such as public safety, healthcare, and diagnosis. Besides, the blockchain-enabled applications such as data platform for sharing valuable data between non-trusted organizations, blockchain-based financial systems, online games, online education system, and identity management system improve reliability and democratization of cities by eliminating centralization. However, majority of applications depends on either digital signature or public key cryptography-based schemes which, in turn, depend on the premise that

---

Corresponding author: pcl2017003@iiita.ac.in

Rajesh Kumar Dhanaraj, Vani Rajasekar, SK Hafizul Islam, Balamurugan Balusamy and Ching-Hsien Hsu (eds.) Quantum Blockchain: An Emerging Cryptographic Paradigm, (263–292)
© 2022 Scrivener Publishing LLC

computation of private key from public key is computationally hard. But with advent of quantum computer, the time complexity of all hard problems such as discrete log problem and integer factorization has reduced from millions of years to few seconds, thus endangering traditional cryptographic mechanism, which includes public key, secret key, and digital signature–based protocols used in blockchain technology–based services in smart cities. The quantum computing which uses law of physics for communication does not depend on mathematically hard problems. In addition, convergence of quantum computing with blockchain technology provides us with amicable solutions for smart cities. This chapter discusses overview of quantum computing, key characteristics, and quantum key distribution and presents an architecture enabling post-quantum blockchain–based applications within smart cities. In addition, the need of various services relying on quantum blockchain in smart cities is presented. Moreover, to enable conceptual architecture for post-quantum blockchain-enabled services in smart cities, smart contracts are designed for implementing transportation application.

Keywords: Blockchain, quantum blind signature, quantum computing, quantum key distribution, security, smart cities

11.1   Introduction

Distributed ledger has become an alternative to cloud computing. The flexibility provided by distributed ledger to store database in local proximity and allowing modification of records only after achieving mutual consensus among peers makes this technology extremely popular in market. In addition, each peer within network possesses synchronized copy of records. Although various work related to smart city application utilizing blockchain is present [1–4], huge scope of improvement in different verticals of society within any smart city still exists. Initially, with aim to store financial transaction history, distributed ledger is proposed in cryptocurrency, namely, Bitcoin. However, the secure implementation of blockchain-based application within any smart city demands combination of consensus and cryptographic techniques. Few popular consensus mechanisms which are widely used in blockchain-based applications are practical Byzantine fault tolerance [5], delegated proof of stake [6], proof of work [7], and proof of stake (PoS) [8], while hash-based and public key cryptography-based techniques are used to achieve security. However, with availability of quantum computer, all cryptographic mechanism using public key techniques becomes vulnerable. In addition, quantum computer capabilities to break mathematically hard problems such as integer factorization have only threatened the existing infrastructure. Quantum computer can easily attack on consensus and cryptographic mechanism in blockchain-based applications. Also, quantum computer has ability to phenomenally reduce complexity of SHA256 hash function used in Bitcoin for mutual consensus [9]. In addition, ECDSA scheme used in Bitcoin has become vulnerable due to advent of quantum computer. The centralized structure of smart city has only fabricated unauthorized data manipulation by powerful groups. Sometimes, with focus to fulfill their malicious agendas, huge accumulation of private data of individuals, transfer of illegitimate message in form of fake news, etc., are performed, thus endangering basic rights of privacy of individuals. Besides, illegitimate sell of retrieve data from centralized application has only boosting dark markets, thereby generating chances of increased crime. Although, decentralized mechanism can alone solve the mentioned issue but coordinated targeting by few industries can be performed with the private information achieved through quantum attacks. A classic example could be need of transportation pattern, vehicle-related information of individuals by few manufacturing companies to sell their specific products.

11.1.1 Motivation and Contribution

Because of the ever increasing population within smart cities, tremendous challenges have been emerged, thus requires quick redressal. One such problem is validation of driver records while driving vehicles to accomplish any journey within smart cities. In addition, government used to charge toll fees, etc., from drivers through toll collection point installed around particular road. Besides, penalties are also charged to vehicle's driver for reckless driving, wrong lane driving, breaking traffic rules, and safety measures. The non-possession of valid driving license, pollution certificate, etc., can lead to generation of penalty for individual vehicle. Also, because of multiple toll points, many junction and crossroads within smart cities, handling of vehicle records and managing penalty related records are tiresome. In addition, transfer of records through different organization is complex. Besides, there does not exist any standard benchmark approach which provides solution to such issue. However, a decentralized network, namely, blockchain network could become fruitful in envisioning solution. In literature, the smart road pricing (SRP) system using blockchain is subsequently introduced guaranteeing enhanced security as data stored in blockchain network is protected from tampering but arrival of quantum computer will also make standard encryption technique vulnerable. Therefore, we proposed a quantum blockchain–enabled SRP system to be used within smart cities. The specific contribution of this chapter is as follows:

- In addition to discussion on the need of post-quantum blockchain–enabled services within any smart city, we have proposed an architecture for post-quantum blockchain–enabled application for transportation application within any smart city.
- We have used distributed ledger to build blockchain network and stored records of each registered vehicle such as owner details, vehicle number, and license detail of driver in the blockchain network with aim to protect the transportation application from single point of failure within smart cities. The proposed work incorporates different roles, namely, vehicle, toll point, district transport agency, and network admin. All roles require permission for accessing data already stored in blockchain network. Besides, different smart contract has been designed to enable the whole SRP system (transportation application) within smart cities. The proposed system incorporates quantum blind signature within smart contract to enable automation of SRP system achieving unconditional communication security within smart cities.

The organization of rest of the chapter includes preliminaries section where quantum computing and blockchain are described. Various recent literature utilizing quantum techniques in different application areas such as healthcare and cloud computing have been explored in Section 11.3. Section 11.4 describes background details of proposed work detailing design goals. Later, the proposed SRP system with detailed system architecture and vehicle records utilizing BB84 protocol along with designed smart contracts are described in Section 11.5. Finally, Section 11.6 concludes the work.

11.2   Preliminaries

This section gives insights about building blocks of proposed protocol, i.e., quantum computing, quantum key distribution (QKD), and blockchain. Besides, the need for amalgamation of quantum computing and blockchain is presented.

11.2.1   Quantum Computing

This section includes overview on quantum computing in addition to specifying details of key characteristic as well as quantum platform and software development kit (SDK) available in market where quantum algorithm can be simulated or executed on real quantum computer. The quantum computer will be made up of quantum chips contrary to silicon-based chips installed in classical computers. Moreover, the potential of quantum computer to break mathematically hard problems such as integer factorization (IF) problem and discrete log (DL) problem made it extremely popular, meanwhile, endangering all existing protocols whose security depends on mathematically hard problems. In addition, exponential increase of curiosity by major multi-national companies (MNCs) in building quantum computer that has not only created the hype rather availability of quantum computer in market is assured. Recently, IBM's roadmap predicts the arrival of 1,000 qubit quantum computer within few years. The announcement by several scientist indicates intense planning for cryptographic agility term used to upgrade existing protocols before they become vulnerable or outdated. In addition, quantum computing is also expected to turn around computationally difficult task such as training of neural network, which are known to be building blocks of several machine learning algorithm. The need of optimization for various deep learning algorithms only fosters the need of availability of quantum processing units (QPUs) to researchers and industry through cloud. It is expected that, similar to graphic processing units (GPUs), QPUs will be available to any individual for deploying their algorithm very soon. Now, what follows are basics of quantum system.

11.2.1.1 Basics of Quantum System

Quantum system depends heavily on quantum mechanics which uses complex number contrary to real numbers. In addition, contrary to bit, which is described with set of states, i.e., either 0 or 1, quantum bits are used by quantum system which could be narrated through 2D system $[c_0, c_1]^T$ where

$$|c_0^2| + |c_1^2| = 1. \tag{11.1}$$

where c_0^2 and c_1^2 signify the probabilities obtained after measuring the qubits in state $|0 >$ and state $|1 >$. A real world implementation of quantum bit in day-to-day life will make switch of a bulb in ON and OFF state at the same time. In fact, the presence of electron in two different orbits around nucleus and existence of photon in any one out of two polarized states established the implementation of quantum bits. Therefore, existence of quantum indeterminancy and superposition effects within all system lies in universe.

11.2.1.2 Architecture of Quantum System

The quantum system possess reversibility property thereby action performed on quantum system must allowed to be reversed. The assurance of reversibility property within architecture of quantum system brought up the need of reversible gates. Reversible gates constitute all operations which are represented by unitary matrices and are not measurement. Example of reversible gate includes identity gate, NOT gate, CNOT gate, Toffoli gate, and Fredkin gate. The widely used AND gate in classical computing is not reversible as with output of $|0 >$ from AND gate in hand, no one can determine whether input was $|00 >$, $|01 >$, or $|10 >$ contrary to NOT gate and identity gates which are reversible.

$$NOT * NOT = I_2 \tag{11.2}$$

$$I_n * I_n = I_n \tag{11.3}$$

Therefore, an operator which acts on qubits and represented by unitary matrices is known as quantum gates. In addition, it may be noted that Toffoli and Fredkin gates are not only reversible but also is universal and unitary. However, all mentioned quantum gates are limited by no-cloning theorem for imitating fanout operation but transportation of quantum states is still feasible between two systems.

11.2.1.3   Key Characteristics of Quantum Computing

The key characteristics of quantum computing include superposition, measurement, and entanglement. Superposition enables quantum system to be in more than one state with some probability at the same time. The quantum state interferes with each other in superposition. Constructive interference enables addition of probability amplitudes of quantum states, while destructive interference cancels out probability amplitudes of each quantum state. Besides, entanglement is achieved due to superposition of quantum states. Because of entanglement of quantum particles a single system is formed thus generating correlation between entangled particles. This generated correlation is so strong that interconnection between particles remains unchanged even separated over light-year distance. Besides, measurement of quantum particle collapses the superposition state of particles producing binary state either state 0 or state 1.

11.2.1.4   Available Quantum Platform

The major corporation of world is investing huge amount of money for research and development of quantum computing applications. Similar to cloud computing as a service, major corporations of world are planning to provide quantum computing as a service. Recently, Microsoft has announced public preview of one product related to quantum computing, namely, Azure Quantum. It will enable developers and researchers to run newly designed applications or algorithm on real quantum computer (upto 40 bit quantum computer) through cloud. They have partnership with companies like Riggeti and Honeywell to make quantum computer accessible through cloud. In addition, Azure quantum SDK is also available which will allow developers to test their newly designed algorithms testing or simulation locally. Similarly, IBM offers open source SDK, namely, Qiskit. It also allows developers to run and test their quantum algorithm either locally or through cloud to real quantum computer. Google also offers a python library, namely, Cirq, to be used while writing quantum algorithm before running them on real quantum computer or simulator. In addition, an open source library, namely, TensorFlow quantum, is available to run quantum classical machine learning applications.

11.2.2   Quantum Key Distribution

QKD is implemented by utilizing non-orthogonal single quantum states. The existing QKD protocols can be classified on the basis of dimensions of source code into discrete variable and continuous variable protocol, whereas, if entanglement of light source is taken into account, then it is classified into prepare and measure as well as entanglement based protocols. The following subsections discuss the classified QKD in detail.

11.2.2.1   Discrete Variable QKD

While encoding and decoding these types of protocol includes finite-dimensional quantum states while, for key distribution, examples include all protocols which use certain number of relative phases of photon. Discrete variable QKD protocol incorporates prepare-and-measure as well as entanglement-based protocol in addition to distributed phase reference (DPR) protocol. With view to practical implementation of discrete variable QKD, first experiment results are revealed by Charles Bennett and Gilles Brassard. Later, extreme interest is shown by industry and governments with aim to improve the experimental results and extended the covered distance of QKD. Till date, discrete variable QKD can cover distance of 200–300 km.

- **Single-Photon Protocols:** A type of quantum protocol which utilizes single photon's different quantum states for encoding and decoding while distributing the keys. Various single-photon protocols includes protocol designed by Bennet and Brassard, namely, BB84 in the year 1984 [10], two-state protocol, namely, B92 [11], and six-state protocol by Bruß [12].
- **Entangled Photon:** A type of quantum protocol which utilizes pair of mutual entangled photon for key distribution. These photons contrary to single photon utilizes entangled states for communication. The few popular protocols under this category are protocols proposed by Bennett *et al.*, namely, BBM92 [13], and by Ekert in 1991 [14].
- **Other Discrete Variable protocols:** Various researchers tried to explore the field and proposed different one way discrete variable protocols such as protocol by Inoue *et al.* in year 2002 [15], "fast and simple one way quantum key

distribution" by Stucki *et al.* [16] in year 2005. Besides, two-way discrete variable QKD protocol are well described through Bostrom and Felbinger [17] and by Lucamarini and Mancini, namely, LM05 protocol [18].

11.2.2.2 Continuous Variable QKD

It is type of QKD where infinite-dimensional quantum states are used while distributing keys. Further classification of continuous variable QKD leads us to squeezed state, entangled state, and coherent state schemes. Examples of squeezed protocols and coherent protocols are [19–21]. Besides, experimental results of continuous variable QKD reveals transmission distance of 25 km. Later, major breakthrough is achieved in year 2013 when Jouguet *et al.* demonstrated successful implementation of QKD covering distance of 80 km [22].

11.2.2.3 Measurement Device-Independent QKD

Under the strict assumption of perfect single photon and photon detector, QKD is proved to be secure but QKD becomes vulnerable under loose assumption. Considering vulnerability under loose assumption, various researchers designed device-independent protocols such as protocol by Acin *et al.* [23]. However, inefficiency of loophole free bell test (LFBT) on which measurement device-independent protocols are based turns out to be serious issue. Later, protocols such as one side independent [24] and semidevice-independent [25] are proposed. In addition, various attacks such as wavelength dependent, faked state, and detector time shift attack are prevented using measurement device-independent QKD. The security proof and experimental analysis of these types of protocol is well described in [26].

11.2.3 Blockchain

It may be defined as list of linked records with properties such as data traceability and tamper-resistance. The list of linked records is known as blocks with each block connecting to previous block. Blockchain employs consensus algorithms for providing guarantee related to consistency of records. The privilege related to read-and-update the ledger leads us to classification of blockchain as public blockchain where strong autonomous

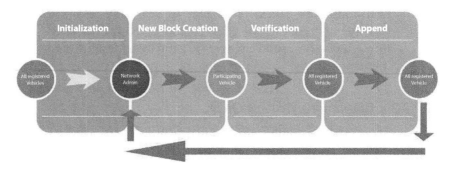

Figure 11.1 Life cycle of transportation application in blockchain.

facilities exist by achieving pure decentralization settings and private blockchain which incorporates control over network up to some extent. Blocks used in blockchain utilize cryptographic hash function to create a chain. However, scalability and efficiency always remain a critical issue during blockchain implementation. Smart contract enables automation of blockchain-based applications in addition to ensuring few popular properties such as atomicity, synchronicity, provenance, availability, immutability, and immortality (no records can be removed) in blockchain, thus opening up scope for designing various application in different industries ranging from healthcare industry, energy industry, robotics energy, agriculture and food industry, and manufacturing industry. In addition, blockchain as a service is expected to completely revolutionize the existing centralized ecosystem. Figure 11.1, shows life cycle of transportation application in blockchain.

11.2.4 Reason for Blend of Blockchain and Quantum-Based Security in Applications Within Smart Cities

All existing applications designed and implemented in smart cities utilize public-key cryptographic techniques to provide security. All public key cryptography-based protocol utilizes the assumption of mathematical hard problems, i.e., the security of existing applications within smart cities depends on mathematically hard problems such as integer factorization (IF). However, the arrival of a few bits quantum chips has indicated the availability of full-fledged quantum computers in the market much sooner than anticipated. The arrival of a full-fledged quantum computer will make existing classical public key-based protocols vulnerable to such an extent that attackers do not require to work very hard to break any system. Besides, utilizing blockchain technology direct access will be provided to every vehicle creating transactions in blockchain network related to vehicle's activities on road. In addition, with use of different available application programming interfaces (APIs) along with smart contract, transmission of data and execution of transaction within blockchain network will be enabled. Also, with vehicle's public identity, all transaction related to vehicle will be entertained, thereby enabling unique identification of all committed transaction in blockchain network. Later, vehicle can verify his records to toll point and district transportation agency whenever asked to verify while moving on road by sharing his secret key. Use of quantum secret based authentication and data sharing will provide unconditional security. Therefore, a decentralized quantum-based security will allow applications within smart cities to become more secure when compared to traditional security techniques.

11.3   Related Work

A blockchain-based architecture to provide security in maintaining electronic health records is presented in [27]. This paper discusses incentive mechanism in detail with frequency of addition of new blocks while giving overview on access control techniques. In addition, a scheme by Yue et al. reveals different architecture utilizing blockchain to store health data records securely [28]. This work includes design of application using blockchain where patient health records can be shared with doctors, clinician, etc., through access control mechanism. Also, in the scheme by Zhang et al. [29], two new protocols are presented, which enables formation of secure connection and sharing of data between different nodes in blockchain network. A scheme by Xia et al. [30] utilizes blockchain to share medical records. The work presents new data sharing scheme which is used by cloud infrastructure providers within blockchain network. In addition, a scheme by Liang et al. [31] discusses medical record sharing implementing blockchain in mobile healthcare applications. The work uses patient's wearable devices, medical inputs manually added by doctors, etc., to constitute medical data record then stores the generated data in cloud, thereby enabling sharing of medical data with healthcare companies as per agreement. Later, a scheme by Lin and Guo [32] discusses a system utilizing quantum blind signature in order to provide identity and message verification. The scheme generates secret keys for messages using quantum bits. Besides, in the scheme by Khodambashi and Zakerolhosseini [33], a smart contract is proposed utilizing quantum blind signature. This work just not only protects the system from quantum attacks but also eliminates the need of trusted third party. A scheme by Lin and Yanlin also uses quantum blind signature to propose quantum circuit which could become a perfect candidate to be used in development of electronic payment as well as electronic voting system [34]. A protocol by Minghui-Zhang *et al.* [35] uses entangled state for quantum blind signature in order to provide traceability, unforgeability, etc. Also, in [36], utilizing light weight quantum blind signature, a smart contract in blockchain network is presented by Cai *et al.*

The availability of quantum computer will definitely boost up number of active applications utilizing quantum computing in various verticals of society. Quantum computing applications are used nowadays in ever growing industries that even blend quantum computing with popular machine learning applications. In addition, in field related to cloud computing, fog computing, and Internet of Things (IoT), vast opportunity is available to design applications that solve specific problems using quantum computing within any smart city. The potential of quantum computing is of extreme importance. Various researchers tried to uncover the hidden potential of quantum computing in different fields such as scheme by Sharma and Kalra [37] in field of cloud computing. The scheme utilizing QKD presented identity-based secure authentication for cloud infrastructure. The scheme ensures identity authentication with unconditional security. In cloud-related application areas, some notable works are also presented by research community such as in schemes [38–40] where properties of QKD are employed to authenticate the entities. The QKD is known to use polarization of photon to encode information. In the scheme by Lohachab and Karambir [41], QKD and payload-based techniques are presented for mutual authentication of IoT devices, employing elliptic curve cryptography (ECC) in application area related to IoT. Also, in applications related to vehicular ad hoc networks (VANETs), identity authentication scheme is introduced for participating vehicles using QKD [42]. In addition, in [43], quantum authentication and communication protocol is designed utilizing one-time pad, while, in the scheme by Mehic *et al.*, detailed discussion on performance of QKD network in widely used network simulator NS-3 is presented [44].

11.4   Background of Proposed Work

This section gives insights on design goals along with fundamental tenets of our work such as conversion mechanism of binary to quantum bit, decision sequence, measurement sequence, template, and encrypted key generation.

11.4.1   Design Goal of Proposed Work

The security and privacy issues play a critical role while envisioning design goal of any protocol. Nowadays, easy availability of high-performance computing infrastructure has enabled any adversary to attack on critical infrastructure very comfortably. In addition, announcement of huge prize money in form of cryptocurrency like Bitcoin on dark web with aim to manifest coordinated attack has threatened any infrastructure like never before. Therefore, with aim to ensure secure communication in the proposed SRP system within smart cities utilizing quantum-blockchain, precautions against the following are designed as goals.

11.4.1.1   Impersonation Attack

It is a form of attack where adversary after manifesting himself to be trusted entity of network shares sensitive information thus creating a confusion within the network. The adversary steals the legal parameters to carry out impersonation attack.

11.4.1.2   Sybil Attack

It is a form of attack where adversary operates multiple pseudonymous identities in order to influence the authority of network. The multiple pseudonymous identities enables adversary to broadcast multiple bogus message, thus allowing him to conduct illegal actions. Examples of Sybil attack include 51% attacks in the blockchain network and generation of multiple fake reviews to any products in e-commerce platform. In order to prevent Sybil attack, different powers to different members need to be assigned. In addition, payment of certain cost for each member who intends to connect in the network should be followed, i.e., cost to create an identity must be accompanied. Also, the direct and indirect validation mechanism should be carried out to members before joining the network.

11.4.1.3   Message Modification Attack

It is a form of active attack where adversary aims to alter, delay, or reorder some segment of message for purpose of fulfilling unintended effect. It involves modifying the packet header and usually performed when adversary wants to either disturb or gain insights about receiver. Whenever instead of altering or reordering the message adversary insert fake data within some section of message, then it leads to bogus information attack.

11.4.1.4   Message Replay Attack

It is the form of attack where adversary delays or resends the intercepted message with aim to generate the mirage of accidents of packet to legal receiver. With proper technique of encryption, timestamping of each message along with small window time, establishing a session with random key which can be utilized only once, could prevent the network from message replay attack.

11.4.1.5   Denial-of-Service Attack

It is the form of attack where adversary floods the network with traffic information, fake requests, or with information that is responsible for triggering a crash. The adversary performs denial-of-service attack with aim to overload the network so that legitimate message cannot be entertained, i.e., intended members are denied with access to network.

11.4.1.6   Source Authentication

The process of ensuring the legitimacy of sender is called as source authentication. It is one of the primary features, which prevents the network from outsider attack.

11.4.1.7   Message Integrity

The process of ensuring that message are not altered or tampered during communication within the network by any adversary. Message digest is widely used to check the message integrity. Message digest is obtained whenever message is passed through hash function. Receiver, after receiving message and digest pair from sender, computes new digest after passing the received message from hash function. In addition, comparison of new computed digest and received digest is performed by receiver to verify integrity of message.

11.4.1.8 Identity Privacy Preservation

The process of preserving real identities of members within the network is known as identity privacy preservation. It is achieved by anonymizing the real identities of members with the help of pseudo identities within the network.

11.4.2 Conversion of Bits From One State to Another

The proposed work uses QKD and thus requires participation of quantum bit. With use of polarization of photon and interconversion rule, conversion of binary bit to quantum bit and vice versa occurs. The proposed protocol denotes photon polarizer through decision sequence and measurement sequence. It may be noted that decision sequence and measurement sequence are alike but do not carry out same function.

11.4.3 Decision Sequence

Decision sequence enables conversion of binary bit into quantum bit. It consists of two types of polarizer, namely, circular and linear polarizer. Horizontal and vertical directions are used to denote linear polarizer, while diagonal direction denotes circular polarizer. In addition, circular and linear polarizer consists of two states which are orthogonal to each other. To be specific, circular and linear polarizer follows orthogonality property.

11.4.4 Interconversion Rule

Interconversion rule is widely used during conversion of bits. In accordance with interconversion rule, sender utilizes decision sequence to find out which polarized photon aligns to zero or one. In proposed work, interconversion rule is defined as follows: $| \rightarrow> \Rightarrow 0$, and $| \uparrow> \Rightarrow 1$. Also, $| \nearrow> \Rightarrow 0$ and $| \nwarrow> \Rightarrow 1$.

11.4.5 Measurement Sequence

Measurement sequence enables restoration of binary bit from quantum bit. It also consists of two types of polarizer, namely, rectilinear and diagonal polarizer similar to linear and circular polarizer of decision sequence.

In fact, the linear and rectilinear polarizer along with circular and diagonal polarizer correlate with each other. Moreover, in accordance with uncertainty principle, decision sequence and measurement sequence are conjugate bases with rectilinear (linear) and diagonal (circular) polarizer as conjugate states, i.e., receiver will only able to retrieve certain results if linear polarizer is measured by rectilinear and circular polarizer are measured by diagonal polarizer. On contrary, uncertain results are obtained. In addition, existence of non-orthogonality property between linear (rectilinear) and circular (diagonal) polarizer makes them indistinguishable. In the Table 11.1, L and R are used to denote linear and rectilinear polarizer, whereas C and D represent circular and diagonal polarizer.

11.4.6   Template and Encrypted Key Generation

Decision sequence and measurement sequence are randomly chosen by sender and receiver during communication. The generation of template occurs in accordance with decision sequence and measurement sequence. In addition, pre-master secret is generated as shown in Table 11.1. The pre-master secret comprises of accurate as well as inaccurate binary bits. Besides, 1/2k denotes selection probability of accurate measurement where k signifies length of bits. The accurate measurement sequence is shown in green color. Moreover, observing pre-master secret and template, encrypted key [0101] is produced as reported in Table 11.2.

11.5   Proposed Work

The proposed quantum blockchain–enabled SRP system includes four roles, namely, vehicles, road side units, network admin, and district

Table 11.1 Generation of pre-master secret.

Binary bit	0	1	1	0	1	0	1	1	1	0
Decision seq	C	L	C	C	L	C	L	L	C	L
Quantum bit	$\vert\nearrow\rangle$	$\vert\uparrow\rangle$	$\vert\nwarrow\rangle$	$\vert\nearrow\rangle$	$\vert\uparrow\rangle$	$\vert\nearrow\rangle$	$\vert\uparrow\rangle$	$\vert\uparrow\rangle$	$\vert\nearrow\rangle$	$\vert\mapsto\rangle$
Measurement seq	D	R	R	D	R	R	D	D	R	D
Pre-master secret	0	1	?	0	1	?	?	?	?	?

Table 11.2 Generation of encrypted key.

Decision seq	C	L	C	C	L	C	L	L	C	L
Measurement seq	D	R	R	D	R	R	D	D	R	D
Template	1	1	0	1	1	0	0	0	0	0
Pre-master secret	0	1	?	0	1	?	?	?	?	?
Encrypted Key	0	1	?	0	1	?	?	?	?	?

transportation agency. The proposed SRP system incorporates QKD and quantum blind signature along with blockchain to fulfill basic security and privacy goals. The implementation of network admin, vehicles, road side units, and district transportation agency is designed through Algorithm 11.1, Algorithm 11.2, Algorithm 11.3, and Algorithm 11.4, respectively.

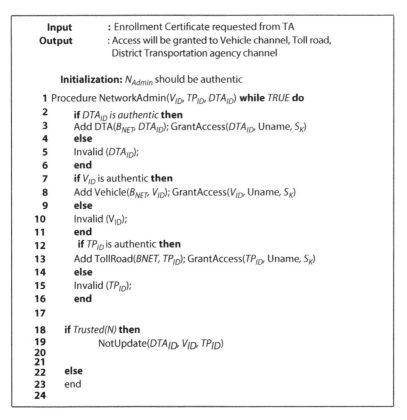

Input	: Enrollment Certificate requested from TA	
Output	: Access will be granted to Vehicle channel, Toll road, District Transportation agency channel	

Initialization: N_{Admin} should be authentic

1 Procedure NetworkAdmin(V_{ID}, TP_{ID}, DTA_{ID}) **while** *TRUE* **do**
2   **if** *DTA_{ID} is authentic* **then**
3   Add DTA(B_{NET}, DTA_{ID}); GrantAccess(DTA_{ID}, Uname, S_K)
4   **else**
5   Invalid (DTA_{ID});
6   **end**
7   **if** *V_{ID} is authentic* **then**
8   Add Vehicle(B_{NET}, V_{ID}); GrantAccess(V_{ID}, Uname, S_K)
9   **else**
10   Invalid (V_{ID});
11   **end**
12   **if** *TP_{ID} is authentic* **then**
13   Add TollRoad(*BNET*, TP_{ID}); GrantAccess(TP_{ID}, Uname, S_K)
14   **else**
15   Invalid (TP_{ID});
16   **end**
17
18   **if** *Trusted(N)* **then**
19   NotUpdate(DTA_{ID}, V_{ID}, TP_{ID})
20
21
22   **else**
23   end
24

Algorithm 11.1 Algorithm for network admin.

```
Input        : Enrollment ID Key requested from N_Admin
Output       : Access will be granted to District Transportation
               Agency Transaction
     Initialization: DTA_ID should be authentic

 1 Procedure DistrictTransportAgency(DTA_ID) while TRUE
do
 2      if Access granted by V_ID then
 3      if Granted M_VID ε C then
 4      RecordsRead (DTA_ID, V_REC, M_VID, B_NET);
 5      RecordsUpdate (DTA_ID, V_REC, M_VID, B_NET);
 6      else
 7      RecordsWrite (DTA_ID, M_VID, B_NET);
 8      RecordsRead (DTA_ID, M_VID, B_NET);
 9      end
10      else
11      Invalid (DTA_ID);
12      end
```

Algorithm 11.2 Algorithm for district transport agency.

```
Input        : Enrollment ID Key requested from
   Output       : Access will be granted to Toll Road hyperledger
Transaction
     Initialization: TR_ID should be authentic

        if Access granted by V_ID
        then if Granted M_VID ε C
           then
                     RecordsRead (TP_ID, V_REC, M_VID, B_NET );

                     RecordsUpdate (TP_ID, V_REC, M_VID, B_NET i.e., (TP_ID, V_REC, M_VID, B_NET);

           else
                     RecordsRead (DTA_ID, M_VID, B_NET);
        end
```

Algorithm 11.3 Algorithm for toll road.

11.5.1   System Architecture

Figure 11.2 illustrates the network model of the transportation application within any smart city that includes the district transportation agency consisting of various toll points. Each toll point covers various roadside units (RSUs). All RSUs are connected to trusted authorities through optical fiber cables for faster connectivity in the real world. The system architecture of the proposed

```
   Input         : Enrollment Key requested from
    Output          : Access will be granted to vehicle for hyperledger
   Transaction
    Initialization: V_ID should be authentic

      if V_ID ∉ B_NET then
          if V_REC/εB_NET then
              RecordsCreated (V_ID, V_REC, B_NET);
              else
                      RecordsUpdated (V_ID, V_REC, B_NET);
          end

      else
      |    Invalid (V_ID);
      end
      if V_ID, Under Speci c Toll Point(M_VID, DTA_ID, TP_ID) then
              M_VID, = TollBill(V_ID,);
              if M_VID εV_CHN then
                      RecordsGranted (M_VID, DTA_ID, TP_ID);
              else
                      (DTA_ID, TP_ID) = Inform("Bill doesn't exist") ;
          end
```

Algorithm 11.4 Algorithm for vehicle.

SRP system gets illustrated in Figure 11.3. There is one district transportation agency within any smart city responsible for maintaining records of all registered vehicles within any city. The district transportation agency handles the collection of money in penalties or taxes by deploying different infrastructures such as toll points. In addition, the generation of driving licenses, pollution certificates, documents related to the vehicle, etc., is also managed by the district transportation agency. In addition, to stop the unlawful driving activities by young drivers, members of the district transportation agency perform strict auditing at any junction or crossroads within the city. The uninformed and instant auditing by members of the district transportation agency leads to an exponential decrement in lane speed violations and hazardous accidents, creating safe and secure transport facilities within the city.

11.5.2   Quantum Information Transmission

QKD is used to exchange keys securely between participating parties. The QKD possesses unconditional security utilizing laws of physics such as superposition, interference, and entanglement. In the proposed protocol,

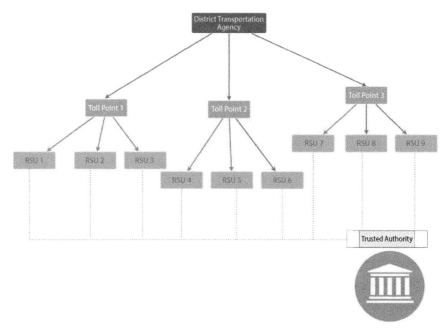

Figure 11.2 Network model of transportation application in smart cities.

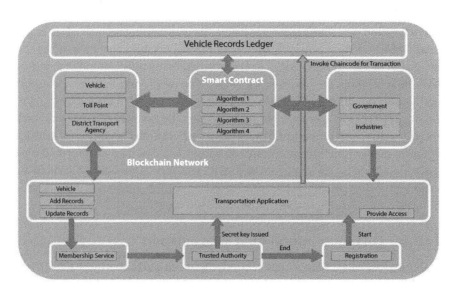

Figure 11.3 Smart road pricing application.

QKD is used within smart contract. Specifically, a quantum communication protocol, namely, BB84, which is proposed by Bennett and Brassard is used. The BB84 allows unconditionally secure exchange of keys between parties as well as enables intrusion detection by prohibiting copying of quantum states in accordance with no-cloning theorem. The implementation of BB84 protocol utilizes polarization photons (linear and circularly polarized photons) in order to encode information. These polarization photons are well known for encoding one bit string to q bit and can retrieve q bit string to traditional binary bits. The high-level description and basics of proposed protocol is already discussed in Section 11.4. Besides, Table 11.3 summaries the notations which are used in the proposed work whereas Table 11.4 reports the time complexity of proposed algorithms. The security of BB84 protocol is well discussed in [45].

11.5.3 Life Cycle of Smart Contract

The proposed quantum blockchain–enabled SRP system for smart cities incorporates smart contracts utilizing quantum blind signature. The quantum blind signature is well discussed in [46]. The post-quantum blockchain-enabled application within any smart city utilizes quantum blind signature to provide unconditional security, which includes three stages, namely, contract development stage, contract release stage, and contract execution stage, as illustrated in Figure 11.4. As the name suggests, contract development

Table 11.3 Notations used in the chapter.

Uname	Username
S_K	Secret key
V_{ID}	Vehicle identity
V_{CHN}	Vehicle channel
TP_{ID}	Toll point identity
TP_{CHN}	Toll point channel
B_{NET}	Blockchain network
DTA_{ID}	District transport agency identity
DTA_{CHN}	District transport agency channel

Table 11.4 Time complexity of proposed algorithm.

Algorithm	Smart contract	Time complexity
Algorithm 1	Implementation of N_{ADMIN}	O(N)
Algorithm 2	Implementation of district transportation agency	$O(DTA_{ID})$
Algorithm 3	Implementation of toll point	$O(TP_{ID})$
Algorithm 4	Implementation of vehicle	$O(V_{ID})$

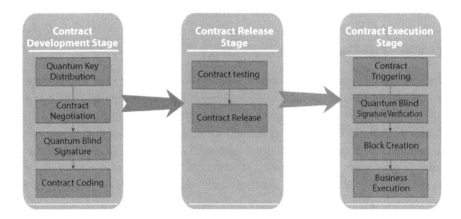

Figure 11.4 Life cycle of smart contract.

stage revolves around development of smart contract. It primarily includes exchange of keys using QKD, contract negotiation, contract coding, and quantum blind signature. The second stage, namely, contract release stage, includes process to perform contract testing thereby performing release of contract. Execution of contract testing will allow transfer of smart contract to each node within the network. As soon as each node receives smart contract due to implementation of contract testing, it performs packing of received smart contract into a set known as contract set. Contract set contains hash value of contract in set and then transfer to different nodes in the blockchain network for further processing. The other nodes, after receiving this contract set, compare the hash with its own contract, leading to decision by all nodes in network regarding release of contract. The third stage, namely, contract execution stage activities, just not only includes triggering of contract and creation of block but also verification of quantum blind signature and execution of protocol. In fact, contract execution is performed using event-based trigger mechanism. As soon as smart contract, which requires verification of quantum blind signature, is received to any node within the network, then verification of quantum blind signature is carried out by respective node. Successful verification will result in creation of new block otherwise not only creation of block gets failed but prohibition of contract execution also takes place.

11.5.4   Algorithm Design and Flow

The QKD occurs between trader and block creator. As soon as utilizing negotiated key, a signed transaction message is received to block creator, utilizing shared key K, the decryption process of signature is performed by block creator, thus producing business request R. It may be noted that since there is chance of collapsing a block creator in any stages of life cycle of smart contract therefore block creator by performing recovery techniques can recover from that particular stage. In addition, automatic execution of contract is enabled in case where business request R and specific signature state b is found to be same otherwise leading to failure of block creation. The steps for execution of smart contract is illustrated through Figure 11.5.

11.5.4.1   Stage 1: Contract Development

The development phase of contract uses QKD for exchange of keys. QKD enables sharing of keys through quantum channel between block creator and trader. In addition, block creator prepares n pair entangled particles in superposition state. Then, negotiation of contract with respect to contract term and quantum keys is carried out. After that, block creator and trader analyze the feasibility of contract term, safety of channel and key. Henceforth, with aim to process business transaction request T_i, blinding factor t and transaction summary k are chosen randomly.

$$T_i = tkT_i'(mod\ n) \tag{11.4}$$

Now, result obtained after blind transformation of transaction request is forwarded to signer. After carefully selecting negotiation particles, signer generates quantum state T_i corresponding to each pair of particles.

$$T_i|(a) >= T_i|(a) >= \alpha|0 > + \beta|1 > where, |\alpha|^2 + |\beta|^2 = 1. \tag{11.5}$$

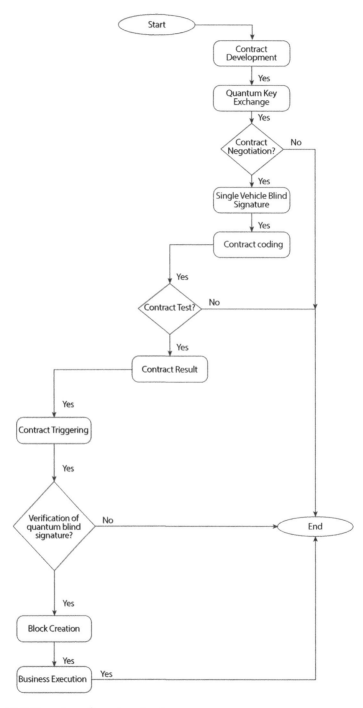

Figure 11.5 Execution of smart contract.

Next, business trader forwards quantum state $T_i(b)$ to block creator while retain $T_i(a)$ to itself. Block creator then verifies the validity of signed transaction request and communicates entangled pairs back to trader. As soon as trader listens back from block creator, calculates particle a_i, T_i, and obtains encrypted result, thereby utilizing bell measurement for generating quantum key corresponding to signature S.

$$S = E_k(T_i) \tag{11.6}$$

11.5.4.2   Stage 2: Contract Release

In this stage, contract testing is done. If testing results is found to be positive, then release of contract is performed.

11.5.4.3   Step 3: Contract Execution

In this stage, triggering of contract is performed after successful fulfillment of conditions. After triggering, the verification process of quantum blind signature is accomplished, leading to conduction of contract evaluation and contract execution. The successful verification will generate a transaction message T_i'. As soon as contract is executed, in addition to creation of a new block, broadcast of message revealing successful transaction to all nodes within the network is performed.

$$T_i' = t^- T_i (mod\ n) \tag{11.7}$$

11.6   Conclusion

The potential of quantum computing has threatened existing infrastructure, thus motivating research community to design new quantum resistant protocols.

Besides, use of blockchain enables complete transformation of various applications in any smart cities. Blockchain eliminates need of trusted third party, thus decentralizing the smart city application with automated secure data collection and sharing while ensuring protection against single point of failure. In addition, the amalgamation of quantum computing with blockchain can do the wonders for any smart cities applications. Therefore, this chapter just not only discusses in detail about quantum computing, blockchain, blend of blockchain, and quantum computing but also describes a post-quantum blockchain architecture for transportation application within any smart city. The description also includes design of a SRP system containing smart contracts with aim to store and share vehicle records securely among four roles, namely, vehicle, toll points, network administrator of network, and district transportation agency. The presented work will not only enable smooth management of vehicle records but also boost up the collaboration between different organization situated within the same city, thereby realizing vision of robust and inclusive smart city.

References

1. Makhdoom, I., Zhou, I., Abolhasan, M., Lipman, J., Ni, W., PrivySharing: A blockchain-based framework for privacy-preserving and secure data sharing in smart cities. *Comput. Secur.*, 88, 101653, 2020, https://doi.org/10.1016/j.cose.2019.101653.
2. Esposito, C., Ficco, M., Gupta, B.B., Blockchain-based authentication and authorization for smart city applications. *Inf. Process. Manage.*, 58, 2, 102468, 2021, ISSN 0306-4573, https://doi.org/10.1016/j.ipm.2020.102468.
3. Kifokeris, D. and Koch, C., A conceptual digital business model for construction logistics consultants, featuring a sociomaterial blockchain solution for integrated economic, material and information flows. *J. Inf. Technol. Construct.*, 25, 500–521, 2020.
4. Khattak, H.A., Tehreem, K., Almogren, A., Ameer, Z., Din, I.U., Adnan, M., Dynamic pricing in industrial internet of things: Blockchain application for energy management in smart cities. *J. Inf. Secur. Appl.*, 55, 102615, 2020, ISSN 2214-2126, https://doi.org/10.1016/j.jisa.2020.102615.
5. Castro, M. and Liskov, B., Practical byzantine fault tolerance and proactive recovery. *ACM Trans. Comput. Syst.*, 20, 4, 398–461, 2002.
6. Yang, F., Zhou, W., Wu, Q., Long, R., Xiong, N. N., Zhou, M., Delegated proof of stake with downgrade: A secure and efficient blockchain consensus algorithm with downgrade mechanism. *IEEE Access*, 7, 118541–118555, 2019.
7. Kumar, D.R., Krishna, T.A., Wahi, A., Health monitoring framework for in time recognition of pulmonary embolism using internet of things. *J. Comput. Theor. Nanosci.*, 15, 5, 1598–1602, 2018.
8. Nguyen, C. T., Hoang, D. T., Nguyen, D. N., Niyato, D., Nguyen, H. T., Dutkiewicz, E., Proof-of-stake consensus mechanisms for future blockchain networks: Fundamentals, applications and opportunities. *IEEE Access*, 7, 85727–85745, 2019.

9. Grover, L.K., A fast quantum mechanical algorithm for database search, in: *Proceedings of the 28th Annual ACM Symposium on Theory of Computing*, pp. 212–219, 1996.

10. Bennett, C.H. and Brassard, G., Quantum cryptography: Publickey distribution and coin tossing. *Proceedings of the IEEE International Conference on Computers, Systems, and Signal Processing*, IEEE, New York, pp. 175–179, 1984.

11. Bennett, C.H., Quantum cryptography using any two nonorthogonal states. *Phys. Rev. Lett.*, 68, 21, 3121–3124, 1992.

12. Bruß, D., Optimal eavesdropping in quantum cryptography with six states. *Phys. Rev. Lett.*, 81, 14, 3018–3021, 1998.

13. Bennett, C.H., Brassard, G., Mermin, N.D., Quantum cryptography without Bell's theorem. *Phys. Rev. Lett.*, 68, 5, 557–559, 1992.

14. Ekert, A.K., Quantum cryptography based on Bell's theorem. *Phys. Rev. Lett.*, 67, 6, 661–663, 1991.

15. Inoue, K., Waks, E., Yamamoto, Y., Differential phase shift quantum key distribution. *Phys. Rev. Lett.*, 89, 3, Article ID 037902, 3 pages, 2002.

16. Stucki, D., Brunner, N., Gisin, N. *et al.*, Fast and simple one-way quantum key distribution. *Appl. Phys. Lett.*, 87, 19, Article ID 194108, 3 pages, 2005.

17. Bostrom, K. and Felbinger, T., Deterministic secure direct communication using entanglement. *Phys. Rev. Lett.*, 89, 18, Article ID 187902, 4 pages, 2002.

18. Lucamarini, M. and Mancini, S., Secure deterministic communication without entanglement. *Phys. Rev. Lett.*, 94, 14, Article ID 140501, 4 pages, 2005.

19. Cerf, N.J., Levy, M., Assche, G.V., Quantum distribution of Gaussian keys using squeezed states. *Phys. Rev. A*, 63, 5, Article ID 052311, 5 pages, 2001.

20. Grosshans, F. and Grangier, P., Continuous variable quantum cryptography using coherent states. *Phys. Rev. Lett.*, 88, 5, Article ID 057902, 4 pages, 2002.

21. Weedbrook, C., Lance, A.M., Bowen, W.P. *et al.*, Quantum cryptography without switching. *Phys. Rev. Lett.*, 93, 17, Article ID 170504, 4 pages, 2004.

22. Jouguet, P., Kunz-Jacques, S., Leverrier, A. *et al.*, Experimental demonstration of long-distance continuous-variable quantum key distribution. *Nat. Photonics*, 7, 5, 378–381, 2013.

23. Acın, A., Massar, S., Pironio, S., Efficient quantum key distribution secure against no-signalling eavesdroppers. *New J. Phys.*, 8, 8, Article ID 126, 11 pages, 2006.

24. Branciard, C., Cavalcanti, E.G., Walborn, S.P. *et al.*, One-sided device-independent quantum key distribution: Security, feasibility, and the connection with steering. *Phys. Rev. A*, 85, 1, Article ID 010301, 5 pages, 2012.

25. Pawlowski, M. and Brunner, N., Semi-device-independent security of one-way quantum key distribution. *Phys. Rev. A*, 84, 1, Article ID 010302, 4 pages, 2011.

26. Liu, Y., Chen, T.Y., Wang, L.J. *et al.*, Experimental measurement-device-independent quantum key distribution. *Phys. Rev. Lett.*, 111, 13, Article ID 130502, 5 pages, 2013.

27. Yang, G. and Li, C., A design of blockchain-based architecture for the security of electronic health record (EHR) systems. *2018 IEEE International Conference on Cloud Computing Technology and Science (CloudCom)*, pp. 261–5, 2018.

28. Yue, X., Wang, H., Jin, D., Li, M., Jiang, W., Healthcare data gateways: found healthcare intelligence on blockchain with novel privacy risk control. *J. Med. Syst.*, 40, 10, 218, 2016.

29. Zhang, J., Xue, N., Huang, X., A secure system for pervasive social network-based healthcare. *IEEE Access*, 4, 9239–50, 2016.

30. Xia, Q., Sifah, E., Smahi, A., Amofa, S., Zhang, X., Bbds: blockchain-based data sharing for electronic medical records in cloud environments. *Information*, 8, 2, 44, 2017, https://doi.org/10.3390/info8020044.

31. Liang, X., Zhao, J., Shetty, S., Liu, J., Li, D., Integrating blockchain for data sharing and collaboration in mobile healthcare applications. *Personal, Indoor, and Mobile Radio Communications (PIMRC), 2017 IEEE 28th Annual International Symposium on*, IEEE, pp. 1–5, 2017.

32. Lin, L. and Guo, Y., Constructions of quantum blind signature based on two-particle-entangled system. *2009 Second International Symposium on Information Science and Engineering*, pp. 355–8, 2009.

33. Khodambashi, S. and Zakerolhosseini, A., A quantum blind signature scheme for electronic payments. *2014 22nd Iranian Conference on Electrical Engineering (ICEE)*, pp. 879–84, 2014.

34. Lin, T., Chen, Y., Chang, T., Lu, C., Kuo, S., Quantum blind signature based on quantum circuit. *14th IEEE International Conference on Nanotechnology*, pp. 868–72, 2014.

35. Minghui-Zhang, Huifang-Li, Yun-Zhou, Xiaoyi-Feng, Zhengwen-Cao, Jinye-Peng, A weak blind quantum signature protocol based on four-particle cluster state. *2017 International Conference on the Frontiers and Advances in Data Science (FADS)*, pp. 125–9, 2017.

36. Cai, Z., Qu, J., Liu, P., Yu, J., A blockchain smart contract based on light-weighted quantum blind signature. *IEEE Access*, 7, 138657–138668, 2019.

37. Sharma, G. and Kalra, S., Identity based secure authentication scheme based on quantum key distribution for cloud computing. *Peer Peer Netw. Appl.*, 11, 2, 220–234, 2018.

38. Kanamori, Y., Yoo, S.M., Gregory, D.A., Sheldon, F.T., On quantum authentication protocols, GLOBECOM '05. *IEEE Global Telecommunications Conference*, pp. 1650–1654, 2005.

39. Dong, Y., Xiao, S., Ma, H., Chen, L., Research on quantum authentication methods for the secure access control among three elements of cloud computing. *Int. J. Theor. Phys.*, 55, 12, 5106–5117, 2016.

40. Murali, G. and Prasad, R.S., Secured cloud authentication using quantum cryptography. *2017 International Conference on Energy, Communication, Data Analytics and Soft Computing (ICECDS)*, Chennai, pp. 3753–3756, 2017.

41. Ankur, L. and Karambir, Using quantum key distribution and ecc for secure inter-device authentication and communication in IoT infrastructure, (April 20, 2018). *Proceedings of 3rd International Conference on Internet of Things and Connected Technologies (ICIoTCT)*, http://dx.doi.org/10.2139/ssrn.3166511.

42. Chen, Z., Zhou, K., Liao, Q., Quantum identity authentication scheme of vehicular ad-hoc networks. *Int. J. Theor. Phys.*, 58, 40–57, 2019.

43. Chang, Y., Xu, C., Zhang, S., Yan, L., Controlled quantum securedirect communication and authentication protocol based on five-particle cluster state and quantum one-time pad. *Chin. Sci. Bull.*, 59, 21, 2541–2546, 2014.

44. Mehic, M., Maurhart, O., Rass, S., Implementation of quantum key distribution network simulation module in the network simulator NS-3. *Quantum Inf. Process.*, 16, 253, 2017.

45. Scarani, V. and Renner, R., Quantum cryptography with finite resources: unconditional security bound for discrete-variable protocols with one-way postprocessing. *Phys. Rev. Lett.*, 100, 20, 200501, 2008.

46. Cai, Z., Qu, J., Liu, P., Yu, J., A blockchain smart contract based on light-weighted quantum blind signature. *IEEE Access*, 7, 138657–138668, 2019.

12

Security Threats and Privacy Challenges in the Quantum Blockchain: A Contemporary Survey

K. Sentamilselvan[1]*, Suresh P.[2], Kamalam G. K.[1], Muthukrishnan H.[1], Logeswaran K.[1] and Keerthika P.[2]

[1]Department of Information Technology, Kongu Engineering College, Perundurai, India
[2]School of Computer Science and Engineering, Vellore Institute of Technology, Vellore, Tamilnadu, India

Abstract

Blockchain is an emerging technology that plays a vital role in the field of banking and financial, government, healthcare, and insurance sector. It is used to store the records behind the cryptocurrencies network. This record keeping technology is decentralized, secure digital records, and public ledger of cryptocurrency transactions, which is collectively well maintained by various users in the world, rather than by one central administration. Only the parties can create the entries and not possible to alter or delete it. Anyone can check the integrity of the transaction record within the network or outside the network by using simple manipulation. Blockchain technology is continuously evolving to its next stage, which is referred to as quantum blockchain. Quantum blockchain is referred to as a distributed, encoded, and decentralized database system based on quantum computation and quantum information theory. It is more securable because, once the data is stored, then it will not have been maliciously tampered. Even though it has more advantages, it has some security threats and privacy issues. Security issues are attacks to unauthorized resources that are protected by some coding or scripts. Privacy issues mean accessing the private information of a person or organization. It involves the security breaches from their vulnerabilities.

*Corresponding author: ksentamilselvan@gmail.com

Rajesh Kumar Dhanaraj, Vani Rajasekar, SK Hafizul Islam, Balamurugan Balusamy and Ching-Hsien Hsu (eds.) Quantum Blockchain: An Emerging Cryptographic Paradigm, (293–316) © 2022 Scrivener Publishing LLC

Security in quantum blockchain is defined as it gives more protection to transactional information and data in the block from various threats such as internal and peripheral, malevolent, and unintentional threats. Typically, security involves finding of threat, the anticipation of threat, and suitable countermeasures to the threats using security policies, tools, and IT services. Security is one of the major concerns to solve the current computational hardness. Many cryptographic systems and algorithms are more vulnerable against quantum computers. Thus, that is breakable by quantum computers. Hence, with the help of quantum computer and quantum technology, we can make the blockchain more secure. Hence, we are in the position to give privacy and security to all the users and groups for their information and perform transactions without leaking identification information. In addition, it allows a user to remain compliant by discerningly revealing themselves without exposing their actions to the whole network. This chapter mainly discusses the security threats and privacy challenges in quantum blockchain applications.

Keywords: Quantum blockchain, security threats, privacy issues, quantum cryptography, cryptocurrency

12.1   Introduction

Blockchain is one of the fastest-growing technologies, which enables the keep storing the digital transaction records. This will transact in the form of cryptocurrencies, like Bitcoin, and Ethereum. All the transactions will be structured, encrypted, and distributed database nature based on the quantum information theory and quantum computing [1]. This technology provides more security than others. Blockchain is storing all digital records of transactions. The name blockchain comes from its natural structure, in which each data records called block is connected together in a single list called a chain. Blockchains are used for documenting the transactions made with the cryptocurrencies like Bitcoin, Ethereum, and Litecoin and have so many other applications.

A classical computer uses NPN or PNP transistors to process the data in the form of binary 0 and 1 to complete the mathematical calculations, and also the processing speed depends on the number of transistors used. At the same time, the quantum computer uses the quantum mechanical states of particles, specifically, the internal angular momentum called spin: at this point, a spin-up (binary 1) and spin-down (binary 0). In physics-based quantum laws, each particle can have multiple states simultaneously. Thus, the spin moving up and down, at that time, introduces the concept of Qbit. In this, Qbit instead of binary 0 and 1 store the proportion of the two values 0 and 1 at the same time. Thus, a quantum computer with n Qbit is producing 2n combinations simultaneously [18]. This performance of quantum computers speeds up the data calculation exponentially and solves difficult problems in very little time [2].

The classical blockchain is developed by linked list data structure and network consensus protocol; initially, the database will be a centralized one and that can be used by everyone. Later days, it will provide the decentralization feature. The main objective of the blockchain is to keep all the records in a centralized single database. This can have all previous records of all existing nodes present in the network and mutually agreed in the contract. In that centralized management, the node is not required to be maintained. It will be more helpful to build a physical model to illustrate this classical information system, i.e., its dynamic and kinematic properties [3].

In Figure 12.1, block 1 consists of block id, nonce value, data, and previous hash values. While mining the block, this will generate the new hash value for this block, and it will forward to the next block. Once the hash value for the particular block is generated and if anyone is trying to modify the data, then, immediately, the value will be changed. Then, the previous block input hash value which is already given and this newly generated hash value will be mismatched. In Figure 12.2, after mining the block, in that, block 1 and block 2 were mined. Here, we can see the hash value that is generated in block 1 (hash) and given to block 2 (previous). Figure 12.3 shows the same for the block 3, block 4, and block 5.

In Figure 12.4, if the attacker is trying to modify the information as "Welcome" to "come", then, immediately, this block 3 and then all upcoming

Figure 12.1 Initial blocks before transaction.

Blockchain

Figure 12.2 Block 1 and block 2 mining.

Blockchain

Figure 12.3 Block 4, block 5, and block 6 mining.

Blockchain

Figure 12.4 Block 3 information modified.

block signatures will be mismatched. After that, all nodes can understand that some block the information has been modified. Figure.12.5 shows how the block was generated, the transaction between the block, and the previous block hash value that are given.

Quantum blockchain is assumed a distributed, heterogeneous, decentralized, and encrypted database with the help of quantum computation and information theory. From the past few years, blockchain security mechanisms such as encryption and hash values can able to reconstruct and tamper with the block of data based on quantum computation and

Block

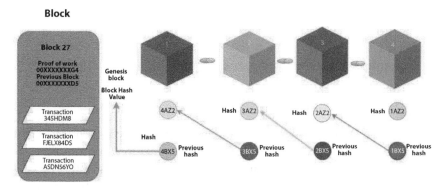

Figure 12.5 Overview of block generation.

quantum information so that the researchers are, nowadays, focusing on the quantum blockchain area.

As discussed, the quantum blockchain has more points of interest so the information structure component of the classical system is supplanted with the quantum framework. In quantum data hypothesis, the different frameworks are created as data carrier, which empowers the encoding and decoding process. In this case of a blockchain, we can capture the idea of the chain through the nonce esteem and parability (ensnarement) of quantum frameworks (e.g., photons).

12.2   Types of Blockchain

The basic necessities of blockchain are used to make transactions or transfer currencies and exchange the information through a secure network. However, the type of blockchain or network varies from application to application. Let us discuss various types of blockchain used in the application field [4].

12.2.1   Public Blockchain

This permission-less blockchain is a non-restrictive and distributed record-keeping system. A public blockchain is a common network to all, i.e., without permission, everyone can access the network and sign in on a blockchain and become a member of the network. The user can view current and historical records, as well as authenticate transactions, mine, and perform proof-of-work (PoW) for newly created blocks. A public block-chain is only secure when the user strictly follows the security methods and rules.

Examples: Ethereum, Bitcoin, and Litecoin.

12.2.2   Private Blockchain

Permissioned blockchain is a closed network where only authenticated and selected members of the network. If anyone wants to enter into the network, then one should get permission from the controlling authority. The amount of security, permission, accessibility, and authorization is in the hand of monitoring and controlling this private network. Private block-chain networks are mainly used for voting digital application asset owner-ship and supply chain management, etc.

Examples: Corda, Multichain, and Hyperledger projects.

12.2.3   Hybrid Blockchain

It is a hybrid of the two previous blockchain types (private and public). It makes use of the benefits of both private (permission-based) and public (permission-less) blockchains. In this blockchain, the authority will define who can access and who can view the records. In this blockchain, some particular section of record or data can be allowed to view in a public network and, at the same time, the remaining data are stored in the private network.

Examples: Bitcoin and Dragonchain.

12.2.4   Consortium Blockchain

It is a special type of permission-based blockchain. The main difference between private and consortium is that consortium blockchains are con-trolled by more than one organization rather than a single organization. It is mainly used by insurance, banks, insurance, medical and government organizations, etc.

Examples: Quorum, corda, R3, and energy web foundation.

12.3   Quantum Blockchain: State of the Art

Blockchain has "n" no of data blocks that are connected in series of the chain. In each data, the block contains many transactions of records [1].

In addition, in each data block contains a) nonce, b) hash value of previously generated data block, c) hash value of the current transaction, and d) timestamp. In the quantum blockchain, the hash value is very essential. Each data block is linked together by a unique hash value. After the data block has been formed, it cannot be changed. Moreover, the transaction record order and data block order are not modified further [1].

Blockchain uses hash functions and digital signatures to verify records and identity redundant storage of multiple nodes to confirm unmodifiable records.

The structure of the classical blockchain is as follows:

Connectivity of BlockChain: Nakamoto [2008] has illustrated the process of the blockchain network,

1. A new transaction will be created using the previous data block hash value.
2. Transaction will be sent into all nodes of the network.
3. Each block will collect some set of transactions and make it as a block (block N).
4. Then, for each block execute the PoW algorithm.
5. Generate the block's hash value, which will be utilized to make another block (block N+1).
6. When a node N satisfies the PoW algorithm, it sends the block hash value to all nodes which are available in the network.
7. All other nodes that accept the block only if all of the transactions are should valid and unused.

Nodes reveal the acceptance of the block by the generation of a new block in the network, by utilizing the previous hash value as the hash value of the newly generated block

$$Block2(H(1)) => block1(H(0))$$

12.3.1 Blockchain Consensus Algorithm

The consensus algorithm is a technique that allows agreement between the participants of the blockchain network. It is decentralized by nature, which means that there is no common authority within the network [17]. Nodes in the network should agree on the transaction validation. Hence, this algorithm ensures that participants in the network follow the rules as well as guarantee trustless transactions in the network system to eliminate the error like double-spending [5].

Characteristics of consensus algorithm

- It operates on the unified understanding between the network members, confirming that the data processed is valid and the information record is up to date.
- This mechanism gives the motivating forces to remunerate clients for great execution and punish bad users.
- It is dependable for the fairness and equity among the network users, i.e., anyone can participate in the network and each one has equal right to vote.
- It allows only verified and valid transactions to eliminate double-spending.
- The consensus algorithm allows the network to continue operating even when major failures, other incidents, and major threats occur [5].

12.3.1.1 Proof of Work

The PoW algorithm allows the nodes to confirm transactions. The participants in the network should work and prove then only he/she add to the network. To be accurate, it is very hard to find the hash value because it has some rules. The person who finds out the right hash value verification gets the chance to add to the network.

PoW gives high computational resources but the main feature is that no one can trust each other in-network participation. As a blockchain the permission is not required, anyone can join the network. The transaction rate is low and scalability is high [6, 7, 17].

12.3.1.2 Proof of Stake

In the proof-of-stake (PoS) algorithm, there is no need for unnecessary and complex calculations. In this, there is no need to compete with others, participants in the network pledge their crypto actives such as Tezos and wait to create a new unit in the network.

In the PoS algorithm, select one participant, based on the share he/she holds. If he/she owns a 4% share, then 4% of transactions will be checked. The increase in the proportion of validators means the interest will be less in the validation process. In comparison with the PoW algorithm, PoS transactions will be relatively fast and mainly probabilistic nature [6, 7, 22].

12.3.1.3 Proof of Activity

To boost the level of protection against prospective assaults, this algorithm combines PoW and PoS. It is a reliable one and another method for Bitcoin miners. Miners in PoA begin by using the PoW consensus procedure to solve the problem. If there are no transactions in the block mined, the system switches to PoS. This algorithm, like PoW and PoS, consumes more energy [7].

Example: Decred coin only is using proof of activity (PoA) right now for the validation process.

12.3.2 Quantum Computation Algorithms

Before we explore quantum blockchain implementation, we must first understand basic algorithms like Grover's and Shor's algorithms.

Grover's approach is primarily an input search algorithm that is faster. It can be compared to brute force search when a unique input is given to the block and inadequate length of the hash function. Shor's algorithm gives factoring numbers with exponential speed when compared to the general classical computer, and also, it can be used for discrete logarithm problems and subgroups. This algorithm is the best-known factoring algorithm. The above problem will break the symmetric and asymmetric ciphers and also things like digital signature and public and private key cryptography. Hence, the above two algorithms will give a major role to systems using quantum blockchain [8].

12.3.2.1 Grover's Algorithm

Blockchain will depend on the hash value which was generated using any of the SHA algorithms like, SHA-1, SHA-2, SHA-256, and SHA-512. The complexity level will increase based on the secure hash algorithms. It will provide more security against the modification of existing blocks. It very a difficult task to reconstruct the existing hash values to modify or alter the existing records. If it is modified or altered any information in the block, then the hash value will be changed.

Grover's algorithm [29, 30] is a specially designed algorithm for finding out the previous block value of a function that is hard to modify. Let us consider a signature that has a hash value of data D2 = Hash(D1), and the function Hash(D1) can be implemented on a quantum computer, then find D1 for a given s in a time of order $O(\sqrt{n})$ n–size of the space of valid hashes.

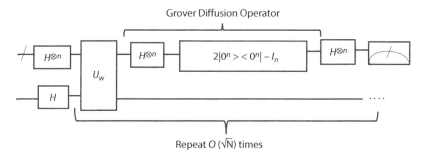

Figure 12.6 Grover's algorithm.

Grover's algorithm produces hash values more efficiently than brute force search, which would be (n).

For example, hash of length n bits means that speedup factor of 2n/2. This value can be very huge for a small value of n as shown in Figure 12.6 [8].

12.3.2.2   Shor's Algorithm

Shor's algorithm [31] is mainly designed quantum computer algorithm to solve prime factors. It takes a number "n" and produces it as a factor. This algorithm takes less number of steps to find numbers prime factors. The difficulty of the general number field is super-polynomial (input length is longer) but sub-exponential (smaller than exponential in the input length). While Shor's algorithm input length is polynomial nature, and getting the output gain speed is exponential.

This algorithm is providing more security and efficiency than Grover's algorithm because it is using public key encryption such as RSA,

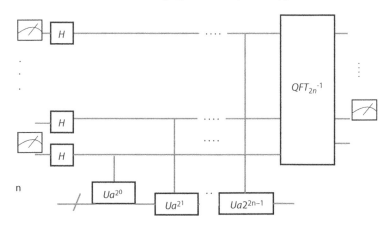

Figure 12.7 Shor's algorithm.

Diffie-Hellman key exchange, and elliptic curve cryptography. Let us consider that Shor's algorithm used RSA for encryption and generated the factoring of large prime numbers as shown in Figure 12.7.

Let us assume that Shor's algorithms were used the RSA encryption algorithm, if the key size is 4,096 bits, then it means that it will not be breakable by normal or classical computation. However, it will be breakable when using quantum computers [8].

12.4 Voting Protocol

Quantum blockchain-based protocol is a simple and secure voting mechanism. This voting protocol satisfies some basic secure characteristics and is also adapted to new technology.

A voting protocol has been successfully developed and applied voting protocol based on classical cryptography. Classical cryptography algorithms (such as factoring large prime factors) complexity is not proved based on the security protocols. Based on much research, the quantum computers factoring of large prime numbers is computed within a short duration because the classical security algorithms are very insecure while using quantum computers. Based on this risk, quantum voting protocols have been developed from a long year ago for quantum computers [9].

To implement in the practical, voting protocol should fulfill the basic requirements, as follows:

1. Obscurity: Only the individual person knows how he/she voted.
2. Binding: Once he or she voted anyone cannot change the ballot.
3. Non-reusability: Everyone should vote only one time.
4. Verifiability: Each voter can easily check whether he/she vote has been numbered or not.
5. Eligibility: Everyone should satisfy the eligibility criteria.
6. Fairness: Before going to the tallying phase no one knows the count of ballots.
7. Self-tallying: Any person who is eager to know the result of voting can tally ballots by his or her individually [9].

The quantum blockchain is primarily used in the voting protocol, and quantum techniques facilitate the design and development of the e-voting system. A quantum bit commitment mechanism is also required to implement the voting protocol in order to ensure certain polling features.

12.4.1   Voting on Quantum Blockchain

Let us consider for voting, n voters vote at a particular time.

Each voter V_i has a private binary value $V_i \in \{0,1\}$, where $V_i = 0$ means disagreement and $V_i = 1$ means agreement [9].

This protocol is more or less similar to the voting protocol on the Bitcoin blockchain, and it has two different phases [17]:

1. Ballot commitment phase
2. Ballot tallying phase

Figure 12.8 shows the simplified model of protocol.

1. Ballot commitment
   - For each value $i \in \{1, ..., n\}$, voter V_i generates the ith row of an n × n matrix of integers $r_{i,1}, ..., r_{i,n}$ of which the sum $\Sigma_j r_{i,j}$ and 0 are congruent modulo n+1.
   - For each, i and j voter sends $r_{i,j}$ to V_j via quantum secure communication.
   - Now for each i voter V_i knows the ith column $r_{1,i}, ..., r_{n,i}$.
   - Then, it can compute his masked ballot $v_i \equiv v_i + \Sigma_j r_{j,i}$ *(mod n + 1)*. V_i commits to $\hat{V_l}$ to each miner of the blockchain by a QBC protocol [9].

Ballot tallying by decommitment:

   - For every *i*, V_i reveals $\widehat{V_l}$ to each miner of the blockchain by opening his commitment.
   - To reach a consensus on the disguised ballot, all miners use the quantum honest-success Byzantine agreement [32] procedure $\widehat{V_l}, ..., \hat{V_l}$.

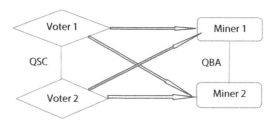

Figure 12.8 Voting protocol model.

- The result of voting is obtained by calculating $\sum_i \widehat{v_i}$, which equals to $\sum_i v_i$

Because,

$$\sum_i \widehat{v_i} \equiv \sum_i \left(v_i + \sum_j r_{j,i} \right) \equiv \sum_i v_i + \sum_{i,j} r_{j,i}$$
$$\equiv \sum_i \left(v_i + \sum_j r_{j,i} \right) \equiv \sum_i v_i (mod\ n+1).$$

12.4.2   Security Requirements

The voting protocol should fulfill the following security prerequisites.

12.4.2.1   Obscurity

Quantum secure communication prevents other users from seeing the original matrix, ensuring security. As a result, the original ballot is unknown, while voters can only see the masked ballot [9, 10].

12.4.2.2   Binding

Quantum key distribution (QKD) is mainly used for authentication purposes in the quantum blockchain because the other voters cannot modify the voter ballot. The binding property of the quantum system says that once the ballot has been submitted cannot change the ballot [9, 10].

12.4.2.3   Non-Reusability

Non-reusability means, if the voter is appended more than one ballot in blockchain, then this will be considered as a violated policy. In a blockchain, this will be treated as a double-spending attack. Hence, we cannot achieve on quantum blockchain [9, 10, 21].

12.4.2.4   Verifiability

It can be easily verified by every voter that is screened ballot is fully uploaded to the network of blockchain. The design of the database is transparent [9, 10, 21].

12.4.2.5   *Eligibility*

Every voter has the eligibility criteria to authenticate into the blockchain. The only eligible persons can communicate to the minors [9, 10].

12.4.2.6   *Fairness*

It cannot be achieved if anyone can partially count the ballots before the counting process. To overcome these, voters have to know the count of screened ballots before the counting process. Hence, the fairness is achieved by the quantum bit commitment property [9, 10, 21].

12.4.2.7   *Self-Tallying*

Because of the transparency of the blockchain every user can easily access all the data in the blockchain. The user can easily count the ballots by manipulating the total masked ballots [9, 10].

12.5   Security and Privacy Issues in Quantum Blockchain

Public key cryptography/asymmetric cryptography, as well as hash functions, are included in the blockchain. Let us discuss this in detail [11].

12.5.1   Public Key Cryptography

Public key cryptography is of great importance to the security of the blockchain [25]. Quantum blockchain uses the public key cryptosystem for sending and receiving information. This can make transactions with the help of digital signatures. It should accept both sender and receiver. This will provide more security to users' information. While generating the signature, both the parties can accept and sign. In every transaction, the sender should sign with the receiver's public key. The receiver should announce his/her public key, and it should be verified [25]. After making the transaction, the receiver should decrypt with the help of his private key. For this case, Elliptic Curve Digital Signature Algorithm (ECDSA) with Koblitz elliptic curve secp256k1 for Bitcoin transactions. It depends on the private and public keys for signing and verifying the messages [11].

In a public key cryptosystem, wallets are used to store the files and simple data which are very useful for blockchain users. It can be associated to a public id, which is the public key's hash value, and the private key is used to sign and validate all transactions. For every Bitcoin transaction, the sender will send the currency with the help of the receiver's public key and, at the same time, receiver can verify with the help of his private key. In this case, the sender and receiver should provide the authenticity. In this case, every currency transaction should verify its digital signature using sender identify [11, 25].

12.5.2   Hash Functions

In the quantum blockchain, hash functions were played an important role. Hash functions, like SHA-1, SHA-2, SHA-3, RIPEMD, RIPEMD-128, RIPEDM-256, RIPEMD-160, MD2, MD4, and MD5, were used to generate the quantum blockchain digital signature. In the following, Figure 12.9 discussed with various hash algorithms strength level in different years [11].

From Figure 12.10, some algorithms were projected as strong and some of them are weak. In the digital signature generation, quantum blockchain users need to provide authenticity to their every currency transaction in front of all users.

To connect its blocks, blockchain employs hash functions. These blocks are connected in a chained hierarchy order, with each block holding the hash of the previous block. Some blockchain like Bitcoin uses the hash value of leading zeros, which may slow down the block addition. At last, the hash functions are used in blockchain for creating public and private user addresses or reducing the size of public addresses.

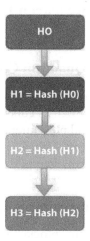

Figure 12.9 Hash value preparation.

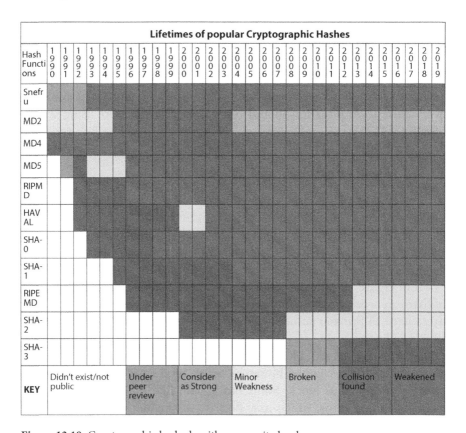

Figure 12.10 Cryptographic hash algorithms security level.

12.6   Challenges and Research Perspective in Quantum Blockchain

12.6.1   Fast Evolution in Quantum Computing

Nowadays, quantum computing is an emerging technology that has played a major role in industry side as well as educational institutions. As a result, more and more new attacking and prevention mechanisms will be developing against the quantum cryptosystems. Hence, researchers will give more importance to quantum blockchain technology and quantum computing [11].

12.6.2   Transition From Pre- to Post-Quantum Blockchain

Pre-quantum to post-quantum blockchain transitions require more attention. For this purpose, many researchers have implemented some methods. In this case, [26] proposed a method to increase the validity of the exiting blockchain block, and the attacker can able to find the hash value or digital signature. For that, the transition from pre-quantum to post-quantum blockchains may use in hard fork and soft fork [27]. In that, hard fork is more secure than a soft-fork because this can be divided into two cryptocurrencies. In addition, another was implemented [28] a simple commit delay reveal protocol. This gives a more secure way to transfer the cryptocurrency from pre- to post-quantum digital signature scheme [11].

12.6.3   Computational and Energy Efficiency

As per various survey results of some posts, quantum methods require significant storage, computational resource, and execution time. Because of that, in the future, they need to increase the energy consumption, so to maintain the efficiency of blockchain the developers should consider novel methods to optimize the cryptosystems [11].

12.6.4   Standardization

From the various surveys, there are many steps were taken to analyze and standardize the post-quantum cryptosystems. If we are using non-standard schemes, then there will be a risk in blockchain compatibility in the post-quantum scene. Hence, the researchers look forward to standardizing and avoid the risk by using appropriate schemes [11].

12.6.5   Hardware Incompatibility in Quantum Blockchain

Only a few types of hardware are available in real-time quantum blockchain implementations, although the same hardware is used in blockchain nodes today. As a result, any post-quantum system must provide computational complexity and security in order for the hardware to be adequate for systems and to connect with the blockchain [11].

12.6.6   Large Cipher Text Overheads

The performance of the blockchain mainly depends on the cryptosystem operation. Some cryptosystems produce large problems; for this reason, quantum blockchain developers will have to reduce the ciphertext problem and use effective compression techniques [11].

12.6.7 Quantum Blockchain

In addition to using cryptosystems to transition from pre-quantum to post-quantum blockchain, many researchers advocated quantum-based blockchain. The author proposes to change from Bitcoin to quantum computing and, at the same time, others explain the mining application by using Grover's algorithm [24]. At the same time, some authors suggest that using quantum cryptography to implement some contracts. Furthermore, the area in which more research is needed is QKD [11].

12.7 Security Threats in Quantum Blockchain

12.7.1 Threats in Smart City Implementation

Blockchain is a point-to-point secure communication network that was adopted by smart cities to manage and monitor data exchange between different components in a smart city. Let us discuss the security and privacy problems in smart cities and how the blockchain is used for the improvement of smart cities [12, 19, 20].

The different characteristic nature of smart city is susceptible to attack. High-level security protocols cannot be applied to the resource devices that

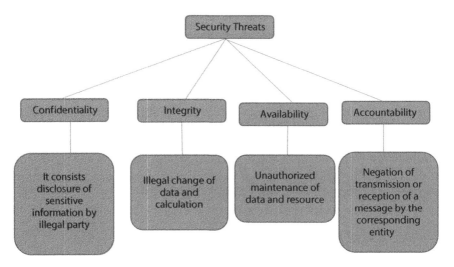

Figure 12.11 Security threats.

are all in the smart cities. The integrated structure of the smart city creates unwanted data and data calculation of certain personal or groups can even deny the exchange of messages from one person to another. Figure 12.11 shows the security threats faced by the integrated smart city [12, 19, 20].

12.8 Applications of Quantum Blockchain

Blockchain can use many applications such as government sector, medical, media, social, digital assets, e-commerce, banking and finance, gambling, games, real estates, asset trading, insurance, entertainment, and blockchain-enabled IoT. Let us discuss few applications in detail [13].

12.8.1 Banking and Finance

Blockchain is used in banking applications, the time taken for the transaction of money will take less than ten minutes, and the time takes to create a new block to the blockchain, regardless of the holiday or day or week. Banks also transfer the funds between institutions using blockchain more and secure and with less amount of time [13, 14, 16, 23].

12.8.2 Healthcare

In the healthcare sector, blockchain is mainly used for storing the patient's medical record, which can be accessible by only authorized personals. Once the new record is created and confirmed, then this will make an entry into the blockchain. It gives hospital patients the evidence and confidence that the record cannot be modified and tampered. Security and privacy are ensured that records could be encrypted and store on the chain of blocks with his private key [13, 14, 16].

12.8.3 Food Industry

In the food industry, the blockchain is played a major role to track the path and safety of food products throughout the farmer to the consumer journey. For example, a farmer produced the milk and that will be packed and delivered to the consumer. If the consumer wants the details such as about the farmer, when this product is packed, and the quantity of the product, then the consumer can able to track their product details [13, 14].

12.8.4   Asset Trading

By using the local register's office, the process of recording their asset and their rights is both time-consuming, and it is very inefficient. In the same way, the blockchain has the potential to eliminate the need for scanning documents and track the physical files in the local registrar's office. If the property record is stored and verified on the blockchain, then owners can trust their data is accurate and permanently recorded [13, 14, 16].

12.8.5   E-Payment

Classical cryptography has more time taken to solve some computational problems, but in QKD, the security is based on the quantum computation theory and any problems such as eavesdropping and intercepting find out between the parties; as a result, the secret key shared between two sides securely [13, 14, 23].

12.8.6   Government Sector

The government can use this blockchain technology, and it will more helpful to keep all confidential government records. Because it can keep the large amount of data, this is also the target of attackers. From that, the government has to take precautions with the help of blockchain data structure. This will gives a minimal risk than other mechanisms. In addition, this will have less failure rate and prevent from the security breach [13, 14].

12.8.7   IOTA in Quantum Blockchain

IOTA is one type of cryptocurrency that will be one of the future enhancements of blockchain technology. This will supports the machine-to-machine communication (M to M) with no processing cost, and it will provide high scalability. In a healthcare system using IOTA, the patents health data and records are stored and can access remotely by using smart devices. Thus, it will store all the records and that is unable to modify the original information. Hence, it gives more security to their patient health records. Similarly, IOTA will support many applications such as automotive and smart city [15].

12.9   Characteristics of Post-Quantum Blockchain Schemes

The main features of the post-quantum blockchain are the following.

12.9.1   Small Key Size

Small key sizes in private and public keys are used by resource devices that can communicate with blockchain to decrease storage space. Hence, the small-size keys require less amount of computational power when managing them. This feature is mainly important for blockchain that uses the IoT, normally, which are required less amount of storage space and computational power. IoT devices also face some challenges in the area of security, which are limiting in the adaptation of blockchain [11].

12.9.2   Small Hash Length and Signature

A blockchain mainly stores data transaction details including data hashes and user signatures. Therefore, if data hash value or signature length increases, then proportionally the blockchain size also will increase as well [11].

12.9.3   Processing Speed of Data

Processing of data is important in the quantum signature scheme, and it would need to be fast enough to process a huge amount of data processing per second. The speed of the execution process is very fast and as usual, it requires less amount computational power complexity which is need to resource devices from blockchain transactions [11].

12.9.4   Low Energy Consumption

The reason behind the power consumption, like adopted security mechanisms, the amount of communication transactions performed, and the hardware used in the network, can get a particular amount of power due to the complexity of the performed operation. Some types of blockchain, like cryptocurrencies, are taken more energy to implement and execute some particular protocols [11].

12.9.5 Low Computational Complexity

Low computational complexity means speed execution of devices; it does not mean that a post-quantum system is a less computational complexity. For example, few signature schemes are executed very fast in few processors (Intel processors) that use the Advanced Vector Extensions 2 (AVX2) instruction set, but the same signature schemes are executed in different processors (ARM processor) the computational speed will be decreased. Therefore, it is necessary to know the connectivity between execution speed, used hardware devices, and computational complexity [11].

12.10 Conclusion

In this chapter, the structure and outline of classical blockchain are introduced. Then, the algorithm used for the implementation of quantum blockchain is introduced. In addition, we will provide the issues based on the security and privacy of quantum blockchain, and the most used post-quantum schemes were analyzed, and their characteristics and main challenges were studied. At the same time, the digital signature was used for the owner authentication purpose in the classical blockchain and the encryption algorithm used for a digital signature like RSA may become unsafe of attacks from quantum computers. Like the basic blockchain, the quantum blockchain also has some advantages like decentralization. The main property of quantum blockchain is safety, efficiency, and security to be ensured. The QKD is mainly used for communication security between the nodes. At last, quantum blockchain has some features like processing speed that is very high compared to classical blockchain and safe transaction based on quantum physics; it will have a variety of practical applications like banking, music, finance, and healthcare systems, and many research ways are also there in future perspective.

References

1. Li, C., Xu, Y., Tang, J., Liu, W., Quantum blockchain: A decentralized, encrypted and distributed database based on quantum mechanics. *J. Quantum Comput. JQC*, 1, 2, 49–63, 2019.
2. Smith, N., Quantum's potential impact on blockchain computing. ISSA developing and connecting cybersecurity leaders globally. *Information Systems Security Association Journal (ISSAJ)*, 12–16, 2020.
3. Rajan, D. and Visser, M., Quantum Blockchain using entanglement in Time. *Quantum Rep.*, 1, 1, 3–11, September, 2019.

4. https://data-flair.training/blogs/types-of-blockchain/
5. https://academy.aaxpro.com/en/consensus-mechanisms-how-pow-pos-dpos-and-other-algorithms-work/
6. Krishnasamy, L., Dhanaraj, R.K., Ganesh Gopal, D., Reddy Gadekallu, T., Aboudaif, M.K., Abouel Nasr, E., A heuristic angular clustering framework for secured statistical data aggregation in sensor networks. *Sensors*, 20, 17, 4937, 2020.
7. https://medium.com/@BangBitTech/what-is-consensus-algorithm-in-blockchain-different- types-of-consensus-models-12cce443fc77
8. Rodenburg, B. and Pappas, S.P., Blockchain and quantum computing, *MITRE TECHNICAL REPORT*, June 2017. MITRE, LINK: https://www.mitre. org/sites/default/files/publications/17-4039-blockchain-and-quantum-computing.pdf
9. Sun, X., Wang, Q., Piotr, A simple voting protocol on quantum block-chain, quantum physics (quant-ph); cryptography and Security (cs.CR), *Int. J. Theor. Phys.*, 58, 1, 275–281, 2019. DOI:10.1007/s10773-018-39. 29-6, arXiv:1805.11979.
10. Gao, S., Zheng, D., Guo, R., Jing, C., Hu, C., An anti-quantum E-voting protocol in blockchain with audit function. *IEEE Access*, 7, 115304–115316, 2019.
11. Fernández-Caramés, T.M. and Fraga-Lamas, P., Towards post-quantum blockchain: A review on blockchain cryptography resistant to quantum computing attacks, *IEEE Emerging Approaches to Cyber Security*, 8, 21091–21116, 2020.
12. El Azzaoui, A. and Park, J.H., Post-quantum blockchain for a scal-able smart city. *J. Internet Technol.*, 21, 4, 1171–1178, 2020, DOI: 10.3966/160792642020072104025.
13. Krishnamoorthi, S., Jayapaul, P., Dhanaraj, R.K. *et al.*, Design of pseudo-random number generator from turbulence padded chaotic map. *Nonlinear Dyn.*, 104, 2, 1627–1643, 2021.
14. Dhiviya, S., Malathy, S., Kumar, D.R., Internet of Things (IoT) elements, trends and Applications. *J. Comput. Theor. Nanosci.*, 15, 5, 1639–1643, 2018.
15. Silvano, W.F. and Marcelino, R., Iota tangle: A cryptocurrency to communicate Internet-of-Things data. *Future Gener. Comput. Syst.*, 112, 307–319, 2020.
16. Crosby, M., Nachiappan, Pattanayak, P., Verma, S., Kalyanaraman, V., *BlockChain Technology: Beyond Bitcoin*, pp. 1–35, Sutardja Center for Entrepreneurship & Technology Technical Report, 2015. https://www. scirp.org/(S(351jmbntvnsjt1aadkposzje))/journal/paperinformation. aspx?paperid=93016
17. Edwards, M., Mashatan, A., Ghose, S., A review of quantum and hybrid quantum/classical blockchain protocols. *Springer Quantum Inf. Process.*, 19, 184, 1–22, 2020, https://doi.org/10.1007/s11128-020-02672-y.
18. Shor, P.W., Polynomial-time algorithms for prime factorization and discrete logarithms on a quantum computer. *SIAM J. Comput.*, 26, 5, 1484–1509, October, 1997.

19. Shanmugam Shoba, M., A survey on post quantum digital signature schemes for blockchain. *Int. J. Comput. Sci. Mob. Computing*, 8, 6, 128–133, June 2019.

20. Biswas, K. and Muthukkumarasamy, V., Securing smart cities using blockchain technology. *2016 IEEE 18th International Conference on High Performance Computing and Communications; IEEE 14th International Conference on Smart City; IEEE 2nd International Conference on Data Science and Systems.*

21. Hillery, M., Ziman, M., Buek, V., Bielikov, M., Towards quantum-based privacy and voting. *Phys. Lett. A*, 349, 1, 75–81, 2006, DOI https://doi.org/10.1016/j.physleta.2005.09.010.   URL   http://www.sciencedirect.com/science/article/pii/S0375960105014738.

22. King, S. and Nadal, S., PPCoin: Peer-to-peer crypto-currency with proof-of-stake, 2012, https://blockchainlab.com/pdf/peercoin-paper.pdf. Accessed 5 May 2020.

23. Nakamoto, S., Bitcoin: A peer-to-peer electronic cash system, 2008, https://bitcoin.org/bitcoin.pdf.

24. Lucamarini, M., Shields, A., Alléaume, R., Chunnilall, C., Degiovanni, I.P., Gramegna, M., Hasekioglu, A., Huttner, B., Kumar, R., Lütkenhaus, N., *Implementation Security of Quantum Cryptography; Introduction, challenges, solutions*, p. 28, ETSI, Sophia Antipolis, France, 2018.

25. Gao, Y.-L., Chen, X.-B., Chen, Y.-L., Sun, Y., Niu, X.-X., Yang, Y.-X., A secure cryptocurrency scheme based on post-quantum blockchain. *IEEE Access*, 6, 27205–27213, April 2018.

26. Sato, M. and Matsuo, S., Long-term public blockchain: Resilience against compromise of underlying cryptography, in: *Proc. Int. Conf. Comput. Commun. Netw.*, Vancouver, BC, Canada, Jul./Aug. 2017.

27. Chen, F., Liu, Z., Long, Y., Liu, Z., Ding, N., Secure scheme against compromised hash in proof-of-work blockchain, in: *Proc. NSS*, Hong Kong, Aug. 2018, p. 1 15.

28. Stewart, I., Ilie, D., Zamyatin, A., Werner, S., Torshizi, M.F., Knottenbelt, W.J., Committing to quantum resistance: A slow defence for Bitcoin against a fast quantum computing attack. *Royal Soc. Open Sci.*, 5, 6, 1–12, Jun. 2018, Art. no. 180410.

29. Long, G.L., Grover algorithm with zero theoretical failure rate. *Phys. Rev. A*, 64, 2, 022307, August 2001.

30. Grover, L.K., A fast quantum mechanical algorithm for database search. *28th Annual ACM Symposium on the Theory of Computing*, pp. 212–219, 1996.

31. Shor, P.W., Algorithms for quantum computation: discrete logarithms and factoring. *35th Annual Symposium on Foundations of Computer Science*, pp. 124–134, 1994.

32. White Paper 27, Jul. 2018, Wan, J. *et al.*, A blockchain-based solution for enhancing security and privacy in smart factory. *IEEE Trans. Ind. Inf.*, 15, 3652–3660, 2019.

13

Exploration of Quantum Blockchain Techniques Towards Sustainable Future Cybersecurity

H. Muthukrishnan[1]*, P. Suresh[2], K. Logeswaran[1] and K. Sentamilselvan[1]

[1]Department of Information Technology, Kongu Engineering College, Erode, India
[2]School of Computer Science and Engineering, Vellore Institute of Technology,
Vellore, Tamilnadu, India

Abstract

When cyberattacks can shut down entire networks, it's important to develop an effective solution to protect data against unauthorized access and tampering. Fortunately, blockchain technology offers an innovative approach to data security that has successfully withstood the fiercest cyberattacks for more than a decade. Many researchers and security experts predict that blockchain technology will revolutionize the cyber security of any business that uses it. Yet though, Blockchain is at particular risk because one-way functions are at the only line of defense. Apparently on the other side, cyber attacks and hackers peaks up in exponential increase of attacks and hacks like cracking digital signatures. Digital signatures pose an eminent and efficient method of securing almost all the bank clients. This is a most imminent threat to all business. Quantum cryptography can strengthen blockchain security. Quantum communication is inherently authenticated - no user can impersonate another. In the quantum blockchain network, each node stores a copy of the blockchain. As in the classical blockchain, the aim of this stage is to add valid blocks in a decentralized manner. To construct the quantum blockchain network, the problem is that the network may consist of dishonest nodes and the generated blocks may come from a dishonest source. Recently developed device-independent quantum communication protocols allow untrusted intermediary quantum stations to relay quantum secured signals between two parties. By which it tightens the one-way function issues and avoids communication between untrusted sources. This chapter provides the different Quantum Blockchain techniques that can be effectively used towards sustainable

*Corresponding author: muthukrishnan.h@outlook.com

Rajesh Kumar Dhanaraj, Vani Rajasekar, SK Hafizul Islam, Balamurugan Balusamy and
Ching-Hsien Hsu (eds.) Quantum Blockchain: An Emerging Cryptographic Paradigm, (317–340)
© 2022 Scrivener Publishing LLC

cyber security. It also provides a detailed survey of cyber security issues and how the recent advancements of Quantum Blockchain are applied to solve these issues.

Keywords: Cyber security, quantum blockchain, security threats, cyber attacks, quantum cryptography

13.1   Introduction to Blockchain

Because of the evolution in chips and chipsets, large-sized processors and sensors were reduced to compact micro mini electronic devices. This miniatures and wireless technologies have elevated the advancements in our society. There is a rapid growth in number of electronic devices in all areas of application where it can be suitably utilized and there is a complete drift in the production cost and toppled this real world into the world of digital communication. Eventually, there falls the conversion in communication surpasses from wireless networks to radio frequency identification (RFID) [1]. Now, IoT had connected the whole world with various devices, and most of them wearable technologies. Various industries have incorporated the smart applications like smart home, wearable devices, smart cities, healthcare, automotive industry, smart agriculture, and smart grid. Characteristics of this application which involves IoT are very peculiar as it generates huge volume of data with considerable amount of power consumption with limited memory and storage. It creates an adorable question for all the researchers, toward unquestionable doubt over the data security, data reliability, and trust. Always, there exists the possibility of tampering data. Data can be altered and modified by anonymous person for their personal benefit.

Only possible way to provide security to the generated data is decentralizing. In the sense, the data has to be distributed over many devices which participate in the eve of communication. Data tampering can be avoided. We may raise a question "How?" How it can be avoided? How data can be secured? Particularly, in this digital world, we do transactions online. In addition, in very recent days, there is a drastic raise in the e-commerce, online transactions, and financial sectors. There is a buzz word name Distributed Ledger Technology (DLT). DLT provides data security and supports reliability over data and its trust. This technique can elevate the existing process in all fields which involves data of huge sizes like big data, fast data, and social media, and, particularly, in finance sector. DLT is a digital system for recording the transactions like who initiated the data transaction, timestamp, with whom it was communicated, *viz.*, in multiple places (participants) at the same time. Bitcoin is the first solvent which potentially used in cryptocurrency for data reliability. Hereby, there created and coined a name called blockchain. Cryptocurrencies illustrate many significances of blockchain [2].

Blockchain technology has proven to be one of the most revolution-ary and disruptive innovations of the last 10 years. However, all political administrations throughout the world and other businesses are starting to look at how other countries can use blockchain to improve organizational standards and processes, a crippling challenge is looming [3].

It is hard to have clarity toward what blockchain is and how it functions in order to comprehend the problems that businesses face when it comes to data security. A blockchain is a distributed digital ledger that keeps track of information through a network. Rather than storing information in a single location, a blockchain replicates it through a huge number of com-puters which are interconnected with each other. It accomplishes this by enrolling the help of specialized computers to provide solution to a cryp-tographic algorithm that authenticates document affairs between two or more people. The solution is then appended as a block of record. Blocks are publicly archived, blockchain document affairs that are not created by a single person but are accessible to anyone [4].

Since the data is available in so many places, it is both easily checked, and, practically, it cannot be hacked even by the most powerful machines on the planet. Its impenetrable degree of protection and capability to pre-serve impersonality rendered it a fundamental building block for cryp-tocurrencies, and Bitcoin trading is almost entirely responsible for its meteoric rise in popularity. Although cryptocurrency is still the most pop-ular use of blockchain today, businesses and organizations are starting to look at other ways to put the technology to work. Supply chains, medical records, and conventional financial transactions may all be managed with blockchains in the near future [5].

However, with all of its potential, blockchain technology has flaws. Another revolutionary methodology on the horizon is not very far distant future, which would jeopardize the safety of any blockchain-based frame-work. Before going through the various disruptive technologies which are going to develop the future digital world in a secured way, let us have a brief discussion about the history of blockchain.

13.1.1 Blockchain History

Later on at the early stages, Internet and its evolution have drastically changed this world. Slowly, the world of digitization has started emerging. Widely many corporate industries and organizations particularly in the finance sector have started using digital documents. Obviously, the chance of data theft, data breach and all sort of damages or data attacks were in existence. In relevance to this, the scientists would prefer dropping a new innovative practical solution for all digital documents such that it can prevent various time stamping issues like backdating and tampering.

In 1992, to enhance the efficiency of the system they upgraded to incorporate Merkle trees; as mentioned in Figure 13.1 thereby, it has enabled the collection of more documents on a one block as a whole. A series of data containing multiple records have been stored and each data record was entirely connected with each other. Thus, now, the upcoming new record which enters the chain will possess the complete history of the entire chain. Therefore, this technology went unutilized, and the patent lapsed in 2004.

In the year 2004, Hal Finney, a computer scientist and cryptographic activist, popularized a system known as Reusable Proof of Work (RPoW) as a prototype for digital money. In the history of cryptocurrencies, it was a smart move. Receiving a non-exchangeable or non-fungible item was how the RPoW system worked. Hashcash has generated an RSA-signed token that may be passed from person to person based on proof of work. In exchange, the participants that participate in the hashcash task will receive a token [6].

We must thank Satoshi Nakamoto, no one knows whether it is a team of member or a single person involved in regaining the short history of Blockchain from the past with latest relevancies in 2008. This technology has evolved from knowing crypto pricing and found its ways into many applications beyond cryptocurrencies. In 2009, this technology was officially introduced in white paper by Satoshi Nakamoto. In that paper, he details about this technology and how it enhances the digital trust by decentralization. After that, Satoshi was a little bit excited and handed

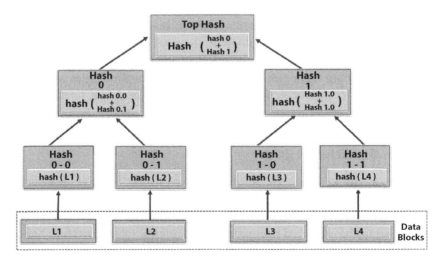

Figure 13.1 Merkle tree.

over Bitcoin development to the other core developers. As a result, digital ledger technology has spawned a new set of applications that make up the blockchain's whole history.

Global nomads are already creating new businesses from their smartphones. It is hard to believe smartphones have only been around for 10 years. Blockchain is a DLT that manages track of continually growing list of organized data known as "blocks," which is undergoing another silent revolution.

Let us see things and innovations happened in just 10 years span.

- The first biggest invention in blockchain was Bitcoin, an experiment of digital currency. Bitcoin has a stock market value of the company of $10–$20 billion USD and is utilized for payments by lakhs and lakhs of people, including a terrific and rapidly growing financial industry.
- The second breakthrough is identifying that the technology which underpins bitcoin could be removed and applied to a range of different interorganizational collaborations. Majority of financial institutions and organizations are in the world is investigating blockchain technology for their future.
- The third breakthrough was the "smart contract," which was reflected in Ethereum, which is a second-generation blockchain technology that inserted small computer programs directly into blockchain to allow financial assets, such as bank credits or deeds, to be replaced instead of just the cash-like tokens of Bitcoin.
- The fourth key breakthrough, which is at the forefront of blockchain thought right now, is known as "proof of stake" (PoS).
- Blockchain scaling is the sixth key innovation on the horizon. Every transaction is currently processed by traditional computer systems in the network of blockchain. It is a sluggish process. By calculating number of computing systems are necessary to validate everydocument and data, and efficiently sorting the job, a scale-up blockchain speeds up the process without compromising security.

Since its inception in the late 1990s, e-commerce has triggered several of these cascades, and blockchain is predicted to do the same. Similarly, these changes are taking us to predict what will happen next? Predictors sometimes exaggerate how quickly stuff can happen while underestimating the long-term consequences. The blockchain industry's notion of scale, on the other hand, is that the upcoming developments will be "as enormous as the initial conception of the internet," which may not be overblown. Blockchain develops and more people become aware of this new way of working together. It is expected to expand into a variety of areas, including supply chains and provably fair online dating (eliminating the possibility of fake profiles and other underhanded techniques)

13.1.2   Why Blockchain?

Technology is constantly changing, and the next decade will be the technological decade. The standard financial transaction activities will begin to fade. Digital currencies like Bitcoin and Blockchain would be at the forefront. Blockchain seems to be a complicated technology, but it is actually very simple. All transactions are held in a digital ledger that is accessed by all participants [7].

These ledgers record global transactions, and the shared database is shared among thousands of devices. Blockchain can be used to store anything, including songs, titles, intellectual properties, and even votes, in addition to monetary value. Both of these assets can be safeguarded using Blockchain technology. People are choosing Blockchain technology because of the high level of protection it offers. Obtaining information or recovering data is extremely difficult. The faith in blockchain technology is built not by powerful forces like governments or institutions but by intelligent code and widespread collaboration [8].

In upcoming years, this blockchain technology is expected to uplift the face of financial transaction in all possible industrial sectors even with a common man. The reason behind is people are tilting toward the blockchain technology due to its security traits. The data can be shared only between the participants. When compared to traditional methods of transaction, the odds of theft or financial robbery are negligible. Blockchain is now extremely essential in the corporate world.

13.2   Insights on Quantum Computing

The blockchain promises unbreakable data encryption in today's technological environment, but this will all be undone on the arrival of quantum computers. The safety of the blockchain can be ensured by building mathematical puzzles that are extremely difficult to solve, even for the most powerful traditional systems. Finding two prime numbers that can be multiplied with each other to make another identical numeral is a popular puzzle, but it gets virtually difficult as the numbers go greater. Shor's algorithm was created by mathematician Peter Shor in 1994 to swiftly determine important components of a number and provide solution the given issue. Anyways, a computer with quantum computing ability is required to execute the algorithm.

Information processing and management in all possible corporates which involves data has been revolutionized by various computing techniques. Traditional computing equipment is referred to as "classical computers" because they follow the laws of classical mechanics. The proposed "quantum computers" are regulated by quantum mechanics laws, resulting in a significant change in computational capacity. Quantum computers will be able to do computations much quicker than contemporary computational devices, and the encryption completely adheres to mathematics to find so difficult to crack, which will be exposed to attacks launched by a quantum computer in seconds [9]. None of them has demonstrated that they have created a quantum computer that works, but major tech companies such as Alibaba, IBM, and Microsoft working on business versions, as well as political administrations of major superpowers such as the United States and China are funding quantum research, the entry of completely functional quantum computers is unavoidable.

13.2.1 Quantum Supremacy

Things that were once unthinkable are now becoming a phenomenon and a part of our lives. One of the most significant achievements that will vastly improve past happenings is achieving quantum dominance [10].

- Quantum computing allows a computer to simulate quantum mechanics.
- Quantum supremacy was claimed by Google researchers.
- However, it will be several years before Ethereum poses a challenge to existing cryptographic signatures.

Obviously, our universe and life on the planet blue is naturally a quantum type; electrons live in various states at the same time, which we cannot properly model with classical computers. It is just too much for them to consider every possibility.

For instance:

10 electron molecules = approximately 1,000 states

20 electron molecules = approximately over 1 million states

In 1982, Feynman delivered a technical talk and justified it with a paper that is the first to specifically discuss the design of a computer depend on the principle of quantum mechanics. He narrated the importance of developing a quantum simulator for universal usage that would employ quantum effects to analyze and execute simulations on other quantum effects.

Tech mammoths are racing with each other to construct the world's first premium quantum computer, a machine capable of trillions of times the computing power of all of the world's computers put together. Google recently announced in a paper surfaced in the scientific magazine that it has achieved quantum supremacy, which was previously thought to be unachievable.

13.2.2   What is Quantum Supremacy?

To understand quantum supremacy, one must first understand how quantum computers work? Classical computers utilize bits that can be in either state 0 or 1 at the same time, whereas quantum computers employ quantum bits (qubits) can be in either state 0 or 1 at the same time. An electron, an atom, or a molecule can all be considered qubits since they display quantum behavior.

Bit:

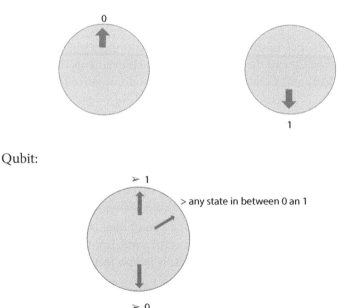

Qubit:

Superposition and entanglement are two important elements of quantum mechanics. The key to the quantum computer's superpower lies in these two principles. Superposition is a quantum mechanics phenomenon that quantum computers take advantage of. Having been associated with chance subatomic occurrence that may or may not happen, this allows to live a particle in two states at the same time.

Let us have an analogy for better understanding of principle 1 superposition.

Geiger counter along with a cat and a bit portion of poison kept in a closed shelter. After a while, quantum mechanics says the cat is both alive and dead. We are not notified if the cat is alive or near to death unless we peep into the shelter. However, if we repeat the experiment with many animals, we will find that the cat lives for half of the time and dies for the other.

Particle entanglement is a term used in quantum mechanics to describe their essential features and their link that could not have occurred by any chance. This may apply to their momentum, location, or polarization, among other things.

Quantum supremacy refers to a quantum computer's ability to perform tasks that classical computers cannot. In this case, the Google paper stated that its QC could complete a work (specific random number generation) in 200 s (3 min and 20 s), when a supercomputer may fetch about 10,000 years.

Google employed Sycamore, a newly constructed quantum processing device with the ability of 53 qubits, to attain quantum dominance. This superconducting device will be utilized to evaluate quantum modeling, optimization, and machine learning, as well as study the error rates of the system and the supportability of their methodology completely developed upon qubits.

13.2.3   Is Quantum Computing a Cybersecurity Threat?

Majority of systems which involve data are predominantly using mathematical models and algorithms to ensure safety and security to the data they utilize. In this regard, a technique is used between two peers who involve communicating with each other and share data to prevent data theft. We use a specific key transfer on both the sides to commence the data transfer and to ensure the data has not been overseen by any other unauthorized person [11]. This is called as Quantum Key Distribution (QKD) technique. Utilizing this technique in blockchain network may provide security the involved data to a greater extent from various attacks [12].

Quantum mechanics, in essence, adds to the current classical mechanics by providing more additive properties. To begin, physical quantities are quantized, which means they cannot be divided. Systems are characterized in terms of superpositions by quantum mechanics, which may allow various inputs at the same time in order to get processed properly, yet although at most one can be seen at the end of the process, obviously, we get probabilistic expected results. Finally, correlations are possible in quantum mechanics that are not possible in conventional physics. Entanglement is a term used to describe such relationships [13].

Quantum computing is a two-sided unleashed force. Single-handedly, it offers a significant step forward in areas such as research and medical advancements, which saves a common man's life from danger and causalities, and sectors, which deals finance. Second flip of the technology is that it has the ability to decrypt information with the help of recent encryption algorithms which are in use.

The expectation of quantum computing is that it would make such speedups for particular difficult problems more widely available. Clearly, this has ramifications in many fields of information science and computation, where a system's functionality is dependent on the complexity of a calculation. This is especially true in the case of cryptographic systems that completely depend on skewed mathematical and analytical endeavor while evaluating a function and its inverse. Multiplication of large primes is simple and thus quick in RSA encryption, however, dividing huge composite numbers into two prime components is a Himalayan task and time-consuming. The important property of hash functions is that they are simple to measure but difficult to invert. It is tough to discover a pre-image that provides a given hash value because they have a quasi-unique fingerprint [14].

Organizations exploring with innovative methods to apply blockchain technology are on the cutting edge, and completely depend on blockchain technology to properly maintain data for the time being may be appropriate. In the cybersecurity room, on the other hand, staying one step ahead of bad actors is a never-ending endeavor. In this scenario, we know what the future holds; the only question is when it will arrive. Those who need to ensure the security of their data in the future should consider the issues that quantum computing will definitely bring.

13.2.4   Quantum Computing is not a Real Threat to Cryptocurrencies

To begin with, let us define known technologies named as quantum computing and the classical computing and examine how the two concepts compare and differ. Quantum computing is simply peer to exemplary standard pre-1900s physics and "modern" physics, which includes theory of relativity and quantum physics insights. Binary computing refers to the computers that we have stretched, accustomed to, as well as the expansions of computations on the basis of Turing's theory, such as portable electronic devices or mobile phones. Physical bits—the well-known 0's and 1's—are frequently used in traditional computing.

Qubits, which are bits that stored smallest increment of data that are stored in quantum systems to be in multiple states, are used in quantum computation to accomplish calculations using quantum principles. The ability of qubits to be in many physical states at the same time (superposition) benefits the information collected or delivered by a quantum system, yet capturing the state of the system causes information decay. A quantum computer must surpass a classical computer at some little and unimportant activity that appears spectacular but is entirely meaningless, similar to a test conducted on machine-generated English by turing, may trick a Ukrainian youngster who does not speak the language. To make "quantum dominance" meaningful, we need to zero in on a characteristic that quantum computers can improve that has a significant influence on cryptocurrencies or the encryption they use [15].

Distinct interest in a zone is Shor's algorithm that can influence big natural numbers into two smaller ones. This is a particularly important trait for breaking encipher because the RSA family of encoding relies on articulating huge natural numbers in this trend. Theory with a large enough quantum computer is the basis for Shor's algorithm functioning, but it is a practical problem that it could be used to crack, RSA encryption, among other things. In response to this, National Institute for Standards and Technology (NIST) has begun accepting manifestos for post quantum cryptography, that would permit encoding to work and not be broken even with quantum computers particularly bigger than those presently available. According to the researchers, quantum computers large enough to overcome classical encryption could be available in the next 20 years.

However a good Shor's Algorithm implementation might not be enough to breach any of Bitcoin's cryptographic rules. For detecting a collision in SHA-256, the theoretically most effective quantum computer implementation is currently less methodical than the long established execution to violate the standard. The file created by Multi bit in the international Bitcoin wallet client utilizes SHA-512 to encrypt private keys (a more stable version than SHA-256).

The majority of modern cryptocurrencies' encryption is based on elliptic curve cryptography rather than RSA, particularly when it comes to signature generation in Bitcoin, which needs ECDSA. This is related to the exponential nature of elliptic curves more difficult to crack than RSA from traditional computers [16]. Both elliptic curve cryptography and elliptic curve encryption are commonly utilized as a variety of other organizations and usage scenarios—in the traditional banking system, RSA-2048 and higher are standards for sending encrypted data.

Accelerating up of mining with a large enough quantum computer logarithmically by Grover's method could be another attack vector. However, it is likely that ASICs bitcoin mining is being done by the sophisticated classical computers. The more comprehensive quantum computer with the initial versions is less fast than classical computers. These and other more unclear attack paths are likely, but post-quantum encryption preparation is currently beginning—and employing post quantum encryption standards by changing cryptocurrencies, and it is also to guard against these fault via forks.

Classical ways of encryption will not be made by adding quantum computers to the mix to obsolete or mine cheap – your encryption is not meant by "quantum supremacy" or Bitcoin's security is in peril immediately.

13.2.5   Need for Quantum Computing in Blockchain

Blockchain has a wide range of applications in digital currency, information security, and smart contracts due to its decentralization, openness, and the fact that the information stored in it cannot be tampered with. The communication and trust between nodes in a distributed blockchain network must always rely on digital signature technology, which primarily enables information identification, authenticity, and integrity verification.

The encryption algorithm used in most blockchain digital signature technology is Elliptic Curves Cryptography (ECC), otherwise called as the large integer factorization problem (RSA). The prevention of certain algorithms is based on the premise that some complex problems are computationally complex. The proof-of-work algorithm is commonly used when adding naive data into the blockchain. The primary motive of this approach is to use calculation to guess a value (once) and solve the hash problem. The advancement of quantum computing could place conventional blockchain technology in trouble. Some quantum algorithms can successfully solve the problems associated with the encryption algorithm, leaving the blockchain's digital signature unreliable. Hence, it would be a good choice to deploy quantum computing in blockchain in order to make it more efficient and effective [17].

13.2.6   Ensuring a Secure, Functioning, and Resilient Critical Infrastructure

The U.S. government has recognized 16 critical infrastructure sectors whose significant properties, networking devices are essential to maintaining daily life and protecting the economic security, public health, and safety of the nation.

Water and waste, energy, oil and gas, telecommunications, and transportation are just a few of the industries that employ Supervisory Control and Data Acquisition (SCADA) systems to control, to be vigilant, and to utilize their devices and plants. Over time, SCADA systems have become increasingly integrated with other third-party systems via the Internet. This has exposed the nation's critical infrastructure to new risks and cyber vulnerabilities as data travels between systems and across vast, large-scale networks.

The North American power grid, for example, is a high-value target under constant attack by malicious actors. Utilities in America and other countries in the world are progressively adopting smart grid technology and the proliferation of IoT devices used by these sectors, the attack surface is expanding causing threat actors and cyber events to grow in frequency and sophistication.

In these highly regulated industries, critical infrastructure operators must look to mitigate new risks that arise from the increased complexity of modern control systems; ensure their network systems remain safeguarded from the risks associated with emerging technologies and supply chain management; adhere to both federal and state cybersecurity regulations; and plan and prepare for future threats including the fast-approaching cryptographic break or Q-Day—when a quantum computer is available to break today's encryption standards [18].

13.2.7   Critical Infrastructure's Unique Threat Landscape

For most commercial businesses, countermeasures against the quantum threat are about preserving data privacy, integrity, and security, keeping critical, high-value data away from the prying eyes of hackers and out of the hands of state-sponsored actors. For networks that manage critical infrastructure, the threat and motivation behind bad acts goes beyond financial motivations. The system itself, and what the system produces, is the high-value target. Service disruptions and the chaos that ensues is the goal of state-sponsored harm or acts of terrorism.

Critical infrastructure and manufacturing is attacked by cyber-attacks is the study by organization of American States. These are more likely to target industrial control systems than data. Fifty-four percent out of the 500 critical infrastructure suppliers polled reporting attempts to control systems. Forty percent reports attempts to shut down system.

As a result, man-in-the-middle attacks are a major concern, as they allow an attacker to insert himself in the middle of a dialogue between a consumer and an application, either to overhear or to impersonate one of the parties, making it appear as if it is a normal information exchange is taking place. When a malicious actor gains control of critical infrastructure, such as the Bowman Avenue Dam in New York in 2013 or three utilities in Ukraine in 2015, the first reported power outage caused by a hostile act, the results can be severe.

While man-in-the-middle attacks are a popular attack vector, critical infrastructure is not immune to other nefarious acts including breaches that look to steal critical data for criminal exploit, or harvesting attack where information is copied and stored waiting for the day when a quantum computer can break its encryption.

13.2.8   Response to the Quantum Threat and Blockchain

Traditional digital networks lack the ability to detect whether someone else is tapping in and reading data. Sending a private key over the network is susceptible to eavesdropping, so public-private key pairs are used. The encrypted tunnel is then created with the exchanged key and the data sent through the tunnel. However, this means the encrypted keys and data travel together. An attacker needs only to compromise one connection to obtain both the key and the information it protects. To make matters more precarious, there is no way to tell whether the attacker is copying data.

With QKD, however, if the stream of photons that delivers the key is tampered with in any way, it changes its quantum state, immediately notifying both parties and terminating the session. QKD then would be a highly effective countermeasure to man-in-the-middle key theft attacks.

The U.S. government has recognized the potential and immediate use case of QKD by critical infrastructure enlisting Oak Ridge and Los Alamos National Labs to work on a multiphase project to make QKD over the North American power grid a reality. The problem is that QKD [12–14] has its limitations which could take several more years to address and overcome—first in the lab, then deployed in a real-world, commercial setting. The most notable challenges include the limited distance a quantum key can travel, point-to-point only transmissions, poor interoperability with equipment and systems from various vendors, and the need for costly dedicated fiber.

Unfortunately, time is a luxury that does not exist. The NIST itself recommended in 2016 that all industries should commence preparing for the quantum-crypto blast. Action is required now to ensure the communication networks of critical infrastructure providers is quantum-safe and capable of addressing new security threats that emerge with the advancement of computing and mathematics.

In this context, it is faced with two things that invalidate blockchain's promises. First, hash inversion is thought to be computationally challenging. No longer, the validity of the upstream blockchain is assured, if a quantum computer can radically simplify this and the trust worthiness of the entries in the blockchain is menaced. Particularly, the old brute force method of generating each output value and comparing it to segregate the given input value, which is slower than the pre-image to a function value, is determined by the Grover's approach.

13.2.9   Ethereum 2.0 will be Quantum Resistant

Their own transaction validation scheme can be chosen by the accounts in the Ethereum 2.0 serenity upgrade. Switching to a quantum safe signature scheme is the option included in this.

ECDSA is regarded to be slower and more difficult than quantum-resistant hash-based signature methods like the Lamport signature. Unfortunately, the scheme's size is an issue. The public key and signature of Lamport are 231 times larger (106 bytes vs. 24KB) than those of ECDSA. As a result, utilizing the Lamport Signature technique will necessitate 231 times the amount of storage required by ECDSA, which is currently unworkable.

Other quantum-resistant signature options being tested by Ethereum developers include the signatures utilized by the Quantum-Resistant Ledger blockchain which includes eXtended Merkle Signature Scheme, hash ladder signatures, and SPHINCS.

Switching to signature schemes which are based on hashes like XMSS has many advantages, including speed and small signatures. XM Signature Scheme is persistent because of many one-time signatures used in Merkle trees method, which is a severe disadvantage. This necessitates the mechanism to store the state to memorize the already used one-time key pairs in constructing signatures. SPHINCS signatures are not persistent, since they use a limited number of signatures with Merkle trees, obviating the necessity to maintain the state because a single signature can be used more than once. RANDAO functions based on hashes, which are utilized in Ethereum 2.0's beacon chain for random number generation, are already regarded to be post-quantum.

13.3   Quantum Computing Algorithms

In the context of understanding quantum computing and quantum enhanced assaults, Grover's and Shor's algorithms would be the fundamental algorithms. The preceding technique is an input search approach for finding a unique input to a black box function that is substantially faster than brute force search, but it may put hash algorithms of insufficient length in jeopardy. In comparison to a standard number field sieve (the most well-known factoring algorithm), the latter offers an exponential speed increase in factoring integers and can also be utilized to manage secret subordinate clusters and discrete logarithmic problems. This might result in a variety of issues. These issues are at the heart of decrypting many established asymmetric cyphers and are thus applicable to decrypting public key cryptography and digital signatures. As a result, these two algorithms address a significant risk to systems when using blockchain to execute work.

13.3.1   Grover's Algorithm

Grover's algorithm demonstrates this. This approach can enhance the run time of an unstructured search issue quadratically, but it can also be used as a general trick or subroutine to speed up a range of other algorithms. It is known as the amplitude amplification trick.

13.3.2   Shor's Algorithm

The general number field has a super polynomial complexity (run time input length is longer than any polynomial) but a subexponential complexity (run time input is exponentially shorter than any polynomial), whereas Shor's algorithm has a polynomial complexity in the input length, resulting in a speed gain of approximately higher. Indeed, 4096-bit RSA keys are impenetrable with the classical computation but can be broken using quantum computation. As a result, Shor's algorithm can be used to solve this issue. It rather boosts the efficiency of factoring huge number by significant margin.

The primary purpose of Shor's approach was to factor huge composite integers that were the product of two large prime numbers. Factoring, on the other hand, is a subset of the larger hidden subgroup problem, and Shor's approach can be tweaked to solve both. This makes problems like the discrete logarithm problem insecure, as well as ElGamal encryption, Diffie-Hellman key exchange, the Digital Signature Algorithm, and elliptic curve cryptography. The existence of Shor's algorithm illustrates that a quantum computer exposes vulnerabilities beyond hash collision creation and Grover's method function inversion.

13.4   Quantum Secured Blockchain

The Hash functions and digital signatures are two one-way computational tools that are used in blockchain. To generate a digital signature, most blockchain platforms use elliptic curve cryptography or the big integer factorization problem. These algorithms' security is based on assumptions about the computational complexity of specific mathematical issues. These problems would be solved by using the universal quantum computing techniques which then makes the digital signatures and the computational techniques followed in blockchain a secure one.

Large integers and discrete logarithms can be factored in polynomial using Shor's quantum algorithm and Grover's search algorithm as a security inability. This gives space for quadratic speedup. The inverse hash function is produced by quadratic speedup. Now, block mining would be possible by a gang of bad parties with a majority of network powers monopolizes. This is called a 51% assault. The other party transactions will be spoiled by the capacity of perpetrators. It sometimes prevents their own spending activities from being recorded in the blockchain.

Blockchains will be more secure if post-quantum digital signature techniques [9, 10] are used to sign transactions. Quantum computer attacks are expected to be resistant to such systems. However, its robustness is predicated on unproven assumptions. Furthermore, it is highly expensive and computationally time consuming to use post-quantum digital signatures, rendering them ineffectual against assaults that control the network's hash rate with a quantum computer.

Authentication can be guaranteed using QKD based in the theoretical correlations based on quantum physics. QKD generates a secret key which will be shared between the peers who involve in the communication through the quantum channel to share the post-processing quantum states in a public channel. This way of utilizing the quantum computing methodology arrived from quantum physics can be widely used for sending the data in the transmission channel. This QKD technique is very intuitive, as this kind of QKD networks are always rely on the nodes based on the trust further transaction may be communicated in the blockchain network. However, this QKD ensures the authenticity between the peers who participate in communication in the quantum channel. Hence, nobody in the network can impersonate, and other classical consensus algorithm may also be used.

13.4.1   Cybersecurity

The initiation and conservation of processes has been covered by cybersecurity in relation to identify the trending cyberthreats, which leads to the reduction of related costs in association with cybersecurity. In reality, it is a prerequisite for adopting the operation of modern and technology-based environment through a sustainable computing ecosystem in which the entire locality which utilizes the data can be safe guarded. In spite of having a true necessity for enhancing the cybersecurity society, there is always a lag in security developments due to constant increase in malicious online activities. Cybersecurity attacks are ranking top among all the attacks in the network when data security is concerned [19]. World economic forum has published a report in 2019 which claims the global risks pertaining toward data security globally. Cyberattacks casually result in huge losses to banking sectors, which involves various data servers. Not only in this sector, whichever the business may be which involves huge amount of data will always be rushed to data breach and hack by various hackers on recent days.

In accordance with the report published by World Economic Forum, it is expected to have approximate calculation for the business value of cybersecurity to be increased from 120 to 300 thousand lakh in the financial year 2024. It is believed that cybersecurity encompasses a broad area that includes anything from building secure networks that withstand attacks to developing methods and systems that aid in the detection of threats and anomalies, as well as ensuring a system's stability and declaring system responses to any assault. Cybersecurity features have been documented systematically by cybersecurity strategies, and it has been rapidly adapted since 2011 across globe.

Throughout the evolution of cybersecurity, there has been a steady increase in the development of these execution plans. According to local needs there evolved the multiple versions of cybersecurity plans over a period of time in countries individually. These modifications apparently point out the momentum in understanding the importance of cybersecurity professionals who are involve in security domain and also by a civilian.

As an initiation, cyber situational awareness has etched new lives and flown high, and security countermeasures have been devised in particular. Finally, as an integral aspect of cyberthreat prevention measures, cybersecurity seeks to protect data from intruders and data thieves and is critical for every individual, public people, and other private business persons. Focusing on the best interest of everyone is on preserving and defending the information involved surroundings from theft and malware—consider the consequences of the recent big waves of ransomware. Cyberthreats are on the rise, thanks to complex and diabolical plans and a desire to break into information systems.

13.4.2   Cyber-Physical Systems

The global upliftment of implemented information and communicating technologies has been set in motion by of cyber-physical systems (CPSes), in which each and every one is mediated as a separate collaborator. Every single stakeholder and organizational levels in a CPS are examined and considered in order to improve communication efficiency and learn about the world. They also boost efficiency, effectiveness, and productivity in industrial situations, government, and academia, while also contributing considerably to the economy and national security. The bulk of people doing crime activities over internet, whose salient motive is to compromise security, profits from the same systems. Unfortunately, workforces that happen through internet attempts to increase the performance, dependability, longevity, and cost have been unmatched with upgraded and uplifted security standards, and a number of issues still exist. It is usually recommended to have a perfectly utilized environment that utilizes advanced technologies to self-protect data by employing precautionary measures such as implementing software that are trust worthy and new models to increase the security alerts.

13.4.3   Cybercrime and Cybersecurity Challenges

A cybercriminal uses social engineering attacks like spam messaging, and distributed denial-of-service attacks (DDoS) to disrupt the entire informational environment and track the device in real time, necessitating the creation of persistent monitoring tactics. Security experts are in high demand around the world to apply such surveillance systems. However, skilled domain specialists are in short supply, stressing the need for enhanced knowledge and related prime degree courses. Cloud computing can aid to provide easy access to distant services for cybersecurity training courses.

There are a variety of meanings for cybercrime and cybersecurity, but no specific term is universally recognized. A concrete well awareness of internet crime and security is required for enabling efficient attacking and protective remedies. In accordance with McAfee, combining implementation of laws and regulatory institutions, education and awareness programs, and highly established technical inventions is the correct strategy to combat internet crime.

Through leveraging entire nations' capabilities, as well as continuous capacity building and growth, a long-term security advantage adds value to security and keeps thieves from exploiting device flaws (aside from zero days). Protecting IT infrastructures is more difficult today because readily available free hacking tools and publicized software endangers are imbalanced with inhibitory solutions that are still in their infancy. This is why the Community Cybersecurity Maturity Model (CCSMM) was designed to bridge the gap by directing practitioners to identify state and community needs and, as a result, develop a viable and long-term cybersecurity program.

13.4.4   Community Cybersecurity Maturity Model

According to the CCSMM, every community member requires three key mechanisms: a "yardstick," a "roadmap," and a common point of reference and terminology. Officials may utilize this to learn about and improve cybersecurity in other states, with local groups sharing their experiences. As states and communities undergo a thorough examination of lists such as cybersecurity awareness, information sharing inside organizations, constructing and running processes, security planning, and the inclusion of cybersecurity in both community and state plans to ensure operation continuity and incident response, CCSMM recognizes the characteristics of states and communities. This model is capable of detecting security variables which can assist nations and local communities improve their cybersecurity maturity levels by incorporating required technology, training, practices, and test plans, as well as policies and plans of action, into security plans and implementing them as needed. This model depicts all aspects of a society at different stages of growth.

Despite having such good models, countries are nevertheless falling behind due to a lack of program implementation support. This methodology has shown to be one of the most powerful and viable for establishing a long-term cybersecurity ecosystem.

The greatest maturity levels, on the other hand, must be given greater attention during implementation in order to be suitably solid. Traditional knowledge sharing allows each partner to discuss their findings, but this is not always feasible or scalable. Collaborative knowledge sharing, on the other hand, will help a group identify cyber-risks and safeguard a system from cyberattacks at an early stage. It also encourages a response to cyber-events, as well as the habits that go with it. To be able to "share, yet protect," access control (AC) must be installed.

A society's common components include business organizations, non-sector entities, and super groupings. A society forms a super group to undertake similar responsibilities, and this group is in charge of obtaining information for the coordination group from non-profit organizations as well as other sources such as nearby communities and the state government. Threats are discovered and detected by intelligence information analysis. Information exchange and cyber-event management can also be coordinated by multiple sector groupings. A smart city is one in which information and communication technology controls all areas of government, people, culture, well-being and education systems, and all other selected parts of a city's surrounds (ICT). This is achieved by combining modern embedded technologies and Internet of Things (IoT) devices with a network that comprises records, tracking and controlling devices, and a variety of choice selection algorithms.

Sharing incident reactions, coping plans, recovery ideas, alarms, and cautions with members of a super community is crucial. This network was founded by cybersecurity experts. Finance, energy, water resources, healthcare, law enforcement, and telecommunications are just a few of the industries involved are just a handful of the major sectors served by a society composed of many different sector classes. Each sector community promotes the exchange of information among the numerous organizations that make up the sector in question. Even for those organizations that are not affiliated with any major sector of a society but may provide crucial information in the event of a cyber-attack, a non-sector organization strengthens and protects itself.

13.4.5 Cybersecurity in Smart Grid Systems

Cybersecurity is a key concern in smart grids because of fiber optic communication technologies and the large number of elements involved, all of which are totally backed by internet services, making them more powerful. As networks become more vulnerable to cyber-risks, smart grids become more brittle as a result of the use of networked devices and the connectivity between them. Symmetric and asymmetric cryptography are used to safeguard the device against hackers.

Simple infrastructure security solutions are available in addition to cryptographic methods. Cryptographic systems and processes should have plans in place to respond rapidly to emergencies and resolve concerns like isolation, elimination, location, and even data recovery. Cyberattacks on smart grids are typically well-planned, and they launch multiple attacks at once, making them very tough to combat and perhaps undermining the overall security system. Security measures applicable to network levels are regarded efficient solutions for a smart grid application like this.

13.4.6 Smart Cities: Sustainable Future

A smart city is one in which information and communication technology controls all areas of government, people, culture, health and education systems, and all other significant parts of a city's surrounds (ICT). This is achieved by combining modern embedded technologies and Internet of Things (IoT) devices with a network that comprises records, tracking and controlling devices, and a variety of choice selection algorithms.

The following are the primary security issues that a smart city faces:

- Radio frequency identification, wireless sensor networks, smart mobile phones, and the grid are examples of Internet of Things tools.
- An insecure system, mobility, and smart device management are all examples of governance causes.
- Intelligent networking, services, privacy, and e-commerce are all aspects of the economy and society.

A Hybrid Smart City Cyber Security Architecture (HSCCA) was proposed to improve efficiency, ease access, and explore the regional level risk management. In general, it only deals with a smart city system that is properly planned when taking into account all security schemes and without any gaps in knowledge, availability, or versatility. This allows for a near-instant response to information and any related incidents. The source development should have direct access to real-time data in order to optimize resource usage at both the department and city levels. HSCCA provides many mechanisms for identifying threats, as well as the protection of public data and intelligent strategies for dealing with threats and risks.

13.5 Conclusion

This technology can make unimaginable strides in fields like materials science, medicine, and science and technology by using the strange laws of quantum mechanics. At the same time, it might generate the highest threat to internet security. Positively, the threat has not yet been arrived. It is out of everyone's knowledge about the commencement of quantum computing, but Ethereum will be ready.

Ethereum developers have begun developing alternative cryptographic signature schemes to replace those that are endangered, in order to create a stable, resilient post-quantum Ethereum protocol.

NIST has also begun the process of identifying, testing, and standardizing some cryptography algorithms that are quantum-resistant. In the next stage of post-quantum cryptography standardization, NIST has picked 26 algorithms for investigation.

As part of post quantum cryptography standardization, listed algorithms have been proposed for research for having right confronted implementation toward the sustainable future world of digital era.

References

1. Reyna, A., Martín, C., Chen, J., Soler, E., Díaz, M., On blockchain and its integration with IoT. Challenges and opportunities. *Futur. Gener. Comput. Syst.*, 88, 173–190, Nov. 2018.
2. Bentov, I., Gabizon, A., Mizrahi, A., Cryptocurrencies without proof of work, in: *Lecture Notes in Computer Science (including subseries Lecture Notes in Artificial Intelligence and Lecture Notes in Bioinformatics)*, vol. 9604, pp. 142–157, LNCS, 2016.
3. Tolstykh, T., Gamidullaeva, L., Shmeleva, N., Lapygin, Y., Regional development in Russia: An ecosystem approach to territorial sustainability assessment. *Sustain.*, 12, 16, 6401, Aug. 2020.
4. Fernández-Caramés, T. M., Blanco-Novoa, O., Froiz-Míguez, I., Fraga-Lamas, P., Towards an autonomous industry 4.0 warehouse: A UAV and blockchain-based system for inventory and traceability applications in big data-driven supply chain management. *Sensors (Basel)*, 19, 10, May 2019.
5. Shin, B. and Lowry, P. B., A review and theoretical explanation of the 'Cyberthreat-Intelligence (CTI) capability' that needs to be fostered in

information security practitioners and how this can be accomplished. *Comput. Sec.*, vol. 92. Elsevier Ltd, May 01, 2020.

6. Androulaki, E. *et al.*, Hyperledger fabric: A distributed operating system for permissioned blockchains, in *Proceedings of the 13th EuroSys Conference, EuroSys 2018*, vol. 2018, 2018-Janua.

7. Fernandez-Carames, T. M. and Fraga-Lamas, P., Towards post-quantum blockchain: A review on blockchain cryptography resistant to quantum computing attacks. *IEEE Access*, 8, 21091–21116, 2020.

8. Tounsi, W. and Rais, H., A survey on technical threat intelligence in the age of sophisticated cyber attacks. *Comput. Sec.*, Elsevier Ltd, 72, 212–233, Jan. 01, 2018.

9. Salman, T., Zolanvari, M., Erbad, A., Jain, R., Samaka, M., Security services using blockchains: A state of the art survey. *IEEE Commun. Surv. Tutorials*, 21, 1, 858–880, Jan. 2019.

10. Wang, S., Ding, W., Li, J., Yuan, Y., Ouyang, L., Wang, F. Y., Decentralized autonomous organizations: Concept, model, and applications. *IEEE Trans. Comput. Soc. Syst.*, 6, 5, 870–878, Oct. 2019.

11. Devi, R. M. *et al.*, Retina biometrics for personal authentication, in: *Machine Learning for Biometrics*, pp. 87–104, Academic Press, 2022.

12. Fernandez-Carames, T. M. and Fraga-Lamas, P., A review on the application of blockchain to the next generation of cybersecure industry 4.0 smart factories. *IEEE Access*, 7, 45201–45218, 2019.

13. Fernández-Caramés, T. M. and Fraga-Lamas, P. A review on the use of blockchain for the Internet of Things, in: *IEEE Access*, vol. 6, pp. 32979–33001, Institute of Electrical and Electronics Engineers Inc., May 30, 2018.

14. Fraga-Lamas, P. and Fernández-Caramés, T. M., Leveraging blockchain for sustainability and open innovation: A cyber-resilient approach toward eu green deal and un sustainable development goals, in: *Computer Security Threats*, IntechOpen, 2020.

15. Cheung, D., Maslov, D., Mathew, J., Pradhan, D. K., On the design and optimization of a quantum polynomial-time attack on elliptic curve cryptography, in: *Lecture Notes in Computer Science (including subseries Lecture Notes in Artificial Intelligence and Lecture Notes in Bioinformatics)*, vol. 5106, pp. 96–104, LNCS, 2008.

16. Kearney, J. J. and Perez-Delgado, C. A., Vulnerability of blockchain technologies to quantum attacks. *Array*, 10, 100065, Jul. 2021.

17. Van Meter, R. and Horsman, C., A blueprint for building a quantum computer. *Commun. ACM*, 56, 10, 84–93, 2013.

18. Mosca, M., Cybersecurity in an era with quantum computers: Will we be ready?, *IEEE Secur. Priv.*, 16, 5, 38–41, Sep. 2018.

19. Suresh, P. *et al.*, Contemporary survey on effectiveness of machine and deep learning techniques for cyber security, in: *Machine Learning for Biometrics*, pp. 177–200, Academic Press, 2022.

14

Estimation of Bitcoin Price Trends Using Supervised Learning Approaches

Prasannavenkatesan Theerthagiri

Department of Computer Science and Engineering, GITAM School of Technology, GITAM University, Bengaluru, India

Abstract

Bitcoin, one of the most well-known cryptocurrencies, soared above $17,000 in November 2020, a 3-year high. Since its inception in 2008, the digital currency has experienced considerable price changes. Due to the instability generated by the epidemic on global equities markets, investors flocked to cryptocurrencies. The goal of this study is to see how well machine learning models can forecast the price of Bitcoin in relation to the US dollar. Among the models are linear regression, Random Forest, Support Vector Machine, Auto-Regressive Integrated Moving Average, Long Short-Term Memory, and Recurrent Neural Network. The findings will contribute to a better understanding of the new and complex cryptocurrency's behavior.

Keywords: Bitcoin, supervised learning, price estimation, LSTM, ARIMA, RNN

14.1 Introduction

14.1.1 Bitcoin

Satoshi Nakamoto created the decentralized cryptocurrency Bitcoin in 2008. The major goal was to allow participants to bargain directly with one another without the need for a mediator [1]. The Bitcoin network verifies all transactions with the nodes that make up the network. The blockchain is a decentralized public ledger that records confirmed transactions.

Email: prasannait91@gmail.com

Rajesh Kumar Dhanaraj, Vani Rajasekar, SK Hafizul Islam, Balamurugan Balusamy and Ching-Hsien Hsu (eds.) Quantum Blockchain: An Emerging Cryptographic Paradigm, (341–356) © 2022 Scrivener Publishing LLC

Bitcoin mining is carried out in order to maintain the blockchain current. Anyone who is prepared to use their computer's processing capacity to solve complicated mathematical problems can earn Bitcoins.

14.1.2   COVID-19 and Bitcoin

COVID-19 has wreaked havoc on capital markets, particularly virtual currency markets [2]. It describes the pandemic's economic and societal consequences. The report emphasizes the impact of the COVID-19 crisis on global financial markets, as well as the pandemic's influence in the financial sector. COVID-19 cases/fatalities are linked to cryptocurrency (e.g., BTC, ETH, and XRP). Initially, there was an inverse relationship between Bitcoin and reported deaths/cases, but this relationship has now shifted to a positive one [3]. The main issue is whether Bitcoin is a dangerous threat or a secure sanctuary. What is the core of Bitcoin during the financial market upheaval caused by the COVID-19 pandemic? Conlon and McGee [4] respond to both concerns and show that Bitcoin does not behave as a safe haven; in fact, Bitcoin's trajectory paralleled that of the S&P 500 when the crisis began.

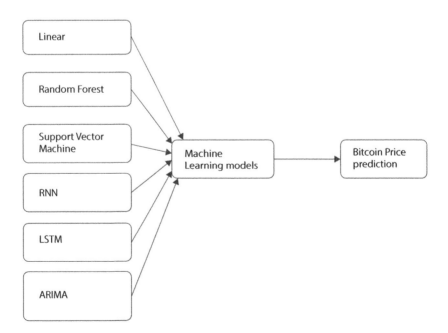

Figure 14.1 Proposed research overview.

14.1.3 Price Prediction

Forecasting prices is not a new phenomenon. Stock price predictions are the subject of a lot of research [5]. Using machine learning algorithms, stock prices with increased accuracy and precision are predicted. For prediction, regression and Long Short-Term Memory (LSTM) models were utilized. Although both models increased accuracy, the LSTM results were more efficient [6]. By studying the relationship between the news stream and stock price movement, the share prices are forecasted.

Using a range of machine learning techniques, this study estimates regular Bitcoin values. Some of the models utilized were Support Vector Machine (SVM), Linear Regression, Recurrent Neural Network (RNN), Random Forest, Autoregressive Integrated Moving Average (ARIMA), and LSTM. Figure 14.1 presents a summary of the research.

14.2 Related Work

The research of Bitcoin price prediction is inadequate due to its young age and considerable volatility. Because of its peer-to-peer design and decentralization, Bitcoin has a large number of users all over the world [7]. The author discovered a relationship between Twitter and Google searches and the price of Bitcoin. The accuracy of Bitcoin price prediction using polynomial regression is 77% per tweet volume and 66.66% using Google trends. Chen [8] suggested the "latent source pattern," which has been used to Bitcoin price forecasting by [9]. The return was 89% in 50 days, with a Sharpe ratio of 4.10. The study also looks into the impact of social media networks on digital currencies like Bitcoin [10]. It investigated the behavior of a SVM, an Artificial Neural Network, and the ensemble method (k-means clustering and RNNs). The assisted vector machine algorithm performs best in terms of pricing estimations. Machine learning patterns such as SVM, Random Forest, LSTM, Quadratic Discriminant Analysis, and XGBoost were employed for regular Bitcoin price prediction [11]. The SVM came out on top with a precision of 65.5%. The authors of [12] looked at the influence of Bitcoin's most prevalent edges on price prediction and discovered that a single–hidden layer feed-forward neural networks (SLFNs) could forecast prices with 60.05% accuracy (approximately).

To anticipate Bitcoin price, the authors employed a RNN and a linear regression model in [13]. Because of its ability to spot long-term dependencies, the RNN model had a mean square error value lower than the regression model. The linear regression, RNN, and Random Forest models are contrasted in [14]. Because the data is very volatile, the RNN with

LSTM has improved the model's efficiency for predicting Bitcoin values. The MAE of the model was 0.0043, which was lower than that of linear regression and random forest [15]. McNally compared the accuracy of the ARIMA, RNN, and LSTM models and discovered that the LSTM network had the greatest accuracy of 52%.

Ladislav [16] investigated the link between Bitcoin prices and Wikipedia and Google searches. The findings also revealed an inconsistency between the increased interest in cryptocurrency and the lower or greater value of the currency in recent trends. For short-term predictions, authors in [17] employed the ARIMA model. The Bitcoin price is more correctly predicted by ARIMA (4,1,4). For day 1 projections, the average absolute error was 0.87, while for day 7 forecasts, it was 5.98. As a result, ARIMA has yielded superior short-term results.

14.3   Methodology

14.3.1   Data Collection

Kaggle, an online community, provided the Bitcoin dataset. From October 8, 2015, until April 10, 2020, this dataset is available. Close, date, high, volume BTC, low, volume USD, and opening price of BTC are all included in each row. Table 14.1 presents the features available in the dataset.

Table 14.1 Features of dataset.

Features	Explanation
Date	Bitcoin price for particular date
Open	Opening price
Close	Closing price at that day
High	High price
Low	Low price
Volume	Volume from top exchange

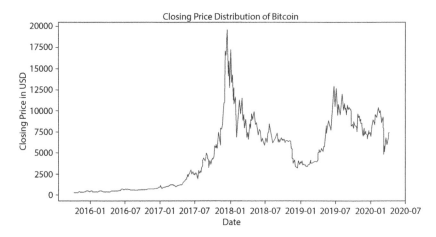

Figure 14.2 Bitcoin closing price distribution.

14.3.2   Feature Engineering and Evaluation

Feature engineering is the process of extracting useful information from data in order to increase the accuracy of machine learning algorithms' predictions. It can be regarded an important component of the data mining process for achieving good outcomes in future assignments. Figure 14.2 depicts the dispersion of closing prices.

14.3.3   Modeling

Data mining is the process of collecting usable information from large amounts of data. The technical underpinning for data extraction is machine learning. As a result, Computer Learning (ML) is a subset of Artificial Intelligence (AI) in which a machine learns from prior experience rather than being explicitly programmed. A dataset is made up of instances that have one or more characteristics. There are two types of machine learning: supervised machine learning and unsupervised machine learning. Supervised learning uses labels to model the dataset. Each instance can be represented by x and y, where x represents a collection of independent variables and y represents a set of dependent characteristics.

Whether the target variable is discrete or continuous makes no difference. If the target attribute is continuous, then the regression model is used; if the target attribute is discrete, then the classification model is employed. Supervised learning includes things like help vector machines and neural networks. Unsupervised learning is used to learn from observations and uncover structures within the data collection. It is used to represent a data collection when one of the attributes is not known. The goal of this study is to forecast Bitcoin prices. As a result, the goal is clear, and supervised machine learning will be applied. Random Forest, Linear Regression, SVM, ARIMA, LSTM, and RNN are the methods employed.

14.3.3.1   Linear Regression

The relationship between dependent and independent variables is shown via linear regression. The following is the equation for fitting data points to a line:

$$Y = a + bX \qquad (14.1)$$

Independent variables are denoted by the letter "X", dependent variables by the letter "Y", slope by the letter "b", and intercept by the letter "a".

14.3.3.2   Random Forest

Random Forest is one of the most prevalent regression and classification issues. For improved results, it combines numerous decision trees. A variety of categorization challenges are addressed by decision trees. The decision tree is a recursively partitioned tree structure in which feature space is partitioned. When splitting adds no value to the forecast or until single class samples are present in each node, recursion ends. The dataset may be connected to leaf nodes in decision trees.

14.3.3.3   Support Vector Machine

The SVM model is employed in binary classification issues [11]. The goal is to find a hyperplane with the smallest possible difference between two classes of data samples. Assume there is a problem with binary classification. The number of data points in the real n-dimensional space is denoted by the letter m.

Matrix A is used to represent Rn (xi is ith row of A). yi € 1,−1 can be used to denote the xi class. As a result, here is the one-dimensional SVM search for the optimal choice hyperplane:

$$x.y + a = 0 \qquad (14.2)$$

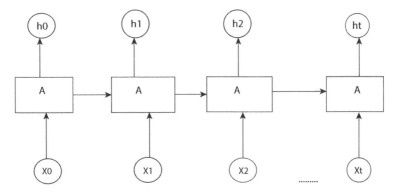

Figure 14.3 Recurrent neural network.

where "y" belongs to Rn, "a" belongs to R, "y" is the normal to the hyper-plane weight vector, and "a" represents bias. Minimization of $\|w\|$ produces the finest hyperplane.

14.3.3.4   Recurrent Neural Network

J.L. Elman is the inventor of RNNs. In these neural networks, signals can move back and forth in a repeating fashion. The context layer makes up these networks. Every layer's output is passed to the context layer, which is subsequently used as input by the next layer. The state is rebuilt at each timestamp. A typical structure of the RNN is shown in Figure 14.3.

14.3.3.5   Long Short-Term Memory

The LSTM model, which consists of three gates: output gate, forget gate, and input gate, solves the RNN's vanishing gradient problem [11]. When it comes to sequence data, LSTM outperforms other methods in terms of extracting long-term dependencies and portraying both future and previous data. The LSTM is written as follows:

$$X = [h - 1] \tag{14.3}$$

$$ft = £ \, (Wf. \, X + bf) \tag{14.4}$$

$$it = £ \, (Wi \, . \, X + bi) \tag{14.5}$$

$$ot = £ \, (Wo. \, X + bo) \tag{14.6}$$

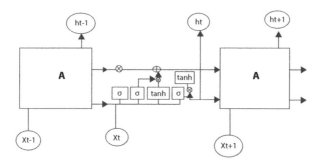

Figure 14.4 Structure of LSTM.

$$\hat{C}t = \tanh (Wc.[ht\text{-}1,xt] + bc) \qquad (14.7)$$

$$Ct = ft \odot C t\text{-}1 + it \odot \hat{C}t \qquad (14.8)$$

$$ht = ot \odot \tanh (Ct) \qquad (14.9)$$

xt is an input at time t, and ht is a hidden state at time t; Wo, Wc, Wf, and Wi are weight matrices, while bc, bi, bf, and bo are LSTM offsets. The activation function is £, and the dot matrix is multiplying operator. Figure 14.4 illustrates the structure of the LSTM.

14.3.3.6 *Autoregressive Integrated Moving Average*

The time series is forecasted and examined using the ARIMA model.

$$AR(p) + MA(q) = ARIMA(p, d, q) \qquad (14.10)$$

ARIMA's three instructions are p, d, and q. p stands for auto regression, d stands for differencing, and q stands for moving average. Autoregression (AR) is a statistical technique for determining the relationship between two periods. The ARIMA (p,0,0) is as follows:

$$Xt = \mu + \emptyset 1Xt\text{-}1 + \emptyset 2Xt\text{-}2 + \ldots\ldots + \emptyset pXt\text{-}p + et \qquad (14.11)$$

Integration (I) is mainly made to make the temporal series stationary. The moving mean (MA) indicates the movement of the previous error values. Therefore, the ARIMA (0,0,q) is

$$Xt= \mu + et - \emptyset 1\ et\text{-}1 - \emptyset 2et\text{-}2 + \ldots\ldots + \emptyset q\ et\text{-}q \qquad (14.12)$$

The ARIMA (p,d,q) is set out below:

$$Xt = \mu + Xt\text{-}1 + Xt\text{-}d + \ldots.. + \emptyset 1\ Xt\text{-}1 + \emptyset 2\ Xt\text{-}2 + \ldots.. + \emptyset p\ Xt\text{-}p$$
$$+ et - \emptyset 1\ et\text{-}1 - \emptyset 2et\text{-}2 + \ldots + \emptyset q\ et\text{-}q \qquad (14.13)$$

14.4 Implementation of the Proposed Work

The dataset was split into two parts: training and research, with the Bitcoin price forecasted for the next 30 days. The actual and predicted graphs are shown in Figures 14.5 to 14.10.

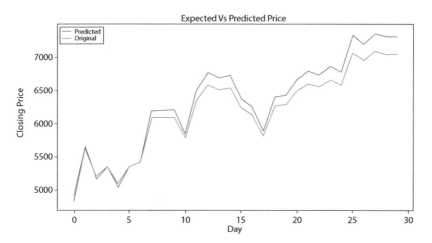

Figure 14.5 Actual and predicted price (linear regression).

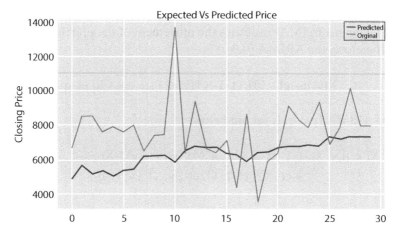

Figure 14.6 Actual and predicted price (random forest).

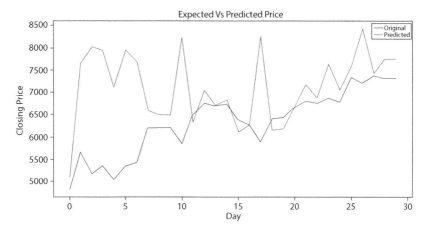

Figure 14.7 Actual and predicted price (SVM).

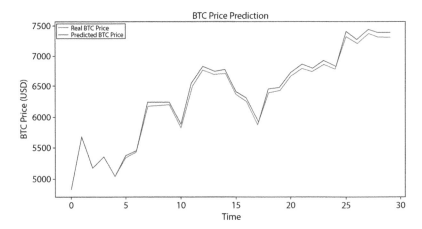

Figure 14.8 Actual and predicted price (RNN).

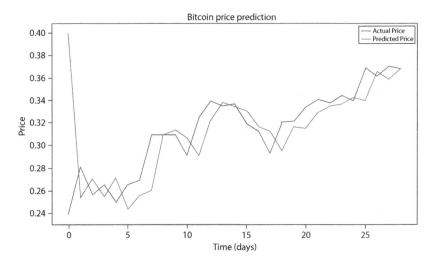

Figure 14.9 Actual and predicted price (LSTM).

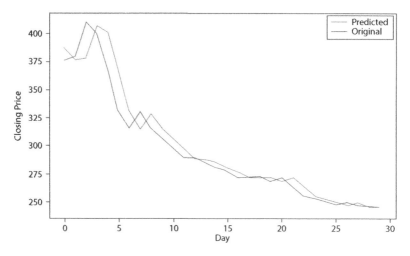

Figure 14.10 Actual and predicted price (ARIMA).

14.5 Results Evaluation and Discussion

The following metrics are used to assess the models' performance:

Mean Absolute Percentage Error (MAPE): The mean of the absolute difference between the initial and expected values is the MAPE. It is a metric for determining the accuracy of a forecasting system [20].

$$MAPE = 100 \, / \, n \sum \mid ni{=}1 \; actual_i - predicted_i/actual_i \mid$$

Root Mean Square Percentage Error (RMSPE): RMSPE tells about the percentage of error with respect to actual values.

$$RMSPE = (np.Sqrt \; (np.Mean \; (np.Square \; ((actual\text{-}predicted)/ \\ actual)))) \, {}^{*}100$$

The goal of this research is to examine and contrast different machine learning models for predicting Bitcoin prices. Figure 14.11 depicts the comparative results of supervised learning algorithms such as linear regression, random forest, SVM, ARIMA, LSTM, and RNN models [18, 19]. With a MAPE of 0.3174 and RMSPE of 0.8853, the RNN produced the greatest results.

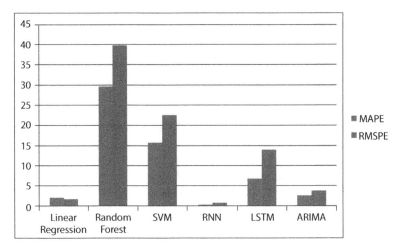

Figure 14.11 Comparison of results of supervised learning algorithms.

14.6   Conclusion

In recent years, the cryptocurrency industry has attracted the interest of businesses and investors. It will aid in comprehending the challenging and fast increasing business by presenting comparison studies and conclusions based on Bitcoin price data. Finally, this study focuses on using machine learning algorithms to forecast Bitcoin prices. The Bitcoin dataset was created with the help of the Google Colaboratory. Other datasets, containing more attributes, might be examined in the future to assist estimate the most exact and trustworthy Bitcoin price.

References

1. Dhanaraj, R.K., Krishnasamy, L., Geman, O., Izdrui, D.R., Black hole and sink hole attack detection in wireless body area networks. *Comput. Mater. Contin.*, 68, 2, 1949–1965, 2021.
2. Goodell, J.W., COVID-19 and finance: Agendas for future research. *Financ. Res. Lett.*, 35, 101512, 2020.
3. Demir, E., The relationship between cryptocurrencies and COVID 19 pandemic. *Eurasian Econ. Rev.*, 10, 349–360, 2020.
4. Colon, and Mc Gee, R.J., Safe haven or risky hazard? Bitcoin during the COVID-19 bear market. *Financ. Res. Lett.*, 35, 101607, 2020.

5. Palmer, *et al.*, Stock Market Prediction Using Machine Learning. *First International Conference on Secure Cyber Computing and Communication (ICSCCC)*, pp. 574–576, 2018.

6. Wang, Z., Ho, S., Lin, Z., Stock Market Prediction Analysis by Incorporating Social and News Opinion and Sentiment. *IEEE International Conference on Data Mining Workshops (ICDMW)*, pp. 1375–1380, 2018.

7. Mittal, A., Dhiman, V., Singh, A., Prakash, C., Short –Term Bitcoin Price Fluctuation Prediction Using Social Media and Web Search, Data. *Twelfth International Conference on Contemporary Computing (IC3)*, pp. 1–6, 2019.

8. Chen, G.H., Nikolov, S., Shah, D., A latent source model for non-parametric time series classification. *Adv. Neural Inf. Process. Syst.*, 26, 1088–1096, 2013.

9. Shah, D. and Zhang, K., Bayesian Regression and Bitcoin, Communication, Control and Computing (Allerton). *52nd Annual Allerton Conference on IEEE*, pp. 409–414, 2014.

10. Mallqui, D.C.A. and Fernandes, R.A.S., Predicting the direction, maximum, minimum and closing prices of daily Bitcoin exchange rate using machine learning techniques. *Appl. Soft Comput. J.*, 75, 596–606, 2018, https://doi.org/10.1016/j.asoc.2018.11.038.

11. Chen, Z., Li, C., Sun, W., Bitcoin price prediction using machine learning: An approach to sample dimension engineering. *J. Comput. Appl. Math.*, 365, 112395, 2020.

12. Kurbucz, M.T., Predicting the price of Bitcoin by the most frequent edges of its transaction network. *Econ. Lett.*, 184, 108655, 2019.

13. Kavitha, H., Sinha, U.K., Jain, S.S., Performance Evaluation Of Machine learning Algorithms for Bitcoin Price Prediction. *Fourth International Conference on Inventive Systems and Control (ICISC)*, pp. 110–114, 2020.

14. Tandon, S., Tripathi, S., Saraswat, P., Dabas, C., Bitcoin Price Forecasting using LSTM and 10 Fold Cross Validation. *International Conference on Signal Processing and Communication (ICSC)*, pp. 323–328, 2019.

15. McNally, S., Roche, J., Caton, S., Predicting the price of Bitcoin Using Machine Learning. *26th Euromicro International Conference on Parallel, Distributed and Network-based Processing (PDP)*, pp. 339–343, 2018.

16. Kristoufek, L., Bitcoin meets google trends and Wikipedia: quantifying the relationship between the phenomena of the internet era. *Sci. Rep.*, 3, 3415, 2013.

17. Wirawan, I.M., Widiyaningtyas, T., Hasan, M.M., Short Term Prediction on Bitcoin Price using ARIMA method. *International Seminar on Application for Technology of information and communication*, pp. 260–265, 2019.

18. Prasannavenkatesan, T., Probable Forecasting of Epidemic COVID-19 in Using COCUDE Model. *EAI Endorsed Trans. Pervasive Health Technol.*, *Online First*, 7, 26, e3, 2021.

19. Theerthagiri, P., Jeena Jacob, I., Usha Ruby, A., Yendapalli, V., Prediction of COVID-19 Possibilities using K-Nearest Neighbour Classification Algorithm. *Int. J. Curr. Res. Rev.*, *13*, 06, 156, 2021.
20. Prasannavenkatesan, T. and Menakadevi, T., Futuristic Speed Prediction Using Auto-Regression and Neural Networks for Mobile Ad hoc Networks. *Int. J. Commun. Syst.*, 32, 9, e3951, 2019.

Index

Printed and bound by CPI Group (UK) Ltd, Croydon, CR0 4YY

27/10/2024

14580173-0003